OH MY GODS

A MODERN RETELLING
of
GREEK AND ROMAN MYTHS

PHILIP FREEMAN

SIMON & SCHUSTER PAPERBACKS

NEW YORK   LONDON   TORONTO   SYDNEY   NEW DELHI

Simon & Schuster Paperbacks
A Division of Simon & Schuster, Inc.
1230 Avenue of the Americas
New York, NY 10020

First Simon & Schuster trade paperback edition January 2013

SIMON & SCHUSTER PAPERBACKS and colophon are registered
trademarks of Simon & Schuster, Inc.

For information about special discounts for bulk purchases,
please contact Simon & Schuster Special Sales at
1-866-506-1949 or business@simonandschuster.com.

The Simon & Schuster Speakers Bureau can bring authors
to your live event. For more information or to book an event,
contact the Simon & Schuster Speakers Bureau at
1-866-248-3049 or visit our website at www.simonspeakers.com.

Designed by Akasha Archer

Manufactured in the United States of America

20   19   18   17   16   15   14   13   12

The Library of Congress has cataloged the hardcover edition as follows:

Freeman, Philip, 1961-
    Oh my gods : a modern retelling of Greek and Roman myths / Philip
Freeman.
        p. cm.
    Includes bibliographical references and index.
    1. Mythology, Greek. 2. Mythology, Roman. I. Title.
BL782.F73 2012
398.20938—dc23
                                                              2011039704
ISBN 978-1-4516-0997-4
ISBN 978-1-4516-0998-1 (pbk)
ISBN 978-1-4516-0999-8 (ebook)

For my students

CONTENTS

HEROES   87

LOVERS   116

HERCULES   136

OH MY GODS

OH MY GOD?

INTRODUCTION

Like most children, I loved stories of ancient gods and heroes. Zeus wielding his mighty thunderbolt, Hercules slaying monsters, battles raging before the walls of Troy—all these were favorite bedtime reading before my mother made me turn out the light. As I grew older, I continued to enjoy classical myths, so much so that I made the ancient world the focus of my life's work as a college teacher. In the classroom I talk about the stories that so enchanted me with students who have signed up for mythology as a much-needed break from chemistry and calculus. They also read the myths as children and are now rediscovering in them the magic of a strange and distant world that echoes so clearly in their favorite modern stories by J. R. R. Tolkien, C. S. Lewis, and J. K. Rowling.

Mythology is every bit as fascinating to the students now as it was when they were younger, but the stories we talk about in class are more surprising and shocking than those they knew from childhood. Likewise when I give presentations to visiting high school students, parents, or members of the community, the room is always full to overflowing if the topic is classical mythology. We talk about the familiar stories they read as boys and girls, but I include all the mayhem, madness, and sensuality of the original tales. Some always linger at the end of a presentation and confess that they still have their childhood book of myths carefully tucked away on a shelf. Then they ask where they can read more about the stories as the Greeks and Romans first told them. I always try to direct them to appropriate books, but aside from scholarly works, there hasn't been much written on classical mythology for readers past childhood.

Thus this book was born. In it I try to present the major Greek and Roman myths with all the sublime beauty and disturbing twists of the original stories so that readers can enjoy and appreciate the ancient tales as they were written long ago. We all know that Zeus was king of the gods, but did he use his immense power solely for good? Was Jason really a great hero who sailed across the sea to find the Golden Fleece or a selfish lout who succeeded only with the help of a clever and resourceful woman he later betrayed? And why did a young Roman wife named Lucretia feel she had to kill herself after she was raped by her husband's best friend? These and many other vital aspects of mythology were understandably left out or glossed over in the stories we read as children. But for anyone ready to dig deeper, they provide astonishing insights into the Greek and Roman imagination.

When we use the word "myth" today we usually mean a story that isn't true, such as the claim that giant alligators live in the sewers of New York City. The ancient Greeks used the word *mythos* to mean anything spoken, though sometimes they applied the term more narrowly to a legendary tale as opposed to a strict historical account. Even modern scholars who spend their lives studying myths can't agree on a precise definition, but most would say that a myth is a traditional story that possesses significant meaning. Whether or not a myth reflects a historical event is beside the point since it is the underlying message that matters. The power of the Trojan War story, for example, does not depend on whether or not there really was such a conflict between Greeks and Trojans at a particular time and place, but lies in the universal themes of love and loss, courage and anguish, life and death, that the tale preserves.

There is a kind of natural selection that takes place among myths. Those that capture something essential to the human condition can be preserved for thousands of years. Those that are relevant only to a few are lost forever. The truly enduring myths may change over time as new generations discover their own lessons from the stories, but the core of the tales remains. The Greeks and Romans told countless stories that do not survive simply because no one found them compelling enough to keep alive. But those myths that spoke to the fundamental hopes and fears of humanity never died. Indeed, this is the very reason we read them still today.

The classical world derived its myths from many sources. When the

Greeks first entered the Balkan peninsula perhaps four thousand years ago, they brought with them stories inherited from their Indo-European ancestors. But these newcomers to the Aegean world were quick to embrace myths from the great centers of Near Eastern and African civilization. Minoans from Crete; Hittites and other Anatolian peoples from modern-day Turkey; Phoenician traders from the eastern Mediterranean; Sumerians, Assyrians, and Babylonians from Mesopotamia; and Egyptians from the Nile valley all deeply influenced Greek mythology. It is no coincidence that Greek myths of creation bear a striking resemblance to the Babylonian *Enuma Elish* epic or that the Kumarbi Cycle of Hittite mythology parallels the struggle for divine supremacy among the Greek gods, just as echoes of the Sumerian hero Gilgamesh are found in Homer. The Romans were likewise great borrowers, whether from their Etruscan neighbors or from the Greeks themselves.

The flow of myth across cultures and through time is one of its most striking features. Mythology is never static, but takes on new shapes as it moves across generations and continents, yet it always preserves its fundamental message as it evolves. The latest Hollywood movies based on classical myths may use spectacular computer-generated effects, but it is the stories they tell as first recorded by ancient authors that bring these movies to life for modern audiences.

When the Greeks arrived on the shores of the Aegean, they encountered far more civilized people than themselves. Foremost among these were the Minoans from the nearby island of Crete, who lived in palaces with grand courtyards, labyrinthine passageways, and beautifully painted frescoes of female figures, raging bulls, and idyllic scenes from nature. Though they spoke a completely different language, the Minoans were great sailors and merchants who traveled the seas bringing luxury goods and undoubtedly stories as well to the Greeks on the mainland. The Minoans were also literate, though their writing system etched on baked clay tablets is still a mystery to scholars. Their civilization was strong enough to survive the tremendous volcanic explosion on the small island of Thera (Santorini) just north of Crete. The memory of this cataclysm may have given birth to the legend of Atlantis, recorded over a thousand years later by Plato.

Two centuries after much of Thera sank beneath the waves, Greeks from the mainland seized control of Crete and established kingdoms at palace centers on the mainland such as Mycenae, Thebes, Pylos, Athens, and Sparta. These were independent realms ruled by aristocratic families who sometimes warred with one another and sometimes cooperated in raids on other kingdoms. It is no coincidence that almost all these Bronze Age towns feature prominently in later Greek myth. They were to the classical Greeks what Camelot is to us today. In the greatest of all Greek stories—the tale of the Trojan War—Agamemnon of Mycenae leads a coalition of other Greek kings against the wealthy city of Troy at the entrance to the Black Sea to recover the fabled princess Helen. While it is doubtful any Greek king would go to war over a woman, the promise of glory and plunder may well have launched a thousand ships (or at least a few dozen) against the Trojans at the end of the Bronze Age.

We have no written myths from Mycenaean times, though the Greeks of the period did make use of a syllabic writing system borrowed from the Minoans. Mycenaean clay tablets are rare as they survived only by accident in the hardening fires of burned palaces, but the limited information they contain is intriguing. They preserve the names of gods well known from later Greek mythology, such as Zeus, Hera, Poseidon, Artemis, Ares, Hermes, and Dionysus. Surprisingly, they don't mention Demeter or Aphrodite, though this may simply be due to the small number of surviving tablets. The Mycenaean records reveal the existence of divine cults and organized worship, perhaps even human sacrifice, though the evidence for this is inconclusive. The tablets also contain names given to heroes in later myths, such as Achilles, Hector, Theseus, and Jason.

Most of the Bronze Age palaces of Greece fell to outside invaders or internal dissension not long after 1200 B.C., but Greek culture and mythology continued to flourish throughout the next three centuries, a period known to modern scholars as the Dark Age of Greek history. It was dark only in the sense that written records disappeared, but in towns and villages throughout Greece and now across the Aegean where Greek colonists settled on the western coast of Asia Minor, the stories of gods and heroes flourished. With increasing contact at this time between

Greeks and peoples of the eastern Mediterranean, stories flowed into Greece from Mesopotamia, Egypt, and the interior of Asia Minor. When Phoenician traders introduced their alphabet to the Aegean about 800 B.C., the Greeks quickly adapted the Semitic symbols to their own language and set the stage for an explosion of creativity.

Sometime around the year 750 B.C., a poet named Homer gathered together the stories of the great war against Troy and its aftermath and wove them into two extraordinary poems, the *Iliad* and the *Odyssey*, that would become the touchstone for all of Greek mythology. These two epics were soon recorded in the new alphabet and quickly spread throughout the expanding Greek world. For later Greeks, who memorized much of the *Iliad* and the *Odyssey* as the foundation of their education, Homer was the master bard who first sang the wrath of Achilles, the love between Helen and Paris, and the adventures of Odysseus against the one-eyed Cyclops, deadly Sirens, and alluring goddesses in his long struggle to find his way home.

But Homer was not the only Greek maker of myth. A shepherd named Hesiod was tending his flock on Mount Helicon one day when he says the Muses called to him to sing the stories of gods and mortals. Whether he was divinely inspired or not, his *Theogony* became the accepted account of creation in the classical world. His *Works and Days*, aside from offering a catalog of pithy advice to young men (i.e., "Marry a virgin who lives nearby," and "Don't urinate while walking down the road"), tells of the god Prometheus, who brought fire from heaven, and the beautiful maiden Pandora, who unleashed woe on men when she foolishly opened a jar full of evil ("box" is a later mistranslation). Soon after Hesiod, a whole collection of short poems erroneously labeled the *Homeric Hymns* spread throughout Greece. These popular songs celebrated the Olympic gods and provide us our earliest narrative stories of divinities such as Demeter, Apollo, and Aphrodite.

By 500 B.C., the Greeks had colonized the Mediterranean and Black seas from the Crimea to Spain. Wherever they went they would establish a polis, a city-state—the root of our word "politics." Many cities abroad and in the Greek homeland were ruled by popular tyrants who lavished state funds on the arts and public theater. In Athens, the family of the tyrant Pisistratus encouraged, among other celebrations, a springtime festival to the god Dionysus in which choruses and actors performed tragedies and comedies. The festivals continued and grew even after the tyranny was overthrown and replaced by Athenian democracy to usher in the celebrated Golden Age of Greece. Many of these productions, such as *Oedipus Rex* by Sophocles, are major sources for Greek mythology. Aside from plays, contemporary writers of the period, such as the lyric poet Pindar and the historian Herodotus, record many enduring myths.

The defeat of Athens by Sparta in the Peloponnesian War at the end of the fifth century B.C. brought an end to the great artistic flowering of the Golden Age, but stories and myths continued to be as popular as ever. The conquests of Alexander the Great less than a century later spread Greek culture to Asia and Africa, especially to the newly founded city of Alexandria in Egypt. There and elsewhere around the Mediterranean, scholars collected and edited centuries of Greek mythology on papyrus scrolls.

Far to the west, a small village on the banks of the Tiber River in central Italy had begun to expand beyond its seven hills. The Romans had inherited a rich mythological tradition from their own ancestors, but they added many other stories when they encountered the cultured Etruscans and Greeks. Native Roman gods were ephemeral deities of field, hearth, and home. While their rituals were faithfully observed, many of the stories behind them were lost. The ancient myths that survived were often disguised as early history, such as the tale of Romulus and Remus. These Roman stories may surprise modern readers in tone and purpose compared with Greek mythology. To a Roman, unwavering loyalty to the state was the greatest virtue, so that many early myths read like stark political propaganda.

The Romans were always ambivalent about the Greeks, admiring their sophisticated culture but dismissing their neighbors to the east as inferior in honor and the manly art of war. However, as their power spread across the Mediterranean and republic grew to empire, the Romans sought to tie their own history to that of the Greeks by claiming an origin from the Trojans. Thus while distancing themselves from the Greeks in lineage, they nevertheless wrote themselves into the greatest of Greek stories—surprisingly as the heirs of the losers. The Latin poet

Virgil crystallized this tradition in his monumental poem the *Aeneid*. In this epic the Trojan refugee Aeneas and his band of hearty followers venture ever westward through countless toils and snares eventually to become the ancestors of the Romans.

Throughout imperial times, both Romans and the Greeks under their dominion continued to retell the ancient myths, often with additions both subtle and bold. The Greek biographer Plutarch preserves many traditional stories in his prolific works, while his countryman Pausanias includes a number of myths in his travelogue of sites he visited throughout Greece. But the greatest of these writers was the Roman poet Ovid, who preserved many Greek myths that would otherwise have been lost forever. His *Metamorphoses* is an epic of mythological tales built around the theme of supernatural changes. Read widely long into medieval and Renaissance times, it became the most influential source of mythology in later art and literature.

There are many ways to write a book on classical mythology, all of which have their strengths and weaknesses. Many contemporary authors choose to explore the myths from a particular thematic angle, such as a function of religious ritual, a reflection of social structure, or an expression of the universal unconscious. These approaches and many more, such as feminist criticism, can be productive ways to look at classical myth, but my goal in this volume is more modest. I simply want to retell the great myths of Greece and Rome for modern readers while remaining as faithful as possible to the original sources. Sometimes this means paraphrasing a single ancient author, while in other cases I merge a number of different classical sources. In some stories I draw on authors centuries apart to create a complete version of a tale. Such an approach is unavoidable as few myths are wholly preserved in just one writer. Often I have had to choose which version of a story or episode within a myth to present as there are usually variants, some of which contradict each other. I describe the ancient authors I use for each tale in the notes at the back of the book. Readers interested in learning more about a particular story are encouraged to read the appropriate primary sources.

For Greek names, I have tried to use the spelling most familiar to contemporary readers rather than a strict transliteration of the Greek.

Thus Hercules instead of Herakles, and Oedipus for Oidipous. With less familiar names I have tried to pick the form I think is most pleasing to the modern eye and tongue. Different forms, along with their Roman equivalents, are listed under each name in the Glossary.

No one should be allowed to have as much fun writing a book as I did while putting together this collection of myths. I have so enjoyed teaching these stories to my students for years that the opportunity to present them to a wider public was irresistible. My heartfelt thanks go out to all who helped me in this endeavor, including the National Endowment for the Humanities and the libraries of Harvard University. But as always, my greatest thanks go to my students, who have so patiently listened to me tell these myths in my classes. Whatever you do in life, may you never lose your love for old stories.

CREATION

In the beginning there was Chaos—a great, bottomless chasm beneath the endless darkness of the cosmos. Out of Chaos came the broad green Earth, unmoving seat of the gods, and the black hole of Tartarus below. Then from Chaos sprung Eros, who overcomes the minds of gods and mortals alike with burning desire. Out of Chaos also flew dark Erebus, the Underworld, and his sister, black Night. Erebus made love to Night and fathered the lofty air called Aether and bright Day.

Earth gave birth to starry Sky, equal to herself, who covered her on every side and became her mate. From Earth came the high mountains and the swelling sea. Then Sky made love with Earth and their children were the gods Coeus, Crius, and shining Hyperion, along with deep Ocean that surrounds the Earth, then Iapetus, Theia, Rhea, and Themis, who brings order to the world. Earth also bore Sky a goddess, Mnemosyne, who never forgets, and golden-crowned Phoebe, as well as lovely Tethys, goddess of the sea. Last of all was born Cronus, youngest of the shining gods, the most willful and crafty of all Earth's children.

The broad Earth bore other creatures, such as the single-eyed Cyclopes, who delight in violence and brute force. These were Brontes of thunder, Steropes of lightning, and Arges, bearer of light. She also bore terrible Cottus, Briareus, and Gyges, huge monsters of enormous strength with a hundred arms springing from their shoulders and fifty heads each.

Father Sky hated all his children. As soon as they came from the womb, he gleefully shoved them into a hole in the ground and would not let them see the light of day. Mother Earth groaned from the pain of her children inside her and hatched a plan for revenge. She crafted a giant sickle from the hardest adamant and showed it to her offspring.

"Dear children of mine," she pleaded, "who will avenge this evil done to you and me by your wicked father? Who will dare to strike back against the power of Sky?"

None of those hiding in her belly said a word, as they were all deathly afraid of their father. Only the youngest of the gods, the clever Cronus, spoke up: "Mother, I will do it. I'm not afraid of Sky, especially since he wronged us first!"

The Earth was thrilled at the courage of her son and gave him the sickle with its jagged teeth. When night was drawing near, Sky at last stretched himself out on the Earth, eager to make love to her. At just the moment they were about to join, Cronus sprang from his hiding place and grabbed his father's genitals with his outstretched hand. With a single swing of the blade, he castrated Sky and threw what he had reaped behind him. Blood splattered everywhere across the face of the Earth. Where it hit the ground, vengeful Furies sprang forth as well as wicked giants decked in shining armor, brandishing great spears. Nymphs also arose from the bloody mud.

The severed testicles of Sky sailed through the air and landed in the sea, where they floated at last to the island of Cyprus. There the pounding waves stirred up a white foam on the beach. Inside the foam the goddess Aphrodite was born, immortal divinity of smiles and sweet delights who urges all to lose themselves in passion.

Now it was Sky who groaned at the pain within him. He called his children Titans and cursed them as ungrateful whelps who had wounded the very father who had given them life. And he swore that in time Cronus would pay dearly for his wicked deed.

The family of Chaos bore untold sons and daughters, some children of beauty and hope but most of darkness and despair. The goddess Night gave birth to hateful Doom, Blame, Distress, Nemesis, Deceit, Strife, Old Age, and Death itself. She also bore Sleep and the tribe of Dreams, for good and ill, and the three Fates who weave our destinies. From her womb also sprang pitiless Furies who hunt down gods and men to seek vengeance. Night's daughter Strife bore Toil, Neglect, Hunger, and Pain, along with War, Murder, Lies, and many other woes. But Sea gave birth to kindly Nereus, who in turn mated with a daughter of Ocean to father fifty nymphs of the wind and waves.

Many other children were born of these early unions, such as Medusa and the Gorgons, along with Echidna, half beautiful nymph with fair cheeks and golden hair and half monstrous serpent. Typhon, mighty son of Tartarus and Earth, lay with Echidna and fathered Orthus, the dog, as well as the monster Geryon and the three-headed hound Cerberus, who guards the door to the Underworld so that no one may ever leave. Echidna also gave birth to Chimaera, a beast who was a lion in front, a goat in the middle, and a dragon in back. Chimaera was raped by her brother Orthus and bore the riddling Sphinx. Tethys, daughter of Sky and Earth, gave birth to all the great rivers of the world and to thousands of nymphs who live in streams and ponds. The daughter of Ocean, Styx, by whom the gods swear, bore Aspiration, Victory, Power, and Strength. Phoebe came to the bed of her brother Coeus and became pregnant with gentle Leto and her sister Asteria, who was the mother of honored Hecate. Theia, sister of Tethys, slept with her brother Hyperion and gave birth to Helios the sun, Selene the moon, and Eos, goddess of dawn. Eos in turn gave birth to the winds and the morning star. Iapetus, son of Sky and Earth, went to the bed of the nymph Clymene and she bore him four sons. These were stern Atlas, proud Menoetius, forward-thinking Prometheus, and foolish Epimetheus. Countless other divinities were conceived in those days, so that no one could number them all, until the world itself was full of gods.

Now that Cronus had defeated his father the Sky, the young Titan ruled all of heaven and earth. He overcame the resistance of his sister, Rhea, and lay with her, fathering six splendid children. There was Hestia, goddess of the hearth, then Demeter, who brings the fruits of the ground to ripeness, and Hera of the golden sandals. Rhea also gave birth to mighty, merciless Hades and Poseidon, shaker of the earth. But Cronus was a jealous god who had learned from his parents that he was destined to be defeated by his own child and lose his power. Thus when each child was born, he snatched it from weeping Rhea and swallowed it whole.

Rhea suffered such grief from having her children eaten that she went to her father and mother to ask how she might have vengeance on crooked-scheming Cronus. They felt pity for her and told her all that they had revealed to Cronus, how he would one day lose his throne to a son yet unborn. Then they told her to go to the island of Crete to bear the child now in her womb. Alone in a cave high on a mountain, she gave birth to Zeus. Her mother, the green Earth, came to her there and took her grandson away to hide in a secret place. But ever-vigilant Cronus was close on the heels of his wife and soon arrived in Crete to demand the newborn child. Earth, however, had given Rhea a great stone wrapped in swaddling clothes that she handed to Cronus in place of her baby boy. Greedy Cronus snatched the bundle and shoved it down his throat, never suspecting that he had been deceived.

As the years passed, Earth raised Zeus on Crete hidden from the eyes of his father. The boy soon grew wise and strong, until one day he emerged from his hiding place. He hatched a plot with the wise goddess Metis. She went to the unsuspecting Cronus and offered him a potion for his health, but it racked his stomach with pain and caused him to vomit up his deathless children. The offspring of Cronus then banded together with Zeus as their leader and challenged their father in the greatest battle the world had ever seen or will ever see.

For ten long years the younger generation of gods battled their elders, with neither side able to gain victory. It seemed as if Zeus would never be able to defeat his father, but then his grandmother Earth came to him with wise advice. Long before the birth of Zeus, his grandfather the Sky had imprisoned the Cyclopes in Tartarus along with the hundred-armed monsters Cottus, Briareus, and Gyges. Cronus and the other Titans, fearful of their power, left them there to live in misery. Now Earth told her grandson that with the help of the Cyclopes and these three monsters, he might be able to overcome his father. Zeus then sped to Tartarus and freed them, bringing them back to Mount Olympus. He fed them nectar and deathless ambrosia to nourish their bodies and spirits. Then he spoke to them: "Children of Sky and Earth, listen to me. For ten years we have been fighting the Titans for control of the world, but neither side can gain an advantage. I call on you now to help us, to remember who it was who freed you from your bonds in the misty darkness of Tartarus."

Cottus spoke for them all and answered: "Son of Cronus, we know that you are wiser than your father and his generation. You have freed us from our prison and we will not forget it. Come, we will fight with you and crush the Titans into dust."

With that the Cyclopes forged lightning bolts for Zeus to serve him in battle and joined with the young Olympians in war. They marched on the Titans and fought until the sky roared, the sea rolled, and the earth quaked. The noise of combat was terrible and filled the earth. Zeus now raged with all his might and threw lightning bolts down on his enemies from the sky. The forests of the world burst into flame and smoke rose to the heavens. At last the tide of battle turned and the young gods began to drive back Cronus and his allies. The Titans turned to run, but were captured and cast down themselves into gloomy Tartarus. There they are guarded by the Cyclopes and will never again see the light of day, save for Atlas, son of Iapetus, who Zeus punished by forcing him to bear the weight of the heavens on his shoulders.

But just when Zeus thought the struggle was over, a new threat emerged. Typhon, son of Tartarus, rose against the young gods. Some say his mother was Earth herself or even Hera, but whatever his origin, he was a grave threat to Zeus. A horrible creature of hideous strength, he had a hundred snake heads with burning eyes. He bellowed like a bull and roared like a lion as he rushed Mount Olympus and began to climb. The immortals shook in fear and panicked. Typhon would have destroyed the gods that day if Zeus had not taken his weapons of thunder and lightning down to face him. He leapt from the mountain and struck the monster again and again with terrible blows. At last Zeus picked up the broken body of the creature and cast him down into Tartarus to dwell forever with the Titans, where Typhon rages still, bellowing typhoons across the seas.

Zeus now lorded over the immortals from the shining heights of Mount Olympus, ever watchful lest he himself should be overthrown as were his father and grandfather before him. He took the stone Cronus had swallowed in his place and set it up at the holy vale of Delphi as a monument to himself for ages to come. He chose this site because when he had released two eagles from opposite ends of the world, they met here beneath Mount Parnassus, marking the navel or center of the earth.

Zeus was the most powerful of the gods, but he knew he could not rule alone. He cast lots with his brothers Poseidon and Hades to divide the world among them. The sea fell to Poseidon and the underworld to

Hades, while Zeus received the sky. The earth and Mount Olympus belonged to the three brothers alike, but all the gods knew that Zeus was their king.

The master of the gods decided he should marry and chose as his first wife Metis, who had forced Cronus to vomit up his brothers and sisters. He did this not out of love but cunning, for Earth and Sky had revealed to him that any son Metis bore to him would surpass him in power. Therefore when Metis was pregnant, Zeus swallowed her whole, just as Cronus had done to his children. He thought he had seen the last of his bride and her child, but soon he began to have a terrible headache. He ordered Prometheus, a nephew of Cronus who had taken his side against the Titans, to split open his head with an ax to relieve the pain—and out came the goddess Athena, wisest of the children of Zeus. Metis, however, remained trapped inside Zeus, where she was a constant source of good advice.

The next wife of Zeus was Themis, goddess of order and justice. Some say she also was the mother of the Fates. Eurynome, daughter of the Ocean, was his next bride and she bore to him the beautiful Graces. Then Zeus married Demeter, fathering Persephone, and afterward took Mnemosyne, goddess of memory, as his wife. He also chose Leto, daughter of Titans, and she bore to him the archer god Apollo and the virgin huntress Artemis. Last of all he married his sister Hera, who became the mother of youthful Hebe, and Eileithyia, goddess of childbirth, and pitiless Ares, god of war. Some say the god of the forge, Hephaestus, was also their son, but others say that he was born of Hera alone.

The earth below Mount Olympus was beautiful, but empty except for wild animals and green plants. All the gods looked down from Olympus and saw no one who could honor and worship them. A few tales say it was Zeus who solved the problem, but most say it was clever Prometheus who first conceived the idea of creating mortals to serve the gods.

According to this story, Prometheus took clay from the earth and mixed it with water, then shaped it into men formed in the image of the gods. He gave them two legs so that unlike animals, they would walk upright and gaze at the stars. There were no women yet, just men who toiled alone.

But another tale says there were different races of humanity created

at different times. There was first a golden age during the reign of
Cronus when the gods fashioned men to dwell on the earth. These
men lived like gods themselves, free from all worries, enjoying the
fruits of the earth without labor. In great old age they died as if they
had fallen asleep and became divine spirits who still walk the world
unseen, granting happiness and wealth to those who deserve it. When
the golden race had passed away, the gods made humans of silver, but
these were not at all like their predecessors. They remained children
for a hundred years in the care of their mothers and died soon after
becoming adults, for they were foolish and violent against each other.
They refused to worship the gods or offer sacrifices on the altars, so
Zeus destroyed them. Then the son of Cronus made a race of bronze
men who cared for nothing but war. They were strong brutes who wore
bronze armor and lived in bronze houses. In time they all killed each
other and went to dwell in Hades. Then Zeus made a fourth race,
but not of metal. These became the great heroes of old who fought at
Thebes and Troy. Most of these went down to Hades at their deaths,
but a few the gods rewarded with eternal life on the Isles of the Blessed
at the ends of the earth. Finally the gods made a race of iron, our own
race, who suffer constant toils and trouble, a people of evil mixed with
little good. The story says it is our fate to destroy ourselves one day,
when children no longer respect their parents and think only of their
own gain. Innocence will disappear, might will become right, and envy
will rule the world. Justice will flee the earth, along with decency and
righteous indignation. We will perish in our own hatred and there will
be no help from the immortal gods.

Yet another tale claims that there were in the beginning three kinds
of human beings. The first kind were male, the second female, and the
third a mixture of the two. The males were offspring of the sun, while
the females came from the earth and the third were children of the
moon. These early humans were completely round creatures with four
arms, four legs, and two faces on opposite sides of a single head. They
had two sets of sexual organs on the outside of their bodies facing away
from each other. All three types walked upright as we do, but when they
ran they used eight limbs to cartwheel across the land faster than anyone

today could hope to move. They were immensely strong, so much so that they threatened the gods just as the Titans had done.

Zeus held a council of the gods to decide what to do about these troublesome humans. After much debate, he decided to cut them in half. Zeus reasoned that this would make them less of a threat as well as doubling the number of people who could offer sacrifices to the gods. They would henceforth walk on two legs instead of four. If they still caused trouble, Zeus warned, he would cut them in half yet again so that they would have to hop about on one leg.

So Zeus split these spherical humans apart, just like cutting an apple in half with a knife. As he divided each one, he ordered the healing god Apollo to turn their faces around so that they could see the gaping wound and remember not to trouble him again. Apollo then took each and gathered the skin on the cut side into a pouch and drew it together in the center of the belly, so that we still have navels to show where the god sewed together our ancestors. However, he left the genitals on the outside near the buttocks.

When Zeus had finished, all the new human beings began frantically searching for their missing halves. Those that had once been all male sought out males and females longed for females, while the children of the moon who had once embodied both genders looked for their opposites. If some found their absent partner, they would throw their arms around each other in a pitiful attempt to reunite and remained that way until they starved to death. Zeus finally had mercy on them and decided to move their genitals to the front of their bodies. Thus when a male half embraced a female half, they would join together in pleasure and produce children. When two males or two females embraced each other, they could at least give each other satisfaction.

We are the children of these formerly joined creatures that Zeus split apart, though we always long for our missing half. Those who seek after the opposite sex come from humans who once were a mixture of male and female. Men and women who seek after the same sex as themselves descend from those who were once all male or all female. Love between people is in fact a pursuit of wholeness, a desire to be complete.

Most say it was indeed Prometheus who created men from clay and that he cared for them from the beginning above all other gods. He taught mortals to build houses for themselves and how to track the movements of the stars across the night sky. He instructed them in mathematics, arts, medicine, metallurgy, divination, and even how to write. He patiently showed them how to yoke oxen and plow fields to grow their food and tame wild horses to pull carts. At last he led them to the shore and taught them how to build ships to sail across the seas.

Men long lived at peace with the gods, even feasting together with them in fellowship. One day when there was a great banquet set at a seaside town, Zeus was invited to join in the celebration. At such festivals, the gods always chose the best portion of meat, leaving mortal men skin and bones, so Prometheus decided to play a trick on Zeus. He arrived early and slaughtered an ox for the feast, then roasted the animal over the fire and placed the choicest cuts of meat inside the ox's ugly stomach. At the same time, he wrapped the white bones in rich, appealing fat and laid both choices on the banquet table. When Zeus arrived and took his seat at the head of the table, he was surprised at how Prometheus had divided the portions.

"Son of Iapetus, my good friend, great among the immortals, this doesn't seem a fair choice."

But Prometheus smiled and flattered him with winning words: "Zeus, greatest and most glorious of all the gods, please choose whichever part you would most desire."

Zeus suspected a trick, but the savory smell of the rich fat was too much to resist. He greedily took it in his hands to devour, only to find that he had chosen a bag of bones. Thus to this day at sacrifices men set aside the bones covered in fat for the gods at the altar while they keep the meat for themselves.

But the cloud-gathering king of the gods became furious at this deception and raged at Prometheus, "Son of Iapetus, clever above all the gods, you are always the trickster!"

Zeus then stormed from the banquet furious at Prometheus and mankind. In his anger he decided to take back the fire that he had given men to roast their food and keep themselves warm. But Prometheus stole fire from heaven and brought it down to men, this time hidden in the stalk of a fennel plant. Zeus was angrier than ever and decided to punish Prometheus in a most terrible way. He ordered Power and Strength, sons of the goddess Styx, to take Prometheus to a distant cliff in the Caucasus Mountains and bind him naked in chains to an immovable pillar of stone. Then he sent a great eagle to tear the god open and eat his liver raw. Being immortal, Prometheus could not die, so that his liver grew again each night, only to be devoured again the next day by the same eagle. Defiant against Zeus, refusing to repent for helping men, Prometheus was bound for eternity alone on a cold mountain at the end of the world.

But the anger of Zeus against men still raged. Rather than destroy the creation of his enemy Prometheus, he decided to inflict on them a much more subtle and insidious punishment. With a wicked smile he ordered Hephaestus, craftsman of the gods, to mix together clay and water to shape a trap for men. He gave this creation life and speech, then molded it into the lovely image of an immortal goddess. It was a new kind of creature, a mortal woman, something never seen before by gods or men. Zeus ordered Aphrodite and the Graces to cover her in beauty, but place inside her the pain of heartbreak and the aching sorrow of love. Athena then taught her weaving and the womanly skills she would need, while all the gods gave her gifts to make her irresistible to men. Her name was thus Pandora, "bearer of all gifts," and every woman is descended from her. Zeus told Hermes to take the woman down to earth and present her to the brother of Prometheus, Epimetheus, who always acted first and thought later. Epimetheus and indeed all mortal men gazed on Pandora in wonder and desire.

Until that time men had lived on the earth free from cares, but Zeus gave the first woman a great jar sealed tightly on top. Unable to resist her curiosity, Pandora broke the seal and opened the jar. Out flew every kind of evil into the world, so that from that day forward the earth has been full of pain, sickness, and woe. Pandora slammed the heavy lid back on, but it was too late. Only feeble Hope remained in the jar, trapped inside, unable to escape.

Zeus had loosed the evils of the world on humanity, but he believed men and women might yet be able to live worthwhile lives of honest labor and worship. To see for himself, one day he left the heights of Mount Olympus and came down to walk upon the earth as a simple peasant.

But everywhere he went he saw nothing but wickedness and impiety. In lush Arcadia he at last came to the kingdom of Lycaon, a savage ruler who terrorized both his neighbors and his own people. The king of the gods appeared before his palace seeking hospitality for the night, as was the sacred custom for wandering strangers. By certain signs, Zeus showed the people of the town that he was no ordinary traveler and they began to worship him, but their king scoffed at the idea that a god had come to visit.

"I'll test this fellow," said Lycaon, "and see if he is divine or mortal."

The king took one of the hostages he had demanded from a nearby kingdom and slit his throat. While the body was still warm, he boiled parts of the dead man and roasted others, then served them to his guest for dinner. Zeus knew immediately what Lycaon had done and stormed in anger. His lightning bolts destroyed the palace and killed all inside except the king. Lycaon he transformed into a creature befitting his cruel nature. The king's skin turned to shaggy gray hair and his arms to legs, then Lycaon began to howl. The wolfish man had become a wolf himself and rushed from the palace to attack his own sheep in their pasture.

The savage behavior of Lycaon was the last straw for Zeus. He summoned the gods to council on Olympus and told them he was going to destroy the entire human race because of their wickedness. The gods agreed with his decision, but some wondered who would offer sacrifices to them and celebrate their rites at the altars. Zeus then assured them that he would create a new race of humanity far better than the doomed people of the earth.

With that, Zeus called down all the waters of the heavens on the earth and ordered his brother Poseidon to raise the ocean waves on the land. The river gods pushed their streams out of their banks and flooded the dry ground. Men, women, and children ran in panic to the hills seeking high ground. Some fled to little boats to ride among the treetops, but the violence of the storm overwhelmed them. Wild lions and bears swam among sheep in the raging waters, but it seemed no creature of the earth, whether animal or human, was able to survive the horrible flood.

As Zeus looked down in satisfaction on the waters covering the earth, he saw a large, sturdy chest floating on the waves. Inside were a single man and woman, Deucalion, son of Prometheus, and his wife,

Pyrrha, daughter of Pandora. Prometheus had somehow warned his son of the coming flood and told him to build the chest to ride out the anger of Zeus. For nine days and nights the couple floated amid the death and destruction of their world until at last they came to rest on the soaring twin peaks of Mount Parnassus above Delphi.

At first Zeus was furious at being deceived again by Prometheus, but he knew Deucalion and Pyrrha alone were righteous on the earth, always honoring the gods and treating strangers with kindness. The ruler of Olympus thus ordered the waters to return to the seas and reveal once more the dry land.

When Deucalion and Pyrrha emerged from their chest, they saw the world was desolate and empty, save for themselves. Deucalion took counsel with his wife about what they should do and both agreed they should seek the guidance of the gods. Nearby was a temple of Themis, goddess of order and justice, still covered with seaweed and debris. They had no animal to sacrifice, so they fell to their knees before the dripping altar and begged the goddess for her help. Themis took pity on the pair and gave this oracle: "Leave here with your heads veiled and robes undone. As you go, throw behind you the bones of your mother."

The couple stood in silence trying to believe their ears. Even if they could find the bones of their mothers it would be the greatest impiety to dig them up and treat them so disrespectfully. Pyrrha collapsed in tears and perplexity, but Deucalion turned the oracle over in his mind. Then at last he spoke to his wife and assured her that the gods would never order sacrilege. The bones the goddess spoke of must be the stones of Mother Earth.

Pyrrha was doubtful, but what harm could it do to try? They picked up rocks from around the altar, veiled their heads, loosened their robes, and began to throw the stones over their shoulders as they left. As soon as they hit the ground, the stones began to soften and grow. The stones thrown by Deucalion took on the form of men, while those tossed behind Pyrrha became women. From these stones the entire human race is descended, forever tough and enduring like the rocks our ancestors sprang from.

GODS

╬╬╬╬╬╬╬╬╬

ZEUS

╬╬╬╬╬╬╬╬╬

Of all the gods on Mount Olympus, Zeus was by far the most powerful. He might have willingly shared some of his power over the universe with his brothers and the other gods, but woe to any divinity who threatened his domination. As he himself warned his fellow gods:

> *Learn how much stronger I am than all the rest of you immortals.*
> *Drop a golden cord from the heavens, if you wish, and I will prove it.*
> *Grab the end of the cord, all of you gods and goddesses, and pull with*
> *all your might. You can try and drag me down from the heavens, but*
> *you won't budge me an inch. I am Zeus, the highest and wisest. If I*
> *wanted to, I could pull that cord and drag all of you up to me with the*
> *land and the sea trailing along behind you. Then I would tie the end*
> *of the cord to Olympus and leave all of you there twisting in the wind.*

Little wonder that Zeus remained largely unchallenged after he defeated the Titans and Typhon. The other gods might grumble and even plot against him, but they knew they could not defeat him.

Zeus was the great god of the sky and the raging thunder. He wielded his lightning bolts against those, mortal or immortal, who challenged the order he had established. Anyone who stepped out of line was punished in most unpleasant ways. He was especially concerned with maintaining justice in the world and caring for strangers. No human ever knew if the lowly beggar who appeared at his door might be Zeus himself in disguise.

Those few mortals who dared to challenge the ruler of the gods soon learned their lesson. Among these was Salmoneus, an arrogant king of Elis in western Greece who believed he was more powerful than Zeus himself. He even tried to convince his subjects that he was Zeus and so attached bronze kettles to his chariot, claiming he was making thunder as they clattered behind him. He would also throw torches into the sky and say they were lightning bolts. Zeus quickly grew tired of this fool and destroyed him along with his entire city in a blaze of genuine lightning.

Another Greek king named Ixion was a cheapskate who refused to pay his father-in-law, Eioneus, the promised bride-price for his daughter. Eioneus seized the prize mares of Ixion as security until payment was made, so his son-in-law invited him to come and collect the money himself. Once his guest arrived, Ixion threw him into a burning pit where he died. Everyone was horrified at this murder of a family member and refused to help ritually purify Ixion of this crime lest they be cursed themselves. However, Zeus had a soft spot for the king—or at least for his beautiful young bride—and invited him to come to Mount Olympus as his guest. While he was in the court of Zeus, Ixion tried unsuccessfully to seduce Hera. When the wife of Zeus told her husband of this shocking breach of hospitality, the ruler of the gods couldn't believe it. Hera insisted it was true, so Zeus tested his guest by fashioning a lifelike Hera out of a cloud and placing the seductive imitation in Ixion's bed. While Zeus watched, Ixion eagerly made love to the cloud. Zeus then grabbed Ixion and chained him to a fiery wheel that revolves forever in the sky.

But the anger of Zeus did not fall just on kings. The great physician Asclepius, a son of the god Apollo himself, was so skilled in his art that few of those he treated failed to recover. He even succeeded in raising mortals from the dead, using drops of blood from the right side of one of the snake-haired Gorgons to bring people back to life—blood from the left side caused death. Zeus could not allow such acts against the natural order to continue for he was afraid that if mortals learned the secret of eternal life they would become gods themselves. And so, much to the dismay of Apollo, Zeus killed the divine physician with a lightning bolt.

Zeus was the enforcer of cosmic justice, but he was noticeably iniquitous in many of his private dealings with mortals, especially young women. Although the king of the gods created women as a punishment for men, he spent a great deal of time seducing them, usually against their will. His human lovers often paid for this attention with severe punishment from Hera, his divine and very jealous wife. Zeus fathered many children with immortal goddesses, but his children by mortal women were even more numerous. Many of these offspring became great heroes of Greek mythology.

One of the first unlucky maidens to catch the eye of Zeus was Io, a virgin priestess at the temple of his own wife, Hera, near Mycenae in the Peloponnesus peninsula of southern Greece. Zeus had already seduced Io's young niece Niobe, but this was not enough to quench his appetite for the beautiful women of her family. Every night he would come to Io in a vision with wooing words: "Most blessed maiden, why stay a virgin so long when you can have me, Zeus, in your bed? I am enflamed with love for you and would give anything to enjoy your pleasures. Go out now, child, to the wild meadows of the river Lerna among the flocks and cattle of your father. There I will come to you!"

The poor, unwilling girl was tormented by these nocturnal visions from Zeus until at last she went to her father Inachus for help. He was sympathetic to the pleas of his daughter and repeatedly sent messengers to the oracles at Delphi and Dodona to learn what he should do. As was often the case, the responses were ambiguous and offered no clear guidance to Inachus. But at last Io's father received a message from an oracle of Zeus telling him to cast his daughter out of the house to wander unprotected on the borders of his land like a cow set aside for sacrifice. If he did not obey, Zeus would annihilate his entire family with a thunderbolt.

The heartbroken father had no choice and so exiled Io to face her fate alone. It did not take long for Zeus to find her. He surrounded her with a mist and raped her there in her father's distant meadow. Hera was ever-watchful of her husband and noticed both his absence and the strange cloud of mist on an otherwise sunny day. She swept down at once from Olympus so fast that Zeus barely had time to hide his philandering, turning Io into a white cow. When Hera arrived at his side, he claimed he was innocent of any wrongdoing and, perish the thought, would never touch a mortal woman when he had such a beautiful goddess as his wife. Hera was buying none of this and asked her husband for the lovely white cow as a gift. As his lust had been satisfied, he happily agreed to give the cow to his wife.

It was now that Io's punishment began. Hera did not kill her, but instead placed her under the guard of the monster Argus, a creature with a hundred eyes. Argus tied her to a nearby olive tree and sat down to watch over her day and night. By this point Zeus was starting to feel guilty about his treatment of Io and sent Hermes, the god of thieves, to steal her away from Argus. But even Hermes had a difficult time as some of the monster's eyes were always open and awake. At last he played a lullaby for Argus on his flute until one by one all his eyes closed. The god then quickly cut off the head of the monster so that Io could escape. When Hera found out about the deed she was furious and swore vengeance, but first she placed the hundred eyes of Argus onto the tail of the peacock, a bird sacred to her ever after.

It wasn't long before Hera found Io wandering nearby and set upon her a gadfly to sting her mercilessly and drive her near to madness. The tormented girl, still in the form of a cow, then began an epic journey to escape the fury of Hera. She fled northwest across Greece to the sea, henceforth named Ionian after her, then beyond the mountains to Macedonia, followed by a long trek through Thrace to the waters separating Europe from Asia at the entrance to the Black Sea. She swam these narrow straits, which were later called the Bosporus, or "cow crossing," for her. She wandered through the wilds of Scythia until at last she came to the barren Caucasus Mountains near the end of the earth and there found the Titan Prometheus chained to a rock.

Io begged the far-seeing Prometheus for news about how long she would have to suffer. Would she ever be free from Hera's anger? In between bouts of having his liver eaten by Zeus' eagle, Prometheus told Io her fate. She still had far to go, over mountains and through deserts, escaping violence and dangers along the way. She would narrowly avoid the Graeae, three gray-haired hags, never young, who dwell in darkness sharing only a single eye and tooth between them. She would also find their sisters, the snake-haired Gorgons, at the ends of the earth. But at last she would find her rest in Egypt. He also revealed that she would be the ancestor of a man thirteen generations hence who would at last free him from his chains. He also told the eager Io that Zeus himself would one day fall to a son of his own loins, just as Father Sky had been defeated by Cronus, and Cronus in turn had been bested by Zeus. The only one who could save Zeus from this destruction was Prometheus himself, though he was in no mind to help someone who had done such evil to him.

Taking heart from the vengeance that she hoped would one day fall on the head of Zeus, Io left the Caucasus and roamed the lands of Europe, Asia, and Africa until she at last came to the banks of the Nile River near Memphis in Egypt. There she collapsed in exhaustion only to be discovered by Zeus once again. This time the god was more gentle and impregnated her with the mere touch of his finger. He also restored Io at last to her human form so that she gave birth as a woman to a child she named Epaphus, meaning "touched by the god." Hera, however, always vigilant and vengeful, sent divine spirits to kidnap the child and take him to Syria. The distraught mother finally found her child there cared for by the queen of Byblos and returned with the boy to Egypt, where she married the Egyptian king Telegonus and settled down to a peaceful life. It was said she brought the worship of Demeter to the Egyptians, who called the Greek goddess of grain Isis in their own language. It was also said that Isis was worshiped in the form of a woman with the horns of a cow in memory of the struggles of long-suffering Io.

As the years went by, Io's son Epaphus grew up and had a daughter of his own named Libya. This girl had twin sons, Agenor and Belus, by the god Poseidon, brother of Zeus. Belus reigned over the land of Egypt, but Agenor went to Lebanon and there married a princess named Telephassa. The royal couple had three sons, Phoenix, Cilix, and Cadmus, along with one daughter, a beautiful maiden named Europa. Like her ancestor Io, Europa was troubled by dreams. In a vision one night, she saw two women fighting over her, one like a woman of her own country trying to hold her and another like a foreign woman from across the sea trying to steal her away. The foreigner said she had been sent by Zeus himself to bring her to a distant country.

When she woke from this troubling vision, she sought out her own friends among the young women of the royal court to ease her mind. They ran to a seaside meadow and there laughed as they chased each other across the grass and gathered flowers.

Zeus looked down from Mount Olympus and spied the girls in the meadow, but his eye lingered on Europa alone. The maiden was every bit as beautiful as Io had once been and his heart was overcome with desire. But how could he go to the girl without Hera discovering him? He immediately hit upon a clever plan and flew down to the seashore, transforming himself into a handsome white bull with horns like the crescent moon. He paused at the edge of the meadow where the young women were playing and walked forward as gentle as a lamb. They had never seen such a lovely animal before and approached slowly so as not to frighten it away. But the bull was not at all afraid and inched toward the girls to stand before Europa. He began gently to lick her neck as she laughed and at last placed a kiss upon its cheek. The bull had a wonderful smell and lowed deeply as it knelt before the princess and urged her with its eyes to mount its back.

The other maidens were too frightened to climb onto an unknown bull, but Europa told her friends not to worry. "Look at this loveable creature," she told them. "He wouldn't hurt a fly." She then sat down on the broad back of the bull—but suddenly it rose up and began to move toward the sea. Her friends called to Europa to jump off, but the bull was in the water before the maiden could move, charging headlong into the waves. Out to sea the bull swam with Europa until the shore of her homeland was left far behind. The terrified girl clasped her purple robe tightly around herself as hour after hour they traveled on. Dolphins accompanied them like wedding guests as the bull made its way west toward the island of Crete, the very place where Zeus had been raised secretly as a child.

"Who are you?" Europa cried at last to the bull. With a bellow the animal answered, "I am Zeus, king of the gods, and I can take any form I wish. I came to you in the meadow because of my burning desire. You won't be a virgin long, for I am taking you to Crete to share my bed." The poor girl was too frightened to say anything more, but clung to the horns of the bull until they at last made their way onto the shore of the distant island. There Zeus wasted no time in taking on human form and stripped Europa of her clothes. He had his way with her until he was at last satisfied, then left her, alone and pregnant, in a foreign land. But he did give her three remarkable gifts. The first was a hound that always caught its prey, the second a spear that never missed its mark, and the third a giant bronze man named Talus who ran around the island of Crete three times each day throwing rocks at any ship that tried to land there. In time, Europa gave birth to three sons by Zeus—Sarpedon, Rhadamanthys, and Minos. The king of Crete, Asterius, took pity on Europa and married her, raising her sons as his own.

Europa's father, Agenor, was distraught when he heard the news of his daughter's disappearance and was determined to recover her at any cost. He sent out his wife along with his three sons to search every land. He warned them not to return without Europa. After endless seeking there was still no sign of her, so the brothers decided to settle abroad to found their own kingdoms. Phoenix stayed close to the shore of Lebanon, afterward named Phoenicia for him, while Cilix established the royal house of Cilicia to the north. Cadmus, however, took his mother all the way to Greece and there founded the city of Thebes on a new continent named after his lost sister.

Of all the places of the earth, the favorite of Zeus was Arcadia, a verdant land of forests, springs, and mountains in the Peloponnesus. One day when Zeus was visiting there he saw a young woman hunting in the woods. Her hair was tied back so that she could chase her prey and a simple brooch held her short dress to her body. In her hand was a polished spear with a quiver and a bow slung over her shoulder. She was Callisto, a sworn virgin dedicated to Artemis, the maiden goddess of the hunt.

As Zeus watched, Callisto removed her weapons, unstrung her bow, and lay down on the soft grass to rest. The king of the gods could not resist such a beautiful and unprotected girl.

"Hera will never see me here in these thick woods," Zeus said to himself. "And even if she does, the pleasure will be worth the price."

Immediately Zeus took on the form of Artemis herself and approached Callisto. The girl sprang up with joy to see her patroness and ran to embrace her.

"Callisto, loveliest of all my maidens," spoke the false Artemis, "where have you been hunting all day long?"

"Here in these woods, my lady, greatest of all the gods—and thus I would call you even if Zeus himself were to hear my words."

Zeus laughed and kissed her, not as one innocent girl might kiss another but with a passion that surprised Callisto. She began to tell the divine visitor about her hunting that day, but before she knew it, the god had returned to his true form and threw her on the ground. She tried to resist but was no match for Zeus. After he had raped her and departed, the shattered young woman struggled to her feet and wandered away in shock, barely remembering to take her quiver and bow.

A few days later the true Artemis with her band of virgin hunters appeared to Callisto and called on her to join them. The distraught girl obeyed, but followed the goddess with downcast eyes, ashamed that she had lost her virginity. Artemis noticed the sadness in Callisto's eyes, but thought little of it as the months went by. After nine moons had come and gone, Artemis and her maidens came one hot day to a pool in the woods where they all stripped for a welcome swim in the cool water. Artemis told Callisto to join them, but the girl hesitated and made excuses. At last the goddess grew angry and demanded Callisto remove her clothing. Her swollen belly told the tale all too clearly and Artemis was in no mood for excuses.

"Get out of here!" the goddess proclaimed. "You defile the purity of our sacred pool with your shameful state. You are no longer one of my followers."

Shattered by this rejection, Callisto ran away in disgrace from her friends and the goddess she loved. Soon she gave birth alone to a son she named Arcas.

Hera saw all of this and realized what had happened. As ever, she could not strike back directly against Zeus, so she vented her fury on his victim.

"You whore!" the wife of Zeus cried when she found Callisto in the woods. "Did you really think you could get away with leading my husband astray and bearing him a son as proof of this scandal? You think you're so pretty, do you? Well, that can change."

With that she caught Callisto by the hair and threw her on the ground. The girl stretched out her arms to beg for mercy, but they were now covered with black, shaggy fur. She grew long claws instead of fingers and her once lovely face was replaced with broad, rough jaws and a large nose. So that she might not call on Zeus for help, Hera took away her voice and gave her a harsh, terrifying growl in its place. Callisto had become a wild bear of the mountains. Only her human mind remained unchanged as she reached her limbs up to the heavens, beseeching the ruler of the gods, but to no avail.

Callisto could no longer care for her son, so she left him to be raised by the local king. As a bear, she wandered the mountains and forests ever fearful of hunters, but equally scared of other bears she found in the woods. The years passed in misery for poor Callisto, until one day when young Arcas, who had grown to manhood, was hunting in the forest with his friends. They suddenly saw a bear watching them from behind a tree with a strange look upon its face. It seemed to know Arcas and moved toward him as if to speak. The young man grabbed his spear and was about to plunge it into his mother's breast when Zeus had pity on Callisto at last and snatched her up into the heavens. He placed her as a constellation of stars in the sky to shine during the night.

This was still too much for Hera. She went to Tethys, goddess of the sea, and her husband Ocean to ask of them a favor.

"Isn't it enough," she sobbed, "that Zeus honors this harlot by placing her in the heavens for all to see? Grant to me that she may not bathe in your waters. Let her forever circle the sky without rest."

And so Tethys and Ocean granted her request. Callisto remains to this day ever wandering, ever revolving around the pole star, a great bear who never vanishes below the horizon.

After Cadmus had founded the city of Thebes, rule of the town passed in time to a Greek named Nycteus, who had a beautiful daughter named Antiope. This maiden caught the eye of Zeus as he looked down from the heavens. He came to her in the form of a satyr, a half-man, half-goat creature known for crazed addiction to wine and sex. As with other young women in the past, he raped her and left her pregnant. When her father discovered her condition, he was furious and drove her away from Thebes. She fled south across Greece to the city of Sicyon, where the king of the city, Epopeus, took her in and married her.

Nycteus was angrier than ever at Antiope when he heard the news of her good fortune and was consumed with shame—not for driving his daughter away but because she had brought such disgrace to her family. He called his brother Lycus to his side, making him pledge to punish Antiope and exact revenge on the king who had treated her so kindly. Nycteus then killed himself. Lycus took the throne of Thebes and set about to follow his late brother's wishes. He marched on Sicyon and destroyed the city, killing Epopeus and hauling Antiope out of the town in chains.

Antiope was nine months pregnant at the time and struggled to walk the rough roads back to Thebes with the victorious army. On the slopes of Mount Cithaeron near Thebes, she went into labor and crawled into the bushes to give birth. She bore twin sons, Amphion and Zethus, who were immediately taken by Lycus and left to die on the mountainside. After the army had marched on with the grieving Antiope trailing behind, a local shepherd found the boys and raised them secretly as his own sons.

At Thebes, Lycus handed Antiope over to his wife Dirce for punishment—a task the new queen took on with great pleasure. Every day for many years Dirce subjected Antiope to every cruel punishment she could think of, then chained her in a filthy hut to spend each miserable night alone.

Meanwhile the sons of Antiope grew into fine young men roaming the wilds of the mountains, unaware of who they were or of their mother's fate. Zethus became a master herdsman and cattle breeder while Amphion excelled all others in playing the lyre. The two brothers were opposites in nature and taunted each other endlessly about their respective talents, but they were devoted to one another nonetheless.

One night after Dirce had tormented Antiope and imprisoned her in her hut, the chains holding her mysteriously fell away, perhaps by the power of Zeus. Not stopping to question this miracle, she ran as fast as she could out of Thebes and into the forests below Mount Cithaeron. Cold and miserable, she at last found a shepherd's hut and knocked softly on the door. Two young men answered and took the poor woman inside to sit by the fireplace. After giving her food and drink, they asked her how she came to such a wretched condition. She then told them her sad story, how Zeus had taken advantage of her, how her kind husband had been slain, how she had suffered endless cruelty at the hands of the Theban queen, but most of all her sorrow at being forced to abandon her newborn children years before near the very spot where they sat that night.

As the two young men listened to the story, they realized they themselves were the sons she spoke of. It was a joyous reunion for all, but Zethus and Amphion soon determined to seek their revenge on the king and queen who had been so cruel to their mother. They attacked the city of Thebes and killed Lycus, taking the throne that was rightfully theirs. Then they found Dirce and tied her to the horns of a bull that dragged the queen through the streets and rocky pathways until she was dead. They took what was left of her body and threw it into a nearby spring that thereafter bore her name.

The brothers ruled Thebes together in peace and harmony, even working together side by side to strengthen the city walls. Zethus used his great strength to carry enormous stones to the town, but Amphion played his lyre so sweetly that he charmed the very stones of the earth to follow him from the quarry to their new home on the walls of Thebes.

Near Sicyon, where Antiope had once found peace with King Epopeus, there is a river that runs from the nearby mountains to the blue waters of the Corinthian Gulf. The god of this river was named Asopus and he had a beautiful daughter named Aegina. Zeus fell in love with the girl and came to her one night in the form of a flame to ravish her. Then he carried her off to an island near Athens where she bore a son named Aeacus.

Asopus was frantic at the kidnapping of his beloved daughter and searched everywhere for her. At last he came to Sisyphus, king of nearby Corinth, who revealed to him that it was Zeus himself who had stolen Aegina away. In thanks Asopus created a stream of fresh water for Sisyphus on top of the Acrocorinth, a previously dry fortress looming over the city. The river god then rashly set out to take back his daughter, but Zeus struck him with a thunderbolt and wounded him severely, forcing him to return home without Aegina. To punish Sisyphus for betraying his secret, Zeus decreed that he would be sent to Hades to roll forever a boulder up a hill, only to have it roll back down again when he reached the top.

As usual, Hera was furious at the latest maiden to catch her husband's fancy. But this time instead of changing the girl into an animal or driving her to endless wandering, she poisoned the water of Aegina's island and killed the girl outright, leaving her son, Aeacus, alive. In memory of his mother, the boy named the island after her. When he grew to manhood and became king of Aegina, Hera struck again and annihilated the inhabitants with a horrible plague, save Aeacus and his own young son, Telamon. Young King Aeacus was left alone with the boy on his island and prayed beneath an oak tree to his father Zeus for help, either to repopulate the island or to strike him dead. Zeus showed his favor by sending a flash of lightning across the sky with a peal of thunder. Aeacus was thrilled and sat down beneath the tree to wait for Zeus to act. While he was there, he saw a column of tiny ants carrying grain to their nest. Aeacus admired their industry and prayed again to Zeus: "O most excellent father, grant to me as many subjects for the walls of my city as there are ants here beneath your sacred oak tree."

The branches of the tree swayed back and forth even though there was no wind. Aeacus shivered at the sight and continued to wait for Zeus to do something. At last evening came and he fell asleep beneath the oak. He dreamed that the ants he had seen earlier suddenly grew in size and took on human form. When he awoke, he found his island was full of men and women laboring hard to build homes and farms. Grateful, Aeacus gave thanks to Zeus and named his subjects Myrmidons, after the *myrmex*, or ant, that each had once been.

Aeacus, son of Zeus, became a man known throughout Greece for his fairness and piety. Kings came to him to be judged and cities appealed to him to intervene with Zeus to restore fertility to their lands. After a long life, Zeus appointed him guardian of Hades itself, where he kept the keys to the kingdom of the dead.

The Titan Atlas fathered seven daughters, known as the Pleiades, after their mother Pleione. One of these sisters, Electra, lived on the island of Samothrace and there was seen by Zeus as he looked down from Mount Olympus. He flew to the island and snatched Electra up, taking

her back to the halls of Olympus in his eagerness. The girl clung to a
sacred wooden statue called the Palladium next to the throne of Zeus for
sanctuary, but this meant little to the ruler of the gods in his fit of lust.
He cast the Palladium out of Olympus and raped Electra then and there.
He then returned her to Samothrace, where in time she bore twin sons,
Iasion and Dardanus. Some say that Iasion later became a god, but others
say Zeus killed him after he, as a mortal, dared to sleep with the goddess
Demeter. Dardanus married the daughter of King Teucer and became the
ancestor of the Trojans.

One of Electra's sisters was named Taygete, who was a nymph living
in the high mountains to the west of Sparta. Like Callisto, she was a virgin devoted to the goddess Artemis. Zeus also fell in love with Taygete,
but this time Artemis did what she could to protect her follower from
Zeus. She transformed Taygete into a doe to disguise her. But this did
not fool Zeus. He found her and raped her, fathering a son by her named
Lacedaemon, who became the ancestor of the Spartans. Taygete was
nonetheless grateful to Artemis for her help and dedicated a doe with
golden horns to the goddess—a sacred deer that became known as the
Cerynitian hind, sought by Hercules in one of his labors.

Zeus placed all seven daughters of Atlas in the sky as the constellation still called the Pleiades. But except to the sharpest eyes on the
darkest nights, only six stars are visible. Some say that the seventh star is
Electra, who veiled herself in mourning when the city of Troy fell.

As the years went by, the descendants of Taygete's son, Lacedaemon,
grew into the powerful kingdom of the Spartans in the Peloponnesus.
A son of this royal house named Tyndareus was driven from his home
and sought refuge with King Thestius in Aetolia near Mount Parnassus.
There he met the king's daughter, a beautiful princess named Leda. They
married and when Tyndareus returned to Sparta to claim his throne, he
took Leda with him as his queen.

The beauty of Leda did not escape Zeus. Hoping that Hera would not
notice, the god came to the queen one night in the form of a swan. He
seized her by the neck and forced himself on her, leaving her pregnant.
That same night, Tyndareus also came to her bed and slept with her.
There are different stories of what happened next. Some say that Leda

gave birth to two eggs. From one came twins fathered by Zeus, Helen and Pollux, and from the other came Clytemnestra and Castor, fathered by her mortal husband, Tyndareus. Others say that Castor and Pollux were both sons of Zeus or that both were fathered by Tyndareus. In any case, the brothers were inseparable and came to be known as the Dioscuri, or "sons of Zeus."

Still another story says that Helen was not the daughter of Leda at all, but was conceived by Zeus with the goddess Nemesis when she turned herself into a bird to flee his advances. She had tried to escape Zeus as a fish, then as various land animals, but at last when she was a goose her pursuer took the form of a swan. When he caught her, he had his way with her and she laid an egg. A shepherd then found the egg and brought it to Leda, who put it in a chest until it hatched. Helen was thus born and Leda brought her up as her own daughter. Whoever was the true mother, the Spartans still showed visitors the broken shell of an egg hanging from the roof of one of their temples, claiming that it was the same from which Helen hatched.

Castor and Pollux grew into brave men who one day would sail with Jason on the *Argo*, then rescue their sister Helen from King Theseus of Athens when he kidnapped her long before Paris stole her away to begin the Trojan War. When Castor was killed on a cattle raid, his divine brother Pollux prayed to Zeus that he might give up half his immortality so that he and Castor could spend alternate days on Olympus and in Hades. In time Zeus transported them to the stars to become the twins of the constellation Gemini.

Like many Greek men, Zeus did not restrict his sexual attention to women, but was drawn to handsome boys as well. One of the first was a youth named Phaenon, sculpted out of clay by Prometheus when he began creating men. Prometheus spared no effort on this boy and crafted a young man so stunning that he hid him away from Zeus, knowing that the ruler of the gods would not be able to resist such a temptation. But the god Eros heard of Phaenon and whispered in the ear of Zeus about the boy, so that he sent Hermes to bring the lad to Olympus. In time he was placed among the stars.

But the most famous male lover of Zeus was a young Trojan prince named Ganymede. Some say he was the grandson of Electra's son

Dardanus, making him a great-grandson of Zeus himself, while others say he was the child of another Trojan king. Most agree his father's name was Tros and that one day while he was watching over his flocks on Mount Ida near Troy, Zeus descended in a whirlwind and snatched the boy up to Olympus. Others say the god sent his eagle to grab the youth and carry him away or that the eagle was Zeus himself.

Tros was frantic at the disappearance of his son and searched everywhere for him, but he seemed lost forever. Zeus took pity on the father and sent Hermes to Troy to console him. The messenger god told Tros that he should rejoice, for Ganymede was now a lover of Zeus and the honored cupbearer to the king of the gods. He would be immortal and live forever in the halls of Olympus. In recompense for the boy, Zeus gave Tros a pair of the finest horses and a golden grapevine crafted by the god Hephaestus. The father took comfort in these words and gifts, glad that his son had found such favor with Zeus. Even Hera showed none of her usual jealousy and accepted Ganymede as a bedmate of her husband and member of the divine household.

POSEIDON

There is an old story once told in the mountains of Arcadia that Zeus was not the only child of Rhea to escape being swallowed by his father, Cronus. The tale says that after Rhea gave birth to the infant Poseidon, elder brother of Zeus, she placed him near a spring among a flock of lambs in the hope that his father would not notice him. When Cronus came to swallow her latest child, she presented him with a foal and told the great god that she had given birth to the young horse. Strangely enough, this seemed believable to Cronus and he swallowed the animal, leaving Poseidon to grow up among the flocks of Arcadia.

Most ancient stories dismiss this version of Poseidon's childhood and say he was indeed swallowed whole along with his brothers and sisters, but it is surely no coincidence that forever after Poseidon was linked with horses. Poseidon was best known as the god of the wine-dark sea, but he also ruled over earthquakes and stallions racing across the plains. As an ancient hymn recounts:

> I first sing of the great god Poseidon, shaker of the earth and the barren sea, lord of the deep, who possesses Helicon and broad Aegae. The gods, earth shaker, gave you two privileges—to be tamer of horses and savior of ships. Hail to you, Poseidon, dark-haired rider of the earth. Be compassionate in your heart and protect those who sail the seas.

Well the Greeks might pray for the mercy of Poseidon. As a people of the sea, they knew better than most that a peaceful voyage could suddenly turn deadly as they traveled among their many islands. The god who shook the land and gloried in horses thundering over the fields could also calm the waves so that sailors might live another day.

The Greeks might pray to Zeus to bring justice and order to the world, but Poseidon was a violent, primal force of nature to be appeased in terror and placated with extravagant vows and sacrifices. The god cared little for the affairs of men and lived in the depths of the sea, emerging only to raise terrible storms or turn cities to rubble. He was jealous of his younger brother Zeus and chafed under his rule. In one of the few uprisings against Zeus, he once joined Hera and Athena to bind and overthrow his brother, but was thwarted when the goddess Thetis summoned a creature some say was Poseidon's own son, the hundred-armed Briareus, from Tartarus to end the revolt. The sea god sometimes competed with other Olympians for the patronage of cities, and was terrible in his wrath when he lost. And like Zeus, he took whatever female he wanted by force, leaving neither immortal goddess nor human maiden safe from his advances.

One ancient poem says that the oracle of Apollo at Delphi once belonged to Poseidon in common with his grandmother the Earth, also known as Gaia or Ge. In those days:

> The voice of Ge spoke words of wisdom,
> and with her Pyrcon, servant of the famed Earth-shaker.

The voice of Earth was a nymph named Daphnis who breathed vapors from the mountainside shrine along with the otherwise unknown Pyrcon and uttered the words of the two gods. Mother Earth later gave her share of the shrine to Themis, who in turn yielded it to Apollo. Poseidon, having little real interest in guiding the lives of men, traded his ownership of the oracle to Apollo in return for the small island of Calaureia south of Athens.

After Poseidon gained dominion over the seas in the division of the world with his brothers Zeus and Hades, he began to fight with other gods to be patron of the most important Greek cities. First of these was Corinth, where he unsuccessfully contested with the sun god Helios for control of the town. Briareus was again summoned to deal with his father, eventually awarding Poseidon the isthmus and nearby lands, but granting Helios the coveted heights of the Acrocorinth. The sea god also fiercely contested rule over Argos with Hera. Three river gods—Inachus, Cephissus, and Asterion—were called in to judge the dispute and awarded the town to Hera. Poseidon was so upset that he shriveled all three rivers, so that thereafter these streams flowed only after a heavy rain.

But the most famous story was the bitter contest for sovereignty over Athens between Poseidon and Athena. The first king of the city was a man named Cecrops, who had the tail of a snake. Zeus cleverly appointed him to judge the dispute between his brother and daughter, thereby avoiding making the difficult decision himself. To prove his powers to the king, Poseidon struck his trident on top of the rocky Acropolis above the town and produced a spring of salt water. When her turn came, Athena caused an olive tree to sprout from the hill, yielding a valued new food for the people of the city. Cecrops rightly decided that olives were more useful than seawater and awarded the patronage of Athens to Athena. Poseidon, in typical fashion, went on a rampage and flooded the whole countryside in revenge.

Poseidon was married to Amphitrite, the daughter of Ocean and Tethys or perhaps of the ancient sea gods Nereus and Doris. Amphitrite, however, at first wanted nothing to do with the unpredictable Poseidon. As soon as he came to her she fled to the Titan Atlas to hide and remained with him in secret to preserve her virginity. But Poseidon did not give up so easily and sent out many spies to find her. At last one of them named Delphinus came upon her on a distant island and persuaded her to marry the god. He even arranged the wedding himself. Poseidon was so grateful that he placed Delphinus among the stars as a constellation shaped like a dolphin. He honored dolphins ever after as they escorted him across the waves.

But like his brother, Poseidon did not confine his sexual urges to his wife. He pursued goddesses and mortal women with a callousness and violence that surpassed even that of Zeus. Even his own sister was not safe from his advances. One day when the goddess Demeter was passing through Arcadia desperately searching for her lost daughter Persephone, Poseidon pursued her in a fit of lust. She had no desire for her brother nor time to put up with his philandering, so she changed herself into a mare and hid among a nearby herd of horses. Poseidon was not fooled and immediately transformed himself into a stallion, then forced himself on Demeter. When the act was done, Demeter was furious but powerless to strike back against her overwhelming brother. She became pregnant and bore the sea god two children. The first was a daughter, Despoina, whose name was told only to those initiated into her cult, but the second was a famous horse called Arion. This stallion belonged in turn to Poseidon, Hercules, and Adrastus, a king of Argos whose life was saved by Arion when he battled against Thebes.

Poseidon also raped Medusa, but this was in the distant past when she was a young maiden instead of a hideous Gorgon. The story says that she was mortal, unlike her two sisters, Stheno and Euryale. Medusa was the most beautiful girl in the world and had many human suitors. Poseidon also desired her and so came to her as she worshiped in the temple of the virgin goddess Athena. He raped her there as Athena turned her eyes away, but the goddess placed the blame on Medusa, not Poseidon. Athena had always been jealous of the girl's good looks, especially her lovely hair, so she turned her flowing locks into writhing snakes so horrible to gaze upon that they transformed anyone who looked at them into stone. Medusa became pregnant from the god but did not give birth until much later, when the hero Perseus cut off her head and out sprang two children, one of whom was the winged horse Pegasus.

Like Medusa, the beautiful virgin Theophrane had many suitors from all over the Greek world. But Poseidon kidnapped the girl and took her to an island to hold her prisoner. When the suitors found out where she was, they gathered together and made an expedition to the island to rescue her. To confuse the would-be heroes, Poseidon changed Theophrane into a ewe and the rest of the islanders into goats. The suitors arrived and searched the island high and low, but there was no sign of anyone except the goats, so they began to slaughter the animals for food. Poseidon then turned the rescuers into wolves, who continued to prey on the flocks. While all this transformation and bloodshed was occurring, Poseidon changed himself into a great ram and ravished Theophrane. The girl-turned-goat became pregnant and gave birth to a remarkable young ram with golden fleece, later sought by Jason and the Argonauts.

Poseidon was known to pursue maidens in the form of a bull, just like his brother Zeus. As such an animal, he came to Canace, the daughter of Aeolus, ruler of Thessaly. She had five children by the god, including Aloeus and Triops. Aloeus married his niece, Iphimedia, a daughter of Triops, but the bride was smitten with her own grandfather, Poseidon. She would often sit on the shore and cup the waters in her hands, then pour them into her lap. Poseidon must have been surprised to find a woman who was actually in love with him and so gladly lay with her. She bore him two sons—who were also his great-grandchildren—named Otus and Ephialtes. By the time they were nine years old they were immensely powerful and handsome giants over fifty feet tall. In their youthful arrogance they decided to build a tower to the heavens and attack the gods themselves. They ripped Mount Ossa in Thessaly from its roots and piled it on top of Mount Olympus, then placed nearby Mount Pelion onto both of them to storm the sky. They threatened to push mountains into the sea and make it dry land, then turn the former land into sea. They did manage to capture Ares, the god of war, and stuff him into a bronze jar for over a year until Hermes rescued him. They also made advances on Hera and the virgin goddess Artemis, but to no avail.

If the pair had been full-grown, they might have conquered heaven and earth, but the gods decided they had had enough. They could not defeat the two through strength, so they used a trick. The brothers were great hunters, so Apollo sent a deer between them as they roamed the island of Naxos. When they saw the animal, they threw their spears at the same instant and struck each other dead. Zeus punished them in Hades by binding the brothers back to back to a pillar with snakes as they spend eternity facing away from each other, watched over by an owl.

Among the final objects of Poseidon's unwanted affection was a girl from Thessaly named Caenis. This beautiful maiden, who had refused to take a husband, was walking along the seaside one day when Poseidon saw her and raped her. When he was finished, Poseidon offered to grant her any request she might make. In sheer contempt the young woman asked to be made into a man so that she might not have to suffer such violation again. Poseidon granted her this favor and in addition made her invulnerable to all weapons. The sex-changed Caenis—now Caeneus—became a clan leader of the Lapith tribe in Thessaly and later battled with a pack of raging, libido-driven half-horse, half-human centaurs at the wedding of the Lapith king Pirithous. The centaurs were unable to strike down Caeneus with their swords and spears, so they pounded him deep into the mud with a tree trunk.

Poseidon also had at least one male lover among mortals, the handsome young prince Pelops, grandfather of the future king Agamemnon. The sea god took him to Olympus to serve as his own cupbearer and catamite, then sent the boy home with the gift of a magnificent chariot Pelops would one day use to win his wife, the princess Hippodamia.

Zeus never forgot that Poseidon had once joined Hera and Athena in rebelling against him. As punishment he sent his brother to the new city of Troy to serve King Laomedon for a year along with Apollo. The two gods were disguised as mortals, but Laomedon recognized their talent and put them to work. Poseidon supervised the construction of Troy's impregnable walls, while Apollo herded the city's cattle on nearby Mount Ida. At the end of the year with the work completed, Poseidon and Apollo came to the king to collect their wages, but Laomedon sent them away unpaid and threatened to cut off their ears and sell them into slavery if they complained. The two gods were angry at being cheated by a mere mortal and quickly carried out their revenge. Apollo sent a plague to ravage the city, then Poseidon sent a sea monster that snatched wandering Trojans off the beach until Laomedon agreed to sacrifice his own daughter, Hesione, to appease the creature. Just in time, Hercules sailed into town and agreed to rescue the girl if he received her as his wife along with some fine Trojan horses. Laomedon agreed and the hero slew the sea monster, but Laomedon broke this bargain as well and refused to surrender the girl. In typical fashion, Hercules killed the king and took his daughter anyway, leaving her young brother Priam on the Trojan throne. Although not given to patience, Poseidon bided his time and held back his own anger at the city of Troy. But someday, he swore, the walls he had built around Troy would fall.

HADES

The Greeks feared Hades even more than his brothers Zeus and Poseidon, though they seldom worshiped him and even avoided mentioning his name. To mortals he was "the god below" or "the invisible one"— titles used to keep from speaking his real name and perhaps drawing his unwanted attention. Sometimes he was called by the Greek *Pluto* ("wealth"), a reference to the riches hidden beneath the earth, or even "the good god" in hope of gaining his benefaction. But in the end, no attempt to hide from Hades or curry his favor worked. All he inspired in humans was terror of the bitter end of life. As the queen Alcestis shouted on her deathbed: "Someone is taking me away—don't you see him?—taking me away to the halls of the dead. It is Hades, staring at me from beneath his dark brows! What do you want? Leave me alone! Such an unhappy journey I must make, the most unhappy of women."

Prayers and pleas did not move him nor did sacrifices appease the merciless god of the dead. All mortals, good and bad alike, eventually went down to the house of death where Hades ruled—his allotment in the three-fold division of the cosmos with his brothers. Hades was not a spiteful or cruel god, simply an implacable force as relentless and inevitable as death itself.

There are few myths about Hades, save for a single story best told in the tales of Demeter. Almost all we know about Hades is the nature of the home that shared his name. It was a dark and brooding place of endless sighs and a vaporous existence for mortals who passed into it. Hades ruled this land while Death dwelled there as well, along with his brother Sleep. There was no punishment in this dark kingdom, save for a few singled out by the gods, simply an endless existence as a bodiless shade without substance or hope.

Every soul that died was led by the god Hermes, or occasionally by Hades himself, to the banks of the River Styx. Souls who had not received a proper burial remained on the far side of the river for at least a hundred years before they could cross. Those who had been given funeral rites were ferried across the stream by the ill-tempered boatman Charon, who charged the dead for their passage—thus Greeks were always buried with a coin in their mouths. On the other side of the Styx they were met by the three-headed dog Cerberus, wagging his tail to greet all who entered, but devouring any soul who tried to leave. The worst of the dead were judged by Minos, his brother Rhadamanthys, or virtuous Aeacus, and condemned to torture, while a blessed few might be allowed into the delightful fields of Elysium. Some stories say the unhappy dead could drink from the waters of the stream Lethe and forget the misery of their lives, but most were left to remember and wander the dismal plains of the underworld for eternity.

But there were some Greeks who rejected this grim view of death and hoped for something more than the shadowy realm of Hades as the next world. They believed the soul might be reborn into a new life on earth—or with proper training and initiation, the cycle of rebirth itself might be broken and the soul could attain a higher existence forever in the realm of the gods.

One story of such a life after death begins on a battlefield. There was once a young man named Er who died in a nameless war and lay among the fallen corpses for ten days. His family came at last for his body and placed his remains on a funeral pyre to be burned. But just before the fire was set, Er rose up alive and well.

The young man said he had been on a journey through the land of the dead and had returned to tell all who would hear about what happens after death. He said that after he had been slain, he joined a multitude of souls in another world walking toward a place of judgment. At this place there were four doors, two above leading to and from heaven and two below leading to and from the underworld. After the judges had ruled on their lives, the dead were led either to the right and the entrance to heaven or to the left, where they passed into the land beneath the earth. At the same time, there were souls leaving both heaven and the underworld through the other doors after a journey of a thousand years. Those who had been to heaven had received a tenfold reward for the good they had done in their previous lives, while those emerging from the underworld told of punishment ten times worse than the sins they had committed on earth. A few, especially wicked men, were not allowed to leave the underworld at all but were bound hand and foot by fiery demons and thrown into Tartarus for eternity.

After the souls exiting from heaven and the underworld had rested on a plain for seven days, they continued on their journey to a place with a shining column stretching all the way to the sky. This axis of the universe held together the cosmos, with Sirens on different levels, each singing a single note of great purity to create the music of the spheres. It was also here that the Fates spun the lives of those who would be reborn, though the gods allowed the souls to choose their own destiny.

The first soul to select his next life was rash and saw only that the life he wanted was that of a powerful king. He did not look closely and see that he was also fated to eat his own children. The next souls were weary of being humans and so chose the life of animals. Some who were men wanted to be women, while some women chose to be men. When at last there was only one soul left, the man came forward and looked at all the possible fates with great care. He was the celebrated hero Odysseus, who had been famous for his cunning and skill in war. At last he found the life he wanted—that of a simple, private man who minded his own business. When some of the souls asked if he was disappointed about such a future, he said that he would have made the same choice if he had been the first in line.

When all the souls had made their selection, they went forward to have them woven into their new lives. Then they were led to the River Lethe to drink and forget their past before they were reborn. At midnight, there was great clap of thunder and an earthquake. Suddenly all the souls shot up into the sky like stars to their new lives. But Er awoke on his funeral pyre, ready to tell his tale to all who would listen.

APOLLO

When Zeus seduced the goddess Leto, daughter of the Titans Coeus and Phoebe, she became pregnant and wandered the world in search of a quiet place to give birth. Jealous Hera had already sent a dragon named Python after her as she passed Delphi, so she left the mainland to find an island refuge safe from all harm. Hera, however, warned all the isles not to allow her to bear children on their shores, so none would welcome her. At last, in great misery, Leto came to the small, barren island of Delos in the Aegean Sea. No one ever paid attention to Delos because of its diminutive size and the fact that it floated about on the waves from place to place, unfixed to the seafloor below.

When she arrived on the island she spoke: "Delos, if you would consent to be the birthplace of my children, my son will build a great temple here. Your soil will blossom with the fruits of the earth. Men will come to your shores from far and wide to offer sacrifice."

And Delos replied, "Leto, glorious daughter of Coeus, I would be honored to host you. But everyone scorns my rocky fields and no one ever comes to my shores. Will you swear that your son will build his temple here?"

And so Leto swore by the River Styx, the unbreakable vow of the gods, that all would come to pass as she promised.

Leto was in agonizing labor for nine days and nine nights, attended by many goddesses—but not Hera. The wife of Zeus stayed on Olympus and kept with her Eileithyia, the goddess who brought comfort to women in childbirth. Those attending Leto at last sent Iris, the divine messenger and goddess of the rainbow, to find Eileithyia and bring her to Delos secretly. The goddess eased Leto's pain, then told her to wrap her arms around a palm tree, lean against its trunk, and push with all her might. Out into the light of day came the infant Apollo. The goddesses all cried with joy and bathed the child in purest water, afterward wrapping him in swaddling clothes. Instead of milk from his mother's breast, they nursed him on deathless ambrosia and nectar of the gods. Still hanging onto the tree, Leto then bore Apollo's sister Artemis and collapsed on the green earth beneath her.

But Leto's troubles were not over. Hera in her anger pursued her and the newborn babes across the sea to Lycia. There Leto was thirsty and asked the local peasants if she might drink from their well, but they foolishly refused, even when her infants stretched out their hands in supplication. In her indignation at this gross breach of hospitality, Leto changed them all into croaking frogs. Then she returned to the mountains near Delphi where a giant named Tityus tried to rape her. She called on her young but miraculously mature children to save her, which they did by slaying Tityus. Zeus afterward punished the giant in the underworld for his crime by staking him to the ground and sending two vultures to eat his bowels for eternity.

Apollo was always quick to come to the defense of his mother, whether for injuries or insults. When he was only four days old, the precocious young god began looking for a place to establish his oracle. He traveled from Mount Olympus to Thebes and along the road to a spring sacred to the nymph Telphusa. He liked the look of the place, so he told the nymph he was going to build his oracular temple there. She welcomed him, but warned the god that the clatter of horses and passing chariots might be distracting. She recommended a quiet spot she knew on the slopes of Mount Parnassus, a suggestion Apollo took to heart. It was only later when he realized Telphusa had been trying to get rid of him that he dried up her spring.

Beneath Mount Parnassus at the site of Delphi, Apollo constructed his temple, taking over the beautiful mountainside shrine from Themis and his uncle Poseidon. But the great serpent Python lived nearby and was determined—some say at the encouragement of Hera—to stop the god from bringing his cult to Delphi. The dragon attacked Apollo, but Apollo, the god of archers, was eager to kill the beast for standing in the way of his plans. He pierced him with a mighty arrow and mortally wounded the serpent. The creature writhed in agony while its screams echoed from the cliff walls, until at last it collapsed and died. The young Apollo gloried in his victory and took on the title "Pythian" after the dragon he had slain.

The temple was built and the oracular site readied, but the god had no priests or prophets to serve him. Gazing out to sea from the towering cliffs of Delphi, he spotted a ship on the waves and flew down to it. The sailors were merchants from Crete, plying their trade up and down the coast. Apollo turned himself into a dolphin and jumped onto the deck of the black ship, surprising the men, who saw this as a sign from the gods. Suddenly the ship began to sail against the wind until it reached port beneath Mount Parnassus. Apollo then reverted to his true form and brought the sailors to his temple, telling them they had been selected as priests for his new shrine. He also chose a young woman named Phenomoe to be the first Pythia, the priestess who would reveal his words to mortals. Thereafter when supplicants came to his oracle she gave responses to their questions from the god's sanctuary, while the priests offered sacrifices and interpreted the utterances of the Pythia for men.

But it was not just monsters that Apollo slew for the sake of his mother's honor. When Niobe, daughter of the king of Lydia, married Amphion, king of Thebes, the couple had seven handsome sons and an equal number of beautiful daughters. She refused to worship Leto as a goddess, for she believed that Apollo's mother had less reason to boast than she did: "I too have divine blood in my veins. Isn't my mother a sister of the Pleiades? Am I not the granddaughter of both Atlas and Zeus himself? Aren't I as beautiful as any goddess? And most of all, why should I worship Leto, mother of only two children, when I have seven times that many?"

When her friends warned her not to tempt the gods, she laughed and said that her very abundance of blessings made her safe. Leto heard her words and was very angry. She called Apollo and Artemis to her side and began to tell them the details of the insults Niobe had made against her.

"Stop, mother," said Apollo. "To continue would be merely to delay her punishment."

With that Apollo and his sister flew to Thebes and came to the plain outside the city. There the sons of Niobe were all riding their fine horses. Suddenly the eldest fell down dead, then the second, then the third, until at last all seven lay on the ground, struck by Apollo's arrows.

When their father, Amphion, heard the news, he rushed to the plain and plunged his own knife into his heart to escape the pain caused by his wife's boasting—but Niobe was unrepentant. She threw herself onto the still-warm bodies of her sons and shouted out to heaven: "Feed yourself on your vengeance, Leto, glut your bloodthirsty heart! I have lost my seven sons, but I still have seven daughters. My children still outnumber yours. After so many deaths, I still win!"

The daughters who stood weeping above the bodies of their brothers and father scarcely had time to look at their mother, when one by one they too began to fall to the arrows of the god. Finally only the youngest remained clinging to her mother's knees. Niobe wrapped her robe around the girl and cried out to Leto, "Please, great goddess, leave me the youngest. Spare me just one, I beg you."

But no sooner had these words left her lips than the maiden fell dead beside her. Niobe collapsed in stony grief surrounded by the bodies of her children and husband. Her face pale, her eyes fixed, she sat staring into space. A whirlwind came and caught her up, carrying her back to her home across the sea in Lydia. There on a mountaintop she sits to this day, a weeping woman of marble, mourning her lost children.

Apollo could also be vengeful when his own honor was insulted. As the god of music, he was fiercely proud of his skill as a flute player. One day his sister Artemis decided to try her hand at the instrument. She crafted a flute out of deer horn and practiced until she was very good, then came to a banquet of the gods to show off her new skill. No sooner did she start to play than Hera and Aphrodite began to laugh at the sight of her cheeks turning blue as she puffed on the flute. Embarrassed, Artemis ran off into the forest and watched her own reflection in a spring as she played a tune, realizing then that indeed she did look strange. She threw the flute into the spring and laid a curse on anyone who ever used the instrument to make music.

One day the satyr Marsyas was watching over his flocks when he came to the spring and saw the flute. He picked it up and was enchanted by the sound it made. He practiced every day for months until he could play the sweetest tunes anyone had ever heard. He became so good, in fact, that he challenged Apollo himself to a contest of skill. Apollo accepted and appointed judges to decide the winner. Some say these were the Muses, but others say he chose King Midas of Phrygia.

Marsyas and Apollo both played beautifully, but the satyr was definitely the better musician, matching every trick and technique that the god could come up with. At last Apollo turned his flute upside down and played just as well—a skill Marsyas could not match. Apollo was judged the winner and the god then turned his attention to Marsyas. He hung the satyr from a tall pine tree and began to strip the skin from his body as his woodland friends watched in horror. He slowly flayed the satyr alive, Marsyas screaming in agony until the end. No one ever again challenged Apollo to a contest of musical skill.

Those who write that Midas was the judge at this contest say that the king had favored Marsyas until the end and that Apollo did not forget this insult. As punishment, the god gave Midas the ears of an ass. The king was so ashamed that he wore a Phrygian cap pulled down over his head thereafter and told no one of his deformity. Only his barber knew and Midas threatened him with death if he told anyone. But the strain of keeping the secret was eventually too much for the poor servant, so he dug a hole in a meadow near a road, whispered the news into it, then covered it back up again. When spring came, reeds grew from the hole. But when anyone passed by, the wind blowing through the reeds gave voice to the secret: "Midas has the ears of an ass"—and soon everyone knew the truth of what Apollo had done to the king.

For a handsome young god, Apollo was often unlucky in love. Unlike his father Zeus and uncle Poseidon, he rarely resorted to outright violence to win the objects of his desire, instead preferring persuasion and gifts. The god's first and most famous romantic failure was his pursuit of the nymph Daphne, daughter of an Arcadian river god. Not long after he had slain the dragon Python, Apollo quarreled with Cupid, son of Aphrodite, saying the lad should leave the handling of bows and arrows to him.

"My arrows may not be able to pierce everything," replied Cupid, "but they can pierce you."

Cupid then flew down to Arcadia, where he spied the beautiful maiden Daphne playing with her friends. He took a special arrow from his bow to make her turn away from love and shot her in the breast. From that moment on the girl wanted nothing to do with men but only to hunt in the woods with her female companions as a follower of Artemis. She was courted by many suitors and her father was anxious for grandchildren, but she pleaded with him, "Father, dearest, please let me remain a virgin all my life. I hate the sight of the wedding torch and detest Hymen, the goddess of marriage."

He at last gave in to his daughter and consented that she would never have to marry. But then Cupid flew to Olympus and shot Apollo with another arrow, this one to make him fall madly in love with Daphne. The god was consumed with desire for the girl, but nothing he did could win her heart.

Apollo was by no means alone in his longing for Daphne. Among her suitors was Leucippus, a young prince from a nearby kingdom. He begged her to be his bride, but she scorned his advances. At last he decided he had to be with her, even if he could not be her husband. He grew his hair long and braided it like a maiden, then put on women's clothing and joined the girls in the woods in disguise. They were all pleased to have such a fine new hunter in their band and welcomed Leucippus warmly. Daphne was especially taken by the latest member of the group and the two became fast friends. But Apollo was watching from above and grew jealous of Leucippus. He arranged for the band of hunters to come to a cool river on a hot day. All the girls gleefully stripped off their clothes and jumped into the water naked, except for the reluctant Leucippus. The maidens teased him for his modesty and chased him until they pinned him down and tore off his clothes. When Daphne and her friends discovered he was a young man instead of a maiden, their laughter turned to fury and they stabbed him to death with their spears.

But Apollo was not discouraged and continued to burn with love for Daphne. Finally he came to her in the hills of Arcadia and tried one last time to speak with her. She fled at once as the god chased her, but Apollo cried out for her to wait and listen to him. Daphne only ran faster through the woods with the god on her heels. Apollo was now determined to take her by force since persuasion had failed, but as he drew near, the girl cried out to her father the river god, "Father, help! If you have the power, let your waters change this beauty of mine into something the god will despise."

In an instant a numbness seized her limbs and her soft skin began to harden. Her hair sprouted into green leaves and her arms turned to branches. The legs that had run so fast through the hills became fixed in the earth and her head became the top of a laurel tree.

But even in this new form Apollo still loved her. He embraced her branches as if they were arms and pressed his lips to the wood. He wept as he spoke to her: "Even though you cannot be my bride, you will always be my love. My hair will forevermore be entwined with your laurel."

The god plucked a sprig from her boughs and wove it into a crown that he placed on his head. Though she still shrank from his embraces, the maiden tree seemed to consent to this honor as she nodded in the breeze.

Another of Apollo's early loves met an unfortunate fate when she rejected his advances. She was a young prophetess named Sibyl from near Troy or perhaps from the Greek colony of Cumae in southern Italy. When the god came to her, he offered her anything she might wish if she would only sleep with him. Sibyl laughed and pointed to a heap of sand.

"Grant me then that I might have as many years of life as there are grains of sand in that pile."

Apollo gladly consented and said the gift was hers even without agreeing to be his lover. He then offered her immortality if she would yield her virginity to him. Sibyl saw little need for this since she had seemingly endless years stretching before her, so she spurned the god's offer and chose to remain a maiden forever.

But Sibyl had forgotten to ask for eternal youth when she received the gift of long life. There were a thousand grains of sand in that pile—a thousand years to grow ever more old and decrepit. In time her hair and teeth fell out, her limbs shriveled from age, and she shrank in size until she was nothing but a speck. Only her voice remained unchanged. Toward the end of her life, she lived in a bottle hanging from the ceiling of her shrine at Cumae. Neighborhood boys would come to the temple and ask, "Sibyl, what do you want?"

To which she would answer: "I want to die."

Many of Apollo's other romantic attempts were just as fruitless. The god fell in love with a young woman named Marpessa, daughter of Evenus, but she was carried off instead by a mortal named Idas on a winged chariot he had received as a gift from Poseidon. When Apollo caught up with Idas, he was ready to kill the young man and steal Marpessa away, but Zeus intervened and granted the girl the right to choose which of the two she wanted as her husband. Marpessa wisely decided that a god would soon tire of her and so chose Idas.

Apollo was likewise disappointed in his wooing of the maiden Sinope. When this girl made him first promise to grant her any request she might make, the god quickly vowed that it would be so. Then Sinope asked to remain a virgin all her life. The god was exasperated at having been so easily deceived, but he kept his word and left Sinope untouched.

Apollo was not so kind to the final maiden who caught his eye, Cassandra, the daughter of King Priam of Troy. Apollo fell in love with her and taught her the art of prophecy hoping to win her favor, but once she had learned to foresee the future, she spurned his advances. In revenge he allowed her to keep her unmatched talent as a soothsayer, but decreed that no one would believe any prediction she made. In time, Cassandra would learn what a terrible price she would pay for rejecting the love of Apollo.

The archer god was just as unlucky with his male lovers. When Apollo fell in love with handsome young Hyacinth, the son of the king of Sparta, he was so smitten that he lost all interest in his bow and lyre. The god and the boy spent every day together in the woods and fields around the town hunting and playing sports. One day they stripped off their clothes, anointed themselves with olive oil, and began a discus-throwing contest. Apollo threw the iron disk so hard it soared through the clouds, much to the delight of Hyacinth. But Zephyrus, the West Wind, was also in love with the lad and jealous of his affair with Apollo. As the discus sailed back down to earth, Zephyrus directed it toward Hyacinth, crushing his skull. Apollo rushed to his mortal lover and used all his skill at medicine to heal him, but to no avail. Hyacinth died in the arms of the god with his blood dripping to the ground. Apollo honored the young man by causing a beautiful flower to spring from the drops of blood on the grass, so from that day forth the flowering hyacinth was a memorial to his lost love.

Likewise young Cyparissus from the small island of Cea was lost to Apollo. There was a magnificent stag sacred to the nymphs that roamed the island and was beloved by all the people there. They decorated its antlers with gold and hung silver and pearls from its ears. The deer was so tame that it would visit homes all around the island and allow even strangers to stroke its neck. But no one loved the animal more than young Cyparissus. He would lead the stag to fresh water and make sure it had the finest grass to eat. The deer gladly allowed the boy to decorate its horns with garlands and even ride on its back.

Apollo loved Cyparissus as much as the young man loved the deer and was delighted to see the lad spending his days with the sacred stag. But one hot summer day, the deer lay down to rest in the cool shade of the forest. Cyparissus was out hunting and had no idea when he threw his spear that the stag was nearby. His weapon pierced the heart of the animal as it lay peacefully on the grass and the boy screamed in horror. He rushed to the stag and held it in his arms as its lifeblood drained away. Apollo tried to comfort the lad, but he was inconsolable. The boy asked only that he might be allowed to grieve without ceasing. Apollo granted his wish and turned him into a cypress tree with dark limbs and drooping branches, forever mourning his lost friend.

Apollo was usually kind to the objects of his love, but at times he could be as brutal and violent as any other god. When the Athenian princess Creusa, daughter of King Erechtheus, refused his advances, he dragged her into a cave beneath the Athenian Acropolis and raped her. The violated young woman became pregnant and somehow hid her condition from her family for nine months. She bore a child, named Ion, alone and in secret, then brought the baby to the same deserted cave where Apollo had ravished her. Weeping, she laid her newborn son in a cradle and left him there to die.

Apollo felt pity for the child, if not his mother, and sent the god Hermes to bring the infant to his shrine at Delphi. There Ion grew up as a servant in Apollo's temple, not knowing where he came from or who his parents were. Creusa meanwhile married a man named Xuthus who became king of Athens, but their union was childless.

Years passed until one day Creusa came to Delphi to discover if she would ever have another child. She met Ion, now a young man, and the two were drawn to each other for reasons neither understood. She told him that years before a friend of hers, raped by Apollo, had left her baby to die in a cave. She wanted to consult the oracle about the child, but was warned that to accuse the god of such an act in his own temple was sacrilege.

Xuthus also arrived at Delphi to ask the oracle if he would ever be a father. The Pythia told him that indeed the first person he met as he left the temple would be his son. As soon as he stepped out of the door, he saw Ion. The boy was as cool to the king as he was kind to Creusa and refused to believe the god had made the king his father. Ion wanted only to remain at Delphi and serve Apollo, but finally Xuthus convinced him to return to Athens as his heir. When Creusa learned of this, she suspected that Ion was in fact a son Xuthus had fathered secretly as part of a plan to place a bastard on the Athenian throne instead of the child she hoped to bear. She therefore decided to poison Ion with a drop of Gorgon's blood, but Apollo intervened and miraculously saved the boy when a bird that sipped from his cup fell over dead.

Ion accused Creusa of attempted murder in spite of his affection for her and she sought sanctuary at the sacred altar of Apollo. The Pythia then entered the temple bearing the very cradle in which Ion had been abandoned. Creusa recognized it at once and confessed that she had left her child in it to die. Ion realized then that Creusa was his mother and the god he had served so faithfully was his father. Unlike most myths of Apollo, the story of Creusa and Ion ended happily with mother and son returning to Athens, where Ion became the ancestor of the Ionian tribe of the Greeks.

There was no happy ending for a fair young maiden named Chione when both Apollo and Hermes fell in love with her. She had just turned fourteen, the marriageable age for a Greek girl, when both gods chanced to see her at the same time as they passed by her town. Apollo decided to wait until night to approach her, but Hermes would not be delayed. He put her to sleep with a magic spell and raped her. When night came, Apollo disguised himself as an old woman to gain her trust, then did the same as Hermes. The young woman therefore became pregnant with the sons of two gods at the same time. To Hermes she bore Autolycus, who became a notable thief and grandfather of the wandering hero Odysseus. Apollo was the father of her son Philammon, a famous musician. Chione was so proud of the fact that she was mother to the children of two gods that she forgot how she had lain with them unwillingly and began to boast of her good fortune. She even mocked Artemis, saying she, Chione, must be more beautiful than the virgin goddess of the hunt. Artemis heard her and promptly shot an arrow through her head, piercing her boastful tongue and killing the foolish girl instantly. When her father came to look for her, he found Chione's body burning on a funeral pyre and tried to embrace her, but was driven off by the flames. In madness he ran to the top of Mount Parnassus and threw himself off the summit, but Apollo in an act of mercy changed him into a hawk to soar among the clouds.

HEPHAESTUS

No one was ever quite sure where Hephaestus came from. Some say he was a child of Zeus and Hera, while others say he was born of Hera alone. Whatever his origin, he was a figure of scorn and laughter in the halls of Mount Olympus—a crippled, lowly craftsman limping among the shining gods. But like human blacksmiths in ancient Greece, Hephaestus was also respected for what seemed like a magical ability to bend metal into any shape he chose. The other gods might mock him, but when they needed a new shield or sword, they would come begging at his door.

Those who say Hera bore Hephaestus without Zeus to father him claim that she was angry at her husband, but when she saw that the infant was lame, she threw him from Mount Olympus in disgust. The goddesses Thetis and Eurynome then rescued the child and raised him secretly in a cave by the sea, where for nine years he learned the art of forging metal. When he was a master of his craft, he sent a gift of magnificent thrones made of gold and adamant to the gods on Olympus. But not forgetting his mother's cruel treatment, he made her a throne that held her fast when she sat in it. Zeus commanded him to free the woman who bore him, but Hephaestus replied that he didn't have a mother. Dionysus then flew down and got Hephaestus drunk, finally persuading him to return to Olympus as an honored god and set Hera free.

Zeus was grateful and offered the crippled god anything he desired, to which Hephaestus replied that he wanted the virgin goddess Athena for his wife. The ruler of the gods consented, but sent word to Athena in her bedroom that Hephaestus was on his way and she should be prepared to defend herself. When he burst into her quarters naked, Athena was ready and not about to let Hephaestus touch her. They wrestled and fought until in his excitement the god spilled his semen on the ground. From this seed was born Erichthonius, half serpent, half man, who became the ancestor of the Athenians.

The other story of Hephaestus' origins says that he was born as a healthy young god from the union of Zeus and Hera, but that one day when the couple were having one of their endless quarrels, Hephaestus stood up to his father to protect his mother. Zeus was so angry that he grabbed Hephaestus by the ankle and hurled him down from Olympus. He fell for a whole day until he crashed onto the island of Lemnos, where the natives healed him of his injuries, though they could not mend his crippled leg.

One of the few myths of Hephaestus tells us that he married the beautiful goddess Aphrodite, although she was ever unfaithful to him. But the god suspected his wife's infidelity and decided to set a trap for her. He forged an unbreakable net as fine as a spider's web and fixed it to the top of his marriage bed. No sooner had he left to visit the mortals of Lemnos who had been so kind to him than Aphrodite welcomed Ares, the god of war, to her bed and the two lost themselves in passionate lovemaking. But just as they were finishing, the net of Hephaestus came down and trapped the pair in their passionate embrace, unable to move.

Warned by the sun god Helios, who sees everything, Hephaestus returned suddenly and caught the two in the act, then went to Zeus to complain. He and all the other gods rushed to the house of Hephaestus to see the sight and laughed as they gazed at Aphrodite and Ares trapped together naked on the bed. Apollo joked with Hermes that it would be worth the embarrassment to sleep with Aphrodite, but Poseidon urged Hephaestus to release the lovers and accept a payment from Ares as compensation. At last the craftsman agreed and freed the divine pair, who swiftly fled away to hide in shame.

ARES

Aside from sneaking into Aphrodite's bed, there are few stories about the god of war. The Greeks detested Ares almost as much as Hades, though they fought many wars among themselves and with foreign nations. To the citizens of Athens, Thebes, and even Sparta, Ares was not so much the god of glorious war as he was the spirit of irrational, destructive conflict for its own sake. Even during the Trojan War, Zeus wanted nothing to do with his own son: "Don't come complaining to me you lying, wretched creature. I hate you more than any of the gods on Olympus. Strife and fighting are all you care about. You're as implacable as your mother Hera!"

Ares was a bully and a coward who came crying to Zeus when he lost a fight. The Greeks much preferred Athena, the goddess of wisdom, as the divinity to rule over martial affairs. With Athena, war was never an end in itself, simply a regrettable but often necessary means of settling conflicts between cities.

Ares had no wife of his own, but behind Hephaestus' back he did father four children with Aphrodite. These were Deimos and Phobus—also known as Fear and Panic—a daughter, Harmonia, and, according to some later authors, Cupid, known as Eros. Ares also slept with mortal women and had many notable children, including several of the Argonauts, who would one day sail with Jason, as well as the Amazon queen Penthesileia and the beautiful maiden Alcippe. When Poseidon's son Halirrhothius raped Alcippe, Ares killed him and was brought to trial for murder in Athens. At a hill just below the Acropolis, he was tried by the gods and acquitted. Thereafter the site was known as the Areopagus, or "Hill of Ares."

ᘓᘓᘓᘓᘓᘓᘓᘓᘓ

HERMES

ᘓᘓᘓᘓᘓᘓᘓᘓᘓ

One of the many loves of Zeus was the nymph Maia, daughter of Atlas, who lived quietly in a cave in Arcadia. Often at night when Hera was fast asleep, Zeus would steal away from their bedroom on Mount Olympus and secretly visit Maia. In time she gave birth to a son named Hermes.

On the morning of his birth, while his mother rested, baby Hermes sprang from his cradle and left the cave to explore the world. The first thing he saw was a tortoise moving slowly across the forest floor. The child laughed in delight and spoke to the creature: "Greetings to you, my little friend. Where did you get that pretty shell you wear? I think you could be useful to me. It's dangerous here in the wild mountains. Let me carry you inside my cave where it's safe. We could make wonderful music together."

And so Hermes picked up his new toy and carried it home. There he took a sharp knife and cut off its legs, then hollowed out its flesh until only the shell remained. He stretched seven strings of sheep gut across the back and plucked them with his fingers. Then he began to sing songs of Zeus and Maia and his own birth, rejoicing in the beautiful sound of the instrument he had invented.

But soon the child grew bored and placed the lyre in his cradle. There was so much more of the world to see. He left the cave again and wandered north until he came to the fertile land of Pieria below Olympus. There he spotted the sacred herd of cattle dear to the god Apollo. With a wicked grin on his face, he separated out fifty of the bellowing beasts and led them away. Looking behind him, the young thief saw that the tracks of the animals would be easy to follow, so he made the cattle walk backward and padded his own feet with leafy sandals so as to leave no trace of his passing.

Hermes met no one along his way except an old shepherd tending his vineyard. The young god spoke to him kindly but firmly, saying that his vines would always bear sweet wine if he told no one what he saw.

Then he continued with the cattle all the way back to Arcadia, where he placed them in a hidden stable, sacrificing two of the animals to the gods. As night had already come, he slipped back into the cave and crawled into his cradle, wrapping his swaddling clothes about him.

To all the world young Hermes looked like an innocent babe, but his mother knew the truth, as mothers always do: "Where have you been, you rascal, sneaking home this time of night? I know what you've been up to. Leto's son Apollo is going to be pounding down our door soon looking for his cattle. Oh, your father is to blame! He begot you to be a nuisance and a trickster to men and gods alike."

Baby Hermes assured his mother that all would be well. It really wasn't fair, he said, that the gods should feast on Olympus while Hermes and Maia starved to death in a drafty cave. If Apollo came to visit, he told his mother that he would handle him.

At that moment as the sun was rising on a new day, Apollo was up searching for his missing cattle. The tracks of the animals seemed to lead him in the wrong direction, so that soon he had lost the trail. He finally came across the old man tending his vines and asked if he had seen anyone passing by with a herd of fifty cows. The man confessed that he had indeed seen a strange sight. A baby with feet wrapped in leaves had come that way yesterday with a herd of horned cattle walking backward. Apollo then followed the strange trail over mountains and through forests until he came at last to the home of Maia.

The god entered the cave and there saw a baby sleeping peacefully in his cradle. The child looked like any other newborn, but Apollo was not fooled: "Get up, you cunning thief! I know you stole my cattle. Tell me what you have done with them or I will hurl you down into Tartarus."

And Hermes replied: "Son of Leto, what are you saying? I'm just a little baby who was born only yesterday. All I care about is my mother's milk and a warm bath. I have no idea where your cattle are."

With that Apollo picked up Hermes and carried him off to Mount Olympus. He brought the child before a council of the gods and accused him of stealing his sacred cattle. After a long speech during which little Hermes looked as innocent as a lamb, Zeus asked the child what had happened. The young god swore that he had never seen the herd of Apollo and, after all, how could a baby steal fifty cattle? He appealed to his father for protection against the anger of Apollo, who, as he related, had made all kinds of terrible threats against him.

Zeus could not help but laugh and admire the guile of little Hermes. But of course he knew the baby was lying, so he ordered him to give Apollo back his cattle. The child then led the archer god to his secret stable and returned his missing animals. Apollo was indeed ready to throw Hermes into Tartarus for his thievery, but suddenly the baby began to pluck his lyre made from the shell of the tortoise. Apollo was enchanted by the sound as the baby sang to him. When the song was finished, Apollo agreed to set aside his grievance if Hermes would give him the lyre and teach him to play—and swear never again to trouble his cattle. The young god gladly agreed and from that day forth Apollo became the patron of music.

Hermes grew to become the trusted messenger of Zeus himself, as well as god of travelers and thieves. He had no wife but fathered many children, including the pastoral god Pan. Hermes was beloved by the Greeks, who erected his image throughout their cities and looked for him at their final breath to guide them down to Hades, just as he had once led the cattle of Apollo to their new home.

PAN

Once Hermes fell in love with a nymph Dryope and soon she became pregnant. When it was time for her to give birth, all her companions gathered around her in the women's quarters of her palace to help in the delivery. They were not prepared, however, for the newborn babe they saw. The laughing child had the feet of a goat and two horns, along with a full beard. The nurse who received him into the world screamed and ran away in fright, but his proud father, Hermes, was there in an instant to take the boy in his arms. He carried him up to the halls of Mount Olympus where he presented him to the other gods, much to their delight. They named him Pan, Greek for "all," because he brought joy to everyone.

True to his goatish nature, Pan grew up with an insatiable appetite for sex. One day when wandering through the forests of Arcadia, he saw the nymph Syrinx, a devotee of the virgin goddess Artemis. She was used to being chased by lustful satyrs, but Pan was faster and far more persistent. Nonetheless she ran as fast as she could until she came to a river she could not cross. With Pan closing in, she prayed to the nymphs of the stream to transform her. The eager god then grabbed her from behind, but all he found in his hands were water reeds, the remains of poor Syrinx. Disappointed but intrigued, Pan took some of the reeds and cut them to different lengths, then sealed them with wax to make a musical instrument he named for the girl he had almost caught. The instrument is also known as the panpipe.

When not pursuing nymphs, Pan was the genial god of goatherds and shepherds. He seldom visited Olympus, but instead preferred to spend his days in the woods and forests. He was a kindly if lecherous god who nevertheless could bring terror to the hearts of anyone who offended him. Among such unlucky souls he inspired uncontrollable fear—better known as "*pan*-ic."

HELIOS

The god of the sun was ancient, not a child of Cronus or Zeus, but born from the union of the Titans Theia and Hyperion when the world was still young. Each morning he would drive his chariot of light across the sky, seeing everything below him done by men and gods, then each evening he journeyed back across the ocean in an enormous golden cup to his palace in the east. There was no rest for this most crucial of gods. Without him all plants, animals, and humans would freeze and die, ice would cover the lands, and darkness would descend upon the world forever. He was so busy in fact that when Zeus was distributing portions of the earth as the special provinces of all the gods, Helios missed receiving his lot. Zeus considered starting all over again to be fair to the sun god, but then he raised the beautiful island of Rhodes from the Aegean Sea to be a sacred land for Helios alone.

Aphrodite was still so angry at Helios for telling Hephaestus about her affair with Ares that she made the sun god fall hopelessly in love with Leucothoe, daughter of the Persian king. Every day as he soared across the sky he would watch her, heartsick with longing. He ignored all other women, including the nymph Clytie, his former lover. At last he could no longer stand to be apart from Leucothoe and came to her one night as she was weaving with twelve of her attendants. He took the form of the girl's mother and dismissed the maids, then revealed himself to the princess and proclaimed his eternal love. Leucothoe was amazed and frightened, but fell willingly into the arms of Helios.

Clytie found out about the affair and burned with jealousy. She sent word to the king that his daughter was no longer a virgin and the ruler exploded with rage. He had Leucothoe buried alive even as she prayed to the sun and protested that the god had practically forced her to submit. The girl was crushed beneath the earth, but Helios could do nothing until he had finished his course across the sky. That night he rushed to the place she was buried and tried to revive her with his warmth, but it was too late. He then sprinkled her with divine nectar until her body put forth a sweet fragrance and turned into a shrub of frankincense, the finest perfume in all the world.

Helios scorned Clytie all the more for her revenge, but the young woman continued to pine away for the sun. Her longing soon turned to madness. She sat naked beneath the open sky, neither eating nor drinking, watching the fiery chariot of her former lover sail across the heavens. As the days passed, her limbs became fixed to the ground and her face burned away until she was nothing but a small violet flower, the heliotrope, forever following the sun across the sky.

Another lover of Helios was Clymene, a daughter of Ocean, who was married to the Egyptian king Merops. She bore him a son named Phaethon, who grew up hearing tales of his conception from his mother. He told these stories to his best friend, but the boy only laughed at him and called him a fool for believing his mother's fantasies. Phaethon went to Clymene in tears and demanded to know the truth about his father. His mother swore by Helios that her words were true and urged the boy to journey to the palace of the sun to ask the god himself if he indeed had sired him.

Phaethon took up the challenge and traveled east from Egypt to the farthest borders of the world. There he found the rising place of the sun with its lofty columns and gold glittering like fire. Phaethon climbed the many steps to the throne room of Helios, but once he entered he could not bear to gaze at the bright god sitting before him.

"Welcome, Phaethon, a son no father would deny," proclaimed Helios.

"If you are really my father," said the boy, "swear to me by the River Styx that you will grant me whatever I wish."

"Gladly, I swear," replied the sun god. "You have only to ask what you will."

"Then let me drive your chariot across the sky."

Helios immediately regretted that he had made such a rash promise to his son. He urged the boy to reconsider and request some other favor. He explained that his horses required the strongest hand, but the impetuous youth would not be moved. As he had sworn an unbreakable vow, Helios reluctantly led Phaethon to the stable and gave him the reins of his chariot.

No sooner did the horses leap into the sky than they realized their master was not the driver. Phaethon was unable to control them and panicked, dropping their reins and crying in terror as the chariot tore across the sky and swerved close to the earth. Mountains burst into flames and seas began to boil away. Cities were consumed in fire, while whole forests went up in smoke. The once lush fields of Africa became the Sahara Desert and the channels of the Nile dried up. Gods and men alike prayed to Zeus to do something quickly before the world was destroyed.

The ruler of the gods took up one of his bolts and cast it with all his might at the chariot of the sun, tearing it into pieces. Phaethon's charred body fell down from the heavens into a river in the far west. There the daughters of Helios wept for him until their tears became amber. They left behind for him an epitaph so that he would always be remembered:

> Here lies the body of Phaethon, who drove the chariot of the sun.
> He failed greatly, but greatly did he dare.

DIONYSUS

In the city of Thebes there once lived a beautiful young woman named Semele. She was the daughter of Cadmus and a niece of Europa, the unlucky maiden kidnapped by Zeus in the form of a bull. The king of the gods also fell in love with Semele and came to her in mortal form, wooing and eventually seducing her. The girl became pregnant but consoled herself that the father of her child was Zeus himself, for this is what he had revealed to her.

When Hera heard of Zeus' latest dalliance, she began to plot her revenge. One night she came to Semele disguised as an old woman with white hair and wrinkled skin, tottering along on a cane. Semele invited her in and the two talked about many things until eventually the young woman revealed the secret of her pregnancy to her visitor. The old woman shook her head. "My dear, I do hope it is Zeus who came to your bed, but you never really know, do you? A man will say anything to spend the night with a fair maiden. If I were you, next time he shows up, I would ask him to reveal himself as a god in all his glory. That should settle the matter once and for all."

After her guest had departed, Semele began to consider her words. How did she know for certain that the man was Zeus? Could the father of her child just be a smooth-talking mortal who had led her astray? She was determined to find out.

When Zeus came to her soon after, Semele brushed aside his embraces.

"If you are really a god," she said, "grant me a wish."

"Anything you want," replied Zeus, eager to take the young woman to bed. "I swear by the River Styx you shall have it."

Then Semele replied, "Show yourself to me as a god, just as you would appear to Hera."

As soon as she spoke these words, Zeus groaned in despair, but he had sworn by the Styx and could not break his vow. He therefore put aside his mortal disguise and appeared to her as Zeus almighty, divine bearer of thunder and lightning. In an instant Semele was reduced to ashes. But before she was burned away, Zeus snatched the unborn child from her womb and sewed it quickly in his thigh to grow until it was ready to be born.

A few months later, Zeus removed the stitches in his leg and took out the baby, whom he named Dionysus. Since the child was delivered from two wombs, as it were, one mortal and one immortal, he became known as "twice-born." Zeus gave the infant to Hermes, who took him to Semele's sister Ino to be raised in secret, secure from the jealous eyes of Hera. The boy's aunt even dressed Dionysus as a girl to keep him safe, but Hera was ever vigilant and vengeful. She drove Ino mad so that she killed her son Melicertes by throwing him into a boiling pot. In grief Ino then took the dead child and leapt into the sea, where she and the now-revived boy became sea gods, prayed to ever after by sailors in storms. Zeus found baby Dionysus before Hera could get her hands on him and turned him into a goat for his own protection. Then he spirited him away to distant Asia, where he was raised by the kindly nymphs of Nysa.

However, there is another story of the infancy of Dionysus told by the people of Laconia near Sparta. They say that Cadmus discovered his daughter was pregnant and scoffed at the idea that Zeus was the father. He was so angry that he took the girl and her newborn son and locked them both in a chest that he threw into the sea. The little craft drifted south along the coast until it was found by local villagers. They looked inside and found a dead girl holding her baby, weak and hungry but still alive. The villagers cared for the child until his aunt Ino came to their country in search of her sister and took the boy to raise herself. She nursed the child in a nearby cave and grove that became known as the Garden of Dionysus.

According to the more widely held tradition, however, after Dionysus had put aside his goat form and grown into a young god, he bade farewell to the nymphs who had raised him and set off to see the world. He had discovered the secret of making wine from grapes during his time in Nysa and wanted to spread this knowledge along with his religious cult throughout the world. He wandered far and wide until he came to the shores of the Aegean Sea. Wishing to cross to the island of Naxos, he hailed a ship of passing Etruscan pirates. Handsome young Dionysus was dressed in rich purple robes with dark hair sweeping down to his sturdy shoulders. The pirates took one look at him and decided they would make a pretty profit selling him into slavery in some distant land. They nodded to each other, then jumped off the ship as it approached the shore and grabbed the boy, forcing him on board. They planned to rape him as soon as they had him tied up, but the bonds kept slipping off his hands and feet. All the while Dionysus sat patiently on the deck, smiling.

The helmsman of the pirates, a pious man named Acoetes, alone understood what was happening and rebuked his shipmates: "You fools, don't you see that you've taken a powerful god on board? No chains can hold him. He must be Poseidon or Apollo or perhaps Zeus himself. We must set him free at once and return him to the mainland or he will surely send a raging tempest to destroy us all."

But the captain of the ship sneered and said, "Acoetes, you are an idiot. Pay attention to your sails and leave this boy to real men."

But when the sails were hoisted, suddenly the mast of the ship began to sprout grapevines and the sails turned to ivy. Sweet wine flowed over the decks of the ship and wild animals appeared all around the pirates. Dionysus turned himself into a lion and roared with all his might. The sailors were terrified and leapt off the ship into the water. Their divine passenger then turned them all into dolphins, save for Acoetes, whom he spared. From that day forward dolphins have been kindly to humans since they themselves were once men.

Hera was not the forgiving sort and continued to pursue Dionysus in her anger. She drove the young god mad so that he wandered aimlessly through Egypt, Syria, and Asia Minor until at last he came to the temple of the Great Mother goddess Cybele in Phrygia. With ecstatic rites of music and dancing, the priests and priestesses of the goddess cured Dionysus of his insanity and sent him gratefully on his way, followed by a faithful band of women known as the Bacchae (after Bacchus, another name for Dionysus), each carrying a thyrsus, a wooden wand wrapped in ivy leaves and crowned with a pine cone.

King Midas of Phrygia had received him warmly, so before he left the land of Cybele, Dionysus offered to grant the ruler his heart's desire. The king was more kind than wise, so he immediately asked his divine visitor to make whatever he touched turned to gold. Dionysus agreed and Midas excitedly began to test his new gift. He touched an oak branch and saw it turn into a golden twig. Then he touched a stone, then the lofty pillars of his palace, all of which turned to gold. The king was thrilled and ran around his city touching everything he could find, to the amazement of his subjects.

At last the king grew weary and called for food and drink. The royal servants brought him platters of delicious food and goblets of sweet wine, but everything turned to gold when it touched the lips of Midas. The king was soon starving and his throat parched, but there was nothing he could do to satisfy his needs. He realized then how foolish he had been and prayed to Dionysus to lift this dreaded power from him. The god heard his prayer and told him to go and wash in a nearby stream. The king did as he was told and plunged into the river. The rocks in the streambed turned to gold, but the gift—or curse—of the golden touch left Midas forever.

Not every king was as welcoming to Dionysus as Midas had been. When the god crossed into Thrace, King Lycurgus seized the Bacchae and chased the young god into the sea. But Dionysus soon had his revenge. He freed his Bacchae and drove Lygurgus mad so that the king struck his own son with an ax, thinking he was a grapevine. Only after the boy was cut to pieces did Lycurgus recover his sanity and realize what he had done. The subjects of the king were so horrified at his actions that they tied the king to horses to be torn apart.

When Dionysus moved south into Greece he was welcomed by the inhabitants of Orchomenus, but the daughters of King Minyas wanted nothing to do with his wild new religion. They remained in their chambers like proper ladies and scorned those who followed the god into the mountains, wearing animal skins to dance and behave in such a vulgar and unseemly manner. Dionysus appeared to them in the form of a young girl and tried to persuade them that his rites were not an affront to the old ways. Wine was not evil, he explained, but was in fact necessary to achieve balance in life.

The daughters of Minyas, however, would hear nothing of it. Dionysus then filled the room with the sound of beating drums and tambourines. Milk and nectar dripped from the ceiling and an irresistible madness seized the women. They selected one of their own children by lot and tore him to pieces, greedily eating the raw flesh with their hands. Then they ran off to the mountains to join the other Bacchae in celebration of the god, after which Dionysus turned them into bats.

The daughters of King Proetus of Argos were just as unreceptive to the new ways of the god. They refused to worship him, so he struck them with madness. Along with the other women of the city, they killed their own children and ran into the mountains, until finally a healer named Melampus cured them in exchange for a large share of their father's kingdom.

When Dionysus returned at last to his hometown of Thebes, he expected to be welcomed with open arms by all—but a prophet is seldom honored in his own country. His grandfather Cadmus and the seer Tiresias embraced his cult, but the women of the city and his cousin Pentheus, now the young king of Thebes, scorned him. Dionysus therefore drove the women mad and sent them into the hills with his followers, but for the king he had other plans.

To Pentheus, the worship of Dionysus was just a silly indulgence of the lustful and irrational nature of women. He believed the adoration of the god by the matrons of Thebes was simply an excuse to have an orgy in the forest: "It's Aphrodite they're devoted to, not Bacchus! I've captured some and put them under guard at the jail, but I'll hunt down the rest in the mountains, even my mother Agave, and throw them into iron cages. I'll put a stop to this filthy business, this worship of the so-called god Dionysus."

Even when wise old Tiresias tried to explain to Pentheus that the proper worship of the god was all about finding balance in life, the king refused to listen. A spy, sent into the woods to report on the activities of the wayward women, reported back that they were merely drinking moderate amounts of wine and dancing to the flute, but Pentheus had already made up his mind that this new god was a dire threat to the social order of the city.

Dionysus then appeared to Pentheus disguised as one of his own priests and offered to take him to the mountains to see the Bacchic worship for himself. But first the king would have to dress as a woman and promise to watch the activities quietly from a tree. Like a lamb led to the slaughter, Pentheus agreed and followed Dionysus into the woods. No sooner had the pair arrived among the Bacchae than the god revealed the king's true identity. The women, driven mad by Dionysus, pulled Pentheus out of the tree and began to tear off his limbs while he was still alive. His mother was at the forefront of the attack, first ripping off his arm at the shoulder then helping to butcher him. The ladies of Thebes laughed as they tossed parts of Pentheus back and forth as if it were all a game.

When at last the bloody affair was over, the women marched back to Thebes, Agave carrying her son's head in her arms, believing that she had killed a lion. She looked all around the palace for Pentheus to show him her prize, but as the spell wore off, she realized the horrible truth. Dionysus then appeared and declared that it was all her fault, along with the rest of the stubborn Thebans, for rejecting him: "If you had only known how to keep your minds balanced, I, the son of Zeus, would have brought good fortune to you—but you would not welcome me."

To drive home his harsh punishment, Dionysus then transformed his faithful grandfather Cadmus into a snake and his gentle grandmother Harmonia into a wild beast before sending them into exile along with Agave.

As cruel as Dionysus was to his grandparents and aunt, however, he loved his mother, Semele, very much. He lamented that she was confined to the dismal realm of Hades while he was allowed to live as a god. He therefore decided to journey to the underworld to rescue Semele and bring her back to the land of the living. The only problem was that he didn't know the way. He searched high and low in vain for an entrance to Hades, until at last he came to an elderly man named Hypolipnus, who offered to show him a secret door. But in return, the lecherous guide demanded that the handsome young god have sex with him. Dionysus was in such a hurry that he agreed, but only after he had returned to the surface. After a long journey, the god found Semele and brought her back, but by this time Hypolipnus had died of old age. Still, a promise was a promise. The god took a branch from a nearby fig tree, carved an impressive likeness of his own penis, and put it in the tomb of Hypolipnus. Then at last he led his mother up to Mount Olympus, where Zeus and the other gods welcomed her and her son ever after as immortals.

CUPID

In some stories Eros was one of the first gods, born from Chaos after Mother Earth herself. This Eros was a primal force of procreation that drove all the other powers of the cosmos to mate and reproduce. But in later stories, Eros was the young son of Aphrodite who flew about the world shooting arrows of love into unwilling victims, such as Apollo or Zeus himself. This Eros was also known as Cupid and of him one of the best-loved myths of ancient times was told.

Once upon a time a king and a queen in a distant land had three young daughters of marriageable age. The oldest two were quite pretty and were sought by many potential husbands, but the youngest girl, named Psyche, possessed a beauty so astonishing that she drew visitors from many lands just for a glimpse of her face. Pilgrims came to the royal city to watch the girl pass by and threw garlands at her feet as if she were a goddess. Soon the temples and shrines of Aphrodite were neglected, for the people could see divine beauty in the mortal girl walking among them. Her sisters soon married, but Psyche was so lovely that no man thought himself worthy to seek her as a wife. She sat alone in her room weeping and miserable, wondering if she would forever be a virgin.

When Aphrodite found out that she was being ignored, she was furious.

"Here I am, the creator of all that is, the origin of the primordial elements, the mother of the whole world, forced to share my worship with a mortal woman!"

The goddess sent for her son Cupid and told him to get his arrows ready. Then she told him to shoot Psyche and make her fall madly in love with the meanest, vilest, most disgusting man who walked the face of the earth. She didn't care who, she didn't care how, as long as it guaranteed her a wretched life.

The girl's father soon began to worry that having such a beautiful daughter might indeed be a curse from the gods. He sent to a sacred oracle and asked what he should do about Psyche. The message he received was frighteningly clear:

*King, put the girl on a lofty mountain cliff dressed in her finest gown
for a wedding—or a funeral. Your son-in-law will come to her there,
but he won't be a mortal. Indeed, he will be a savage, wild, and evil
beast that flies through the air on wings and troubles the world with
fire and sword. He is so terrible that Zeus and the gods shake at his
approach, the rivers roll back, and all the shades in Hades tremble.*

The poor father loved his daughter dearly and could not bear to
abandon her to such a fate, but it was Psyche herself who led the way to
the cliff dressed as a bride of death. She saw in the oracle the vengeful
hand of Aphrodite and knew that it was pointless to resist. Then her
brokenhearted parents and sisters left her there on the mountain to
face her doom alone, knowing that it was impossible to fight the will of
heaven.

For a long time Psyche waited for something terrible to happen, when
without warning a gentle wind lifted her from the cliff and carried her
down to the valley far below. There she saw a beautiful palace that she
knew immediately was created by divine hands. She entered and saw
that the walls were made of gold and even the floors were covered with
precious jewels. A voice then spoke from somewhere in the castle saying that he was one of many servants of his lord and all she beheld was
hers. If she desired anything, she had only to ask. The invisible servants
prepared a fine dinner for their new mistress and drew her bath, then
showed her the way to her bedchamber.

Alone in her room, Psyche began to fear for what would happen next.
She had been instructed by her mother and sisters how to behave on her
wedding night, but as a maiden she had no experience with ordinary
men let alone gods or monsters, whoever might be the master of this
house. The sun slowly set and the room grew dark as the hours passed,
but still Psyche lay in her bed waiting. Suddenly she felt a presence next
to her and gasped as an unseen man took her in his arms. Her husband
made passionate love to her all through the night, but was gone before
the first rays of the sun entered the windows of the chamber. This happened again the next night, then again the next, until at last Psyche
began to look forward to the visits of her invisible lover.

One night as they lay together, Psyche's unseen husband warned her that under no circumstances could she ever see his face. She was pregnant, he revealed, and her child would be a god—if she made no attempt to discover his identity. Psyche was reluctant, but promised she would obey. But please, please, couldn't she bring her sisters here for a visit just to show them she was safe?

Her lover agreed but urged her yet again not to give into temptation. The next day, when the two sisters of Psyche arrived at the very cliff where she had waited for her doom, the wind gently picked them up and carried them to the castle far below where Psyche was waiting. She embraced them and eagerly showed both the wonders of the grand palace. Her visitors sat down to a glorious feast and enjoyed luxuries they could never have imagined. As the sun began to set, Psyche bade them farewell and the wind carried them back to the top of the mountain.

It was then that envy seized the two sisters.

"Cruel fate," said the elder of the pair. "Our little sister enjoys the life of a goddess while I share my bed with a fat old husband as bald as a pumpkin!"

"That's nothing," replied the other. "My husband is bent double with arthritis. I spend my days more as a nurse than wife, rubbing his joints with some disgusting salve that burns my delicate hands. I don't care if she is our sister, it's not fair that Psyche should share the embraces of a handsome young god in a glorious palace. If it's the last thing I do, I'll see that she loses everything she has!"

The elder sister agreed and they began to make their plans. The next day the wind bore them from the cliff to visit Psyche again, but this time the evil pair were determined to strike fear into their sister's heart. They told her stories of neighboring farmers who had seen a giant snake slithering through the forest on his way to her castle. They warned the girl that he was just waiting until she was ready to deliver her child so that he could eat her alive as a plump, tasty meal. Psyche was horrified and denied it was true, but when the sisters had left, she began to wonder.

That night after her husband had fallen asleep beside her, she took an oil lamp and sharp knife and approached the still figure. Holding the lamp up to his face, she was ready to cut off the monster's head—but she saw instead the loveliest man she could ever imagine lying in her bed. His cheeks were fair and rosy, while his hair flowed down in ringlets onto his perfect body. At his feet were a bow and arrow that she picked up, pricking herself on the sharp point of one dart. As if she needed any prodding, immediately she fell deeply in love with her sleeping husband, whom she now knew was Cupid himself.

But as she drew near to kiss him, a drop of hot oil fell from the lamp onto his bare shoulder and woke him with a start.

"Psyche, why didn't you listen to me?" Cupid cried in despair. "Don't you know what you've done? I can never see you again—never. My love, all that we had is now lost."

With that the god disappeared and left Psyche alone. She ran from the bedroom and fled into the woods, seeking only to end her newfound misery by drowning herself in a river. But the waters of the stream would not receive her. She lay on the grass weeping until the god Pan, who was in the same woods chasing a nymph, saw her and told her she should forget about suicide. He then led her to the home of one of her sisters. Once safely inside, Psyche collapsed in tears and told her sister everything that had happened. But instead of comforting Psyche, the wicked woman saw the girl's misery as a golden opportunity. She ran all the way to the cliff above the god's castle and launched herself into the air, crying, "Take me, Cupid! I will be a worthy wife to you." But instead of the gentle wind that had previously carried her to the castle grounds, she felt only the rush of cold air as she fell down on the jagged rocks below. The other sister did the same when Psyche found her and told her the story of losing her husband forever.

Soon a bird flying over the earth saw Psyche wandering distraught through the forests and came to tell Aphrodite. The goddess was furious: "So, my precious son has a girlfriend, does he? Instead of doing his job he took up with that little bitch and got her pregnant! Did he think I was a common madam finding a harlot for him to play with? Besides, I'm too young to be a grandmother!"

Aphrodite found Psyche and brought her to her palace, but instead of servants and fine meals she received only beatings and abuse. At last the goddess, weary of tormenting the girl, told her she would be freed if she could complete a few tasks. She was first placed in a granary full of mixed wheat, barley, millet, poppy seeds, chickpeas, lentils, and beans and told to sort each grain into a separate pile by morning. If not, she would die.

Psyche knew the goddess was only looking for an excuse to kill her, so she sat on the floor of the barn and waited for death. But a little ant passing by saw the girl and took pity on her. He brought all his friends to the granary and they began to sort the seeds according to kind. By morning, all the grains were separated as Aphrodite had ordered.

The goddess was furious at Psyche's success and next ordered her to go among a flock of sheep whose fleece shone with gold. The only problem was, the sheep were vicious killers that would tear into pieces anyone who approached them. She was nonetheless to gather some of their wool and bring it to her or she would die. Again Psyche sat down to wait for death, but a slender reed growing from the banks of a nearby stream felt sorry for her and told her a secret. The sheep, it said, were ferocious in the heat of the day, but if she waited until evening she could gather some of their wool from the branches of trees they had brushed against in passing. Grateful, Psyche did this and dutifully brought the wool to Aphrodite, who was fit to be tied.

"You think you're so clever, do you?" asked the goddess. "Well, for your next task you must draw a cup of water from a spring of the river Styx. It's at the bottom of an impassable gorge in the mountains, but I'm sure that won't be any trouble for you, my dear." She laughed in wicked delight, then handed Psyche a crystal chalice and sent her on her way.

Psyche knew she could never descend the precipitous gorge, so she climbed instead to the cliff above it to throw herself off and end her life. Just then, however, the eagle who served Zeus was flying by and saw the girl about to jump. Cupid had once done him a favor, so he swooped down to the young god's bride and told her to stop. Then he took the cup and filled it from the spring in the gorge below. Psyche ran back with the goblet and presented it to the goddess.

To Aphrodite, it was beyond all belief that this young girl could complete these deadly travails, so she decided on a final test so impossible, so dangerous, that Psyche would never be able to finish it alive. She was to go down into the land of the dead and fetch back some of the perfume of Persephone, wife of Hades. Aphrodite gave the girl a jar and kicked her out of her palace, confident that she would never see her again.

Psyche was just as certain that she could not complete this task since no mortal could journey to the realm of Hades and return alive. She climbed to the top of a tall tower to cast herself off, but the tower spoke to her and told her all was not lost. The journey to the underworld and back was difficult, but not impossible if she followed the tower's instructions exactly. She was to go to a remote grove near Sparta, where she would find an entrance to the land of Hades. Going down into the cave, she was to carry two barley cakes in her hands and two coins in her mouth. She was to ignore all requests made to her by anyone she met on her journey through the shadowy kingdom. Only when she arrived at the house of Persephone was she to speak and make her request for the perfume—but under no circumstances was she to open the jar and look inside.

Psyche listened carefully and thanked the tower for its kindness. She found the entrance to the underworld and, taking her cakes and coins, entered into the dark world below. She met a crippled man with a lame ass who asked for her help, but she passed him by. Then she came to the river Styx and found the greedy ferryman Charon, who poled her across for one of the coins he took from her mouth. In midstream, she looked down into the water and saw a dead man who begged her to pull him into the boat, but she closed her eyes and ignored him. Then the girl came to some old women weaving who urged her to stay and spin with them, but Psyche walked on. Later she came to the vicious three-headed dog Cerberus, to whom she tossed one of the barley cakes so that she could pass by. At last she came to the palace of Persephone, who greeted her warmly and offered her a fine meal. Psyche declined and asked only for some of her precious perfume. Smiling, the goddess of the underworld agreed and filled the jar, sealing it tightly.

Returning the way she had come, Psyche gave her other cake to Cerberus and final coin to Charon for passage back across the Styx. The girl then labored back up the long, dark path and emerged at last into the land of the living. But then she began to wonder, if the perfume of Persephone was so powerful, perhaps it could help her win again the love of Cupid. She wanted so badly to have her husband back that she opened the jar, only to fall immediately into a sleep like death.

There in the forest Cupid found her and held her in his arms. He woke her with a gentle prick from his arrow and carried her to Olympus. After giving the perfume to his mother, he addressed Zeus and the rest of the gods, asking that his courageous bride be made a goddess to live with him forever. By this time even Aphrodite was impressed by Psyche's bravery and devotion to her son, so she reluctantly consented to a formal marriage. With a nod from Zeus, Hermes brought forward a cup of divine ambrosia and gave it to Psyche. She drank deeply from the goblet and immediately felt the fire of immortality coursing through her veins. She kissed Cupid and everyone cheered the new goddess. Satyrs played their flutes, the Muses sang wedding songs, and Aphrodite herself danced to the music. In due time, the child of Cupid and Psyche was born, a daughter named Happiness.

GODDESSES

⌘⌘⌘⌘⌘⌘⌘⌘⌘

HERA

⌘⌘⌘⌘⌘⌘⌘⌘⌘

The queen of heaven was the patron of marriage and childbirth, but she was also the goddess whom troubled women turned to in all phases of their lives. Hera was worshiped as a young girl, as a bride, and as an old woman. Whatever pain and sorrow a mortal woman might feel, she could always count on Hera's sympathetic ear, whether she wanted to find a husband, become pregnant, or face life alone as an aging widow. Although a mother of several children herself, Hera became a virgin again each year at her temple in Argos so that she could better serve the needs of young women. Hera was a goddess of renewal, of comfort throughout a woman's life, and of hope for women young and old in a world dominated by men.

But in spite of her sympathy for women in distress—or perhaps because of it—she could be an implacable shrew when it came to her own husband. Io, Callisto, and Leda were only a few of the many innocent lovers of Zeus she tracked down and tormented to assert her rights as his legitimate wife.

Hera was never shy about confronting Zeus, especially when she thought he was up to something. One day when the sea goddess Thetis had come to the king of the gods seeking his favor for her son, Hera burst in and starting screaming at Zeus, "Which of the gods is plotting with you now? You never tell me anything! You and all your secret plans. Why don't you have the guts to let me know what you're up to?"

Zeus shot back: "Woman, I've had just about enough of you! Always suspicious, always prying into my business. If you keep on nagging me, I swear, you're going to regret it, even if you are my wife. I'm the ruler of the gods, not you. I'm going to do what I think is right whether you like it or not!"

There are few myths that feature Hera in a predominant role, but stories of domestic quarrels between her and Zeus are frequent. One time they even argued about whether men or women enjoyed sex more. They decided to let the soothsayer Tiresias settle the matter since he had experienced lovemaking as both a male and female. This happened because once when he was walking through the woods he came upon two snakes mating and struck them with his cane, then was changed into a woman for seven years as punishment. After living life as a female for this time, Tiresias saw the snakes again and thought that perhaps striking them once more might change him back to a man, as it indeed did. Thus when the ruler of the gods asked him if men or women received more pleasure from intimacy, he was able to reveal that it was in fact women who enjoyed sex more—ten times more than men. Hera hated that this secret had been revealed and she struck Tiresias blind as punishment, but in compensation Zeus gave him the power of foresight so that he became a great prophet.

Like all goddesses, Hera was jealous of her famous beauty. When Side, the wife of the hunter Orion, boasted that she was fairer than the wife of Zeus, Hera cast her down into Hades forever. Likewise after Gerana, the queen of the Pygmies, claimed her own beauty was beyond compare, Hera transformed her into a crane. Some stories also claim that the daughters of the Argive king Proetus were not driven mad by Dionysus, but were in fact turned into cows by Hera because they thought they were more beautiful than her.

DEMETER

Like her sister Hera, Demeter was also a child of the Titans Cronus and Rhea. But unlike Hera, Demeter cared little for love affairs or contests of beauty. Her domain was the fertile, green earth, where she presided over life-giving grain.

Not that she was wholly immune to matters of the heart. Once when she joined the other gods at the marriage of King Cadmus of Thebes and his bride, Harmonia, she fell madly in love with a mortal man named Iasion. True to her nature, the goddess lay with him not in a perfumed bed but in a thrice-plowed field. Some stories say that when Zeus found out he struck down Iasion with a thunderbolt for daring to sleep with a goddess. But other stories say that he lived a long life while Demeter sadly watched his hair grow ever more gray. The couple had two sons, Plutus, a god of riches under the earth, and Philomelus, a poor mortal farmer who nonetheless pleased Demeter by inventing the wagon.

However, Demeter could be terrible in her anger when she was offended. One mortal who dared to offend her was Erysichthon from Thessaly. Once when he was out cutting firewood he came upon a sacred grove of Demeter and took out his ax. The wood nymphs who were embodied in the trees cried out as he chopped and hacked at their limbs, but he ignored their cries and the blood dripping from their leaves. The surviving trees prayed to Demeter for vengeance and the goddess heard their prayer. She inflicted Erysichthon with an insatiable hunger. He fell to eating everything in his house, then he sold his daughter Mestra into slavery so he could buy more food. She was able to change shapes, a gift granted her by Poseidon, who had once made love to her. With this ability the dutiful daughter returned again and again to her father to be sold in new forms. Even so, the money they gained from this deceit was not enough. Soon Erysichthon began to gnaw at his own flesh and eventually ate himself alive.

But by far the best-known tale of Demeter is the story of what happened when her daughter Persephone was kidnapped by Hades, the lord of the dead. It began one day when the maiden was gathering violets and roses in a grassy meadow far from home. Persephone stooped down to pick a particularly beautiful flower when suddenly a giant chasm opened in the ground before her. Out of it flew the god Hades in a chariot of gold drawn by immortal horses and he grabbed the girl. She fought back and called out to her father Zeus for help, but it seemed that no one heard her cries. Hades quickly flew back into the earth with his prize and closed the ground above him, leaving no trace of his shameful deed.

Persephone was taken to the dark palace of the underworld ruler where she sat weeping, longing to see again the light of day. Her sobs echoed throughout the realm of the dead but could not reach the land of the living. Still, somehow, Demeter sensed that her daughter was calling to her, though she could not tell where she was.

With an urgency only a mother could feel, the goddess flew down from Mount Olympus and began to search the world for Persephone. She looked everywhere and asked everyone she saw, mortal and god alike, if they had seen her daughter, but no one could tell her where Persephone was. For nine days she frantically raced across the whole earth seeking her child. At last she came upon the goddess Hecate, who told her an astonishing tale: "Noble Demeter, goddess of the fruits of the earth, giver of gifts, you wish to know who of mortals or gods has carried off Persephone and brought pain to your heart? I wish I could tell you, but I only heard her cry out. I did not see who stole her away."

Demeter then sought out the sun god, Helios, who sees all from his chariot traveling across the sky. She came to his radiant home and begged him for news. Helios was reluctant at first, but finally told her the truth: "Daughter of Rhea, I am moved by your sorrow. It is none other than Zeus who is to blame for her disappearance. He allowed his brother Hades to seize the maiden while she gathered flowers. The lord of the dead now holds her in his underworld kingdom and will not let her go. She is there by the will of Zeus and there is nothing you can do to help her."

Demeter was so angry at Zeus and Hades that she swore she would never return to Olympus. She put aside the appearance of a goddess and took on the form of an old woman. In this guise she wandered the earth in sorrow, mourning the daughter she would never see again.

One day she came to the town of Eleusis north of Athens and sat down in a shady spot by a well near the palace of King Celeus. It was the place to which all the women of the town came to draw water and it wasn't long until the four daughters of Celeus came to fill their own brass pitchers. They greeted her politely and asked what brought a stranger such as herself to their town. Demeter said that she had been kidnapped from Crete by pirates, but that she had escaped in a nearby port. All she wanted now was a quiet place to live out her remaining days. Perhaps the girls knew a household that needed a nurse for a child?

The daughters said that indeed their own mother had recently given birth to a son and they were sure their parents would be happy to have such a distinguished-looking woman as herself to care for him. They led her back to the palace to meet their mother, who welcomed her and gladly offered her the job. When Demeter saw the small child, she loved him at once and promised his mother she would care for him as if he were her own.

From then on every night while the palace slept, the goddess nursed the baby on ambrosia and buried him in the hearth fire to burn away his mortality. But one night his mother walked in and screamed when she saw what Demeter was doing. The goddess reached into the fire and pulled the baby out, then addressed the mother: "I am Demeter, you foolish woman! I would have made your son free from old age and death. Now he will know the pain of life as a mortal."

The goddess then ordered the people of Eleusis to build her a temple so that she could establish her cult in their city. The boy may have lost his chance at immortality, but she would show her followers the secret of how to escape the dismal land of Hades after death.

The king and citizens of Eleusis happily agreed and built Demeter a wondrous temple in their city. When it was finished and all the workers had gone home, the goddess entered and closed the doors. There she remained, mourning for her daughter and neglecting the care of earth's bountiful harvests.

No seeds ripened, oxen plowed the fields in vain, and famine spread across the world. People began to starve as they called to the gods to help them—but none of them had the power to make grain grow. Only Demeter could restore fertility to the earth.

Zeus heard the cries of humanity and sent golden-winged Iris down to urge Demeter to return, but the heart of the goddess was unmoved. All the gods then made their way to her temple in Eleusis to beg her to make the earth bloom again, offering her fabulous gifts if only she would relent. They pleaded that without grain the people of the earth would die and there would be no one to offer sacrifices to the gods.

But Demeter said no. She would never—never—set foot on Olympus again or send forth the fruits of the earth until with her own eyes she saw her daughter Persephone.

Zeus then sent Hermes down to plead with Hades to release Persephone. The ruler of the underworld was surprisingly agreeable and yoked
his golden chariot to drive her back to her mother. When they arrived
in Eleusis, Demeter threw her arms around her daughter and held her as
if she would never let her go. But then she asked Persephone if she had
eaten anything while she was with Hades. Her daughter replied that no,
she had eaten nothing, except for one small pomegranate seed since
Hades had insisted. With a groan Demeter explained to Persephone
that since she had tasted the food of the underworld they could not
remain together always. She would have to spend a third of each year
with Hades, then she could return in the spring to the land of the living.
Demeter was not happy with this arrangement, but she agreed to restore
the earth to its fruitfulness, although she declared that each winter forevermore she would mourn for her daughter and the fields would produce
no crops. Thus in autumn when Persephone journeys to the underworld,
the land turns brown and the sky grows cold and dark until spring, when
Demeter and Persephone are together once again.

ARTEMIS

Daughter of Zeus and Leto, sister of Apollo, Artemis was the maiden
goddess of the hunt. She honored those who devoted themselves and
their chastity to her, but condemned her followers, like Callisto, who by
their own choice or by force lost their virtue to a man or god. Artemis
was even more harsh with those who attempted to steal her own virginity or even get a glimpse of her naked body.

A young man named Actaeon discovered this one day when he
was hunting in the forest with his dogs. He was the grandson of King
Cadmus of Thebes and had the finest pack of hounds in all of Greece.
Artemis was tracking deer in the same forest that day with her nymphs
and had stopped to swim in a cool, inviting spring. The goddess had set
aside her clothes and was splashing in the water with her followers when
suddenly they saw a man's face staring at them from behind a tree.

Actaeon was entranced by the sight of the beautiful Artemis before him in all her glory. The nymphs quickly gathered around their mistress to shield her from the eyes of the intruder, but the goddess proudly rose up naked before Actaeon and spoke to him: "Take a good look, my eager young friend. You can tell all your friends that you saw the virgin goddess of the hunt naked with your own eyes. Tell them—if you can."

With these words she splashed Actaeon with springwater so that he suddenly began to change shape. Antlers spouted from his head, his ears became pointed, and his arms and legs turned into those of a deer. He tried to cry out for mercy, but his human voice was gone. He ran from the spring in terror, only to find his own hounds in a nearby glade. He called to them, or tried to—Melampus, Ichnobates, Pamphagus!—but the dogs heard only the sound of their favorite prey. They rushed him and sank their teeth into his hide. "I am Actaeon," he tried to say, but they had him by the throat and pulled him down. Quickly the hounds ripped the life from the deer, wondering only where their master was, who would be so pleased at the stag they had caught. But the only witness was Artemis, who stood on the edge of the glade watching and smiling.

One foolish hunter named Buphagus even tried to rape Artemis when he found her wandering through the woods of Arcadia, but she killed him with an arrow from her quiver. Another great hunter, the giant Orion, met the same fate when he offended the goddess. Orion was the son of the king of Thrace who had once royally entertained Zeus, Poseidon, and Hermes. As a reward the gods promised the childless king that he would soon have a son if he gave them the hide of a bull he had sacrificed. The king did so and all three gods promptly urinated on the skin, then buried it. Nine months later, a baby was born from that spot of ground, whom the proud father named Urion, or Orion ("urine boy").

The cause of Orion's death varies widely according to different stories. Some say it was because he tried to rape Artemis, but others say she was in love with him and killed him in a fit of jealousy when he went to live with Eos, the goddess of the dawn. Still others say the goddess was angry when he beat her in a contest or because he tried to seduce one of her followers. In any case, most agree that Artemis killed him by forcing a scorpion to sting him. She later placed him in the sky as a constellation accompanied by his faithful dog Sirius, along with the scorpion that had caused his death.

Instead of lust, the goddess inspired in some men the desire to seek a life of chastity as one of her followers. Such an enthusiast was Hippolytus, an illegitimate son of Theseus, king of Athens, and the Amazon queen Antiope. Aphrodite, however, was much offended by Hippolytus, who scorned the goddess of love. In revenge, she caused the wife of Theseus, Phaedra, to fall madly in love with Hippolytus, though the young man wanted nothing to do with her. Phaedra in despair and anger then hung herself, but first left a note for Theseus that Hippolytus had tried to rape her. When Theseus read the note he called on his own father, Poseidon, to strike down Hippolytus. The god of the sea did so, mortally wounding him by driving his chariot onto rocks near the shore. But before Hippolytus died, Artemis revealed the truth to Theseus and reconciled son and tearful father, then promised eternal honors for Hippolytus.

APHRODITE

Making love to a goddess is a dangerous business. A young Trojan nobleman named Anchises learned this one night when he was tending cattle alone on Mount Ida, far above his city.

The gods had all grown tired of being driven to distraction by Aphrodite's wiles, so in revenge Zeus struck her with an irresistible longing to lie with a mortal man. One look at young Anchises was all it took. She was smitten and raced to her temple at Paphos on the island of Cyprus, where she had once sprung from sea foam. There her attendants bathed her and anointed her with sweet perfume, then dressed her in a beautiful gown. When all was ready, she flew down to Mount Ida, where Anchises was playing his lyre. As she passed through the forest and meadows, wild animals caught her scent and were overcome with the urge to mate with one another, much to the delight of the goddess.

Aphrodite put aside her divine glory and appeared suddenly before Anchises as a young maiden. Her silky robe was fastened by a single flower-shaped brooch, while her ears were adorned with finely crafted earrings and a beautiful necklace circled her lovely throat and came to rest between her soft breasts.

Anchises jumped up so fast he almost dropped his lyre: "Welcome, goddess on earth, whoever you are, whether Artemis, Athena, or even golden Aphrodite. I will build you an altar here and worship you forever."

Aphrodite smiled at the young man and said, "Dear Anchises, I am no goddess. Why would you think that I am? I'm just a mortal girl, daughter of King Otreus of Phrygia. I was dancing with my friends when suddenly Hermes whisked me away and brought me here. He said I was to be the wife of Prince Anchises and mother to his children. I hope that you'll find me worthy of you, innocent virgin that I am, and take me home to meet your parents, But first, perhaps, we could spend the night here, just the two of us?"

Anchises was so much in love that his heart almost beat out of his chest: "If you are truly a mortal woman, gladly I would take you for my wife. Indeed, you are so beautiful that I would happily trade my life for a single night with you."

The goddess smiled at him like a shy young girl and took his hand. Seemingly untried in the arts of love, she hesitated as he led her inside. There he first removed her jewelry and laid it aside, then loosened her brooch so that her gown slipped gently to the floor about her feet. Innocent like a lamb, she stood naked before him with eyes lowered modestly to the floor. Then he took her into his bed, where they made love the whole night through.

When dawn at last came, Aphrodite arose and once again put on the shining form of a goddess. The mad passion sent by Zeus had passed and she saw before her only a mortal man "Get up, Anchises! Take a look at me and see if I've changed since last night. Aphrodite, goddess of love, now stands before you."

Anchises fell out of the bed when he saw her. He bowed down before Aphrodite in terror and trembled. "I knew when I first beheld you that you had to be a goddess. Please, I implore you by Zeus himself, have mercy on me! No man can sleep with a goddess and live. I know you'll at least strike me with impotence!"

And Aphrodite answered him: "Oh, Anchises, calm down. You are loved by the gods as are your people. No harm will come to you for enjoying my divine charms. But know well that if you ever tell anyone that you spent the night with me you will suffer. I am disgraced that

I slept with a mortal man. Worse still, you have made me pregnant! I will bring the boy to you to raise when he is born. You can tell him his mother was some mountain nymph, but if you ever mention my name, you are a dead man."

Aphrodite flew back to Cyprus, but returned nine months later with the newborn son of Anchises, whom his father named Aeneas and raised as a prince of Troy. In time Aphrodite forgot her anger and claimed Aeneas as her son, but she always resented her night with a mortal man.

Aphrodite could be harsh, but she was sympathetic to true love, even among mortals. Such was the case with Pygmalion, a king on her home island of Cyprus. The young ruler could not find a woman to live up to his high standards, so he lived in his palace without a queen and went to his bed alone every night.

But Pygmalion knew what he wanted in a woman. He sculpted his image of ideal feminine beauty in precious ivory so that soon he had a life-size statue of a maiden more perfect than any woman ever born. His creation was so flawless that he fell deeply in love with it. He would often lift his hands to her face and caress her cheeks, then kiss her lips and imagine that she was kissing him in return. He brought the statue gifts of pretty shells, sweet flowers, and amber jewelry. He dressed her in fine robes and put rings upon her fingers, all the while pretending that she loved him as well. When evening came he would gently lay the statue down in bed beside him and spend the night dreaming that she was real.

One day during a festival of Aphrodite, Pygmalion approached the altar of the goddess to pray. More than anything he wished for his statue to be a real woman, but he dared not ask the goddess of love for such a favor. Instead he implored Aphrodite to give him a woman like his ivory maiden. The goddess heard his prayer and knew what was in his heart. When the king returned to his palace he went to his room and looked longingly at the statue still lying in his bed. He bent over and kissed her gently on the cheek. She seemed warm to his lips, but surely this was his imagination. He kissed her again and stroked her breasts, which now seemed soft to his touch. At last he placed his hand on her chest and felt her heart beating. The goddess had indeed granted his wish and made the ivory maiden into a living, breathing woman. She opened her eyes and for the first time saw the light of day at the same instant she beheld Pygmalion before her. She then smiled and embraced him, gladly consenting to be his wife.

Some say that Pygmalion and his bride had among their children a daughter named Metharme who was the mother of a boy named Adonis. But most say that the child was a son of Cinyras, king of Assyria, by his own daughter Myrrha. This incestuous union came about when Myrrha refused to give due honor to Aphrodite. The goddess punished the girl by making her consumed with an unnatural passion for her father. With the help of her nurse, the princess shared the bed of her father for twelve nights without his knowledge and became pregnant. When Cinyras found out, he took his sword to slay his daughter, but the gods had mercy on her and changed her to a sweet-smelling myrrh tree. Nine months later, the tree burst open and out came a baby boy.

The child was so beautiful that Aphrodite placed him in a chest and gave it to the underworld goddess Persephone to hide him from the world. But Persephone also loved the child and wanted to keep him for herself. They called on Zeus to settle the dispute, but he wisely chose the muse Calliope to judge the case. She directed that Adonis would spend one third of the year with Persephone, one third with Aphrodite, and the other third as he chose. But the boy so loved Aphrodite that he spent his own time with that goddess as well.

When Adonis became a young man, he and Aphrodite spent most of their days hunting in the forests and mountains. He always wanted to chase large game, but the goddess warned him to stick with smaller animals such as rabbits. This was no challenge for the youth, however, so one day when he was by himself he saw a wild boar running through the woods and chased it with his spear. The boar suddenly turned and charged him, suffering only a glancing blow from Adonis, but sinking his razor-sharp tusks deep into the young man's groin. He was lying on the ground bleeding his life away when Aphrodite arrived to take him in her arms. It was too late to save her beloved, but from his blood she caused a bright red blossom, the anemone, to rise up. It lives only a short time, but while it blooms it is the most beautiful flower in the world.

Aphrodite once made love to Hermes and bore a son whose name, Hermaphroditus, was a blending of the two gods. She gave the boy to the nymphs on Mount Ida to be raised and there he remained until he was fifteen years old. But as childhood gave way to maturity, he longed to see the world and so left his peaceful home. He wandered south to the land of Caria, where he came upon a beautiful pool one hot day. He stripped off his clothes and jumped into the delightfully cool water, splashing and swimming in the bright sun. But there was a nymph who lived in the pool named Salmacis. She saw the boy and immediately fell in love with him, longing to be his wife. She put on her finest robes and approached the lad at the edge of the pool, but Hermaphroditus was overcome with shyness and was terrified as he stood naked before the beautiful young nymph. She pleaded with him to take her as his mate, but the youth had no experience with women and tried to flee. She then threw aside her own clothes and jumped into the pool to follow him. She caught him and clung to him, naked body on naked body, entwining herself like a snake around the young man's flesh. She called on the gods never to let them be separated—and they heard her prayer. Suddenly their two bodies melted together into one. Hermaphroditus was horrified at the unmanly creature he had become and prayed to the gods that anyone who entered the pool would share his fate. He then went on his way, a handsome and beautiful youth with the breasts of a woman and the genitals of a man, eventually to become a god sharing male and female features forever.

Aphrodite also had an unusual son named Priapus with Dionysus. He was an ugly little god with enormous genitals and a nasty disposition. One day he got into an argument with an ass his father had given human voice to. The ass claimed to be better endowed than the god, but Priapus was proud of his own equipment and boasted that his was larger. After some careful measurements, it was determined that the ass was indeed the winner. Priapus was so angry that he beat the animal to death with a stick. Dionysus, however, felt sorry for the ass and placed him as a star in the heavens.

HECATE

If there was a goddess of mystery in the ancient world, it was Hecate. According to one early story she was the daughter of the Titans Perses and

Asteria. When most of the other Titans were overthrown by Zeus and cast down into Tartarus, Hecate was spared and was in fact greatly honored by the ruler of the gods. She was praised as protector of horsemen, sailors, and fishermen, as well as herdsmen and hunters.

But there is surprisingly little mythology about Hecate. She appears briefly to help Demeter find her daughter Persephone, but then quickly disappears. And yet, she was worshiped everywhere as a goddess of the underworld who ruled over crossroads and was a patroness of dark magic. She was called the keeper of the keys that hold the hellhound Cerberus and the wearer of the sandals of she who rules Tartarus. Her favorite sacrifices were red mullet fish, little cakes with candles, and fresh young puppies. At the time of the full moon, meals of garbage made up of old bread, rotten eggs, spoiled cheese, and dog meat were offered to the goddess. Those who wished to curse their enemies or make magic spells more potent invoked the name of Hecate, but as for myths, tales of Hecate are noticeably and ominously lacking. She was, like Hades, a god best worshiped with grave respect but otherwise treated with reverent silence.

HESTIA

Another goddess mentioned in few myths is Hestia, though this divinity of the hearth was welcomed in every household. She was a daughter of Cronus and Rhea as were Zeus and Hera, but Hestia's only task was to guard the life-giving fire at the center of every home. She had refused marriage to both Poseidon and Apollo, devoting herself to perpetual virginity. Her lack of mythology is a result of her chosen occupation, for as guardian of the hearth, she was never able to leave the sacred fire unguarded.

But Hestia was nonetheless greatly revered. As one early hymn sings:

Hestia, you who dwell in the lofty halls with undying gods and with men who walk the earth, you have gained an everlasting home and highest honor. Your portion among the gods is precious and everlasting. Without you, there would be no feasts for mortals. To you, the first and last drops of sweet wine are poured in sacrifice.

ATHENA

Most stories say that Athena was the daughter of the wise goddess Metis, whom Zeus swallowed after getting her pregnant, only to give birth to her daughter Athena from his forehead months later. The child leapt fully grown and armored from the head of Zeus and took her place among the gods of Mount Olympus. But other tales say she was born from a river named Triton in Boeotia or Arcadia. The Ausean tribe of north Africa even claimed she was the daughter of Poseidon and their Lake Tritonis, but that she shunned the sea god and was adopted by Zeus.

Whatever her origins, Athena was a goddess both of warfare and the feminine arts. As the presiding goddess of Athens, she was celebrated as Athena the Virgin (*parthenos*) and honored with the grand temple of the Parthenon on the Acropolis.

Most of Athena's myths involve battles, aiding heroes in their quests, or helping warriors return home, but there are a few stories in which she shows herself as patroness of crafts. The most famous of these begins with a young peasant woman of Lydia named Arachne. This maiden was so skilled at weaving that the nymphs would gather around to watch her work. She moved with grace and consummate skill as her fingers flew across the loom, drawing the long threads and giving a twist with a practiced thumb to the spindle. Everyone thought she must have been taught by Athena herself. But Arachne was indignant at the suggestion: "I taught myself. If the goddess thinks she is better than me, let her come to a contest."

Athena heard the girl's boasting and decided to pay her a visit. The goddess took on the form of an old woman with gray hair leaning on a cane. She then came to Arachne's cottage and spoke to the maiden: "Take my advice, young lady, and don't be so proud. You're good, no doubt, but you are only a mortal. You shouldn't pit yourself against a goddess. Pray to Athena for forgiveness for your pride and I'm sure she will grant it."

But Arachne was indignant.

"Mind your own business, old woman. Go give advice to your own daughter, if you have one, and leave me alone. If Athena is so great at weaving, let her come and challenge me."

The goddess then threw aside her disguise and revealed herself to Arachne. The nymphs all fell to their knees in worship, but the girl remained defiant and insisted on a competition. Two looms were set up next to each other and the goddess and maiden began to weave. Athena moved with lightning speed as she wove stories with her threads. She told tales in cloth of foolish mortals who had dared to challenge the gods and had suffered the consequences. Arachne countered with images of vain and cruel gods deceiving and abusing men and women. When the girl finished, Athena could not find even the smallest imperfection in her weaving. The goddess was so furious that she grabbed a wooden shuttle and began to beat the girl senseless. Arachne was in such pain that she took a rope and hanged herself from the cottage roof.

Athena at last calmed down and felt sorry for what she had done. She sprinkled the dead girl with divine herbs and watched as her hair fell away. The maiden's nose and ears also disappeared and her whole body shrank, leaving only a tiny head, a large belly, and eight long legs. Arachne was restored to life, but as a spider, the mother of all her descendants ever weaving beautiful patterns in their webs.

EOS

The goddess of dawn was rosy-fingered Eos, daughter of the Titans Hyperion and Theia. She was an unusually amorous deity who delighted in kidnapping mortal men to serve as her lovers. One of these was Orion, hunting companion of Artemis, whom the dawn goddess once transported to her love nest on the island of Ortygia before he died of a scorpion bite. She also snatched away a young man named Cleitus to warm her bed because of his beauty.

More of a challenge was Cephalus, a prince who was deeply in love with his wife, Procris. The couple had exchanged a vow that they would always be faithful to each other. One morning when Cephalus was out hunting, Eos came and offered to sleep with him. He refused, telling the goddess of his promise to his wife. Eos was patient, however, and assured the prince that she had no desire for him to break his vow—unless, of course, Procris broke hers first. Cephalus swore this would never happen, so Eos proposed a test. She changed his appearance and gave him many fine gifts, then dared him to try, as a stranger, to seduce his own wife.

Cephalus took up the challenge and went to his palace. There he met Procris and charmed her with sweet words of love and wonderful presents. At last, to his surprise, his wife was won over and went to bed with him.

The next morning Eos returned Cephalus to his own form and Procris was deeply ashamed. She fled to Crete, where one story says she tried to become a follower of Artemis, but was rebuked by the goddess because she was not a virgin. Another story says she cured the womanizing King Minos of an unfortunate curse his wife had placed on him—he ejaculated spiders and scorpions instead of semen—and gained the royal favor.

Either Artemis or Minos then gave her a magnificent spear and hunting dog and sent her back to her husband in disguise, for Procris had cut her hair short and dressed in the clothes of a man. Once home, she challenged Cephalus to a hunting contest and easily defeated him. The prince was so surprised that he offered to buy the spear and the dog from the stranger, but Procris refused. Still, Cephalus just had to have those prizes, so he asked if there was anything he might do to obtain them. The stranger smiled and said he could have both the spear and the dog if he would go to bed with him. Although Cephalus knew it was shameful to prostitute himself to another man, he agreed.

The two went to the bedroom of Cephalus and the prince removed his clothes. Then Procris slowly took off her tunic and revealed herself both as a woman and his wife. Cephalus then realized he was no better than his wayward bride. The two embraced and kissed, forgiving each other and finding love again.

However, the most famous paramour of the dawn goddess was Tithonus, a young and handsome prince of Troy. Eos took him away to her palace in the east where she enjoyed his pleasures every night. She so loved Tithonus that she asked Zeus to give him eternal life, which the god granted. But like Sibyl, she forgot to request eternal youth along with immortality for her love. While he was still in the bloom of youth, the couple were rapturously happy and had several children. But when the hair of Tithonus began to turn gray, Eos grew tired of him and sent him from her bed. As the years passed, the man grew aged, crippled, and senile. All he could do was lie in his bed alone and babble endlessly. Eventually the goddess wearied of his chattering and turned him into a cicada, an insect that never stops making noise.

THE MUSES

The nine sisters who inspired poets, artists, musicians, scientists, and writers were the Muses. They were Calliope (epic poetry), Erato (lyric poetry), Polyhymnia (hymns), Clio (history), Euterpe (flute playing), Terpsichore (dancing), Melpomene (tragedy), Thalia (comedy), and Urania (astronomy). They were the daughters of Zeus and Mnemosyne, the goddess of memory. They appear in just a handful of myths and had few places of worship, but one temple below their home on Mount Helicon housing archives and historical objects came to be known as the first *mouseion*, or museum.

Like all gods, the Muses were jealous of their reputations. When the celebrated bard Thamyris challenged them to a singing contest, they easily won and took away both his poetic gift and—more devastating for a bard—his memory. The nine foolish daughters of Pierus thought themselves equal to the Muses and also challenged them to a contest of song, but were beaten and turned into magpies for their insolence.

The nine sisters were not maidens and among themselves had several famous sons. Clio bore Hyacinth, and Calliope was the mother of the famous singer Orpheus, while Melpomene gave birth to the dreaded Sirens, who would one day sing so sweetly to Odysseus.

THE FATES

The three daughters of Night who spun, wove, and cut the thread of life for each person on earth were known as the Moerae, or Fates. Their

names were Clotho, Lachesis, and Atropos, and even the gods feared
them. No one could master or outwit them, not even Zeus. When every
child was born, the three sisters determined how long it would live and
when it would die.

Like Hades, the Fates were not cruel, but merely performed their
job as part of the order of the cosmos. At times they would even leave
their dark lair and come to the aid of the gods, such as when the great
monster Typhon attacked Olympus and threatened to overthrow Zeus.
The sisters pretended to be on Typhon's side and offered him human
food to eat, claiming it would make him even stronger, but it only made
him easier to defeat.

The Fates did not usually reveal a person's destiny, but there were exceptions. When the prince Meleager was born, they came to his mother,
Althaea, and told her he would die when the log burning in her hearth
was consumed. The frantic mother quickly grabbed the wood from the
fire and put it away carefully in a chest. There it safely remained for
many years until her son went on a hunt for the Calydonian Boar. He
killed the beast and gave its hide to his female companion Atalanta,
but one of Althaea's brothers was also on the hunt and tried to steal the
skin, prompting Meleager to kill him in anger. When Althaea found out,
she took the log from the chest and threw it into the fire. Meleager then
died in burning agony, proving that no one could cheat the Fates.

CYBELE

One day when Zeus was visiting the land of Phrygia, he fell asleep in a
grassy field. While he was sleeping, he ejaculated on the ground. From
this spilled seed, a creature arose named Agdistis who had both male
and female sexual organs. All the gods were fearful of what might happen if such a child grew up, so they cut off the male parts of Agdistis and
turned the androgynous being into a woman. As a female, she became
the goddess Cybele.

From the male genitals of Agdistis grew an almond tree. The daughter of a local river god was walking past the tree one afternoon when
she stopped beneath its shade to rest. This young woman, named Nana,

took a nut from the tree and put it in her lap, but it disappeared. Soon afterward, she realized she was pregnant. She gave birth to a baby boy named Attis several months later, but the mother realized she could not raise him and so left him to die on a nearby mountain. A he-goat found the child and somehow suckled him, so that Attis grew up to be a handsome young man.

Cybele saw Attis one day and fell in love with him, even though by then he was promised in marriage to a princess of Phrygia. Just as the wedding ceremony was about to begin, Cybele appeared and drove Attis mad. He took his knife and castrated himself in front of his bride, but bled so much that he died. Cybele felt bad about this afterward and prayed to Zeus that the body of Attis might not decay, a prayer that the ruler of the gods granted.

Cybele was never a member of the family of gods on Olympus, but was always seen as an outsider, an exotic goddess from the lands of the east. Nonetheless, she was greatly honored throughout the classical world. Sometimes she was associated with Rhea, the mother of Zeus, or with Demeter, but most worshiped her simply as Cybele, "Mother of the gods and all humanity, who delights in the sound of drums and tambourines, the playing of flutes and the howling of wolves, and in the roar of the mighty lion."

Like Dionysus, she was a god of emotional release. Young men danced in her honor dressed in full armor, clashing their spears on their shields. Worshipers male and female bathed in the blood of bulls sacrificed in her honor and sang songs of ecstasy. But the most loyal of her followers were her male priests, called the Galli. These men, wishing to be initiated into her cult, would long prepare themselves by fasting, purification, and baptism. Then, on a warm spring day, they would take out knives and castrate themselves, just as Attis had done. Such was the price of devotion to the great goddess.

HEROES

PERSEUS

𐤟𐤟𐤟𐤟𐤟𐤟𐤟𐤟𐤟

The broad and fertile plains of Argos were once the home of Io, who was forced to flee as a tormented cow from Hera's wrath. From Io came many descendants, such as Europa, kidnapped by Zeus when he was disguised as a bull, but the most famous of her heirs was Perseus, the son of Danae and grandson of the Argive king Acrisius.

Acrisius had always wanted a son, so he asked an oracle if he would ever have a male heir. The news was not good. "Not only will you not have a son," the oracle revealed, "but if your daughter Danae does, he will kill you." Fearful of this fate but not wishing to be cursed for killing his own child, Acrisius locked his virgin daughter in an underground chamber made of bronze with only a small window in the top through which servants could lower food and drink. There Danae passed her days, untouched by any man.

But one night while she was lying in bed, she saw a strange and beautiful sight. Through the opening of her cell came a shower of golden coins that fell gently into her lap. It was not long afterward that Danae realized she was pregnant. The shower of gold was in fact Zeus himself who had come to the maiden.

The young woman was terrified at what her father would do when he found out—and with good cause. Acrisius was furious and scoffed at his daughter's story of a god getting her pregnant. As soon as she gave birth, he took both mother and child and placed them in a chest, then cast it into the sea.

The pair was tossed about by storms while Danae held little Perseus in her arms. The frightened girl prayed for help: "Dear gods, save us from our great peril. Father Zeus, with a humble heart I implore you! But you, little one, warm and well fed, sleep on as we sail through the night in our prison. Crashing waves and the dangers of the deep mean nothing to you, my innocent babe."

Zeus must have heard her prayer, for soon they washed up safely on the tiny island of Seriphus. There a kindly fisherman named Dictys found them and took them into his home. He treated Danae as a father would his own daughter and he loved little Perseus as well, watching proudly as the boy grew into a strong young man.

Danae was a beautiful woman and caught the eye of Polydectes, ruler of Seriphus and brother of the fisherman Dictys. He tried to win her as his bride, but she had no interest in the man and Polydectes was too afraid of Perseus to seize her by force. He was clever, however, and announced that he was planning to court a princess named Hippodamia and therefore required all his subjects to contribute wedding gifts for her dowry. Polydectes had no chance of winning the hand of this famous beauty, but he wanted an excuse to get Perseus out of the way. The men of the island brought horses to contribute, but Perseus was poor and had nothing to offer. Still, he was a brave young man and had once rashly bragged that he could do anything, even fetch the head of the dreaded Gorgon Medusa. Polydectes therefore told him to do so, if he dared.

Perseus was nothing if not confident, so he set off on his quest to kill and decapitate the most dangerous monster in all the world. Not only were Medusa and her two sisters vicious creatures with hair made of writhing snakes, but the slightest glance at their faces would turn anyone to stone. They could also fly, so that even if by some miracle Perseus managed to slay Medusa, the other two would easily catch and kill him. Fortunately for Perseus, Athena detested Medusa, who had once been a lovely maiden who rivaled the goddess in beauty. Athena thus appeared to the young hero and told him how he might slay her.

Perseus first went to distant Africa to find the cave of the Graeae, eternally old sisters of the Gorgons who shared a single eye among them. They were suspicious of Perseus, but with so few visitors they were willing to talk with him for a little while. Suddenly, as one sister passed the eye to another, Perseus grabbed it and rendered the Graeae blind. The sisters cursed and threatened the young thief, but at last they calmed down and asked what he wanted in return for their eye. Perseus said that all he required were directions to the home of some nymphs Athena had told him about. These divine ladies had three magical objects he would need to slay Medusa. The Graeae reluctantly agreed and revealed the dwelling place of the nymphs, after which Perseus returned their eye—though some stories say he threw it into a lake.

Once he found the nymphs, they gladly gave him the objects he needed—a large pouch in which to carry Medusa's head, a pair of sandals with wings, and a cap that rendered the wearer invisible. Leaving the nymphs, he was soon met by the god Hermes, who gave him yet another gift, a sword made of the hardest adamant with which to cut off Medusa's head. Sword at his side, bag over his shoulder, cap on his head, and sandals on his feet, Perseus flew off to face the Gorgons.

Even with magical tools to help him, the three sisters were formidable foes, with scales like dragons and sharp tusks like wild boars. But most difficult to overcome was their power to change men into stone, a threat from which no sword or shoes could protect Perseus. But Athena was soon on hand with more advice. "Approach them at night while they are sleeping," the goddess advised, "and take with you a polished bronze shield." Perseus did so and, wearing his invisibility cap, he crept up on the sleeping Gorgons with the greatest of care. Before he saw their faces, he turned around and began walking backward towards Medusa while gazing at her reflection in the shield. With one slash of the adamantine sword, Perseus sliced off her head and threw it into his pouch. Much to his surprise, the young foal Pegasus flew out from the gaping wound along with Chrysaor, who would one day father the monster Geryon. Both were children of Poseidon, engendered when the god had long ago raped Medusa as a beautiful young woman.

Perseus had no time to marvel at this turn of events, for the other two Gorgon sisters were awake in an instant. They saw the headless body of their sister lying on the ground before them and screamed for blood, but there was no trace of her murderer. They searched for hours, but finally returned to their cave as Perseus flew away on his magical sandals.

Some say the young hero next stopped at the house of the god Atlas, who carried the heavens on his shoulders. However, this Titan was most unfriendly to his guest since he had been warned by the goddess Themis that a son of Zeus would one day steal his most precious possession, a tree bearing golden apples. Atlas grabbed him and threw him against a stone wall like a toy. Perseus expected better treatment from his host and wanted to kill him then and there, but knew he was no match for the giant. So he said, "Even though you are rude to me, great Atlas, I have a gift for you." With that he pulled the head of Medusa from his pouch and held it in front of him. The Titan shuddered and tried to close his eyes, but it was too late. As he watched helplessly, his arms and legs turned to stone, followed by the rest of his body. At last he was nothing but rock, the African peak we know today as Mount Atlas.

As Perseus continued on his way home, he flew over Ethiopia and saw far below him a beautiful, naked girl tied to a rock. This was Andromeda, his distant cousin, left on the barren shore as a sacrifice to a sea monster by her parents, King Cepheus and Queen Cassiopeia. The trouble had begun when Cassiopeia boasted to the Nereids, sea nymph daughters of Poseidon, that she was more beautiful than they. They were irate and complained to their father, who sent both a flood and the monster to ravage the coast. Cepheus asked the oracle of Zeus at the Egyptian oasis of Siwa how he might appease the god, but the oracle proclaimed that Poseidon would relent only if the king sacrificed his own daughter to the sea monster. Reluctantly, the grieving father ordered Andromeda bound to the rock. Both he and Cassiopeia then stood by weeping and waiting for their daughter to die.

Perseus fell in love with the girl the instant he saw her and flew down to strike a deal with her father. He offered to kill the sea monster if Cepheus would promise him Andromeda's hand in marriage and give him a kingdom of his own. The king gladly agreed, so the young hero put himself between the sea and the maiden to wait for the creature that would soon appear. When the monster breached the waves, Perseus could see that it was enormous and fast with fangs like a snake, but not very bright. Invisible under his magical cap and flying with his winged sandals, Perseus easily evaded the beast while it attacked his shadow on the surface of the sea. At just the right moment, Perseus flew in close and plunged his sword deep into the monster's neck. The wounded creature bellowed and vomited blood, but its unseen attacker kept stabbing it relentlessly until it was dead.

Perseus freed Andromeda and presented her to her mother and father, who were overjoyed at her unexpected rescue. They held a banquet for the visiting hero that went well until it was interrupted by Phineus, brother of Cepheus. The king had forgotten to mention to Perseus that his daughter was already engaged to be married to her own uncle. Phineus had brought many supporters with him when he burst into the dinner so that Perseus was soon surrounded by an angry mob. A battle ensued between the followers of Phineus and the few Ethiopians on the side of Perseus. The young hero slew his fair share of men, but was outnumbered and finally shouted that any friends of his still alive in the hall should close their eyes. He then reached in his pouch and pulled out the head of Medusa, turning two hundred men into stone. Phineus was quick enough to look away and remain unchanged, but Perseus found him. The challenger begged for mercy, but the young man was not moved. He grabbed Phineus and forced him to look at the head, then watched his rival turn to stone even as he pleaded pathetically for his life.

Perseus stayed in Ethiopia only long enough to father a child with Andromeda. The boy was named Perses and was left to inherit the throne from Cepheus. Perseus was anxious to return to his mother on Seriphus, so he and Andromeda sailed back to the island, only to find that the conniving Polydectes had been busy while he was away. Some say he had forced Perseus' mother, Danae, to marry him, but others say she and her protector Dictys had taken refuge at the altar of one of the gods. Perseus marched into the palace and played his usual trick on Polydectes by pulling out the head of Medusa and turning the king and his entire court to stone. He then made Dictys ruler of Seriphus.

Now that his tasks were done, Perseus gave all his magical tools to Hermes, while he presented Athena with the head of Medusa. The goddess was so pleased with the gift that she placed the hideous object in the center of her own shield. Perseus, Danae, and Andromeda then sailed back to Argos, from which he and his mother had been exiled by his grandfather Acrisius years before. The old man heard that Perseus was returning and feared for his life, so he fled north to the town of Larissa in Thessaly. Perseus followed him there and arrived just as the local king Teutamides was holding funeral games in honor of his father. The young hero couldn't resist the urge to prove himself in competition, so he joined in the games and competed in throwing the discus. Perseus launched his discus farther than anyone, but the wind caught it and turned it back toward the crowd. It flew at terrific speed and struck an old man who had been secretly watching—none other than Acrisius himself.

With his grandfather dead and the prophecy fulfilled, Perseus was free to return to Argos and claim the throne, but he felt guilty since he had accidentally killed a blood relative. He therefore went to the nearby town of Tiryns and persuaded his cousin, Megapenthes, who ruled there, to trade kingdoms with him. Perseus then became king of Tiryns while Megapenthes ruled over Argos. In the years to come, Perseus also built the great palace of Mycenae on the hills overlooking the Argive plain. When he and Andromeda had lived a long and happy life together with many children, Athena placed them among the stars along with his in-laws Cepheus and Cassiopeia.

THESEUS

Perseus was a champion known and loved by the people of Argos, but the city of Athens celebrated its own native hero whom the Athenians claimed was even more daring and brave—and, unlike Perseus, did his deeds with a minimum of divine help.

The story begins when Aegeus, king of Athens, went to the oracle at Delphi to ask if he would ever have a child. In her typically obscure manner, the priestess of Apollo went into a trance and proclaimed to the king: "Open not the swollen mouth of the wineskin, O king of the people, until you come once more to the city of Athens."

Aegeus had no idea what this meant since he wasn't even carrying a wineskin, so he left the temple scratching his head. Seeking advice, he journeyed home by way of the city of Troezen to ask its wise king Pittheus if he understood the riddle. His host was much quicker than Aegeus and realized at once that the god was telling the Athenian king not to have sex until he returned home. Pittheus understood that whatever woman Aegeus first lay with was bound to give birth to a mighty hero. But, claiming he could not interpret the oracle, the king then got his visitor drunk and guided him to the bed of his own daughter, Aethra.

When he woke up the next morning, Aegeus had a terrible headache and a beautiful young woman beside him. He still didn't understand the oracle, but he had a hunch he might have gotten this girl pregnant. When he found out she was the daughter of the king, he gave her secret instructions before leaving: "If you have a son," he whispered, "send him to me in Athens when he grows up—if he can retrieve these." Aegeus then took a sword and a pair of sandals and placed them underneath an enormous boulder. He declared that if she bore a son worthy of him, the boy would be able to lift the stone and take the tokens he had left. He was to bring these to Athens and claim his throne.

Some stories say that unknown to Aegeus, the sea god Poseidon raped the princess soon thereafter. The girl indeed became pregnant, but whether by mortal man or god, she could never quite be sure. In any case, nine months later Aethra gave birth to a baby boy and named him Theseus.

Aethra raised her son to believe he was the offspring of Poseidon. The boy was certainly strong and clever enough to be the son of a god, but when he reached young manhood, his mother led him to the rock under which Aegeus had buried his tokens and told him the alternate story of his conception. She confessed she did not know for certain who his real father was, though she advised him to try to lift the stone and claim his rightful place in Athens. Theseus put his shoulder to the giant rock and pushed with all his might, rolling it over and revealing both the sword and sandals.

Theseus was determined to make the trip to Athens by land, even though the sea route was safer by far. This was because a series of notorious savage outlaws haunted the road that led across the Isthmus of Corinth between Troezen and Athens. Travelers who took that route seldom lived to tell the tale. But to Theseus, such challenges were merely ways to prove himself a true hero. So in spite of the pleas of both his mother and grandfather, the boy took the sword and sandals, then set off down the dangerous road.

It wasn't long until Theseus came to Epidaurus, where he met a large, crippled man named Periphetes. This outlaw was nicknamed Clubman because of the giant iron club he used as a cane. Whenever anyone passed by on the road, Periphetes would shuffle out of his home to greet his guest, then beat the surprised visitor to death. This villain was strong but slow, whereas Theseus was smart and fast. He barely dodged the first blow, but quickly came up behind Periphetes and grabbed the club from his hands. He then pounded Periphetes to a pulp with his own weapon.

Not far down the road was another outlaw named Sinis, called the Pine-Bender. This scoundrel seized unwary visitors and tied their legs to a supple pine tree bent to the ground. He would then take their arms and tie these to another tree bent down from the opposite direction. When all was ready he would cut the cord holding the trees together and gleefully tear his victims apart. Theseus quickly realized what his plan was and took hold of the outlaw before he could be captured himself. Then with Sinis begging and pleading for his life, Theseus tied him between two pine trees in the same manner as all those he had murdered and cut the cord.

Perigune, the beautiful daughter of Sinis, watched all this in horror from her hiding place in some nearby asparagus bushes. Theseus saw her and promised she would not be harmed if she surrendered. The girl was so grateful she emerged from the bushes and wrapped her arms around the handsome hero. He had never been with a woman before, but he learned quickly, leaving her pregnant as he went on his way. Generations later, the descendants of Perigune were still venerating asparagus.

Theseus crossed the narrow Isthmus of Corinth and continued on his journey to Athens, detouring along the coast to seek out a creature known as the Crommyonian Sow. Some say she was a wicked, murderous woman who had the manners of a pig, but most agree that she was indeed a sow of immense size and fierce nature bred by a local woman named Phaea. This beast was a deadly threat to the peaceful seaside town of Crommyon and to anyone who came across her path. Theseus could have easily taken a side road and avoided the animal, but he was determined to make a name for himself. After a brief struggle, the young hero killed the sow and continued on his way.

Near the town of Megara, Theseus next came across the outlaw

Sciron who lived on a cliff above the sea. It was his peculiar habit to capture travelers and force them to wash his feet. In the middle of this humiliating task, he would kick them over the edge of the cliff into the sea where a giant turtle was waiting to eat them. Theseus let himself be taken by Sciron, then pretended to bend down and wash his feet, but instead he grabbed the outlaw by his legs and threw him over the cliff to be devoured by the turtle.

Drawing near to Athens, Theseus arrived at Eleusis, where Demeter had established her cult. At this time the city was ruled by a wicked king named Cercyon who forced all travelers to wrestle him, usually killing them during the match. Theseus, however, was a skilled wrestler himself and, lifting Cercyon above his head, dashed him on the ground and killed him.

Theseus had almost reached his destination when darkness fell. He was at the village of Erineus and met a kindly man named Procrustes who offered him a room for the night. This villager frequently took visitors into his home, but he had a very exacting nature. After feeding his guests a good meal, he would lead them to a comfortable bed. But before they knew it, they were tightly bound on their backs while their host pulled out his saw and ropes. He was insistent that his guests fit the bed exactly, so those too tall were trimmed to size, while those too short were stretched with cords. Theseus, however, turned the tables on Procrustes and fatally adjusted him to fit his own bed.

By the time Theseus walked through the gates of Athens, everyone knew that the young hero who had cleared the road of outlaws was in the city, but they did not know who he was. This became clear when the handsome young man passed beneath the unfinished temple of Apollo on the Acropolis. His appearance was foreign to the Athenians as he wore a long tunic reaching to his feet and had his hair neatly plaited. The workmen who were finishing the roof of the temple saw him below and mockingly called out asking why such a beautiful maiden was walking around by herself. Saying nothing, Theseus unyoked a pair of oxen from a nearby cart and threw both of them onto the roof with his bare hands. No one in Athens ever teased him again.

The one person suspicious of Theseus was Medea, a sorceress from the distant land of Colchis who had taken refuge in Athens years before.

She had obtained sanctuary from Aegeus and was now the king's influential advisor and lover. She and the king had a son together named Medus who stood to inherit his father's throne, but as soon as Medea saw Theseus, she realized who he must be and the threat he posed to her own son's succession. She therefore whispered to Aegeus that the presence of this celebrated visitor in the city was a grave danger. Aegeus was already wary of challenges to his power since he had a brother named Pallas, the father of fifty grown sons, who was eager to topple him. In this mood of general suspicion, it was easy for Medea to persuade Aegeus to get rid of Theseus permanently.

Nearby on the plain of Marathon lived a dangerous bull brought to Greece years before. Aegeus, at Medea's suggestion, sent Theseus to slay this animal. The king fully expected the young man to be killed, but it was the bull who died at the hands of Theseus. Surprised but impressed, the king invited Theseus to a celebratory feast and placed him on the seat of honor. With the king's approval, Medea now mixed deadly aconite into a goblet of wine and offered it to Theseus. The young hero was just about to drink the poison when Aegeus saw the sword hanging from his belt. He recognized it as the very weapon he had left under the stone at Troezen years before and quickly knocked the cup from the hands of his guest. Aegeus embraced the lad and proclaimed that the visitor was none other than his own son, the rightful heir to the throne of Athens.

Medea was driven far away into exile with her son, but Theseus' uncle Pallas was not so easily removed. He and his fifty sons realized that with Theseus as prince, they would never inherit power in Athens. Therefore they laid an ambush to slay the hero, but were defeated by him and killed to a man. With all competition now removed, Theseus was certain to be the next king.

Every nine years the king of Athens was obligated to send seven young men and seven maidens to Crete as victims for the monstrous, man-eating Minotaur. This was because many years earlier Minos, king of Crete and son of Europa by Zeus, had attacked Athens and forced its surrender with the help of the gods. One of the terms of the city's capitulation was that fourteen young people would be sent without fail to his palace to meet a most gruesome end.

The Minotaur was a creature born of the disobedience of Minos to the god Poseidon. After the old king of the island had died, Minos drove away his own brothers, claiming he was best suited to rule. He asked that the sea god prove this to everyone by sending a magnificent bull from the sea as a sign, an animal Minos promised to sacrifice to Poseidon. The bull duly arose, but it was so splendid that Minos couldn't bear to kill it, so he sent it to his own herd and substituted a lesser beast. Poseidon was not pleased and in an act of perverse revenge caused Pasiphae, the wife of Minos, to fall madly in love with the bull he had sent. The poor woman was torn between sexual desire for the animal and shame at her own bestial lust. But in the end, passion was stronger than prudence and the queen decided she must give herself to the bull at any cost.

There was a skilled Athenian builder on the island named Daedalus who Pasiphae persuaded to help her. This craftsman built a lifelike wooden cow big enough for the queen to crawl inside. It had an opening in the back in just the right place for a bull to mate with it. Pasiphae climbed inside and Daedalus wheeled the contraption out to the pasture. The great bull saw it and snorted with desire, then hurried over and mounted the strange creature. The queen became pregnant by the bull and in due time gave birth to an ill-tempered creature with the head of a bull and the body of a man.

Minos was deeply ashamed at being cuckolded by a beast, but he didn't want to offend the gods by killing the monster who was, in a sense, part of the family. He therefore ordered Daedalus to build a complex maze called the Labyrinth to hide the creature and serve as a punishment for prisoners. Those unfortunates who were forced into the complex passageway full of twists and turns could not find their way out—at least not before the Minotaur found and devoured them.

When Minos sailed to Athens announcing that it was time to send the boys and girls to feed the Minotaur, all the Athenians prayed their children would not be chosen in the lottery. However, the new prince Theseus, indignant at the injustice imposed on his people, volunteered to be one of the victims, much to the horror of his father, Aegeus. The king begged him to reconsider, but the young man was determined to prove himself by killing the monster and preventing any further deaths. Aegeus wept at his son's audacity, but Minos laughed and encouraged the boy in his hopeless quest. Aegeus made the captain of the ship taking the young victims to Crete promise, on his return to Athens, to unfurl a white sail if his son still lived, but to enter the harbor with a black sail of mourning if Theseus was dead.

Minos and Theseus quarreled during the voyage to Crete after the young hero defended one of the maidens on the ship from the notoriously lustful king. Minos grew so angry that he challenged Theseus to prove he was really the son of Poseidon by throwing his ring into the depths of the sea and demanding that the youth retrieve it. Theseus dove in and almost immediately met a group of sea nymphs who not only gave him the ring, but also a crown that Aphrodite had given to Thetis at her wedding to Peleus. Minos was indignant when Theseus returned with both prizes.

When the ship finally reached Crete, Minos held athletic contests that Theseus begged to join. This was most unusual since most victims-to-be were not in the mood for games, but the king granted the prince's request if for no other reason than he hoped the youth would defeat his own general Taurus, an insufferable but popular braggart who always won every event. Theseus defeated Taurus in wrestling and disgraced the general, much to the delight of Minos. Also impressed was the king's daughter, Ariadne, who fell passionately in love with Theseus on the spot.

Ariadne couldn't bear the thought of Theseus being devoured by the Minotaur, so she went to Daedalus to see if he knew a way out of the maze he had built. The architect said that not even he could escape from the Labyrinth unaided, but he suggested a clever ploy. Take a ball of thread, he told the girl, and have Theseus tie it to the entrance of the maze. He should unroll it after him as he worked his way deeper into the Labyrinth, then, if he managed actually to kill the Minotaur, follow the thread back out. Theseus did as Ariadne told him and made his way into the depths of the maze at the head of the Athenian victims. He found the Minotaur and killed him with his bare hands. He then took the ball of thread and led the grateful youths and maidens out of the twisting Labyrinth, escaping with them to the Athenian ship. With Ariadne at his side, he sailed quickly away from Crete.

Some stories say Theseus stopped at the island of Naxos on his way home. By then Ariadne was pregnant with his child, but, depending on the story, he either forgot her or abandoned her on the beach, in either case leaving behind the young woman who had given up everything to save him.

Theseus was so anxious to get home to his father and tell him the good news that he forgot to tell the captain to raise the white sail as agreed. Aegeus had been waiting every day on the heights of the Acropolis for his son to return, but when he saw the black-sailed ship in the distance, he assumed Theseus was dead and threw himself onto the rocks below. When the prince rushed from the port up to the city, he saw that everyone was in mourning. With a chill of foreboding, he asked why and heard the sad news that Aegeus was dead. Theseus was now king of Athens.

With his popularity high as a result of his success in Crete, Theseus set about to reform Athens. Up to that time, the countryside around the city, known as Attica, was made up of dozens of quarreling villages that could rarely agree on anything. Every settlement had its own council and cooperated with the capital city of Athens grudgingly, if at all. As a result, Athens was weak in the face of foreign incursions and barely able to hold Attica together. Therefore Theseus—at least as Athenians later told the tale—established tight control over all the surrounding communities of Attica. He eliminated local councils and centralized all government functions in the capital city, where he founded a democratic assembly of all male citizens. He also insisted on absolute command for himself in time of war. Gone were the days of clan politics and autonomous villages. Theseus made sure everyone in Attica was an Athenian, whether they liked it or not.

Civic improvement and the mundane affairs of state held no lasting interest for Theseus, however. No sooner had he established centralized government in Athens than he sought out a new adventure. The young king had long heard of women warriors called the Amazons who lived on the distant shores of the Black Sea. These females were the exact opposite of everything a proper Greek woman should be—aggressive rather than submissive, promiscuous instead of chaste—and they spent their spare time practicing war rather than weaving. They would take visiting men into their beds only when it suited them. If a boy was born as a result of this encounter, they would kill it, but if the child was a healthy girl they would raise her as one of their own. When a daughter reached puberty, they would cut off her right breast so that she might better draw a bow—thus the name Amazon, from a ("no") and mazos ("breast").

After a long sea voyage, Theseus arrived in the land of the Amazons and was greeted respectfully by their queen, Antiope. But at the end of his visit, when she bade Theseus farewell on the shore, he treacherously seized her and sailed away. If the king had hoped the women warriors would meekly let him take their leader, he was sadly mistaken. One morning soon after he arrived back in Athens, he saw thousands of mounted Amazon warriors galloping toward his city from the north led by Hippolyte, the sister of Antiope. There followed a brutal war lasting months in which Theseus and the Athenian men defended their city bravely, but were unable to defeat the relentless women, who attacked them on every side. The Amazons at last forced their way into the very heart of Athens in a valiant effort to take the city and rescue their queen. Theseus knew everything depended on this final battle, so he called together his men and sacrificed to the god Fear, praying that they might not falter. When the Amazons attacked, the Athenians fought until the temples and marketplace were covered with blood, but the brave female warriors from the north were at last defeated. Even as the surviving Amazons made their way back home to the steppes of the north, Antiope bore Theseus a son, Hippolytus, and died soon thereafter. Many centuries later, the Athenians were still proudly showing visitors the graves of their vanquished foes in the center of their city.

As the years went by, Theseus married Phaedra, a daughter of Minos, and had two sons by her. He also fatally cursed his son Hippolytus by Antiope after Phaedra accused the chaste young man of trying to rape her. Father and son were reconciled before the death of Hippolytus, but the pain of his loss drove the king to a notable disregard for his own life.

Theseus sought out reckless adventures, often with his friend Pirithous, king of the Lapith tribe in Thessaly. Like most male bonding between heroes, the two began their friendship by almost killing each other. Pirithous had raided Attica to steal breeding stock from the herds of Theseus in a time-honored tradition. The king caught him in the act and was ready to slay him, but instead each saw a kindred spirit in the other and swore eternal friendship.

Pirithous had become king of the Lapiths after his father, Ixion, had tried unsuccessfully to seduce Hera and ended up making love with a cloud. The ancestor of the Centaurs who sprung from this nebulous union sired many offspring, all of whom lived peaceably near the Lapiths. When the time came, both Theseus and the Centaurs were invited to the wedding of Pirithous and the maiden Hippodamia, but the Centaurs drank too much and tried to rape the bride, provoking a fierce battle in which Theseus helped his friend defeat them. In gratitude, Perithous agreed to help Theseus abduct a new bride of his own, the young princess Helen. The two friends went to Sparta and saw the maiden Helen dancing there in the temple of Aphrodite. When no one was looking, they grabbed her and took her back to Athens. As Helen was still a young girl, Theseus left her with his mother, Aethra, until she reached marriageable age.

As soon as Helen was safely settled in Athens, Pirithous asked Theseus if he would accompany him on another quest, again for a woman. No one knows what had happened to his first wife, Hippodamia, but the king of the Lapiths was even bolder than Theseus in his search for a new bride. He was determined to journey to the underworld and kidnap Persephone, the immortal wife of Hades, and make her his own. Theseus thought Pirithous was out of his mind, but ever-anxious to prove himself a true hero, he could not resist such a challenge. The two journeyed down to the land of the dead and came at last to the palace of Hades. In the ultimate act of hubris, they told the god of their purpose, then sat down in two fine chairs near his throne. As soon as they were seated, however, snakes wrapped around their limbs, holding them tightly in place. They might have stayed there forever had not Hercules come down to the underworld soon afterward on one of his labors. He freed Theseus, who was his cousin, and tried to free Pirithous as well, but could not. Hercules returned Theseus to the surface, while Pirithous remained seated forever in the land of the dead.

When Theseus returned to Athens, he found the city in chaos after a disastrous war brought on by the Spartans, who had come to retrieve Helen. The girl's brothers, Castor and Pollux, had taken their sister back after devastating Attica. They had also seized Theseus' mother to serve as Helen's slave in Sparta. As their king had been engaged in heroic folly instead of defending his city, the citizens of Athens banished him.

Theseus cursed the people for their ingratitude and sailed to the island of Scyrus, where he was welcomed by the local king Lycomedes. After a good dinner and much wine, his host invited Theseus to take a walk with him along the beautiful cliffs of the island, to help forget his troubles. Lycomedes, however, was secretly jealous of the fame of Theseus. When they came to the cliffs, he pushed his guest over the edge, ending the hero's life in a most inglorious manner.

For many years Theseus was forgotten by the Athenians until, it was said, his ghost led them to victory against the Persians at the battle of Marathon. Then the citizens brought his bones home and honored him ever after as a divine hero, founder of democracy, and savior of Athens.

DAEDALUS AND ICARUS

When Theseus fled from Crete with Ariadne, Minos was so angry that he threw Daedalus into prison along with his son Icarus. The king knew that only Daedalus could have come up with a plan for the young hero to escape the very maze he had constructed. While he was incarcerated, the builder of the Labyrinth had plenty of time to reflect on the twists and turns of his own life.

Daedalus had been born in Athens, where from his earliest days he had shown great promise as a sculptor and inventor. By the time he was grown, he was a master craftsman with the best apprentices in the land eager to study under him. One of these was his own nephew Perdix. The boy showed such skill that he threatened to surpass his master, especially after he learned to saw a thin stick in half with the serrated jawbone of a snake. Daedalus could not bear talent rivaling his own and so tossed the lad off the Acropolis. He was put on trial for murder, but fled to Crete and was given refuge there by Minos.

But now, years later, far from home and in prison, Daedalus was desperate to flee from Crete. He knew he could never escape by ship since Minos was patrolling the coast with his navy, but he realized that the king did not rule the sky. He therefore began to construct wings of feathers and wax for both himself and his son. When these were ready, he warned Icarus to proceed with great care. He should not fly too close to the sea, lest the waves get his wings wet and render them useless. He was also not to fly so high that the heat of the sun melted the wax holding the feathers. The boy promised faithfully to obey his father's instructions, so one clear night the pair set out from the prison roof.

No mortal had ever sailed through the sky like a bird before, save for Perseus on his winged sandals. Daedalus was grimly determined to escape the island and headed west to Sicily, but Icarus was simply enthralled by the joy of flight. As the sun rose in the east, he swooped up and down like an eagle, ignoring the constant warnings of his father. Even as Daedalus shouted at him to set a steady course, the boy flew higher and higher into the bright sky. It wasn't long before the heat of the sun began to loosen the wax of his wings. Before he realized what was happening, he began to fall toward the sea. As his father watched in horror, Icarus plunged to his death in the waves below.

Daedalus was heartbroken, but there was nothing he could do for his foolish son. He continued on his way until he arrived at last at the court of Cocalus in Sicily. The king was pleased to have such a famous builder at his disposal and granted Daedalus asylum, keeping him carefully hidden. Even so, it wasn't long before Minos came to Sicily in search of him. The Cretan king had been sailing the whole Mediterranean looking for his escaped architect. Instead of threats, he gave each ruler he visited an intricate spiral shell and promised him a great reward if he could pass a thread all the way through it. No one had been able to accomplish this impossible task, but when he came to Cocalus, the Sicilian king was so eager to win the treasure that he gave the puzzle to his secret guest. This was exactly what Minos was hoping for. He knew only Daedalus had the skill to thread the shell, so that whichever king claimed the reward would surely be hiding him in his palace.

Daedalus looked at the intricate spirals of the shell—so much like his own Labyrinth—and knew immediately what to do. He tied a thread to a tiny ant and coaxed the insect to crawl all the way through the shell until it came out the other end. When Cocalus went to collect his prize, Minos knew he had found Daedalus. He demanded the Sicilian king surrender the architect under threat of war. Cocalus quickly agreed, but asked Minos if he couldn't first prepare a grand feast for him as way of apology. He also promised to have his beautiful daughters give the visiting king a bath he would never forget—an offer the lascivious ruler could not refuse.

After a fine banquet, the lovely girls led him away to the tub and removed the king's clothing. As he lay there anticipating the wonderful evening ahead, the young women all brought large jars of water to fill the tub. On signal, the sisters poured them over Minos. The screams of the king filled the palace and echoed through the town. The daughters of Cocalus, at the direction of their father, had filled the jars with boiling water. The man who had caused the death and misery of so many met his own painful end in a humble bathtub at the hand of beautiful young maidens.

BELLEROPHON

Argos and Athens had their native heroes, but the city of Corinth also sired famous men. One of the most celebrated of these was a handsome young champion named Bellerophon, grandson of Sisyphus. Like many heroes, he often acted rashly. In one particularly violent outburst, he murdered his own brother. He then fled Corinth and made his way to the town of Tiryns in Argos, where Proetus ruled in the days before his daughters were driven mad by the god Dionysus. Bellerophon beseeched the king to ritually purify him of homicide against his own blood. Proetus granted his request and carried out the ceremony so that Bellerophon would not be cursed by the gods.

But just as Theseus' wife Phaedra had fallen in love with Hippolytus, Stheneboea, the wife of Proetus, tried to seduce Bellerophon. Stheneboea was likewise rejected by her would-be lover and eagerly sought his death. She rushed into the throne room of Proetus and demanded that he slay this criminal who tried to violate her. The king was suitably outraged by these false accusations and was determined to kill Bellerophon, but was hesitant to slay a guest who had taken refuge under his roof. He therefore came up with an ingenious plan to get rid of the young man without polluting himself. He called in Bellerophon and asked if he would mind delivering a very important letter to his father-in-law, King

Iobates of Lycia, across the Aegean Sea. The young man was eager for a journey to a distant land, so gladly agreed.

Bellerophon sailed across the sea and traveled to the court of Iobates, where he was welcomed and treated royally. Protocol forbade hosts from questioning noble guests until they had been suitably wined and dined, so the Lycian king did not dare ask his visitor his business until nine days had passed. At last, Iobates inquired what he might do for Bellerophon and thus received the letter. The king was always glad to hear from Proetus and quickly broke the wax seal. His eyes could not believe the few words of the message: *King Iobates, please kill the man who brought you this letter.*

The Lycian ruler was now in the same difficult position that Proetus had so cleverly avoided. He was under an obligation to honor the wishes of a relative, but he also feared the curse of Zeus for slaying a guest in his own home.

After several days, Iobates hit upon the perfect solution—the monster known as the Chimaera. This fearsome creature, the offspring of Typhon and Echidna, was a lion in front, a fire-breathing goat in the middle, and a serpent behind. It had long been ravaging the countryside of Lycia, killing both cattle and men. The king sent Bellerophon on a quest to slay the monster, knowing very well that he could not hope to survive. This neatly solved his problem as he was able to fulfill his duty to Proetus without having the blood of a guest on his hands. But Iobates underestimated Bellerophon. The young hero, with the help of Athena, tamed the winged horse Pegasus and flew against the Chimaera with bow in hand. He easily slew the monster and returned to the king ready for his next adventure. Iobates tried again to end Bellerophon's life by sending him against a powerful enemy, the fierce Solymi, who were always at war with the Lycians on their borders. Again using Pegasus, Bellerophon swept down on the Solymi from above and slew them all. Having failed twice, Iobates sent Bellerophon against the Amazon women to the north, but they too were defeated. In desperation, the king set an ambush for the young hero, picking the best and bravest of all his warriors for the deed. Bellerophon, however, fought all the more ferociously for being caught in a trap and cut down all the Lycian soldiers set against him.

At last Iobates realized he could not kill this young hero, so instead he showed him the letter from Proetus and explained he had only been trying to do his duty to his son-in-law. He then offered Bellerophon his daughter Philonoe in marriage along with half his kingdom.

The couple lived happily in Lycia and had many children, but Bellerophon could not forget that he had been wronged by Proetus and his deceitful wife, Stheneboea. He flew back to Tiryns on Pegasus and offered to give the queen a ride on his magic horse to show there were no hard feelings. She gladly agreed and the pair sailed high into the sky. Just as Stheneboea was most enjoying the ride, Bellerophon pushed her off.

Some stories also say that Bellerophon was not content just to be a mortal hero, but desired to live among the gods. He flew on Pegasus up into the heavens to Mount Olympus, but Zeus sent a gadfly to sting the flying horse and cause him to throw his rider to the ground. Bellerophon survived his plunge to earth, but was crippled by the fall. After his injury, the story of his attempt to storm Olympus spread. Thereafter no one would welcome this man who had dared to challenge the gods. He ended his days without home or family, an outcast doomed to wander the earth alone.

MELAMPUS

Not all heroes relied on superhuman strength and flying horses to slay monsters and rescue fair maidens. Some, such as the seer Melampus from the town of Pylos, used magic to accomplish great deeds.

Melampus and his brother Bias grew up the best of friends, but Melampus longed for the country life and went to live in a rural part of the kingdom far from the hustle and bustle of the busy port. In front of his quiet house was a large oak tree in which a family of snakes had built its lair. Melampus killed the older snakes and burned their bodies, but took their young and raised them as pets, feeding them by hand until they could hunt on their own. The snakes became so tame that they slept next to him on his own bed.

One night when the moon was high in the sky, Melampus awoke suddenly to discover that the snakes were licking his ears. Though surprised, he thought little of it until the next morning when he heard the birds singing outside his window. He was amazed to find that he could understand their speech. He also understood the chattering of mice in the barn and the braying of his goats in his yard. The hidden language of every animal was now revealed to him, but it was the birds that interested him the most. Flying as they did between heaven and earth, they heard the voices of the gods and shared with each other the secrets of what was to come. By listening carefully to birds, Melampus could discover the future. Later he happened upon Apollo at the river Alpheus, who taught him the further mysteries of soothsaying by means of examining animal entrails.

Melampus' brother Bias was deeply in love with Pero, the daughter of Neleus, king of Pylos, but the princess had many wealthy suitors. Neleus liked young Bias, however, and told him he could have his daughter's hand in marriage if he brought to him the cattle of Phylacus, king of Thessaly. But these animals were guarded by a fierce and wondrous dog who never slept, making it impossible for anyone to approach them. Bias turned to his brother for help and was not refused. Even though Melampus knew from the birds that he would be captured and imprisoned for a year if he attempted this cattle raid, he nonetheless loved Bias so much that he had to try. Sure enough, he was quickly seized by the herdsmen of Phylacus as he tried to sneak up on the cattle.

Melampus spent the next year in a dark and gloomy hut on the estate of Phylacus, waiting until the prescribed twelve months had passed. At last one evening he heard two worms in the rafters talking to each other. One said that he had just finished chewing through the main beam holding up the roof of the hut. Melampus called to his guards and asked to be transferred to a new cell as some worms had just revealed his roof was about to fall in. The guards laughed but did as he asked, then the next day were amazed to see the sturdy roof of the hut collapse to the ground. King Phylacus received word of this strange event and was duly impressed by the soothsaying skill of his prisoner. He called Melampus to his court and offered to release him if he would reveal how his grown son, Iphiclus, might have a child. The young man was a great athlete and so fast he could run over the top of a wheat field without crushing the heads of grain, but he was impotent. Melampus offered to discover the reason for this affliction if Phylacus would give him his cattle as a wedding gift for his brother. The king gladly agreed.

Melampus held a sacrifice of two bulls and allowed the birds of the air to come and feast on the meat. Flocks flew in from all directions for the meal, but last to arrive was a single vulture. The soothsayer asked the vulture if he knew why Iphiclus was unable to father a child and the old carrion bird nodded. He said that many years ago he had watched from a nearby branch while Phylacus was castrating rams with a sharp knife. Iphiclus was just a young boy then and had been frightened when he came upon his father covered in blood. The lad cried out and ran away so fast that Phylacus, in an effort to comfort him, had stuck the knife into a sacred oak as he ran after his son. As the years passed, the bark of the oak grew over the knife, hiding it deep inside the tree. The vulture revealed that the gods were displeased by this violation of the holy oak. To make things right, Phylacus needed to dig the knife out of the tree and scrape away the rust from the blade. If he fed this rust to Iphiclus in a drink over a period of ten days, his impotence would be cured. Phylacus consented and performed the ritual. Nine months later, the wife of Iphiclus gave birth to a baby boy.

Melampus returned to Pylos with the cattle and Bias married the princess Pero. The seer lived a happy life honored by all, having many children and called on by kings throughout Greece for his skills in prophecy and magic. When Dionysus came to Argos and the daughters of Proetus refused to worship him and were driven mad, it was Melampus the king called on to return sanity to his girls. Melampus did so through the skillful use of herbs, but only after he made Proetus swear to give him a large part of his kingdom. He shared this land with his brother Bias so that both grew old as lords of Argos.

ATALANTA

Although most women in Greek myths spent their days weaving and raising children, there were a few female characters who managed to break the bonds of tradition to accomplish amazing deeds. One of the most famous of these was a young woman named Atalanta, who had a very rough start in life. Her father, Iasus, wanted only sons and so left his newborn daughter to die alone in a dark forest. Fortunately, a she-bear took her back to her den and nursed her with her own cubs. Not long after, a band of hunters found the child and raised her in their village until she had grown into a beautiful young woman.

Atalanta lived a carefree life roaming the mountains and hunting with male friends, and although she enjoyed the company of men, she wanted nothing to do with marriage. She dedicated herself as a virgin to the goddess Artemis, swearing she would never be intimate with a man. Most of her male companions accepted this with regret, but some were determined to have her at any cost. One day when she was hunting with the Centaurs Rhoecus and Hylaeus, the pair tried to rape her. Atalanta, however, fought them off and killed them with her swift arrows.

Atalanta was the only woman allowed to participate in the great Calydonian Boar hunt along with Meleager and Theseus. Some stories say it was she who first shot the boar, though many of her fellow hunters were outraged that a female could do such a thing and claimed it was one of her companions who killed this dangerous beast. Not long after, Atalanta defeated the great king Peleus, father of Achilles, in a wrestling contest. Some stories even claim that she sailed with the Argonauts in search of the Golden Fleece, but most agree that Jason, the leader of the expedition, declined her request to accompany the male heroes on the journey, fearing that having a woman on the expedition would only cause trouble.

Atalanta was making such a name for herself that soon her father, Iasus, heard about her and realized she was the same girl he had left to die in the woods years before. Belatedly, he welcomed his daughter home and tried, much to the anguish of Atalanta, to take up his fatherly duties. Chief among these was to arrange a proper marriage for his daughter. The young woman reluctantly agreed, but convinced Iasus that potential grooms should vie for her hand by competing against her in a footrace. If a man won, she would marry him—if he lost, she would kill him on the spot.

Atalanta knew very well that no man alive could beat her, but she was so beautiful and desirable that many men came to race against her.

They all believed the previous competitors must have been weaklings to lose to a mere woman and that they would do better. Yet at the end of each race, Atalanta was waiting for them at the finish line with a sword in her hand.

One young man deeply in love with Atalanta was Melanion from the mountains of Arcadia. He was wise enough to know he could not defeat her in a fair race, so he turned to the gods. He went to the temple of Aphrodite and prayed that she might help him gain his heart's true love. The goddess of sex had never particularly liked Atalanta since she had sworn to remain chaste all her life, so she gave Melanion three golden apples and a plan to win the race.

Not long afterward, the young man arrived at the palace of Iasus and asked if he might have the honor of competing for the hand of his lovely daughter. Iasus felt pity for Melanion and urged him to reconsider, but he was determined to try. Atalanta eagerly stripped to her tunic and took her place beside Melanion at the starting line, flashing him a charming smile, knowing he would soon be dead.

The race began and Melanion took off ahead of his rival. Atalanta was in no hurry and let the foolish lad get ahead of her for a short stretch to get his hopes up. Then she began to fly down the course and was soon passing her competitor. But just at this point, Melanion pulled one of the golden apples from his cloak and tossed it on the ground before her. Atalanta had never seen anything so beautiful. She stopped and picked it up, letting Melanion pull ahead of her in the race.

It didn't take long for Atalanta to catch up again with her would-be lover, but just as she did he took out another apple and dropped it in front of her. It was as irresistible as the first, and the young woman couldn't help but stop and pick it up.

They were now nearing the finish line and Atalanta was rapidly over-taking her competitor from behind. Melanion therefore took his final apple and threw it far to the side of the track. Try as she might, Atalanta could not resist the golden fruit. She ran to the edge of the path, swooped up the apple, and flew toward the end of the race. But it was too late—Melanion crossed the finish line just ahead of her.

Iasus presented his daughter to Melanion and gave the couple his blessing. The young groom was eager to return home with his prize, so he and his new bride left immediately on the journey back to Arcadia. Melanion could not believe his good fortune at winning such a beautiful woman as his wife. But they were only a short way down the road when overwhelming desire got the best of him and he led Atalanta to the only private place available, a small temple of Zeus by the side of the road. Although it was sacrilege, Melanion made love to his bride on the floor before the holy altar of Zeus.

Such an insult to his temple did not escape the ruler of the gods. Zeus immediately turned both Melanion and Atalanta into lions—a suitable punishment, as it was said lions do not mate with one another, only with leopards. Thus the couple lived out their days roaming the mountains and hunting their prey, but never coming together to mate. It was a cruel fate for Melanion, but for Atalanta it was a wonderful life.

PROCNE AND PHILOMELA

There was once a king of Athens named Pandion who had two beautiful daughters, Procne and Philomela. Although his family life was peaceful and happy, his reign was threatened by relentless barbarian raids on his city. When the bloodthirsty hordes were almost inside his gates, Pandion's friend and fellow king Tereus from Thrace arrived and drove away the invaders. Tereus was a great warrior as was fitting since he was a son of the god Ares. The Athenian king was so grateful that he promised his friend the hand of his eldest daughter in marriage.

Procne bade farewell to her father and sister with many tears, then boarded the ship with Tereus to sail to her new home in Thrace. In due season a son was born and the boy, named Itys, became his father's pride and joy.

When Itys was five years old, Procne asked Tereus if she might make the journey back to Athens for a short visit with her family: "If I have found any favor in your eyes, allow me to travel to my home. Or, if you prefer, let my sister come here to visit me. You can promise my father that after a brief stay she will return safe and sound. It would mean so much to me, dear Tereus, if you allowed her to come."

This seemed like a reasonable request to the Thracian king, so he ordered his ship readied so that he might go and fetch the princess Philomela himself. The journey to Athens was swift, with favorable winds, and soon the king was sailing into the port of Piraeus with the Acropolis towering in the distance. Pandion greeted his son-in-law warmly and eagerly sought news of his daughter. The kings talked and drank late into the evening, when suddenly Philomela walked into the room. She had been just an awkward girl on his previous trip, but now Tereus saw a stunning young woman standing before him, even more beautiful, if possible, than her sister.

The moment Tereus saw Philomela he was consumed with desire. More than anything in the world he wanted to possess this woman. He was tempted to sneak into her quarters and take her by force that very night, but he knew the consequences would be war. Yet his passion was so overwhelming that for a moment he would have gladly given up his kingdom to lie with Philomela. Instead Tereus decided to bide his time and greeted her as if he were the kindest and most proper of brothers-in-law. He then turned to Pandion and explained the reason for his visit. He told of how lonely Procne was in his humble home—not really a suitable place for such a lovely and civilized lady, in spite of his efforts to make her happy. She longed to have her sister visit even if just for a short while. Tears streamed down his face as he urged Pandion to allow his younger daughter to return with him to Thrace for a brief stay. He wanted only to make his beloved wife happy and swore he would protect the maiden Philomela from all harm with his very life. Everyone in the court was deeply touched by the tender love of Tereus for Procne. Even Philomela, as much as she hated to leave her aging father, begged that she might be allowed to return with dear Tereus.

There was something about his friend that made Pandion hesitate, some father's instinct that caused him to pause. But with the winning pleas of his daughter and the earnest vows of Tereus to the gods that he would watch over her, Pandion at last agreed to let Philomela go. Not long after, the king of Athens waved good-bye as a second daughter sailed away to the distant north, though he felt a terrible foreboding in his heart.

As soon as the ship was away from Athens, Tereus shouted with glee.

Unknown to her, the poor girl was sailing to an awful fate, like a rabbit caught in the talons of an eagle. When they landed in Thrace, Tereus abandoned all pretense and dragged Philomela off to a hut hidden deep in the woods. The maiden, trembling with fear, begged to see her sister. The king only laughed, then savagely raped her, even as she cried out to the gods for help.

When he was finished, Philomela stood before Tereus shaking, with torn clothing and disheveled hair, but unbroken: "You monster! Do you care nothing for your friendship with my father? Does my sister's love mean nothing to you? You have violated not only me but the sacred bonds of family. I would prefer that you had killed me. You can shut me up alone in this prison, but I will shout out your foul deed until the very trees and rocks cry out your infamy."

Tereus then grabbed Philomela by the hair and twisted her arms behind her back. He pulled out his razor-sharp sword, only to have the young woman eagerly offer him her throat. But the king did not want to kill his captive. Instead he held her tongue with pincers from the fireplace and sliced it off with his blade. Then, as Philomela lay bleeding, speechless, and mutilated, he raped her again.

Tereus placed a guard outside the hut of Philomela and returned to his palace to greet Procne. He came into her presence with the look of a man in utter despair. He explained to his wife between sobs that her dear sister had perished on the voyage back from Athens. Procne was devastated and put on black clothes of mourning. She then built a memorial to Philomela and offered sacrifices there so that her spirit might find rest.

A year passed while Philomela was imprisoned in her wretched hut. The guards outside her door were ever watchful and the woods beyond dark and deep. Even if she could somehow escape and find Procne, how could she explain what had happened without words? But pain brings sharp wits and from suffering cunning is born. There was an old loom in her hut, so Philomela made the guards understand that she would like to weave upon it. As this seemed like a harmless activity, she was granted the materials needed and began her work.

On the tapestry she skillfully wove the story of her voyage from Athens, her arrival at Thrace, the vicious attack by Tereus, and her lonely captivity. She showed how her tongue had been cut from her head and how she had suffered, longing for her sister and home. When she finished, she rolled up the weaving and gave it to an old woman to deliver to the queen. The messenger bore the tapestry to Procne, who unrolled it and read the story it told. Then, without a word to her attendants, she withdrew to her room.

Normally she was not allowed beyond the palace grounds unescorted, but that night was the annual celebration of Dionysus, when women could move freely to worship the god in the nearby woods. Procne dressed as a devotee of the god and joined in the festivities with her companions as they ran through the forest. When all the rest were occupied, she slipped away and came to the small hut woven so clearly into the tapestry. In her Bacchic disguise, the guards did not recognize her and so the queen slipped inside.

Philomela cowered in the corner, not recognizing her unexpected visitor, but then Procne removed her coverings. Philomela was overjoyed to see Procne and the two embraced. Procne told Philomela to ready herself for vengeance: "This is no time for tears, only for the sword and swift action. I will burn Tereus alive in his palace or cut out his own tongue and eyes. Better yet, I will cut off the organ by which he wronged you. I will do anything to punish him for what he did to you."

Procne then spirited her sister back to the palace and hid her in her own quarters. When Philomela was safely concealed, Procne's young son Itys appeared in the hall and ran to his mother. She hugged him and exclaimed, "How like your father you are." Then a terrible plan began to form in her mind.

Later that evening, Procne sent a message to her husband inviting him to a banquet. This was a special feast of her homeland, she said, in which only the lord of the house dined, served by his wife. Once he was seated, she brought him platters of meat cooked with tasty herbs. The king was ravenous, so he ate to his heart's content, enjoying every bite. When he finished, he praised his wife for the delicious meal and asked her to call their son, Itys, to join him. But she proclaimed, "That won't be necessary, my lord, for the one you seek is now inside you."

Tereus didn't understand what she meant, but then Philomela walked into the room covered in blood and holding the knife mother and aunt had used to butcher the boy. She then hurled the severed head of Itys into the lap of Tereus.

When he realized what had happened, he screamed in agony, cursing the sisters and evoking the pitiless Furies to witness what a monstrous deed they had done. He would gladly have ripped open his own belly and taken out the horrid food he had dined on, but all he could do was weep.

Procne and Philomela fled from the castle, running into the forest as fast as birds in flight. But Tereus soon recovered himself and raced after them, anxious to slay them both. The gods, however, took pity on the sisters and transformed Tereus into a hoopoe—a small bird with a stiff crest like a war helmet, fitting for a man with such a violent nature. They also changed Procne into a swallow and, at last, Philomela became a nightingale, who sings sweetly for all to hear.

LOVERS

NARCISSUS AND ECHO

Tiresias of Thebes became the most famous soothsayer in all of Greece. People from far and wide would travel to him to discover what the future held for them and their children. One supplicant was the nymph Liriope, who became pregnant after she had been raped by the river god Cephissus. She gave birth to the most beautiful baby anyone had ever seen and named him Narcissus. Liriope was worried about the fate of such an extraordinary child and asked Tiresias if her son would live a long and happy life. "Only if he never knows himself," was the seer's enigmatic reply.

By the time Narcissus was sixteen years old he was famous for his astounding good looks and was sought after by women and men everywhere. But he wanted nothing to do with love. He scorned every handsome youth and fair maiden who pursued him, claiming that no one would ever touch his heart.

Among his many would-be lovers was the nymph Echo, who had once been a faithful attendant of the goddess Hera. No one could talk as endlessly as Echo—a trait Zeus took advantage of. Whenever the ruler of the gods saw the loquacious nymph in the company of Hera, he would fly down from Olympus to seek the bed of a mortal woman or goddess, knowing he would have plenty of time for love. Hera grew so angry at Echo for distracting her that she punished the talkative maiden in a most unusual fashion. She made it so that the nymph could only repeat the last few words spoken to her.

Banished from the presence of the gods, Echo wandered the fields and forests alone. One day she came upon Narcissus while he was hunting with his friends. She had never seen such a gorgeous young man in all her life and was consumed with a burning passion for the youth. But how could she tell him of her love if she could only repeat the words he spoke to her? Nonetheless she followed him through the woods until by chance he became separated from his companions. He called out to his friends hoping to find them:

"Is anyone here?"

"Here," said Echo.

Narcissus was surprised by the sound of a woman's voice.

"Please, come to me," he urged.

"Come to me," replied Echo.

The youth searched all around him but could find no one.

"Why do you run away from me?" he shouted, only to have Echo repeat his words back to him.

"I'm here, let's meet together," Narcissus pleaded.

"Let's meet together," responded Echo.

The nymph was so consumed by love that she could wait no longer, but emerged from her hiding place and ran to Narcissus. She threw her arms around him and covered him with kisses.

"Get off me," commanded the young man. "I would die before I give you power over me."

"I give you power over me," Echo cried.

But Narcissus pushed her away in disgust and ran from her presence. Rejected, but still hopelessly in love, Echo remained hidden in the forest longing for just a glimpse of Narcissus as he hunted in the woods. She was ashamed of her infatuation but so consumed by passion that she lost all interest in eating and sleeping. She became thinner and more gaunt until she was nothing but bones, then even these turned to dust until she was just a disembodied voice haunting the forests and mountain glades.

Narcissus had scorned Echo as he did all who tried to win his love. But one bitter young man rejected by the youth raised his hands to heaven and prayed to that most terrible of goddesses, Nemesis. From the dark places of the earth she heard his cry and sealed the fate of Narcissus.

There was a crystal-clear pond in the woods frequented by the handsome son of Liriope. One day after he was weary from a long hunt, Narcissus came to the pool to slake his thirst. He cupped his hands to bring the pure water to his lips, when suddenly he saw his reflection in the pond. The young man had never seen anyone so beautiful in his whole life. In speechless wonder he gazed at the image before him, longing to touch his face and kiss his lips. He leaned over to embrace the figure, but every time his fingers touched the surface of the water the reflection disappeared in the ripples.

Narcissus sat by the pool unable to tear his eyes away from his own reflection. Night came and the bright moon rose, but the young man took no notice. Food and drink meant nothing to him as he sat gazing at his image day after day. From the edge of the woods, Echo watched her love as he wasted away. Narcissus did not see her or hear her voice as he cried out and begged the reflection to come to him.

"You are so near, but I cannot touch you, alas," he moaned.

"Alas," Echo sighed.

Even when Narcissus had withered to skin and bones, he could not help but gaze hopelessly at his image. Then with his last breath he looked into the pond and whispered, "Farewell."

"Farewell," cried the sad voice of Echo.

The youth died at the edge of the pool, his weary head drooping over the water. The gods took pity on the lad and transformed his broken body into a beautiful flower bearing his name that bends ever downward. But even in Hades, the soul of Narcissus spends eternity gazing at his own image in the river Styx.

PYRAMUS AND THISBE

In the great city of Babylon lived two young lovers side by side but far apart. They were Pyramus, the most handsome youth in the land, and Thisbe, the most beautiful maiden. Although their houses shared a common wall, their families hated each other and forbade the two ever to speak to each other. But love always finds a way.

There was a small crack in their shared wall that no one had ever noticed. Pyramus and Thisbe soon found this opening and began to whisper through it when everyone else in both houses was fast asleep. Each evening when they parted they would kiss their side of the wall and promise to meet again the next night. Soon the two could no longer bear to be apart no matter the enmity between their families. They made plans to slip away from their homes the next evening and meet at an ancient tomb outside the city beside a cool spring with a tall mulberry tree. Beneath that tree they would at last be able to lie in each other's arms.

Thisbe carefully opened her door the next evening and walked quietly through the streets of Babylon. Once outside the gates, she came to the tree and sat down to wait for Pyramus. But suddenly she saw a lion in the darkness. It had just killed a cow from a nearby herd and its face was covered in blood. As it approached the spring to quench its thirst, Thisbe ran away in terror, but she dropped her cloak on the ground as she fled. The lion found the cloak after it had drunk its fill and tore it with its bloody jaws, though it left the cloth on the ground beside the tree.

Pyramus arrived at the pool just as the lion left and saw its tracks along with the bloody cloak of his dear Thisbe laying on the ground. He recognized the garment at once and knew that a lion had slain the maiden. He collapsed in grief, believing that it was his fault she had died. He then pulled out his sword and plunged it into his side. As he fell on the ground, his blood shot into the air, turning the white berries of the tree bright red.

It was then that Thisbe came back to the pool. She saw a body lying there and was frightened, but realized it was her own Pyramus. She ran to him and held him in hers arms, crying out his name. At the sound of her voice, Pyramus used the last of his strength to open his eyes and gaze on her one final time, then he closed them forever. Thisbe wept over the body of her beloved long into the night, then took his sword and stabbed herself in the heart.

The gods took pity on the two lovers and decreed that from that day forward, the fruit of the mulberry would always turn crimson when it was ripe. Even their parents were touched by the devotion their children had shown each other and placed their ashes in a common urn.

CEYX AND ALCYONE

Over the mountains to the north of the sacred site of Delphi was the small kingdom of Trachis, ruled over by Ceyx, son of Lucifer, the morning star. Ceyx was a good king who loved peace more than war and welcomed refugees to his realm without question. He took in Peleus, father of Achilles, after he killed his brother by accident and once gave shelter to Hercules when he was weary from his labors. Both guests repaid their host with courage. Peleus helped to slay a monstrous wolf ravaging the countryside and Hercules drove away hostile invaders from Ceyx's borders.

Ceyx was deeply troubled by all his kingdom had suffered of late and decided to seek the council of Apollo at Delphi. The overland journey was blocked by violent tribes to the south, so the king decided to travel to the oracle by sea. His beautiful and faithful wife, Alcyone, daughter of Aeolus, god of the winds, begged him to reconsider. She urged him not to leave her to make such a long journey. Like all Greeks, she knew the sea was a dangerous and unpredictable force that could rise against a ship and crush it at a moment's notice, dragging every man on board down to its depths.

Ceyx loved his wife deeply and was moved by her tears, but he felt he had to consult with the god for the good of his kingdom: "I swear to you by the bright fire of my father, I will return to you before two months have passed—if the Fates allow."

Alcyone was not comforted by these words, but when she saw she could not change her husband's mind, she embraced him and bade him a sad farewell. She stood on the shore and watched him sail away, while he waved to her for as long as he could keep her in sight.

A few days later when the ship was far from land, a terrible storm began to blow. The captain ordered the crew to lower the sails and let the ship run before the wind, but the tempest grew ever worse. Rain fell in torrents, lightning lit the sky, and the rolling waves rose like mountains over the little craft as every man, King Ceyx included, tried with all their might to hold the ship together. Water poured into the hold faster than the sailors could bail it out. Men prayed and wept and cursed to no avail until at last an enormous wave crashed over the ship and broke it to pieces.

A few men, including Ceyx, clung to timbers hoping to outlast the storm, but the force of the waves was too strong. In their last moments, they thought of family and children they would leave behind and offered a final prayer to the gods. Then one by one they slipped beneath the raging water until only Ceyx remained, clinging to a broken plank. He thought only of Alcyone, the sound of her voice, the touch of her lips. He wished he could see her one last time, then prayed that at least his body might wash onto his native shore so that he might be buried by her dear hands. Finally the waves closed over him and he thought of Alcyone no more.

Alcyone had been praying earnestly to Hera every day that her husband might safely return to her. She passed the endless hours weaving a robe to present to him when he sailed at last into the harbor. But the wife of Zeus could not bear to hear her fruitless prayers. She went to the home of the god Sleep and asked him to send a vision to Alcyone revealing to her the sad fate of her husband. Sleep then called his son Morpheus, skilled in assuming any form, and ordered him to enter the dreams of Alcyone disguised as Ceyx and reveal the truth. Thus he appeared before her in her uneasy sleep wearing the form of her husband, naked and battered with water dripping from his hair: "Sweet Alcyone, cease your prayers for my safe return. There is nothing more you can do for me. I was caught in a raging storm and dragged down to my death by the cruel sea. I called out your name with my final breath, but you could not hear me. Good-bye, my love."

Alcyone awoke crying, "Wait for me! Wait, I will come with you!" but the vision of Ceyx was gone. Her attendants ran into the room and told her that it was just a dream, but she would hear none of it. "My husband is dead," she cried. "The gods have sent me a message. He is gone and I will never see him again."

Even though the morning star had barely risen above the eastern horizon, she made her way down to the shore where she had last seen Ceyx alive. She knelt in the sand weeping and looking out to sea. Suddenly she saw something in the distance floating on the water. As it drew nearer, she saw at last that it was the body of her husband drifting on the waves. She leapt into the sea, trying in vain to reach him—but then, by the will of the gods, her arms became wings. She flew to him and kissed him, though she knew he could not feel her lips on his. But somehow, though dead, he did feel her touch and opened his eyes to see her.

The gods took pity on the lovers and revived Ceyx, then they changed both husband and wife into birds, the bright halcyons, or kingfishers. In this form Ceyx and Alcyone lived together in love. It was said that Alcyone's father, Aeolus, caused the winds to cease for a week each winter. During these seven halcyon days, the pair floated peacefully in their nest on the waves of the sea.

GLAUCUS AND SCYLLA

The sea was also home to a god named Glaucus, who fell deeply in love with a beautiful young maiden named Scylla. Glaucus had not always lived beneath the waves, nor indeed had he always been a god. He was once a simple fisherman who plied his trade off a quiet shore seldom visited by other men. One day he took his modest catch and laid them on the meadow of an unknown island to count them. But as soon as the dead fish touched the grass they began to stir, then jumped back into the water before Glaucus could grab them. He had never seen such a sight before and wondered if it was the will of some god or if the grass itself had magical powers. He decided to test it and nibbled just a tiny blade. Suddenly he wanted more than anything to leap into the sea. He ran to the shore and jumped into the waves, gladly leaving the land behind forever.

The sea nymphs saw him and welcomed him to their realm. They brought him to the ancient gods Oceanus and Tethys to purge away his mortal nature. The gods instructed the nymphs to sing a magic song nine times over him and bathe him in the waters of a hundred streams. When this was done, Glaucus awoke to find his body had changed. His beard was green, his arms blue, and he had the long tail of a fish in place of his legs.

Glaucus enjoyed his new life in the sea, swimming with the nymphs and sailing over the waves. But one day his travels took him to a secluded cove where he spied a mortal woman of extraordinary beauty. This was Scylla, who had taken off her clothes to swim in the refreshing water of the hidden inlet. Glaucus took one long look at her and fell in love. More than anything he wanted to lie with this enchanting maiden, so he swam into the cove and greeted her.

Scylla sprang from the water so fast she left all her clothes behind and sprinted up the side of a nearby cliff overhanging the sea. Hiding behind a rock, she looked down at this strange creature not knowing if he was a monster or a god. Glaucus stretched his arms out to her and pleaded, "Dear maiden, please don't run away. I am no wild creature of the sea, but a god. I was once human like you, but was changed to what you see before you. Until I saw you I thought I was happy, but what good is it to be divine if you are frightened of me? Please come down so that we might speak face-to-face."

Scylla ran away before he had even finished speaking. Glaucus was despondent and did not know how to win her love, but then he remembered Circe.

The famous sea witch Circe was the daughter of Helios the sun and granddaughter of Oceanus himself. She lived on an island in the west where she plied her magic turning men into beasts. Glaucus swam to her hidden isle and begged her for a love potion to make Scylla adore him as he did her. However, Circe took one look at Glaucus and decided she wanted him for herself: "Why seek after some mortal woman when you can have a goddess? Come to my bed and I will show you things no human maiden ever could. Forget this girl and be mine."

Glaucus answered, "Trees will grow upon the waves and seaweed spring from the mountaintops before I forsake my love for Scylla."

Hell hath no fury like a witch scorned. Circe flew into a rage and ran to her room of potions. She knew she could not harm Glaucus, god that he now was, but she could destroy his dreams of ever being with that wretched girl. She mixed together dreadful herbs and roots, then sung over them the charms of Hecate herself. At last when all was ready, she placed the vile juice in a bottle and made her way to Scylla's cove.

The maiden had just come down to her secret pool to swim—looking around carefully first to make sure no one else was there. She did not see Circe pour her poison into the peaceful water, then fly away. Glaucus arrived just as the witch left and watched his love from a hiding place, not wishing to frighten her again. If all he could have was a glimpse of her beauty as she bathed in the water, then that would be enough.

The water was cool and wonderful on Scylla's skin in the heat of the day. She waded into the cove up to her waist and delighted at the feeling of the warm sun on her face. But then something strange began to happen. Her body began to change so that monstrous heads sprang from her loins. Six snarling beasts like wolves with horrid teeth and long, snakelike necks shot forth from her as she screamed in terror. Soon she was transformed into a hideous monster with only the head and torso of a woman remaining. She ran to the overhanging cliff nearby in hope that somehow she would leave the beasts behind, but she soon found that she was rooted to the rock and could not move. The maiden who had once been so radiant and lovely had become the most repulsive monster anyone could imagine. Scylla screamed and screamed until she lost her mind. In her madness and hatred of herself, she struck out at anyone who chanced to sail near, tearing them to pieces. She became a legend among sailors, who avoided her at all costs. Only Glaucus wept for her, knowing what she had once been and what she had become, all because of his love.

HERO AND LEANDER

On the shores of the narrow straits of the Hellespont opposite the city of Troy there lived a young priestess of Aphrodite named Hero. She was from a rich and noble family in the city of Sestus and there she served the goddess faithfully in her temple, though she herself knew nothing of love. The maiden was exceptionally beautiful so that all the men from the surrounding towns dreamed of being with her, saying:

"I've been to Sparta and seen Helen herself, but I've never beheld a girl as lovely as her."

"O Aphrodite, send me a woman like that!"

"I would die a happy man if I could first climb into her sweet bed."

But there was one young man who longed for Hero more than any other. His name was Leander and he lived just across the Hellespont in Asia in the seaside town of Abydos. He was just a poor youth from a humble family, but when he first saw the maiden at the temple, a fire kindled inside him that could not be extinguished. He dreamed of her day and night, wanting only to be with her and hold her in his arms. But he was afraid to talk with a girl who had rejected the advances of so many men. What did he have to offer that might appeal to someone as beautiful as a goddess?

One day at the temple he knew he had to talk to her or die of longing. He walked up to Hero and stood trembling before her. When she looked at him, he felt as if he would lose himself in those lovely eyes. He trembled and searched for words to express his love. Hero found herself moved by this shy young man as she had never been by any other suitor. She gently reached down and grasped his hand in her own, then smiled at him and began to speak, teasing him: "Stranger, what is it you want of me? I'm just a girl unschooled in the ways of men. Is there something you want to tell me? I can't say my father would be pleased that such a handsome young man is trying to seduce me. Oh, and the goddess I serve would be none too happy either. Are you hoping to lure me into your bed, then abandon me in shame before Aphrodite and my family?"

At last Leander found his voice: "Most excellent maiden, fairest flower that ever bloomed on these shores, I swear that my intentions are nothing but honorable. I have admired you for so long and love you with all my heart. I would never treat you with anything but respect. The goddess you serve is dear to me as well and I have the highest regard for your father and mother. But consider, is it right to serve Aphrodite when you have never known the touch of a man? I know I am only a poor boy, but my love is pure. Your parents would never allow me to marry you in a proper ceremony, but I pledge before the goddess herself that I would be a faithful husband who would love you as long as I draw breath."

Hero saw that Leander meant every word he spoke and she was

deeply touched. Her heart swelled inside her and she knew that this was the man for her. But her father would never permit her to take this humble lad from across the straits as her husband, so the two made a secret plan to consummate their love.

Every night when she was able, Hero would hang a lamp from her bedroom window in Sestus that would shine across the narrow Hellespont from Europe to Asia. When Leander saw this, he would follow the guiding light and swim the channel to come to her. They swore their love to each other and vowed to live in their hearts as husband and wife forever.

All that summer and autumn, every night when the sky was clear, Hero would light her lamp and place it in her window. Then Leander, gazing across the straits, would dive into the waves and follow the light to the home of his true love. He would arrive dripping and wet, but Hero was eager to see him once again. The two would make love all night long, then Leander would reluctantly leave just as the dawn was breaking and swim back to his home in Abydos. They told no one of their secret marriage, so that by day Hero continued to serve the goddess as if she were a chaste maiden, but by night she joined in passion with Leander.

When winter came, gales blew down the Hellespont and stirred the frosty seas. Hero begged Leander to wait until spring to return to her, but he would not allow wind and waves to separate him from his love. One stormy night, the lamp blew out while the young man was midway across the straits. The waves crashed against him and the wind blew him back, but still he struggled on. Without the light of Hero to guide him, however, Leander became lost and could not find his way to shore. The bitter wind blinded him and the water poured down his throat, yet he swam with all his might to find his beloved.

Day finally came and Hero looked desperately from her window to the sea below, hoping to catch a glimpse of her lover swimming to her. But her worst fear came true when she saw, on the rocks below, the lifeless body of her dear Leander. Unable to live without his love, she threw herself headlong from the window to her death. There the townspeople found the couple lying together, gently tossed by the waves of the sea.

HYPERMNESTRA AND LYNCEUS

One of the many descendants of Io was Danaus, son of Belus. Danaus had a twin brother named Egyptus, who had fifty sons by many wives. Danaus himself had a number of wives, but had only daughters, also fifty in number. Egyptus ruled over his powerful namesake country while Danaus was king of the smaller land of Libya. Each brother was suspicious of the other and saw treachery in every move his sibling made.

One day Egyptus sent a message to his brother offering to make peace. He proposed sealing the bargain with the marriage of all fifty of his sons to their maiden cousins. Danaus suspected this was a trick and prelude to an attack on his kingdom, so with the advice of Athena he fled Libya with his daughters and settled in Greece near Argos, where he became king of the region.

But Egyptus was persistent and sent his sons to Argos to try to convince his brother to allow the mass wedding to take place. Danaus still did not trust Egyptus, so he decided to use the wedding as a trap to eliminate any future threat from his nephews at one stroke. The king of Argos consented to the wedding and celebrated the ceremonies, after which he gave careful instructions and a sharp dagger to each of his daughters. At the conclusion of the marriage feast that evening, each of the sons led his new bride back to his quarters in great anticipation. All fifty daughters joined their eager grooms in bed, but then each maiden suddenly pulled the dagger from beneath her pillow and slit her husband's throat.

All except for one. The eldest daughter, Hypermnestra, had been given to her cousin Lynceus as a bride to carry out her duty to her father just like her other sisters. But when she entered the chamber with Lynceus, she was touched by how solicitous he was. He told her he realized that she had no say in the marriage and indeed did not know him at all. He said had no desire to force himself upon her that night, but preferred to wait to make love to her when she was ready. Hypermnestra was so taken back by his kindness that she could not go through with the plan.

"Get up! Go, flee from this place before you sleep forever. Don't let my father or wicked sisters catch you. They have pounced on their new husbands like lionesses on bull calves and slaughtered each one. My father can do what he wants with me, but I cannot kill someone so gentle and compassionate. Go, don't look back! We will find each other again someday."

Hypermnestra then helped him escape from the palace to a nearby village. There, by prearranged signal, he lit a beacon to show he was safe, then fled the country.

The other forty-nine daughters of Danaus brought the heads of their husbands to their father, but Hypermnestra arrived empty-handed. Her father put her in chains for her disobedience, though in time they were reconciled and he allowed his daughter to join her husband, who eventually became king of Argos.

The sisters of Hypermnestra had more difficulty finding good men. Their father searched for new husbands for them, but potential grooms were understandably reluctant to marry women with such a bloody past. Finally, with a great deal of bribery, Danaus did obtain husbands for them—though their deeds caught up with the daughters eventually. When at last they died and went down to Hades, they were forced to spend eternity pouring water into leaky jars that had to be constantly refilled.

BAUCIS AND PHILEMON

Once long ago in the rolling hills of Phrygia there was a remarkable tree. From a single trunk grew a sturdy oak and a broad linden, both rising above an enormous marsh. How it came to be there is a story of true love and a reminder always to show kindness to strangers.

Zeus, the ruler of the gods, was greatly concerned with hospitality and the proper care of strangers. From time to time he would disguise himself as a humble beggar and wander the roads of the world to test how the inhabitants of a land would receive him. On one occasion he took with him the god Hermes, also in disguise, and visited the country of Phrygia, where Midas once ruled. The divine pair went from house to house, but when they asked for a simple cup of water or a crust of bread, they were always sent away empty-handed.

At last they came to a hut on a hill that was smaller and more decrepit than any they had seen. The roof was covered with straw and the cracks in the walls were so big the fierce winter wind blew into the tiny hovel. Zeus knocked on the door and was welcomed by an old couple who invited their unexpected guests inside. These were Baucis and Philemon, a poor but happy couple who made light of their poverty and enjoyed their life of endless struggle together, as they had for many years.

The old man set out a bench for their visitors and offered them a seat. Baucis blew on the fire with her feeble breath and fed it twigs and dried bark to heat the water in her single pot. She collected a few leaves of cabbage from her garden and placed them in the boiling water to make soup, along with a few strips of bacon Philemon cut from a precious side of pork hanging from their rafters.

While they worked the aged couple entertained their guests with tales and local gossip until the broth was ready. They then pulled up a table and invited them to recline on a rickety couch stuffed with straw and covered with a worn blanket full of holes. The guests took their place on the wooden frame, which threatened to break any second, as Baucis placed a piece of broken pottery under one of the table legs that was too short. She wiped the table with mint leaves she had collected and placed the few food stores they had before the strangers—olives, eggs, wild nuts, figs, radishes, and a small piece of cheese. Then she put the soup before them in earthen bowls along with a cup each of sour wine mixed with water. The old couple were so proud to be able to lay out what for them was a grand feast.

Baucis and Philemon waited eagerly on their guests, but noticed that as often as the wine cups were drained, they never became empty. It was then that the couple began to suspect their visitors were more than just a pair of wandering beggars. They raised their hands in prayer and begged their guests to wait while they roasted a goose in their honor. This priceless bird was both the source of their eggs and the vigilant guardian of their humble estate, but they were gladly willing to sacrifice it. Zeus and Hermes looked on laughing as old Philemon and Baucis chased the goose around their yard in vain. Then at last Zeus spoke: "Please forget about the goose, dear friends. We are gods and have no need of such food. None of your wicked neighbors welcomed us when we came to their doors, even though they had far more to give than you. They have already been punished—come outside and see for yourselves."

As they left their cottage, the couple were amazed to see water everywhere. The entire countryside of fields and houses was covered with a great flood. The husband and wife wept for their neighbors, who had never showed them any kindness, then turned back to look at their hut. It was now a grand palace with marble columns and a golden roof.

Zeus told them to ask any favor they wished and it would be granted. Baucis and Philemon requested only that they be allowed to be priests of the gods in their new home and, when the time came, to die together so that one might never have to live without the other.

Zeus granted their wishes and the couple lived together into extreme old age in their grand home, still enjoying each other's company as much as ever. One evening when they were standing together talking about old times, Baucis saw Philemon starting to sprout leaves, even as Philemon watched his companion of so many years begin to shoot forth green limbs. The change was so fast that all they had time to say to each other was, "Farewell, my dear love!" and then the bark closed over their lips.

The tree long stood, an oak and a linden entwined together. Peasants often came and laid boughs beneath the tree as an offering to the gods and as a memorial to the pious and loving couple.

ALPHEUS AND ARETHUSA

Few love affairs have so happy an ending as that of Baucis and Philemon. Often, as in the case of Echo and Narcissus, the feelings were not mutual. Such was the unrequited love of the river god Alpheus for the beautiful nymph Arethusa.

This fair maiden lived in the forested hills of southern Greece, where she was devoted to the service of the virgin goddess Artemis. Even for a nymph, Arethusa was extraordinarily lovely and so had numerous suitors for her hand. But she took no joy from her beauty or from the attention it brought her. All she wanted was to roam the hills and valleys serving the goddess and frolicking with her companions in the woods.

One hot summer's day when she had been chasing game on her own, she came to a cool stream flowing silently with crystal-clear water. Willows with drooping branches lined the banks and gave pleasing shade to a pool in the river. Since no one was near, Arethusa came to the water's edge and dipped her toe in the stream. The water was so inviting that the nymph removed all her clothes and lay them on a branch, then waded naked into the refreshing brook. She swam with joy, diving and splashing, until suddenly she thought she heard a voice coming from somewhere deep in the pool. She jumped out of the water on the far bank and stood in terror.

"Where are you going, Arethusa? Why in such a hurry? I so enjoyed having you swim through my waters." The voice called out twice, frightening the maiden, but she was reluctant to flee since her clothes were on the opposite side of the stream. Then she saw the river-god Alpheus rise in human form from the pool.

Clothes or not, Arethusa was not going to wait around for what she knew would come next. She set off across the forest at a speed no man could equal—but she was not being chased by a man. As fast as the nymph was, the god was even swifter. Alpheus pursued her across the forest and over mountains, then down through valleys and up towering cliffs. Arethusa managed to keep just ahead of her pursuer, but she was tiring even as he seemed to gain strength. At last she called out in prayer to her patron Artemis, "Great goddess, hear me! If ever I have served you faithfully as armor-bearer or carried your bow and quiver on the hunt, help me escape this god or my virtue is lost forever."

Arethusa could run no more. Exhausted, she stood with sweat dripping from her naked body as Alpheus drew near. Then she felt the sweat begin to flow so fast that she seemed to be melting. Her entire body quickly turned to a stream of water that sank into the ground just as the god came to her. Artemis then transported her from Greece to safety on an island just off the coast of Sicily, where the nymph became a spring.

Such was the burning passion of Alpheus that he would not be dissuaded. He turned back into his watery form and followed the maiden

through a passage deep under the sea until he reached her island. There
he mingled his waters with her own so that the two became one.

⊟⊒⊓⊟⊒⊓⊟⊒⊓⊟⊒⊓⊟⊒⊓

POMONA AND VERTUMNUS

⊟⊒⊓⊟⊒⊓⊟⊒⊓⊟⊒⊓⊟⊒⊓

In ancient Italy there lived a beautiful nymph who cared nothing for
fields and forests, but spent all her time tending the fruit trees of her beloved orchard. Her name was Pomona and she carried no hunting spear
in her hand, but instead a pruning hook to trim carefully the branches of
the trees she grew. She spent her days grafting twigs and gathering fruit,
caring nothing for the embrace of the many gods who tried to woo her.
She built high the walls of her garden so that no one would interrupt her
care of the trees with foolish talk of love.

But there was someone who loved Pomona more than all others. His
name was Vertumnus and he was a local god of the countryside. Pomona
had scorned him so many times that he began disguising himself just so
he could catch a glimpse of her. One day he would be a farmer hauling
a basket of barley to the orchard, the next he was a reaper fresh from
cutting hay, or a drover with a pair of oxen. Sometimes he dressed as a
gardener with a ladder on his shoulders so that he could spend the day
near Pomona helping her care for her trees.

One day the god transformed himself into an old woman and entered
the orchard leaning on a cane. Pomona saw the gentle figure with white
hair and invited her unexpected guest to sit down in the cool shade of
an apple tree. The visitor talked of how beautiful Pomona's trees were,
but said the maiden herself was even fairer. The old woman dared to
kiss the nymph as a grandmother would, though with such passion that
Pomona began to grow suspicious.

Then her guest began to speak: "Look at that tree standing over
there holding up the vine that grows next to it. Such a vine is not
ashamed to seek the support of a sturdy elm, for otherwise it would lie
flat on the ground and be trampled. Is it really so different for a maiden
such as you? If you would take the advice of someone who has lived
many years, you should not try to live your life standing on your own. I

know young Vertumnus loves you with all his heart. He's a fine fellow—I will vouch for him myself—and would gladly help you care for your beautiful orchard."

The old woman then told Pomona a story of a stubborn girl named Anaxarete who was a proud princess in a nearby land. She was loved by men throughout the kingdom and beyond, but coldly rejected all suitors as beneath her. A poor youth named Iphis loved her more than anyone, but she savagely scorned him, dismissing him as unworthy of her attention. The lad was crushed and took a rope to the palace the next morning. There he hung himself from a doorpost until he was dead. His own mother found him and wept over his still-warm body as Anaxarete happened to glance out the window. Not even this tragic scene could touch her heart as she stood like stone looking down on the corpse of the man who could not bear to live without her. She then tried to turn away, but found she was fixed to the spot where she stood. Her limbs turned to marble, then her heart to stone, until she was nothing but a cold statue, feeling nothing forevermore.

The old woman in the orchard then cautioned Pomona not to be like the foolish princess but to allow love into her life. Then the god resumed his true form and stood before the nymph as Vertumnus, the one who cared for her more than any other. Pomona looked at him as if for the first time and felt love stirring in her heart at last, then reached out and took his hand.

ENDYMION AND SELENE

The goddess of the moon was Selene, who traveled across the sky at night looking down on the people of the earth as they slept. One evening her eyes fell upon Endymion, the handsome king of Elis in southern Greece. Although the king was married, Selene came to him many times and bore him fifty daughters. The love of the moon goddess for Endymion was so strong that she persuaded Zeus to grant him anything he might wish. The king considered the generous offer and finally asked that he be allowed to sleep forever, never aging. The ruler of the gods agreed and so Endymion retired to a mountain cave in Caria across the Aegean Sea where he lay his head on a pillow and closed his eyes for the last time. There he rested in peace, always young, always fair. But on moonless nights, Selene would come to him and kiss her mortal lover gently in his endless sleep.

ORPHEUS AND EURYDICE

The greatest of all ancient bards was Orpheus, a singer from Thrace so skilled with the lyre that whenever he played, wild animals stopped to listen and the very rocks of the earth followed after him. He was the son of the god Apollo, who taught him to play, and Calliope, the leader of the Muses. Orpheus had many adventures, including a journey with the Argonauts to seek the Golden Fleece, but his greatest quest was because of love.

Orpheus fell in love with a nymph named Eurydice and the two planned a grand wedding. But as the bride was walking through the meadow on her way to the marriage ceremony, she was bitten on the ankle by a poisonous serpent and died. The wedding turned into a funeral, with Orpheus himself singing a lament for Eurydice with bitter tears.

Orpheus could not bear the thought of living without his Eurydice, so he decided to make the dangerous journey to the underworld to bring her back. He found an entrance to the gloomy realm of Hades and followed the long path ever downward. When he came at last to the boatman Charon, the old man was so moved by his music that he rowed him across the Styx without payment. At the sound of his harp, the three-headed dog Cerberus became quiet, the Furies ceased their shrieking, and even Sisyphus stopped rolling his stone endlessly up his hill. All the bloodless shades of Hades wept with unaccustomed joy at the magical sound of Orpheus.

When the bard came to the palace of Hades and stood before the god and his consort Persephone, the king and queen of the underworld were also deeply touched by his song. Orpheus then spoke and asked if he might be allowed to bring his bride back to the world of the living. If this was not possible, then he wished to remain in the pale underworld with her forever rather than live without her. Hades granted his request, on the condition that as he journeyed back to the world of light, Orpheus not turn around to look at Eurydice but to trust that she was there behind him.

The poet gladly agreed and started up the steep path. As the hours went by, Orpheus climbed up the long trail with nothing but silence behind him. The thought that Eurydice was not really following him weighed ever more heavily on his mind. What if Hades had tricked him? At last, just as he neared the surface, the urge to see his bride overpowered him. He stopped and turned around, only to see the ghost of Eurydice fading away. His bride looked at him with infinite sadness in her eyes and spoke a single word—"Farewell."

Orpheus ran back down the path, but no one may enter Hades twice while living. Charon refused him passage and Hades himself barred his gates against him. For seven days Orpheus sat on the banks of the Styx and wept, then made his way slowly back to the land of the living. There he shunned all contact with his fellow men and women, seeking only to play sad songs alone in the forest. A wandering group of women came upon him there, worshipers of Dionysus, and, perhaps because they became so enamored of him, they fought over him and tore his body to pieces. His severed head fell into a stream and floated down to the sea, but his tongue found breath one final time and whispered the name of his beloved Eurydice.

HERCULES

The hero Perseus had many children with his wife, Andromeda, after he rescued her from the sea monster. Three of the sons they raised in Argos were Alcaeus, Electryon, and Sthenelus. In time Alcaeus grew up and had a son of his own named Amphitryon, while Electryon had nine sons and a daughter he named Alcmene.

When Perseus died, Electryon became king of Mycenae. The coast of Argos in those days was plagued by pirates and one day they attacked Electryon's sons while they were tending cattle. Unfortunately for the princes, they were no match for the raiders. The king himself then decided to seek revenge on the pirates for their crime. He entrusted Mycenae to his nephew Amphitryon as regent along with the care of his daughter—but gave him a stern warning that her virtue had better be intact when he returned. Nephew and uncle then quarreled, with words leading to drawn swords. In the passion of the moment, Amphitryon slew Electryon.

Electryon's brother Sthenelus took the throne and banished Amphitryon from the kingdom. Alcmene willingly accompanied him into exile and the two made their way north to the city of Thebes, where King Creon purified Amphitryon of blood guilt from the slaying of his uncle. Amphitryon was now eager to marry Alcmene and enjoy the pleasures of her bed, but his beautiful cousin had other ideas. Yes, she would gladly marry him, but—as a matter of honor—he first had to hunt down the pirates who had killed her brothers. Amphitryon was only too happy to seek vengeance against the men who had murdered his cousins, but he was also eager to make love to his new wife. Thus with great urgency, he collected together a band of warriors and set off to destroy the pirates.

Amphitryon was successful, but on the night of his return, Zeus took on his appearance and entered the chamber of Alcmene disguised as her husband. The god showed his bride trophies of his victory over the pirates and said it was time at last for a real honeymoon. Zeus lengthened the night to three times its normal length as he made love to Alcmene again and again.

No sooner had the god left than the real Amphitryon entered the palace. He ran upstairs to Alcmene's bedroom and embraced his wife at last. The exhausted Alcmene couldn't understand how her husband still had such energy after the long night of passion they had already enjoyed. When dawn came, the poor woman asked why he had come to her twice in a single night as if it were the first time. Amphitryon was furious, so he decided to seek out Tiresias the prophet to discover who had slept with Alcmene before him. The seer revealed that it was in fact Zeus who had shared her bed. Amphitryon was none too pleased with this news, but he could hardly blame his wife for the amorous encounter and it was pointless to rage against the god. Reluctantly he accepted the fact that both he and Zeus had enjoyed her favors that night.

Hera was angry as always that Zeus had cheated on her. She determined to make Alcmene and her child pay for the philandering of her husband. The goddess was even more eager to do this when after nine months Zeus rose from his throne on Olympus and declared that the fruit of his loins born that day would rule over the fertile plain of Argos. Hera made him swear that this would be so, then she slipped away and sped down to Mycenae, where the young wife of Sthenelus was seven months pregnant. The goddess caused her to go into early labor so that her son would be born first in fulfillment of the prophesy instead of Alcmene's. As Sthenelus was the grandson of Zeus, his son was also the offspring of Hera's husband and could fulfill the prophecy.

Meanwhile, to buy time until the wife of Sthenelus gave birth, Hera had sent Eileithyia, the goddess of childbirth, to wait outside the bedchamber of Alcmene. Instead of easing her delivery, Eileithyia sat with her legs and fingers tightly crossed in an act of sympathetic magic to prolong her labor. The screams of Alcmene went on for many hours as the pain increased. At last one of her servants, a clever old woman named Galanthis, noticed the stranger in the shadows and understood what this mysterious figure was doing. Galanthis then shouted, "Rejoice, a child is born! Alcmene has given birth!"

"Impossible," cried out Eileithyia, but the distraction was enough to break her concentration and end the spell. Eileithyia was so angry at the trick that she immediately turned the old woman into a weasel. The long-suffering Alcmene then at last gave birth not to one but two sons. One was Iphicles, fathered by the mortal Amphitryon, but the other was sired on the same night by Zeus. His name was Hercules.

After Hercules was born, his mother Alcmene was afraid that Hera would kill her just as she had so many of Zeus' lovers. She therefore took her baby and left him to die in a deserted field, hoping that this would satisfy the vengeance of the goddess. By no coincidence, Athena happened upon the infant and took him to Mount Olympus. She brought him to Hera and asked if she would nurse the beautiful baby she had found. Hera did not know who the boy was and always had a soft spot for children, so she gladly agreed and put the child to her breast. All went well until the precociously strong Hercules bit his divine nursemaid hard on the nipple. Hera screamed in pain and jumped up, spurting milk everywhere. Athena then took the child back to his mother in Thebes and persuaded her to raise him. Hera's milk meanwhile spread across the heavens and came to be known as the Milky Way.

Hercules was just a few months old when Hera first tried to kill him. He was in his crib with his brother, Iphicles, one night when the goddess sent two large and poisonous serpents into their room. The snakes silently moved across the floor until they came to the bed, then climbed up until they were on top of the babies. Iphicles awoke and screamed, but Hercules grabbed a serpent in each of his chubby hands and squeezed. Alcmene and Amphitryon rushed in to find baby Hercules laughing as he held two dead snakes by the neck.

From his earliest days Hercules excelled in physical activities, especially since his teachers were the best Greece had to offer. His mortal father, Amphitryon, taught him to drive a chariot, while a king named Eurytus instructed him in the use of the bow. Helen's brother Castor taught him to fight with a sword and Hermes' son Harpalycus showed him how to wrestle. Linus, the brother of Orpheus, tried to teach him to sing and play the lyre, but Hercules was a poor student of music. Linus grew so frustrated with his pupil that one day he boxed him on the ears. Hercules flew into a rage and smashed the lyre on top of his teacher's head, killing him. Young Hercules was put on trial for murder, but argued that by ancient custom a man was allowed to kill anyone who struck him first. The judges were impressed by this clever youth and acquitted him of all charges.

Amphitryon then wisely decided he should send Hercules out into the country to vent his energy doing chores on a farm. The boy loved this rural life and outdid all of his companions in performing farm tasks and hunting in the woods. By the time he was a young man, he was taller by a head than all his fellows and his eyes gleamed with fire. No one could beat him in contests of skill, whether shooting arrows or throwing the javelin.

When Hercules was eighteen, word reached him that an enormous lion was ravaging the flocks of King Thespius on nearby Mount Cithaeron. The beast was very hard to track, so Hercules spent fifty nights in the home of Thespius while he hunted. The king was so impressed by this young man that he decided he wanted each of his fifty daughters to bear his child. Hercules was potent but not very bright. Every night while he stayed with the king, a different girl slipped into his dark bedroom. Hercules—thinking that it was the same young woman each time coming back for more—gladly made love with each one. Some stories even say that Thespius got Hercules drunk and sent in all fifty daughters at once. But whether in a single night or over a period of weeks, Hercules impregnated each girl. Somehow he also found time to kill the lion.

In the days when young Hercules lived in the city, Thebes was dominated by the Minyans to the north. The king of the Minyans was Erginus, who ruled at Orchomenus and demanded that each year the Thebans send him a hundred of their best cattle. As Hercules was returning home after he had killed the lion of Mount Cithaeron, he happened to meet the Minyan heralds on their way to Thebes to collect their annual tribute. Hercules was so incensed by this humiliation of his town that he cut off the ears, noses, and hands of the heralds and sent them back to Orchomenus mutilated. King Erginus was furious at this outrageous insult and gathered his powerful army to march against Thebes. When he reached the walls of the city he demanded that Creon send out Hercules to be punished. The king of Thebes was seriously considering this when Hercules gathered the young men of the town and broke into a local temple. There the Thebans had long ago dedicated their weapons to the gods and hung them on a wall where they had gathered dust for years. With Hercules leading them, the youthful warriors took up the ancient arms and marched out against the Minyans. The band of Thebans not only slew Erginus and killed almost everyone in the Minyan army, but they also proceeded to the capital of their enemy and burned Orchomenus to the ground. Thanks to Hercules, the Thebans were now free.

Creon was so grateful to Hercules that he gave him his own daughter Megara to be his bride. The young couple lived happily together and had three sons, but Hera had not forgotten her anger against Hercules and was not about to let this happy domestic scene continue. She whispered in the ear of Hercules that he was nothing, a nobody from a small town who was a grave disappointment to his divine father. A true son of Zeus would have accomplished more than kill a mangy lion and defeat the Minyan rabble in a minor war. In visions of the night and in his darkest thoughts, she told him he was no hero.

Hercules wanted to be so much more than a husband and father. Hearth and home had their rewards, but he longed for danger and adventure to prove himself. The conflict between his dreams and the responsibilities of family life caused him such frustration that he didn't know which way to turn. Hera fanned this frenzy until at last Hercules lost his mind.

One day he was performing a sacrifice to the gods with his wife and sons in attendance. His beautiful young children looked up at him in silent reverence as he carried the sacred basket of barley around the altar. Hercules stood ready to quench the flame of the altar torch in a basin so that he could sprinkle the holy water on his family as a blessing. Suddenly, without a word, he froze. Megara and the children stared at him wondering what was wrong. His bloodshot eyes rolled wildly in his head, drool dribbled into his beard, and then he screamed out with manic laughter: "Why should I sacrifice before I slay Eurystheus, son of Sthenelus, king of Mycenae? I'll kill that miserable usurper with a single blow. Throw away the basket, pour out the water, and someone get my bow! I'm off to Mycenae. I'll knock down those mighty walls with my bare hands."

Hercules grabbed his bow and club, then climbed into an imaginary chariot and whipped invisible horses to a gallop. His servants didn't know if he had gone insane or if this were some kind of joke. Their master cried out that he was crossing the Isthmus of Corinth and was nearing his goal. He then jumped on the ground and began running around the altar looking for his enemies. His children were now terrified and cried out, catching the attention of their father. He drew his bow on his eldest son, thinking he was a child of Eurystheus.

"Stop!" cried Megara as she threw herself in front of her son. "You gave this child life. Will you now take it away?"

But Hercules was in a world of his own and could not hear her. He chased the boy around the yard and caught him at last, then stabbed him through the heart with the sacrificial knife. The blood of the young child spurted from his small body as he collapsed into his mother's arms.

"That's one of your brood, Eurystheus," cried Hercules. "Now for the rest!"

His second son tried to hide behind the altar, but his father found him there and dragged him away. As Hercules raised his club to crush his head, the boy grasped his father's knees and begged him, "Daddy, please, don't kill me! I'm your own little boy."

But like a blacksmith at the forge, Hercules brought down his club on the boy's fair hair and crushed his skull.

Megara grabbed her last child and ran into their house, barring the door. But Hercules burst through and drew his bow on mother and child crouched in the corner. Without a word, he shot them both through with a single arrow.

He would have killed everyone present, but Athena suddenly appeared before him and tossed a huge stone at his chest, knocking the breath from his body and driving away Hera's madness. Hercules slowly rose from the ground and gazed in horror at the scene before him. Then he sank to his knees and wept.

For weeks Hercules was beyond consolation. He had murdered his own wife and children—madness or not, he could not forgive himself. Friends and family came to sit with him, but he wanted nothing to do with anyone. His grief consumed him until he was a shell of his former self.

Although time cannot heal all wounds, as the months passed Hercules realized he would have to move on or die alone in a dark and empty house. At last he roused himself and left Thebes behind to seek the counsel of the oracle at Delphi. He made his way west over the mountains until he came to the temple of Apollo beneath Mount Parnassus. Sacrifices performed, he entered the sanctuary and asked the priestess what he must do to be healed of his pain and find forgiveness. The message she gave him was not pleasing. He must return to his ancestral home in Argos and there serve his young uncle Eurystheus, performing whatever twelve labors this hated king would assign him. This was a bitter pill for Hercules to swallow and a powerful lesson in humility. Not only would he be reduced to the level of a slave, but his master would be the very man who had stolen the rightful throne of Argos from him. Still, there was nothing he could do except follow the will of the god. He left the slopes of Parnassus and walked slowly down the road to Argos.

The cowardly Eurystheus was terrified when he heard that Hercules was on his way to Mycenae. He thought that his nephew was planning to kill him and steal the throne. As Hercules entered the massive gates of the citadel with stone lions on each side, Eurystheus hid himself in a large bronze jar buried in the ground and hoped that his nephew wouldn't find him. But Hercules marched into the palace grounds and tore the lid off the jar, hauling Eurystheus to his feet. The king begged for mercy with his hands raised in supplication, but finally calmed down when Hercules explained his mission. The ruler of Argos then determined to assign his nephew the most dangerous tasks he could think of, hoping that he would be killed quickly and never enter Mycenae again.

Seated on his throne but still shaking, Eurystheus commanded Hercules to seek out and slay a great lion that was ravaging the country around Nemea, to the north of Mycenae. Hercules did not think this first labor would be difficult. He had already killed a fierce lion on Mount Cithaeron and supposed this animal would be no different. He began a leisurely stroll toward Nemea and arrived at the little town of Cleone along the way. A poor man named Molorchus invited him to spend the night in his house and served him the best food his humble means allowed. He was so impressed by his mighty guest that when he was leaving the next morning, Molorchus asked if he might sacrifice to him. Hercules laughed and told him to wait thirty days. If he returned having slain the lion, he advised his host to make an offering to Zeus as savior. If he didn't return, then he might make a small sacrifice to his spirit as a hero.

Hercules arrived in the region of Nemea and found the lair of the beast. The lion made its home in a cave stretching through the rock to the other side of the mountain. He found the lion lounging outside the entrance and notched his arrow for an easy kill. The shaft flew straight at the heart of the animal, but it merely bounced off his hide. The lion yawned as Hercules let fly another arrow, but the result was the same, for this was no ordinary lion. It was none other than a child of the ancient monsters Typhon and Echidna. The skin of the Nemean lion could not be pierced by any shaft or blade.

Hercules considered his options and came up with a plan. He went to the far side of the mountain and blocked the exit to the cave, then he returned to the entrance where the lion slept. He cut a huge club from a nearby tree and rushed the animal, yelling and making such a racket that the lion made its way into the cave to get away from the noisy intruder. Hercules followed the lion and grabbed it around the throat. By now the beast was angry and tried to tear him apart, but Hercules was so strong that he choked the lion to death with his bare hands. Since no blade could cut its hide, he used one of the razor-sharp claws of the lion itself to skin the animal. He then draped it across his shoulders as a cloak with the lion's scalp serving as a kind of helmet. This skin and the club Hercules carved at Nemea became his emblems thereafter.

As he walked back to Mycenae, he passed through Cleone and saw Molorchus about to sacrifice to him as a dead hero. Instead, Molorchus made an offering of thanksgiving to Zeus. Hercules then continued to Mycenae, where Eurystheus was once again hiding in his jar. He was more terrified of Hercules than ever and forbade him to enter the city gates in the future. From now on he would convey his royal orders through a herald named Copreus—a calculated insult on the part of the king since his name in Greek meant "manure man."

Eurystheus quickly sent Hercules away on his second labor, to kill the enormous Hydra that lived in the swamps of Lerna south of Mycenae. This monster had a hundred heads and a wicked temper. On certain nights it would crawl out of its swamp and ravage the farms and fields around Lerna with the help of its sidekick, a giant crab. Hercules, along with his nephew Iolaus, made his way to the Lernean swamp, but the muck and mire were so thick that the he had to use burning arrows to drive the Hydra from its hiding place. It was huge and as mean as any monster could be, but Hercules believed he could easily kill it. He rushed it with sword drawn and sliced off one of its heads in a single stroke. Proud of himself, he stood looking at the poisonous blood dripping from the beast when suddenly he saw two new heads burst from the severed neck. He attacked the Hydra again and cut off more heads, but from each stump came two additional heads, all raging against him. He then discovered that its central head was immortal and could not be destroyed by any means. To add injury to insult, the giant crab that was the Hydra's best friend crawled out of the swamp and began biting his foot.

A strategic retreat seemed in order. Hercules ran from the marsh and found Iolaus standing by his chariot. He ordered the young man to grab a torch and follow him. The pair made their way to the Hydra, which by now was fully recovered with more angry heads than ever. Hercules first killed the giant crab nipping at his heels, then told Iolaus to stand by with the torch. He cut off one of the Hydra's heads and yelled at his nephew to cauterize the wound quickly with fire. This had the desired effect—no new heads grew from the burned stumps. One by one Hercules cut at the monster until only the immortal head remained. He chopped this cleanly off at its vulnerable neck and buried it alive under a large rock. He then collected the poisonous blood of the Hydra and dipped all his arrows into the black liquid for future use.

The third labor Eurystheus assigned to Hercules was to track down and bring back alive the deer of Mount Ceryneia. This animal had horns of gold and was sacred to the goddess Artemis. Since he was not allowed to kill or wound the deer, Hercules spent a full year chasing it over the mountains of the Peloponnesus. At last he wore it down near a beautiful stream called the Ladon in Arcadia. He crept up on the deer while it slept and grabbed it, then threw it over his shoulders for the journey back to Mycenae.

As Hercules was making his way to Eurystheus, Artemis suddenly appeared before him. The goddess was furious that he had caught her sacred deer and was ready to kill Hercules, but he quickly explained that he had no wish to harm the animal and that he was acting under orders of the king. Artemis finally calmed down and let him continue on his way with a stern warning that he was to release her deer as soon as he reached Mycenae. Hercules agreed and made his way to the city, where he showed the deer to the herald Copreus and then let it go.

For the fourth labor, Eurystheus ordered Hercules to return to Arcadia and bring another living animal back to him, this time the terrible boar of Mount Erymanthus. This huge beast was ravaging the countryside, killing anyone who dared approach him.

Hercules followed the mountain paths to the southwest until he came to the cave of the friendly centaur Pholus, who welcomed him for the night. His host customarily ate his own meat raw, but he cooked a fine meal for his guest. Hercules asked for wine, but Pholus said the only wine available was in a jar hidden in his cave that belonged to all centaurs in common. It wasn't really his to open and if he did, the other centaurs would smell it and go wild because of their craving for the drink. Hercules assured Pholus everything would be fine, so out of hospitality the centaur broke the seal on the jar.

The fragrant smell of the ancient vintage filled the cave and spread throughout the countryside. Soon centaurs descended on the home of Pholus from all directions. They were armed for war and ready to kill anyone who stood between them and the wine. Hercules shot any who dared to enter the cave, then ran out to chase the rest away. But the centaurs were not easily intimidated. They were fearsome creatures of great strength who tore up whole trees from their roots to use as clubs. It was a tremendous battle that lasted for hours until the hero finally killed the last of the wine-crazed centaurs and returned to the cave of his host.

Hercules found Pholus burying the bodies of the centaurs who had fallen around his home. Pholus pulled an arrow from one of the creatures and marveled at how such a small thing could have killed his companions. Then he accidentally let the point fall on his bare foot. Kindly Pholus died in agony, after which Hercules buried him beside his kinsmen and continued his hunt for the boar.

He found the beast at last in its mountain hideout and chased it until it fled into a deep snowbank and became stuck. Hercules then wrestled it into submission and carried it back to Eurystheus alive, just as he had been ordered. The king could not believe Hercules had survived yet another dangerous mission. As he hid in his jar, he tried to think of a different kind of task, one that would be both impossible and humiliating. If Hercules was unable to accomplish such a labor or too embarrassed to carry it out, the trials would be over and Eurystheus would be rid of him forever.

No job in ancient Greece was lower than cleaning up the excrement of farm animals. Only slaves and the poorest laborers shoveled dung from a barn. For his fifth labor, therefore, Eurystheus ordered Hercules to clean the infamous stables of King Augeas, son of the god Helios. This ruler was a mighty cattle lord with vast herds, but he cared little that the animal excrement in his huge barn had been building up for years. The piles of dung were deeper than a man's knees and the stench was unimaginable. Eurystheus also stipulated that Hercules had to accomplish this humiliating labor all by himself.

Hercules was no stranger to farm life, but he recoiled at the thought of shoveling dung. He also knew it was impossible for him to cleanse the stables of Augeas alone by this method. But as he was under the command of the oracle at Delphi, he dared not offend the god by refusing to try. He made his way to the palace of Augeas to offer his services to the king. As he passed the swift Alpheus River along the way, he had a marvelous idea.

When he reached the palace, he was so confident he could accomplish the task that he told Augeas he would clean his stables in a single day if Augeas would give him a tenth of his cattle when the deed was complete. The king knew this was impossible, but he decided to let the young fool try. Hercules conveniently forgot to tell Augeas that he was acting under the orders of Eurystheus and had to clean the stables even with no payment. He made Phyleus, son of Augeas, witness the agreement and then set to work.

The next morning Hercules went to one wall of the stables and knocked a large hole in the side. Then he strolled through the muck to the other end and made another opening. After this, he went to the nearby banks of the Alpheus and diverted the stream into a channel he had dug into the barn. Thousands of gallons of fresh river water poured through the stables and washed away years of dung in a matter of minutes. Hercules then closed the channel, patched up the holes in the barn, and demanded his payment.

Augeas was incredulous, especially as he had discovered in the meantime that Hercules had come to him under orders of Eurystheus. The king refused to give him a single cow as he claimed to have been deceived. Hercules called on Phyleus as witness, with the king's son confirming that his father should pay. Augeas angrily ordered both Hercules and Phyleus to leave his kingdom forever.

Hercules made his way back to Mycenae without any cattle. In a bad mood, he stopped at the home of a local king named Dexamenus. This ruler had been bullied into promising his daughter in marriage to a centaur named Eurytion, who was coming that very day to claim her. Hercules had no use for centaurs after his encounter with them during the hunt for the Erymanthian Boar, so he killed Eurytion on the spot and then made his way back to Mycenae.

The sixth labor of Hercules was again not particularly dangerous, but Eurystheus considered it impossible. In Arcadia, in a dense forest near the town of Stymphalus, a flock of birds countless in number had settled on a lake and fouled it beyond use. Some say the birds shot their feathers like deadly arrows at anyone who approached, but most stories agree they were simply an enormous nuisance. The inhabitants of the region had tried many times to drive them away, but to no avail. The king therefore ordered Hercules to clear the lake, believing he would surely fail.

Hercules made his way back to Arcadia and gazed in wonder at the number of birds before him. He knew he could never kill them all, so he sat down on the shore and came up with a clever plan. He carefully fashioned a pair of bronze rattles that made a horrendous noise when he shook them. With these he ran around the lake causing such a ruckus that the birds took to the sky and never came back.

By now Eurystheus must have thought he would never get rid of Hercules, so for his seventh labor the king decided to send him on a mission across the sea to Crete, far from Mycenae, where the king hoped Hercules would be killed. His task was to capture alive the bull that had once emerged from the sea at the prayer of Minos to Poseidon. When the Cretan king refused to sacrifice it as he had promised, the god made Minos' queen, Pasiphae, fall in love with it and mate with the animal, producing the murderous Minotaur. After knowing the queen intimately, the bull had escaped the fields of Minos and was terrorizing the island.

Hercules found the bull without much difficulty and wrestled it to the ground, but getting the wild creature back to the mainland would not be easy. However, Hercules borrowed a trick that his father Zeus had used with Europa and rode the swimming bull all the way across the sea. Once he had shown it to the herald Copreus, he released it to wander around Greece until it eventually settled on the plain of Marathon near Athens and was slain by Theseus.

Eurystheus had failed to kill Hercules by sending him south to Crete, so Hercules' eighth labor was to go north to the wild land of Thrace and bring back alive the man-eating mares of King Diomedes. These ravenous horses had been reared on human flesh by the king and would eat nothing else. They were so fierce that their feeding troughs were made of bronze and so strong they were held in their stables by iron chains. Eurystheus hoped that Hercules would be their next meal.

On his way to Thrace, Hercules passed through the kingdom of Admetus who ruled over Thessaly. He noticed that the whole palace was in mourning. When he inquired why, he was told only that a woman not of the king's blood had passed away. Hercules couldn't understand why there should be such a fuss over someone not even related to the royal family. He therefore demanded wine and food be brought to him, then spent the evening laughing and joking with the tearful king.

Finally Admetus explained to his guest that it was indeed his own wife, Alcestis, who had died that very day. He had not wanted to be a poor host for Hercules, so he had tried to hide his sorrow. Hercules was profuse in his apologies and asked how such a young woman had died so suddenly. Admetus then told him the whole story.

Zeus had been angry with Apollo for killing some of the Cyclopes, so the ruler of the gods made him a slave of Admetus for a whole year. The king had been so kind to the god that at the end of his service Apollo granted the king a special favor—he need not die at his appointed time if he could find someone to die in his place.

Admetus searched throughout his kingdom for a person who would willingly die for him. He went to wealthy nobles who owed him their fortunes and to poor beggars living in squalor on the streets, but no one would take his place. He then went to his brothers and sisters, uncles and aunts, nephews and nieces, seeking desperately for someone who would make the long journey to Hades for him, but they all turned away. At last he went to his aged parents, hoping that they, nearing the end of their lives, would be willing. But his father spoke for both when he said, "Admetus, the light of the sun is all the more sweet to us because it is fading fast. We gave you life, but we will not die for you."

The king had almost given up hope when at last his lovely wife, Alcestis, came to him: "My husband, you have searched high and low for someone to take your place in Hades' pale realm, but you did not ask the one who loves you most. Admetus, I will die for you."

The king sadly consented, then sat beside her on her deathbed as she breathed her last.

Hercules was deeply moved by this story and swore to Admetus that he would find a way to make things right. He rushed to the tomb of Alcestis and there found Death, who had come to claim her spirit. He wrestled the grim specter to the ground and took back the soul of Alcestis, reuniting it with her body. He then led the living queen back to the throne room and presented her to Admetus.

After a good night's sleep in the joyful palace, Hercules continued on his way to Thrace with a few of his companions, including a young man named Abderus, who was his lover. Hercules promptly found the horses and calmed them by feeding them their own master, Diomedes. He then led them to the beach to take them by ship back to Argos. The Thracians launched an attack on the Greeks as they were leaving, so Hercules left the horses with Abderus on the shore while he and his friends put the natives to flight. By the time he returned, the horses had eaten most of his boyfriend. In his memory, Hercules founded a town named Abdera and instituted an athletic festival with every sort of game and contest—except for horse races.

Hercules returned to Eurystheus with the mares, but the king of Mycenae did not want the savage animals in his own land. He let them go so that they ran away north to the forests below Mount Olympus, where they were eaten by wolves.

King Eurystheus had a daughter named Admete who knew how to wrap her father around her little finger. This princess demanded that Hercules sail to the distant land of the fierce Amazons and bring back the belt of the warrior queen Hippolyte. Sometimes called a girdle, a maiden's belt was the symbol of her sexuality. Since it held her clothing in place, to freely loosen it for a man was a most intimate act. To have it forcibly taken was a prelude to rape.

Admete got her wish and soon Hercules was on his way north with a band of volunteers across the Aegean and into the Black Sea. Along the way he laid siege to unfriendly islands, battled newfound enemies, and killed two sons of King Minos, but at last he arrived at the town of Themiscyra in the kingdom of the Amazons.

Hippolyte received the visiting hero kindly and, most impressed by her handsome guest, offered to freely give her belt to him. Hercules was looking forward to this when suddenly the other Amazons attacked his ship. Hera had enflamed the warrior women against the Greeks, claiming they were there to kidnap the queen. Hercules mistakenly believed that he had fallen into a trap set by Hippolyte, so he killed her at once and took her belt by force. Fleeing arrows and spears, Hercules and his companions quickly sailed away.

The voyage home was full of trials as well, with Hercules rescuing the princess Hesione from a sea monster at Troy, killing Poseidon's son Sarpedon, and invading the island of Thasos off the coast of Thrace. Finally he arrived back in Mycenae, where he gave the belt of Hippolyte to the herald Copreus, who presented it to Eurystheus for his daughter Admete.

The tenth labor of Hercules was to capture the cattle of the monster Geryon, a ferocious creature with three bodies joined together at the waist. This dangerous beast lived in the farthest west on an island that lay in the great Ocean encircling the earth. No one had ever traveled so far from Greece before, thus Eurystheus was hoping Hercules would either be killed by the monster or become lost and perish in the land of the setting sun.

The hero journeyed alone across the Mediterranean to Africa, then west across the desert until he came to the land of the giant Antaeus. This enormous bully was the son of Poseidon and Earth, and it was his custom to challenge every stranger who came to his land to a wrestling match. In spite of his size, Antaeus was not a particularly good wrestler and was frequently thrown to the ground. But each time he touched his mother the Earth, his strength was renewed. With this advantage, he eventually defeated and killed every opponent. He then took their skulls and used them to decorate the temple of his father Poseidon.

Antaeus was eager to add Hercules' head to his collection, so he demanded the usual wrestling contest. Hercules easily threw him time and again, but each time Antaeus arose he seemed stronger even as Hercules was growing ever weaker. At last Hercules understood the connection between his opponent and the earth beneath him, so he grabbed Antaeus and held him high above his head so that he could not touch the ground. Unable to reach his mother, the giant grew weak. Hercules then snapped him in half like a dry twig.

After many weeks of travel, Hercules reached the western end of the Mediterranean and saw the vast Atlantic before him. He was so impressed by the sight that he decided to erect two pillars on opposite sides of the narrow passage to the Ocean, one in Europe and the other in Africa. These enormous rocks became known as the Pillars of Hercules and marked the boundary of the world.

As he worked erecting the pillars, Hercules grew so hot under the withering heat of the sun that in anger he shot an arrow at Helios as he drove his chariot across the sky. The sun god laughed at his folly but he admired the audacity of the hero so much that he loaned him his own golden bowl. This was a large vessel in which Helios journeyed with his horses every night from the sunset lands to his home in the east to rise again the next day. Hercules was grateful not to have to walk the rest of his way, so he climbed into the bowl and followed the Iberian coast north until he came to the island kingdom of Geryon.

He found the cattle he sought grazing on the banks of a river and crept up on them silently. But nothing could escape the notice of the guard dog, Orthus, who was another ancient offspring of the monster Typhon and the half-nymph, half-serpent Echidna. The terrible hound rushed at Hercules with teeth bared, but the son of Zeus swung his club at the dog and smashed his skull with one blow. This caught the attention of the herdsman of Geryon, Eurytion, who came running, only to be killed in turn.

Hades also had a herd of cattle nearby, watched over by his servant Menoetius. Standing on a hill, this herdsman saw everything that had happened and warned Geryon that a thief was stealing his cattle. The three-bodied monster stormed into the meadow near the river and attacked the cattle raider, but he was struck down by Hercules' poisonous arrows. Hercules then herded the cattle into his golden bowl and ferried them across the sea to the mainland near Tartessus. Safely ashore, he returned the vessel to the sun god and began the long journey by land back to Greece.

Hercules led the cattle across the Iberian peninsula, then over the Pyrenees to the land of Liguria below the Alps. There he was attacked by two brothers, Ialebion and Dercynus, sons of Poseidon, who tried to steal the cattle from him. Hercules pounded them and their followers with so many stones that they were all killed and the land was covered with rocks.

For some reason, Hercules decided to turn south into Italy instead of taking the obvious route beyond the Po River into Greece. He crossed the Alps and followed the shore of the Tyrrhenian Sea past the cities of the Etruscans until he came to a quiet valley beneath seven hills on the banks of the Tiber River.

In a cave there under a rocky crag lived the half-human, fire-breathing monster Cacus, whose very name means evil. The ground around his dwelling was covered with blood and gore, while the rotting heads of his victims decorated the entrance to his dark home. The valley was deserted and Hercules had no idea anything lived there, so he placed the cattle in a pasture and retired for the night. While he lay sleeping, Cacus snuck up on the herd and grabbed four bulls and four heifers by the tails, forcing them to walk backward just as Hermes had done with the cattle of Apollo. He then led them into his black cave.

The next morning Hercules woke up and realized eight of his best animals were gone. He saw their tracks, but was baffled since they didn't lead away from the herd. He searched in vain and was at last ready to move on, when one of the cows in the cave let forth a mournful *Mooooo.*

Hercules heard this, grabbed his club, and ran toward the sound. Cacus panicked and piled giant boulders at the entrance of his cave, but Hercules diverted the Tiber River to reveal a back door to the cavern.

Cacus tried to escape, belching black smoke to create a thick cloud to hide behind, but to no avail. Hercules grabbed him by the neck and strangled him until his eyes popped out. He then soothed his missing cattle and herded them out of the cave to rejoin the herd and continue on their way.

Hercules apparently had a poor grasp of geography and made his way south to the straits separating Italy from Sicily, then realized at last that this was not the route to Greece. After retrieving a missing bull and killing a local king in a wrestling match, he made his way back up the Italian shore of the Adriatic and returned finally to the northern borders of Greece. There Hera, reverting to the trick she had used with Io, drove some of the cows mad with a gadfly so that they escaped across Thrace and swam the Hellespont to Asia. Hercules took the remainder of the herd south through Macedonia and Thessaly until he crossed the Isthmus of Corinth and came to Mycenae. After he had given the cattle to Eurystheus, the king added insult to injury by sacrificing the entire herd to Hercules' nemesis, the goddess Hera.

Hercules had now worked for Eurystheus for over eight years, fighting monsters and performing impossible deeds to purge himself of guilt for the murder of his wife and children. The king of Mycenae had almost given up trying to kill his unwanted servant and instead tried to keep him away for as long as possible in distant lands. With this in mind, the next labor he assigned Hercules was to fetch the golden apples of the Hesperides. The Hesperides were nymphs who lived somewhere in a remote region of the earth, though few knew where to look for them. Their apples were of pure gold growing on a tree given by Mother Earth to Zeus and Hera as a wedding present. They were guarded by a hundred-headed serpent named Ladon who could speak with a multitude of voices. But the surest protection of the apples was their unknown location. For Hercules to seize them, he would first have to find them.

He began by seeking out some sister nymphs of the Hesperides and asking them for directions. They had no idea where to look and sent him on to the ancient sea god Nereus. The shape-shifter did not care to be disturbed, so Hercules snuck up on him while he was sleeping and held him fast. Nereus changed into many different, terrifying forms to frighten him away, but Hercules held the god tight until he relented and revealed the location of the golden apples.

Nereus either gave very poor directions or Hercules was continuing his habit of getting lost, for his search for the Hesperides took him over most of the known world and beyond. His first stop was Egypt, where he entered the kingdom of Busiris. Years before when Egypt had suffered a famine for nine years, a soothsayer had come from the island of Cyprus and told the king the only way to restore the land was to sacrifice a foreigner to Zeus. Busiris took his advice and killed the Cypriot seer on his altar. Fertility returned to the land of the Nile, so the king decided thereafter to sacrifice every foreigner who came his way. When Hercules crossed into Egypt, he was seized by the king's soldiers and led to Busiris. While the king prepared for the sacrifice, Hercules broke through the ropes holding him and grabbed one of the priests by the ankles. He used him like a club to smash his countrymen, then killed Busiris and his sons.

Hercules next sailed north to the Greek island of Lindos, where he arrived famished. The first sight that met his eyes was a cart pulled by two bulls and a driver whipping them on. The man was terrified and ran away when Hercules came running toward him, so the hero helped himself to one of the bulls and, after dedicating the offering to Zeus, roasted and ate the animal. The angry driver stood on a nearby hill the whole time calling Hercules every foul name he could think of for stealing his bull. For generations afterward, the people of Lindos offered sacrifices to Hercules, but always with curses instead of prayers.

Hercules next wandered east to the Caucasus Mountains, where he found Prometheus chained to a rock, the eagle of Zeus gnawing at his liver. Just as the Titan had foreseen long before, the son of Zeus killed the eagle, broke his chains, and set him free. As thanks, Prometheus pointed out to his rescuer a fact obvious to any Greek, that Hesperides meant "nymphs of the west" and therefore he should direct his search in that direction. He also told him that once he arrived at the garden he should not try to retrieve the apples himself, but find a way to have mighty Atlas do the deed for him.

After a long march across the northern coast of Africa, Hercules arrived in the distant west and found Atlas holding up the sky. He asked the Titan if he would fetch the golden apples if Hercules took Atlas' place while he was gone. Atlas gladly agreed and handed the weight of the heavens to Hercules to bear on his shoulders. It didn't take Atlas long to return with the fruit, but he told Hercules that he had no desire to take the sky back and would deliver the apples to Eurystheus himself. Hercules groaned underneath the burden and asked Atlas if he would take back the sky for just a minute while he placed a pillow on his shoulders as padding. Atlas was strong but not very smart, so he agreed. Once the transfer was made, Hercules thanked Atlas kindly and went on his way, leaving the foolish Titan to hold up the heavens for eternity.

After a long journey, Hercules arrived back at Mycenae and presented the apples to the king. Eurystheus marveled at their beauty, but was so frightened at the prospect of having them in his possession that he refused to keep them. Hercules therefore gave them to Athena, who returned them to the Hesperides.

The final labor of Hercules was the most difficult and terrifying of all. Eurystheus ordered him to go to the underworld and bring back Cerberus, the three-headed, snake-tailed guardian of the kingdom of Hades. If Hercules failed at this task, as seemed likely, he would be trapped forever among the shades of the dead.

This was not a journey to be taken lightly, even by a man who had slain monsters and traveled to the ends of the earth. Hercules had a great deal of innocent blood on his hands—blood that might cause the lord of the underworld to keep him in his realm rather than allow him to return to the land of the living. Thus before he started down the long path to Hades, he went to the city of Eleusis to be initiated into the mysteries of Demeter. The goddess had shown her followers how their spirits might escape the eternal night of the underworld. Hercules very much wanted this knowledge in case things did not go well on his last labor.

Leaving Eleusis, Hercules proceeded to the cave of Taenarum near Sparta and began his journey down into the earth. For what seemed like days he walked through darkness until at last he reached the kingdom of shades. All the souls fled before him except for the Gorgon Medusa.

Hercules drew his sword against her, but she was only an empty phantom who could not harm him. The hero felt such pity for the shades that he slaughtered one of the cattle of Hades and gave its blood to the grateful souls of the dead. He also found Theseus and Pirithous sitting trapped on their chairs after trying to steal Persephone from her husband, Hades. They reached out to him for help, but he could release only Theseus, sending him on his way to the surface.

Finally Hercules came before the throne of Hades and asked if he might take Cerberus in fulfillment of his duty to Eurystheus and the oracle of Apollo. Hades agreed, provided he use none of his weapons to capture the hound. Thus Hercules approached the beast with only his lion skin and bare hands. They wrestled and fought, but the serpent fangs on the tail of Cerberus could not penetrate the skin of the Nemean Lion. At last Hercules grabbed Cerberus around his neck and held him so tight that the creature yielded. He then carried him all the way to the upper world and presented him to Eurystheus. The frightened king hiding in his jar pronounced the labors complete, then ordered Hercules to take Ceberus and leave, never to return. The hero, now purged of his guilt for killing his wife and sons, bade his uncle a bitter farewell and returned the guardian of the underworld to his dismal home.

Now that Hercules was finally finished with his labors, he decided it was time to marry again. He heard that his old archery teacher, King Eurytus of Oechalia, was offering his daughter Iole to anyone who could best him and his sons in a contest with the bow. Hercules went to the kingdom and won, but Eurytus refused to give him his daughter as his bride. The king was afraid that the girl and any children she might bear would end up dead at the hands of the unstable Hercules, as had Megara and her sons. Iphitus, a son of Eurytus, stood up for Hercules, proclaiming that his hero would never do anything so base. The king still refused and so Hercules stormed out of Oechalia swearing vengeance. He settled in the town of Tiryns on a rocky outcropping of the Argos plain not far from Mycenae.

Only a short time later someone noticed twelve of the prize horses of Eurytus were missing. The suspect was obvious, but again Iphitus defended Hercules to his father, saying he would journey to Tiryns himself to prove his innocence. Hercules welcomed the young man when he arrived and promised to take him on a tour of the surrounding countryside to show he was hiding no horses. He then gave him a fine meal and led him to the top of the high walls of Tiryns to see the beautiful view. While Iphitus was admiring the scenery, Hercules pushed him off to his death on the rocks below. He then went down to the nearby pasture to admire his new horses.

Hercules believed he could get away with anything and so went to King Neleus in Pylos to be purified of the crime of killing Iphitus. But the ruler refused as Eurytus was a friend of his. The frustrated Hercules soon realized he was developing a horrid disease, undoubtedly as a punishment for the murder. He once again made his way to Delphi to consult the oracle on what he must do to wash away the guilt of his impetuous actions, but the priestess of Apollo wanted nothing to do with him. She was disgusted that he would kill an innocent man and expect to be purified so easily. Hercules grew angry and grabbed a sacred tripod from the temple and began running down the road with it. He cried out that he would establish his own oracle if the god would not help him. Apollo saw this from his home on Olympus and flew down to Delphi, grabbing the tripod and fighting with the hero to take it back. Zeus finally had to send a lightning bolt to break up the squabble between his sons. Apollo then reluctantly told Hercules he could be cured of his disease if he would again serve as a slave, this time for three years. The god led him in chains to the nearest slave market, where he was purchased by the visiting queen Omphale of Lydia, who thought he would serve her quite well in bed.

During his three years as a slave, Hercules delighted in dressing up in Omphale's clothes for their romantic evenings together. One night the couple slept in a woodland cave after making love and were spied by the insatiable Pan. The goat god crept up on the pair in the dark and felt a woman's nightgown. Thinking he could rape Omphale as she slept, he mounted the bed, only to crawl on top of Hercules, who smashed him against the wall of the cave.

Hercules also had more traditional heroic adventures during his time as a slave, such as clearing the Lydian countryside of bandits and assorted evildoers. One such pair were the Cercopes, bandits who assaulted travelers along the road. One day they saw Hercules sleeping beside the road and decided to rob him. But before they knew what was happening, he had grabbed both of them and hung them upside down by their feet from a pole over his shoulders. As he carried them down the road, the two began to joke with each other. The hero was sunburned on his backside from all his journeys through the desert, so the Cercopes began to chant, "Beware the big black butt! Beware the big black butt!" Hercules laughed so hard at this that he decided to let them go. Zeus later turned the pair into monkeys.

After he had served his years as a slave with Omphale, Hercules decided it was time to settle some old scores. The first was against King Laomedon of Troy, who had cheated Hercules of his reward when he had rescued Laomedon's daughter Hesione from a sea monster. Hercules recruited enough soldiers to fill eighteen ships to attack the city, including Telamon, ruler of the island of Salamis near Athens. At first the Trojans got the better of the invaders and pushed them back from their city, but at last Telamon breached the walls and entered. Hercules was so upset that someone besides himself was first into Troy that he advanced on Telamon with his sword drawn. But the savvy king of Salamis quickly began to gather stones and pile them up. When Hercules saw the stones, he asked what Telamon was doing. "Building an altar to you as victor," calmly replied Telamon. Hercules was so flattered that he let Telamon live. Hercules then killed Laomedon and all the princes of Troy save one, a young boy named Podarces. When the princess Hesione was brought before Hercules, he offered to let her buy the freedom of one of the Trojan captives. Hesione cleverly chose her brother Podarces to preserve the royal line, giving Hercules her veil as his price. The lad was thereafter known as Priam, Greek for "ransomed one." He later became king of Troy and as an old man ruled the city during the Trojan War.

After assaults on other kings and princes who had once offended him, Hercules at last collected a large army and marched against Augeas, who had refused his promised reward when he had cleaned his filthy stables. He killed the king and his sons, then instituted a series of athletic contests in nearby Olympia in celebration. These were afterward repeated every four years and came to be known as the Olympic Games.

• • •

After so many adventures, romances, and bitter disappointments, Hercules still did not have a wife. But then he heard of a beautiful princess named Deianira in western Greece and determined to make her his own. However, the maiden had another powerful suitor, a river god named Achelous. Hercules eagerly fought him for the hand of Deianira. It was a difficult contest, as the river god had the body of a water serpent and a deadly horn on his forehead. The two suitors wrestled and grappled and butted heads until at last Hercules grabbed Achelous by his horn and ripped it from his head, ending the fight.

Hercules took his new bride and traveled east to settle the city of Trachis near the pass of Thermopylae. Along the way they came to the swift Evanus River, where the centaur Nessus made a meager living ferrying passengers across the stream on his back. He had lived in Arcadia years before until Hercules drove him out after the battle at the cave of the centaur Pholus. Since then Nessus had lived a humiliating existence serving as a beast of burden for travelers. The last person he had wanted to see was Hercules, but when the hero appeared at the banks of his stream, Nessus had little choice but to ferry Deianira across as Hercules demanded.

Perhaps it was his lascivious centaur nature or perhaps it was a foolish act of vengeance, but halfway across the river Nessus began to fondle Deianira and then tried to rape her. In an instant Hercules shot him through with one of his poisoned arrows. As he lay dying on the far bank, Nessus seemed contrite. "Take some of my blood," he told the woman. "It is a powerful love potion in case you ever need it." Deianira trusted Hercules and believed he would never leave her for another woman, but decided to keep some of the blood just in case.

After they reached Trachis, Hercules made a home for himself and Deianira, but in time decided on one last act of revenge. He was still angry at his old archery teacher Eurytus, who had refused to give him his daughter Iole after he had won her fairly in a contest with his bow. He therefore raised an army and took the king's city, killing Eurytus and his surviving sons. He then took Iole home to Trachis as a concubine.

Deianira took one look at the beautiful young maiden and knew it was time to use the blood of Nessus. She smeared it on a cloak and presented it to Hercules as he was about to sacrifice to his father Zeus. Her husband was grateful and draped it around his shoulders—but then something terrible began to happen. The cloak burned his skin like a blazing fire. Hercules screamed in agony and writhed on the earth, but he could not remove the cloak. He begged someone to kill him to end the pain, but no one dared approach him. Slowly the poisonous blood of deceitful Nessus ate away his flesh until at last Hercules built a funeral pyre for himself and ascended it. He dragged himself to the top and asked a young man named Philoctetes to set it ablaze, giving him his bows and arrows for his service. In an instant the hero was consumed by the flames and his torture finally ended.

When his friends and family went to collect his bones and ashes after the fire had cooled, they could find nothing. Zeus had snatched up his son and taken his soul to Mount Olympus, where he became an immortal god. He was reconciled with his stepmother Hera and married Hebe, the goddess of youth. There in the heavens, honored by gods and mortals alike, Hercules at last found the eternal glory he had sought all his life. In the words of an early Greek hymn:

> I will sing a song of Hercules, son of Zeus, mightiest of all the men who walked the earth. Alcmene bore him in Thebes, the city of beautiful dances, when the dark-clouded son of Cronus lay with her. The hero wandered over the earth at the orders of King Eurystheus. He performed many dangerous tasks and suffered much, but now he dwells in snowcapped Olympus with slim-ankled Hebe as his wife. Hail to you, lord, son of Zeus. Grant us prosperity and excellence.

OEDIPUS

L ong before Hercules was born at Thebes, the city had been founded because of a wandering cow and an ill-tempered dragon. Cadmus had come from Lebanon to look for his sister Europa, who had been kidnapped from her home by Zeus disguised as a bull. After searching high and low, he at last went to the oracle at Delphi to ask Apollo where he might find his sister. The oracle said to forget about Europa and instead seek out a heifer. Once he found this animal, he should follow it until it collapsed from exhaustion. Wherever the cow finally stopped, he should sacrifice the animal and establish a new city.

This all seemed very strange to Cadmus, but one did not lightly ignore the instructions of a god. He left Delphi and walked down the mountain road leading east until he came upon a herd of cattle. He had no idea which cow he was supposed to follow, but he noticed that one had an unusual mark on its side like the orb of a full moon. This seemed like a sign, so he bought the beast from the herdsman and began to follow it as it wandered away. Often it would stop to eat grass or drink from a stream, but it slowly made its way down the mountain and past lakes, over hills and across plains, until at last it lay down on a ridge above a broad plain in the land of Boeotia north of Athens.

It was a good spot for a city, with a citadel for protection and well-watered fields all around. Cadmus built an altar and sent some of his companions to a nearby spring to draw water for a sacrifice. Suddenly he heard a scream and rushed toward the sound, only to find his friends lying dead at the feet of a mighty, hissing dragon. This guardian of the spring was said to be the offspring of Ares himself, but Cadmus did not hesitate to attack the serpent with his spear and sword. After a fierce battle, the Phoenician prince slew the dragon and avenged the death of his companions. Athena then appeared to him and told him to knock the teeth out of the creature and sow them in a field like seeds. Cadmus was used to strange orders from divinities by now, so he removed the teeth and planted them in a furrow.

He had no sooner sown the last tooth than something began to rise from the field. First Cadmus saw the tips of hundreds of spears break the ground, then crested helmets, then the faces, chests, and legs of men clad in shining armor. A whole army of grim-faced warriors had risen from the dragon's teeth. Cadmus was so startled that he grabbed his own sword to defend himself. "Don't draw it," said the soldier closest to him. "Stay out of things that aren't your business." And with that the newborn warriors took to fighting and killing one another. Blood covered the field as Cadmus watched in amazement until at last only five fighters were left alive. At the command of Athena, the survivors ceased from battle and laid aside their weapons. These five became the founding fathers of the leading families of Thebes, under the rule of Cadmus their king.

But a city of men alone has no future, so women were found for the warriors and a queen for Cadmus. Her name was Harmonia, the beautiful daughter of Ares and Aphrodite. The gods themselves attended the wedding and presented gifts to the happy couple, including an exquisite necklace and robe for Harmonia. Afterward they lived a long and tragic life together. All four of their daughters—Autonoe, Ino, Semele, and Agave—led lives marked by violence, insanity, or bereavement. Autonoe's son Actaeon was torn apart by his own hounds when he saw Artemis naked. Semele was destroyed by the radiant glory of Zeus after becoming pregnant with Dionysus. Ino went mad and jumped into the sea, while Agave unwittingly tore apart her own son Pentheus after he refused to honor Dionysus. Only Polydorus, the son of Cadmus and Harmonia, passed his days in peace, fathering a son named Labdacus, who in turn fathered a future king of Thebes named Laius. Cadmus and his wife, Harmonia, ended their days in a most unharmonious fashion, exiled to Illyria and finally turned into snakes. But the family of Cadmus thrived until his descendant Menoeceus bore two children, Creon and his sister Jocasta, who in time married her distant cousin Laius and bore a son.

Laius never meant to make love to his bride. After he became king of Thebes, the oracle at Delphi told him that he would die at the hands of his own son. He was therefore determined never to impregnate Jocasta, but one night he had too much to drink and slept with her anyway. When she gave birth, Laius ordered the baby exposed on the slopes of Mount Cithaeron. He fastened the poor child's feet together with an iron pin and gave him to a trusted shepherd to abandon in the wilderness. Laius was certain he would never see his son again.

But the kindly shepherd could not bear to leave the baby to die, so he gave the infant to a visiting friend from the city of Corinth who promised to take him far from Thebes. The friend in turn gave the boy to Polybus, the childless king of Corinth, and his wife, Merope. They loved him as their own and gave him the name Oedipus ("swollen foot") because of the injury from his pierced ankles. Oedipus grew up happily as a prince of Corinth, but when he entered adulthood one of his friends drank too much at a party and said he was not a true son of the king. Oedipus went to Polybus, but neither he nor the queen would tell him anything about his origins. Eager to discover the truth at any cost, he journeyed to the oracle at Delphi to find out if he was adopted. The priestess dismissed his question and instead gave him the terrible news that he was going to kill his own father and marry his mother. Rather than commit such unthinkable acts of murder and incest against his beloved parents in Corinth, he fled Delphi, vowing he would never return home.

Oedipus made his way east full of despair. At a place where three roads met, he was forced into the ditch by a man in a chariot who ran over his foot, then hit him with a stick. Oedipus had been in a bad mood ever since Delphi and this incident did not improve his disposition. He angrily pulled the man from the chariot and killed him with his sword, then turned on the rest of the party and slew all but one, who fled in panic.

When Oedipus came at last to Thebes, he found the city in an uproar. A creature called the Sphinx had arrived in town and was terrorizing the citizens. This beast—with the head of a woman, the body of a lion, and the wings of an eagle—was yet another offspring of the ancient monsters Typhon and Echidna. She perched on a mountain outside the city and swooped in whenever she saw a likely victim. Being fair-minded, the creature always asked the terrified citizen a riddle first, promising she would let him go if he answered correctly. No one knew the answer and so all were quickly devoured by the Sphinx. The Theban king Laius had left town to ask the oracle at Delphi what the city could do to rid itself of the murderous beast, but had not returned and was presumed dead. In desperation, the regent Creon had offered the kingdom and the hand of the queen Jocasta to anyone who could solve the riddle and drive the Sphinx away.

When Oedipus arrived at Thebes, the winged creature saw him and flew down to block his way. The Sphinx had expected him to be terrified, but he calmly sat down on a stone and waited. The monster explained the rules and consequences of her contest, then posed the riddle:

> What walks on four legs in the morning,
> two legs at midday,
> and three in the evening?

The Sphinx was licking her lips in anticipation of her next meal, but Oedipus said:

> The answer is man.
> An infant crawls on all fours during the morning of its life,
> then walks on two legs as an adult,
> then finally uses the third leg of a cane in his twilight years.

The Sphinx could not believe he had solved the riddle. Defeated, she threw herself off a cliff to her death. Oedipus then entered Thebes as a triumphant hero, happily taking the crown and marrying the still-youthful queen Jocasta. In time the happy couple had four fine children, two boys and two girls. It seemed to Oedipus as if all his troubles were over.

Oedipus ruled a happy and prosperous Thebes for many years. But one day things began to go terribly wrong. The cattle stopped bearing young and the women of the town could not bring a child to term. A plague then descended on the city killing young and old alike. It seemed as if Thebes was under a curse, but no one knew what to do. Rich sacrifices to the gods changed nothing, while all the local oracles were silent. Finally a delegation of city elders came to the palace to beseech Oedipus to do something. He had saved them from the Sphinx—could he not also rescue them from this new pestilence? "Oedipus, mightiest man in the sight of all, we implore you to protect us. Come, save our city! You have brought nothing but good fortune to us. If you can't help us, you will soon rule over a wilderness."

Oedipus replied, "My friends, believe me, I know about the ills that plague this city, but no one is more sick than I. As king, I bear the burden of all. I have sent my brother-in-law Creon to the oracle of Apollo at Delphi to see if the god might reveal to us the cause of this evil."

Creon soon returned to Thebes and brought news to the king. The oracle had said the citizens were suffering because they allowed the murder of their old king Laius to go unpunished. Unless Thebes brought his murderer to justice, the curse would remain and the city would wither away. Oedipus confessed that he knew very little about the previous king, so Creon explained to him that Laius had been killed by a band of robbers years earlier while he was on the way to Delphi to seek news on how to rid city of the Sphinx. His whole party had been killed, save for one servant who ran away. The city would have pursued the murderers, but they were suffering so under the Sphinx that they could not spare any men at the time. After the monster was gone and a new king on the throne, it seemed best to forget the murder and move on.

When he heard this, Oedipus chastised the people of Thebes for failing to avenge their king. He vowed to the gods that he would find the murderer and cleanse the city of its pollution, no matter the consequences. If the killer was found inside the walls of the city, even among the royal household, he would exile that man and make Thebes whole again.

The first thing Oedipus did was call together the citizens and issue a proclamation. Whoever had any information on the death of Laius was to come forward and tell everything he knew. Even if he was guilty of the crime, he would be allowed to leave Thebes unharmed. Anyone who revealed who the guilty party was would be richly rewarded. On the other hand, if someone withheld information, he would be driven from his home, have all his property confiscated, and be denied participation in sacrifices to the gods.

No one came forward, but the elders suggested the king seek the counsel of the prophet Tiresias, who spoke for the gods. Oedipus assured them he had already sent for the seer and expected him at any moment. Soon Tiresias arrived in the presence of the king, but was most reluctant to speak. Oedipus implored him, "Tiresias, you must help me. I implore you not to turn away from your city in this time of trouble. Tell us who killed Laius."

"Let me go home, Oedipus. The words I have to say would not please you, but only add to your sorrows."

"My sorrows? How could you make matters worse for me when my city is suffering so? I charge you by the gods to reveal what you know or face my wrath."

"All right, I'll speak then—it's you, Oedipus. You're the murderer you seek!"

"That's impossible, you pathetic liar! Did Creon pay you to say this? Is this a plot to seize my throne?"

"Forget Creon. This is all about you, Oedipus. I may be blind in my eyes, but you are blind in your ears and mind! Let me leave or I'll tell you things even worse."

"Get out of here and never let me see you again! Prophets are nothing but trouble, greedy liars who care more about gold than gods!"

After Tiresias had departed, Oedipus sent for Creon. When his brother-in-law arrived, the king harangued him with cruel words and biting accusations. Creon proclaimed his innocence, but Oedipus would hear none of it. Jocasta, the wife of Oedipus and sister of Creon, arrived and chastised both men for engaging in such an unseemly display in public. Creon stormed away and Jocasta demanded to know what the trouble was. After Oedipus said that Creon was plotting against him, his wife assured him he was being foolish. Moreover, the words of so-called prophets were worthless. Seers and oracles were for the ignorant rabble—and she could prove it. Laius had once received an oracle that he would be killed by his own son, but this was ignorant folly since his only offspring had perished as a baby years before. Laius had been murdered by a band of brigands at a place where three roads met.

A chill went down the spine of Oedipus when he heard these words. He demanded details from Jocasta. Where did it happen? How many bandits? How many were in the king's party? Were any witnesses still alive? She said there was a shepherd, a family slave, who had witnessed the murder and fled, but he had requested to be sent far into the fields when he saw that Oedipus was ruling Thebes. She could send for him, but it hardly seemed worth the bother. Oedipus insisted, however, and then explained why he was so scared. He had in fact once killed a man at a crossing place of three roads, but he had been alone. If the witness could confirm it was a group of men who had murdered Laius, then his fears would disappear. But if there was a solitary killer, Oedipus feared he might have indeed slain the king, though of course the man could not have been his father.

Before the servant could arrive, an elderly messenger from Corinth entered the gates of Thebes. He bore the sad news that King Polybus, the father of Oedipus, had died of old age. Oedipus wept to hear about the death of the man who had raised him, but he also rejoiced that the bitter prophecy of Delphi could not now come true. He could not kill his father Polybus if the king was already dead of natural causes. Jocasta told him she had been right all along and that he surely realized now that oracles were worthless. He told her he still harbored some fear that he might commit incest with his mother, Merope, by some horrible twist of fate, but Jocasta once again dismissed such a notion: "Oedipus, seers have no knowledge of the future. It's best to enjoy one's life not worrying about the fears buried deep inside us. Many men have bedded their own mothers in their dreams. The one who takes such fears seriously will be miserable."

The messenger from Corinth saw that the king was upset and asked if there was anything he could do to ease his mind. Oedipus told the old man about the dual prophecies of murder and incest and how he had fled from Corinth to assure that they would not come true. The old man took him by the arm and said he could put his mind at ease. Polybus was dead, but he need not fear fulfilling the oracle's second prediction of sleeping with his mother, Merope. He knew for certain that Polybus and Merope were not his true parents. He himself had given Oedipus as a baby to the king and queen since they could not have children of their own. The messenger had received him from a shepherd—near Thebes, in fact—who had rescued him from abandonment.

He could prove it, since the baby he brought to Corinth had pierced ankles, a wound that would still be visible. He assured Oedipus that he should give no more thought to dark prophecies.

Jocasta had turned white as a ghost while she listened to the Corinthian messenger. She then begged Oedipus to let the matter go and inquire no further. He thought the queen was worried that he, as the father of her children, might have been low-born, but he assured her it was the quality of a man, not his lineage, that mattered. She ran into the palace crying out that he should never learn who he really was. But Oedipus was determined to unravel the mystery of his origins.

The shepherd who had witnessed the murder of Laius at last arrived, so Oedipus began to question him in the presence of the old messenger from Corinth. The Theban slave hesitated to answer the king's questions, but he finally confessed what he knew. Yes, he had received Oedipus from his father as a baby. Yes, he had given him as an infant to the Corinthian messenger. Yes, he had seen him kill King Laius alone. Oedipus then demanded to know who his real father was, but the shepherd would not answer. Finally, with threats of dire punishment, the king forced the slave to tell him the truth. The shepherd confessed it was King Laius himself who had told him to dispose of his son, since he had received an oracle that the child would one day kill him.

The agony of Oedipus was almost beyond words: "No! No! No! Everything is clear now. O radiant sun, may I look on you today for the last time. I am cursed in my birth, cursed in my marriage, cursed in my killing."

Jocasta had been so distraught to discover the truth that she had gone to her incestuous marriage bed and hung herself from the rafters. When Oedipus saw his wife and mother dead, he pulled the golden pins from her dress and gouged out his own eyes so that he might see no more suffering. Oedipus vowed he would abide by his own decree and exile himself from Thebes to roam the earth as a penniless beggar, accompanied only by his daughter Antigone. He left the kingdom and the care of his other children, Ismene, Eteocles, and Polynices, in the charge of Creon, then was led out of the gates of the city, a man cursed by the gods above all others.

• • •

For years Oedipus and Antigone wandered the land of Greece, shunned by all and welcomed nowhere. The former king was reduced to the life of a beggar by the side of the road. But in Thebes, his sons Eteocles and Polynices had inherited rule of the city from their uncle Creon once they came of age. The brothers agreed to share the throne, alternating as king year by year. It was an equitable arrangement, but when the first year was over and Polynices was ready to take over, Eteocles refused to step down and drove his brother from the city. Polynices fled to Argos, but not before he stole the necklace and robe the gods had given to his ancestor Harmonia. All this turmoil seemed fitting to Oedipus when he heard the news, for he had cursed both sons for turning their backs on him since his exile.

In those days Adrastus ruled over Argos. He welcomed refugees from many Greek cities in hope that he might use them someday to expand his own influence. Aside from Polynices, the city sheltered Tydeus, a son of the late King Oeneus of Calydon. Tydeus had murdered a relative in anger and fled to Adrastus for protection, but neither he nor Polynices was happy in exile. The pair often fought, more in frustration of being deprived of their kingdoms than in anger with the other. One day when they had set on each other with swords drawn, Adrastus came to the courtyard hoping either to stop the fight or encourage the two to kill each other and finally rid him of their tiresome company. Suddenly he noticed that Polynices had a lion painted on his shield, while the shield of Tydeus was decorated with a boar. The oracle at Delphi had once advised him to "yoke his daughters to a lion and boar," but he had not understood the cryptic message until now. He married his two daughters to Polynices and Tydeus, then promised both young men he would help them regain their kingdoms, starting with Thebes.

Adrastus recruited the finest warriors in Argos for the expedition, including his brother-in-law Amphiaraus, a gifted seer. Because of his ability, Amphiaraus could foresee the grim outcome of the war and so at first refused to go. But the soothsayer's wife, Eriphyle, was long used to settling quarrels between her husband and brother. She also had an eye for fine gifts. Polynices therefore came to her secretly one evening and offered her the necklace and robe of Harmonia if she would convince Amphiaraus to support the expedition. She took the bribe and reconciled her husband to his fate, but he made his son vow to avenge what he knew would be his certain death before the walls of Thebes.

With preparations complete, the seven warriors set out leading a vast army. They were King Adrastus, the seer Amphiaraus, Polynices, Tydeus, and three nobles from Argos and Arcadia named Capaneus, Parthenopaeus, and Hippomedon. Each warrior would lead an assault on one of the fabled seven gates of Thebes.

The oracle of Delphi had long played a major role in the life of Oedipus and his family. Now, with an army marching on Thebes, the god once again spoke through his priestess and declared that whichever side possessed Oedipus—or at least his bones—would win the war. Oedipus, long reviled and cursed by all, had suddenly become a prize much desired by both his sons.

The wanderings of Oedipus and Antigone had taken them to an outlying district of Athens called Colonus. Here the old blind man sat down on a rock in a sacred grove and declared to his daughter he would never leave. He had been told long before that one day he would come to a place sacred to the dark Furies and there he would die, bringing a blessing to that town. The local people were horrified when they discovered who had taken up residence among them, but it would be an offense to the gods to drive a supplicant away. Theseus, the king of Athens, arrived and promised he would protect the visitor from all harm. Oedipus thanked him and said that his body, wretched as it was, would bring great benefits to his city.

After Theseus left, Ismene, the other daughter of Oedipus, found her father there and told him of recent events in Thebes. She also revealed that both her brothers were anxious to bring him to their side in the upcoming war. Soon Creon arrived from Thebes to speak for Eteocles and all the citizens in the besieged town. He urged Oedipus to look beyond the troubles of the old days and think well of Thebes, even though it had brought so much pain to him. Oedipus flatly refused and told Creon to leave him alone. He then called for his daughters, but Creon revealed that he was holding them as hostages nearby to ensure that Oedipus would return to Thebes with him. The old man cursed Creon, but was powerless to help Antigone and Ismene. Fortunately Theseus returned at this point, rescuing the young women and driving Creon away.

It wasn't long before Oedipus' son Polynices showed up at Colonus and begged his father to help him retake Thebes. He was the elder son, he argued, and therefore Eteocles should yield the throne to him: "I know I have been a poor son, Father, but that can change. Give me another chance, join my army in honor. We are both exiles, you and I, driven from our city unjustly. Eteocles is a tyrant who mocks us both. Please, come with me and we will win!"

Oedipus not only refused Polynices but spat at his son and cursed him, saying he and his brother were doomed to slay each before the walls of Thebes. Polynices knew the power of a father's curse and realized his fate was sealed. He left Colonus, making his sisters promise to give him a decent burial.

With only Theseus in attendance, Oedipus walked to a hidden part of the grove and prepared to die. He saluted the life-giving earth and the shining sky, then suddenly, without crashing thunderbolts or a whirlwind from the heavens, Oedipus was gone. By what manner he died or where his body lay, none could say except Theseus, who was pledged to silence. With Oedipus perished all hope for his sons at Thebes. For his daughters, it seemed that only suffering lay ahead.

When Polynices and the Argive army arrived at Thebes, the seven captains met before the city to sacrifice to the gods for victory. They cut the throat of a bull over an overturned iron shield and dipped their hands in the blood. They swore by Ares, Hera, and the god Panic that they would either reduce Thebes to rubble or they themselves would die there. Then they drew lots to see which gate each leader would attack. By chance or by the curse of Oedipus, Polynices was assigned the gate held by his brother, Eteocles.

The Thebans also made preparations with sacrifices and solemn vows. The seer Tiresias informed them that the only way they could save their city was by human sacrifice. The victim must be from one of the leading families, a descendant of the warriors who grew from dragon's teeth, and he must never have lain with a woman. The only man who fit this description was young Menoeceus, a son of Creon. His father refused to offer him up to the gods, but Menoeceus had a deep love for Thebes and so killed himself outside the walls in full view of the enemy.

The slaughter that followed was brutal on both sides. The Argive leader Capaneus heroically scaled the walls of the town, shouting that not even Zeus could stop him from taking Thebes. In answer, a lightning bolt shot down from a clear sky and killed the boastful warrior. A huge boulder crushed the skull of another Argive captain, Parthenopaeus, while his fellow captain Hippomedon was also slain. A Theban warrior named Melanippus attacked Tydeus and mortally wounded him, but not before the Argive leader slew him first. As Tydeus lay dying on the battlefield, Athena, who had always favored the brave warrior, went to Zeus and asked if he would make him immortal. The ruler of the gods consented, but the seer Amphiaraus knew Athena's intentions. He hated Tydeus for dragging him into this futile war and was determined to thwart the goddess, so he cut off the head of Melanippus and brought it to his dying enemy. Tydeus so despised Melanippus that he broke open his skull and began to eat his brains raw. Athena was disgusted at this bestial sight and smashed the vial containing the potion of immortality, leaving Tydeus to perish in the dirt. Soon after this, the seer Amphiaraus avoided a spear in the back only to be swallowed by a great fissure that opened in the earth.

Of the seven who had marched against Thebes, only Adrastus and Polynices now remained. The king of Argos fled the battlefield on the divine horse Arion, offspring of Demeter when she was raped by Poseidon. But Polynices stood firm before the walls of the city and called forth Eteocles to fight him in single combat. In the no-man's-land between the two armies the brothers met. Polynices prayed to Hera that he might soak his hands in the blood of his fallen brother, just as Eteocles prayed to Zeus that he might pierce the heart of his sibling.

With trumpets echoing the call to battle, Polynices and Eteocles ran at each other with spears ready. They threw and missed, then clashed like wild boars with swords drawn. Whenever one would strike with his weapon, the other would meet it with his shield. Neither was able to break through the defenses of the other and gain advantage. But then Eteocles slipped on a pebble and gave Polynices the chance to drive his spear through his brother's calf. Wounded, but not down, Eteocles hurled his own spear through the breast of his opponent, but Polynices did not fall. Both wounded men stumbled across the dust in agony, then took up their swords to continue the fight. Eteocles stepped back with his left foot feigning retreat, then swung his sword with his right arm against Polynices, piercing his side and shattering his spine. The elder brother fell to the ground seemingly dead, but just as Eteocles dropped his own weapon to strip his armor, Polynices rose up with his last breath and plunged his sword into his brother's bowels. Side by side the two sons of Oedipus lay in death, ruling the bloody battlefield together amid a sea of corpses.

After the dust had settled, Creon once again assumed rule of Thebes and gathered all the bodies of the fallen Theban warriors for a proper burial. But contrary to all custom, he ordered that the corpses of the enemy—including his nephew Polynices—be left to rot on the battlefield. Moreover he ordered that anyone who buried any of them would be executed. Everyone was shocked at this decree. If someone was buried, even with a sprinkling of dust over his body, he could cross the river Styx and enter the underworld at peace. But without burial, he was doomed to wander the far bank of the river for a hundred years in misery. No Greek would deny burial to even his worst enemy for fear of offending the gods.

Antigone and Ismene returned to Thebes, having nowhere else to go, and heard the proclamation of Creon in horror. Ismene was mortified at the thought of her brother's corpse lying on the plain, a feast for birds and dogs, but she accepted the decree. Antigone, however, placed family honor above impious rules and determined to give Polynices a decent burial. Even her engagement to Creon's son Haemon and the pleas of Ismene to reconsider would not change her mind.

When Creon received news that someone had sprinkled dust on the body of Polynices, he launched a search for the culprit. He was shocked to discover that it was his own niece who had disobeyed him: "Antigone, do you admit that you did this shameful deed or do you deny it?"

"I admit it proudly. I knew about your decree, but there are laws more ancient and binding than those you proclaim. Zeus and Justice demand a proper burial for the dead, no matter what you say. You are a fool to think you can stand against the gods!"

"And you are a fool to think you can stand against me! The city will fall apart if I let a mere woman scorn my laws. You will pay the price for what you have done."

"Go ahead and kill me! I would rather die honoring the gods than live under your wicked rules."

Creon then ordered her to be sealed in a cave until she was dead. Haemon pleaded with his father to rescind his judgment and spare his bride, but not even the words of his own son could bend his will. Tiresias then appeared before the new king and told him he was offending the gods by his impious actions. Relent, he warned, or you will suffer more than you can imagine. Creon hesitated but by the time he had changed his mind, it was too late. Antigone had hung herself in her cave and Haemon, seeing his love dead, struck out at his father with his sword, then plunged it into his own heart. When Creon's wife heard that their son was dead, she committed suicide as well. Like Oedipus before him, Creon at last realized in sorrow that men were helpless before the will of the gods.

ARGONAUTS

Aeolus was the grandson of Deucalion and Pyrrha, the pair who had escaped the great flood sent by Zeus to destroy humanity. He ruled over Magnesia in Thessaly, south of Mount Olympus, and had seven sons, including a boy named Athamas. This young man migrated to Boeotia and became king of Orchomenus, not far from Thebes. A king needs a queen, so he married a woman named Nephele ("cloud") and by her had a son named Phrixus and a daughter Helle. In time Athamas noticed Nephele was looking older, so he sent her away and married young Ino, daughter of King Cadmus of Thebes. She bore Athamas two sons, then began to plot the death of Phrixus to put her own boys on the throne.

Ino went to the women who stored seed grain for the kingdom and bribed them to parch it before planting. Naturally the grain did not grow and Orchomenus soon faced starvation, so Athamas sent heralds to Delphi to ask Apollo how he could save his kingdom. Ino intercepted the messengers on their return and persuaded them to give a false report to the king. They told Athamas that the oracle had said the only way to save Orchomenus was to sacrifice his firstborn son, Phrixus, to Zeus.

The king was horrified at the thought of killing his child, but the people of the land cried out that Phrixus must die so they could live. Athamas therefore led Phrixus to the altar with a sharpened knife in hand and began to bind him for the sacrifice. At that moment, a golden ram appeared beside the altar—some say it was sent by Nephele, who had received it as a gift from Hermes—and both Phrixus and his sister Helle climbed on its back. As Athamas watched in relief and Ino in outrage, the two children flew away on the ram high into the sky.

While the brother and sister soared over the sea near Troy, Helle lost her grip and fell to her death in the straits between Europe and Asia.

This passage was known ever after as the Hellespont. But Phrixus flew on across the Black Sea until he came to the land of Colchis beneath the Caucasus Mountains. The ruler of this kingdom was Aeetes, a son of Helios the sun god. One of the king's sisters was the powerful witch Circe and the other was Pasiphae, wife of Minos of Crete and mate of his favorite bull. Aeetes happily received Phrixus and gave him one of his own daughters to be his wife. In gratitude for his escape from certain death, Phrixus sacrificed the golden ram to Zeus and gave its fleece to Aeetes. The king of Colchis hung the priceless gift on a tree in a local grove sacred to Ares. There it was guarded by a fierce dragon that killed anyone who dared approach.

Athamas had a brother named Salmoneus who fathered a beautiful daughter named Tyro. This princess was married to a cousin Cretheus, but she was in love with a local river god named Enipeus. She would often sneak away from her household duties and wander alone by her lover's river, waiting for him to come to her. There Poseidon saw Tyro and determined to have her. He disguised himself as Enipeus and made love with her on the soft grass, a giant purple wave hanging over the pair to hide their amorous encounter from prying eyes. When he was done, Poseidon revealed his true identity to Tyro and told her she would soon have twin sons. Then he dove back into the sea and did not think of her again.

In due time Tyro bore Pelias and Neleus, handsome boys who grew into strong men born to rule. Pelias became king of Iolcus on the coast of Thessaly, a land rich in cattle and horses, but he drove away his brother Neleus, who founded a dynasty in sandy Pylos in the far southwest of Greece. Tyro also had two sons, Aeson and Pheres, by her mortal husband.

Pelias kept his half brother Aeson under careful watch in Iolcus as he was considered by many to be the rightful heir to the kingdom. Aeson knew his life depended on keeping quiet and so caused no trouble for King Pelias. When Aeson's wife bore him a son, the couple announced that the infant had died so that Pelias would fear no future threat to his throne. But Aeson secretly took the baby to be raised by the wise centaur Chiron on the slopes of nearby Mount Pelion, where the boy, named Jason, was educated and grew into manhood.

Pelias was ever-vigilant against threats to his power as the years went by. He had learned from an oracle that if a man wearing only one sandal ever arrived in his kingdom, his rule was in grave danger. He was therefore always on guard for such a strange sight.

When Jason reached maturity, he boldly decided to journey down the mountain to the town of Iolcus and claim the throne from his uncle Pelias. Soon he came to a stream swollen with spring rains. He saw there a feeble old woman who approached him and asked if he might carry her across. She had sought the help of many before him, but all had scorned her. Jason was in a great hurry, but he took the woman on his back and bore her safely to the far shore, although he did slip and lose a sandal in the mud midway across. She thanked him for his kindness and he went on his way, not realizing he had just met the goddess Hera. The wife of Zeus was angry at King Pelias for failing to sacrifice to her properly, so she was testing Jason at the river to see if he was worthy to replace his uncle. After he had showed her such kindness, Hera set in motion an elaborate scheme to do away with Pelias.

Jason arrived in Iolcus just as the king was conducting a grand sacrifice to his father, Poseidon. When Pelias was finished, he was startled to notice a young man in the crowd wearing only one sandal. After discovering who he was, he approached Jason and welcomed his nephew to Iolcus. He then posed to him a hypothetical question—what would you do, as king, if you knew a certain subject of yours was going to kill you?

Jason laughed and thought of the most outrageous method possible to get rid of such a man: "I would send him off to fetch the fabled Golden Fleece."

"An excellent idea," responded the king. He then looked Jason in the eye and said, "Go fetch the Golden Fleece."

As a young man eager to prove himself, Jason gladly accepted the challenge from his uncle and began his preparations. He knew he would need an extraordinary ship for such a long and dangerous journey, so he asked a distant cousin named Argus to build a fifty-oared craft to sail to Colchis. The goddess Athena herself advised Argus on the construction and fitted a special prow made of oak onto the ship. The wood of the prow came from the sacred grove of Zeus at Dodona in western Greece and had the miraculous gift of speech. When the craft was finally complete, Jason christened it the *Argo* in honor of its builder.

There are many different stories about who accompanied Jason on the *Argo*, but all agree that he invited the greatest warriors in Greece into his fellowship. First there was Hercules, who interrupted one of his labors to make the journey. Next were the great bard Orpheus and the two brothers of Helen, Castor and Pollux. Zetes and Calais also came, two winged sons of Boreas, god of the north wind. Peleus, the grandson of Zeus and father of Achilles, was there, as was his brother Telamon, the sire of Ajax. Some say Theseus of Athens sailed with Jason, while others say the famous female warrior Atalanta also accompanied the men—though most claim they would never have included a woman on such an adventure. Everyone agrees that Meleager, brother of Hercules' wife Deianira, joined Jason. Idmon the seer was also among the chosen, as was Tiphys, who served as helmsman. There were many others who joined the band of sailors, all great men of valor, known ever after as the Argonauts.

The sailors unanimously elected Hercules as their leader, but the hero refused such an honor. He said he would go on the quest only if Jason acted as their captain. The young prince accepted and made a long speech promising the men undying glory. Soon even the ship was tired of listening and the oak prow shouted out that they should begin. The men all took their places on the rowing benches and cast off. The *Argo* then slipped away from the port of Iolcus and set out into the Aegean Sea, while King Pelias watched from shore, certain he would never see Jason again.

After a few days, the Argonauts came to Lemnos in the northern Aegean. The arrival of the ship threw the inhabitants of the island into a panic, for they believed the Thracians were descending on them to seek revenge. The men of Lemnos had long raided Thrace for treasure and slaves, especially the exotic women of that northern land. The island pirates grew so fond of their Thracian captives that they rejected their legitimate wives. Some say this was revenge from Aphrodite because the Lemnian women had neglected to sacrifice to her, but whatever the cause, the island wives soon had had enough. They killed their husbands along with their Thracian concubines. Ever since, Lemnos had been an island of women alone.

The widows soon discovered that life without men was not so bad. Previously they had spent their long days cooking, washing, and weaving for husbands who cared little for them. Now they herded their own cattle and plowed their own fields. Their husbands had always complained that men had the more difficult lot, but the women found that their previous domestic duties were far more onerous and confining than their new life.

The men of the *Argo* knew none of this when they sailed into the harbor of Lemnos looking for fresh water, but the eerie stillness of the island unnerved them. They sent their herald, Aethalides, a son of the god Hermes, to speak to the ruler, who turned out to be the beautiful Hypsipyle. Although he was surprised to find himself speaking to a woman leader and her armored companions, Aethalides explained that the Argonauts were no threat to Lemnos and simply wanted to take on supplies. Hypsipyle summoned an assembly of island women to discuss the matter. She was in favor of giving the sailors what they needed and sending them on their way immediately, but a wise old woman of the island named Polyxo rose and suggested a different plan. She said they were all doing well since the Lemnian men had been killed, but they should think of the future. Did they want to grow old without children and grandchildren? Should those among them who were virgins never know the touch of a man or the joys of motherhood? Polyxo urged them to welcome the Argonauts into their homes and beds, then, when their handsome visitors had done their job, send them on their way.

This proposal met with rousing approval from the Lemnian women, who, although they had no desire for husbands again, dearly missed the pleasures of making love. They dressed in their most seductive clothing and each invited an Argonaut into her home. Jason put on his own finery and went eagerly with Hypsipyle, while the others were shared among the island women. After a fine meal and good wine, all the men enjoyed the intimate company of the Lemnians until dawn.

A night turned to a week and a week to a month as the Argonauts made their rounds among the women of Lemnos. It was Hercules who finally brought them to their senses. He had stayed on the boat with a young boyfriend he had brought on the voyage named Hylas and cared nothing for the native women: "You fools! Are we on this voyage to sail distant seas and accomplish deeds worthy of eternal glory or to sleep with the first women we meet? The Golden Fleece lies there, beyond the far sunrise, not on this island. If Jason wants to play the gigolo and waste away his life in Hypsipyle's bed, let him. I'm sailing to Colchis!"

The Argonauts were ashamed of themselves when they heard Hercules' words. They gathered their gear and said farewell to the fair women of Lemnos, who by this time were ready to see them go. They had gotten what they wanted, most being pregnant by now, and were looking forward to a normal life without men to bother with. They waved a fond farewell as the *Argo* sailed away, then happily returned to their work.

From Lemnos the Argonauts sailed northeast across the Aegean to the Hellespont, the first of two narrow passages leading to the Black Sea. The winds were strong and the waves choppy as they fought their way up the straits past Abydos, where Leander had once swum the rough waters to spend the night with his secret love Hero. Once beyond the Hellespont, they entered the inland sea of the Propontis, then sailed along its southern coast until they came to a place called Bear Mountain, barely connected to the mainland by a narrow isthmus. On this mountain lived fearsome creatures of great strength known as the Earthmen, each brandishing six powerful arms.

But instead of monsters, the Argonauts were met on the beach by a friendly folk called the Doliones, led by a young king named Cyzicus, who had just married a beautiful maiden named Cleite. He had been advised once by an oracle that if a boatload of foreign heroes ever landed on his shore, he should welcome them with open arms. Cyzicus did so and immediately struck up a warm friendship with Jason, who was the same age as the king.

Jason and his men once again left Hercules and his lover Hylas to guard the ship in a sheltered cove and entered the town of the Doliones to be treated like royalty. The Earthmen looking down from Bear Mountain saw the ship all alone and decided it was an easy target for a raid. The creatures did not bother the Doliones, who were protected by their patron Poseidon, but strangers to their shores were fair game. The Earthmen began to toss huge boulders into the mouth of the cove to prevent the *Argo* from escaping, but this served only to stir Hercules to action. He pulled out his bow and began to shoot down every Earthman in sight. The Argonauts heard the uproar and rushed back to join the battle. Soon there was a pile of dead monsters lying on the beach.

Cyzicus had described to Jason the kingdoms and lands that lay ahead on their journey, at least as far as the entrance to the Black Sea, so the next morning the Argonauts cast off with many thanks and pledges of friendship to Cyzicus and the Doliones. They sailed around the great bulk of Bear Mountain all day until they passed the northern point of the peninsula and headed due east. But when evening came, a great storm arose and blew them back to the west. The wind was so strong and the rain so heavy they had no idea where they were, only that they had to find land or perish. Finally they saw a harbor in the distance and arrived with their ship and lives intact. But the men of that unknown land had seen the strangers make shore. In the darkness they could not tell who they were, but unwelcome guests from the east could only mean Pelasgian raiders come to steal their women and sack their town. A fierce battle in the darkness erupted between the natives and the Argonauts, who also had no idea who they were killing.

When the sun finally rose, Jason and his men were horrified to see that they had been fighting their friends the Doliones. The winds had driven them back to the opposite side of the narrow isthmus they had set out from the previous morning. The Argonauts were heartbroken to see the dead Doliones at their feet, no one more than Jason, who beheld his own spear piercing the chest of Cyzicus. The Argonauts wept and cut their hair in mourning for the terrible mistake they had made, then built funeral pyres for the Doliones with their own hands. They laid out a special tomb for Cyzicus and marched around it three times in their bronze armor to honor him. Cleite, the young bride of Cyzicus, could not bear the thought of life without her husband and killed herself in their home. With this pain added to that they already bore, the Argonauts sailed away, leaving the Doliones alone in their grief.

To help forget the recent disaster, the Argonauts vied with one another to see who could row the longest and hardest up the coast of the Propontis. One by one the men dropped away, but Hercules kept going until he alone was propelling the ship swiftly over the calm sea. Just as they reached the land of Mysia, the oar of Hercules suddenly snapped in two, sending the hero sprawling onto the deck amid the laughter of his companions. It was the end of the day, in any case, so the voyagers pulled to shore at the mouth of the Cius River and were welcomed by the native Mysians with a feast of roasted mutton and sweet wine.

Hercules, however, was in no mood to eat, so he told his companions to enjoy themselves while he and his boyfriend Hylas went into the woods to cut a new oar. He surveyed many trees until he found a towering pine that was just the right size. The son of Zeus lay aside his lion skin and club, then grabbed the tree around its base and pulled it out of the ground with his bare hands, roots and all. Taking it on his shoulder, he headed back to the ship to shape it into an oar.

Hylas, meanwhile, had gotten bored watching Hercules look at trees and so went in search of fresh water. As the sun was setting, he found a beautiful spring on the far side of a hill and bent down to fill his bronze pitcher. A water nymph who lived in the spring saw Hylas and immediately fell in love with him. She had never seen such a handsome young lad, especially with the moon casting its soft rays on him as it rose in the sky. She suddenly leapt out of the water and grabbed him around the neck to kiss him, then pulled on his arm until he fell into the dark water.

One of the Argonauts named Polyphemus heard Hylas scream and rushed to the spring. All he could see were ripples on the surface of the water, so he began to shout for the young man, but to no avail. He ran to Hercules, who immediately dropped his tree and began a frantic search for his lover through the night, crazed at the thought that he might lose him forever.

When dawn broke, the Argonauts, bleary-headed from too much wine, stumbled to the ship and cast off with a fair wind behind them. It was several hours before they realized that three of their crewmen were missing. A fierce argument broke out about what they should do, with most urging they turn the ship around. But Calais and Zetes, sons of the North Wind, declared that such a fair breeze was a gift of the gods and should not be scorned. The men turned to Jason for leadership, but he sat helpless in the stern of the ship, unable to make any decision. Suddenly out of the waves rose Glaucus, the former fisherman who had turned into a sea god after eating magical grass. Glaucus told them not to turn the *Argo* around as everything had unfolded according to the will of Zeus. Polyphemus was to found a great city among the Mysians, while Hercules had to get back to his labors for Eurystheus and forget about the long voyage to Colchis. As for Hylas, he was now the husband of a water nymph and was forever lost to the world of men. Reluctantly, the Argonauts consented and continued on their way without their companions.

Back on land, Hercules was beside himself with grief and threatened to destroy all of Mysia unless the Mysians found Hylas for him. He took the sons of the local nobility as hostages back to Thessaly and told the Mysians he would kill them unless they swore to continue the hunt for Hylas. The families solemnly vowed they would keep up the search. For centuries thereafter, every year on a special day, the people of Mysia would wander through the countryside calling the name of Hylas long into the night, though the young man never answered.

For almost two days a west wind blew the *Argo* across the Propontis, until at last the sailors came to the land of the Bebryces near the entrance to the Bosporus straits. A brutish king named Amycus ruled that land. He was large, rude, and bad-tempered, a son of Poseidon and a local nymph. He met the Argonauts at the shore with a party of his henchmen and told them it was the law of his country that strangers must fight in a boxing match with him. They should pick their champion, but choose carefully, for the bones of all his previous opponents lay bleaching in the sun.

Pollux, the twin of Castor, jumped up immediately and accepted the challenge. He was the best boxer of the expedition despite that he was only a youth of average size. The king laughed at this foolish boy, but his companions laid out a ring in the sand for the contest. Both men wrapped rawhide thongs around their wrists, then faced each other for a match to the death. Amycus was the stronger of the two by far, but Pollux was quick and smart. He soon learned to dodge the blows of the king and keep him off balance. Like an old bull fighting a young challenger, Amycus raged and threatened, but could not lay hold of his opponent. Pollux waited until just the right moment, when the king charged him with all his might, then stepped aside at the last second and struck him a swift blow on the back of the head as he passed, crushing his skull behind the ear and killing him in an instant.

The Bebrycian men howled in rage, then rushed at the Argonauts with spears and swords. But Jason and his comrades began to drive them back. Pollux joined in the fight even though he was exhausted from his match with the king. When two of the brutes attacked him at once, he threw one into the dust and grabbed the other by the eyebrow, ripping off the side of his face and leaving his eyeball exposed. Soon the Greeks had finished off the men of Amycus and stood around the bodies, slapping each other on the back. They made camp on the beach to rest and patch up their wounded, while Orpheus sang songs of victory late into the night. When morning came, they pushed off and sailed into the swirling Bosporus, the final obstacle before they entered the mysterious Black Sea.

On the west side of the Bosporus straits was the land of the Thynians, ruled over by old king Phineus. He was said to be a son of Phoenician Agenor and brother to King Cadmus of Thebes. Like that of his sibling in Greece, his was a life of great suffering. Apollo had given him the gift of prophesy, but Phineus abused it by revealing too much of the future to the eager ears of men. Zeus grew angry and punished the king by blinding him, but this was just the beginning. The ruler of the gods also sent Harpies to torment him constantly. These hideous creatures had the heads of women, but the bodies of large carrion birds. Whenever food was set before Phineus, the Harpies would swoop down and snatch it in their talons, sometimes from his very lips, leaving a filth of putrid decay in their wake. Occasionally they would leave him a morsel to gnaw on, but only enough to keep him barely alive to prolong his pain. Phineus was little more than skin and bones, trembling from weakness and old age, limping around the grounds of his palace caked in the foul droppings of the Harpies.

When the Argonauts stopped to pay their respects to the king, they were appalled to see his wretched state. He motioned them to come closer to him, but they could barely stand the smell. He told them with a quivering voice that he had foreseen their coming and had a favor to ask, one he would repay in turn. If they would drive away the Harpies, he would tell them what lay ahead on their journey. Jason and his companions had great compassion for the king and agreed. The two winged sons of the North Wind, Zetes and Calais, were particularly sympathetic as he was their maternal uncle.

The Argonauts prepared a handsome feast for Phineus and waited for the Harpies to appear. When they did, Zetes and Calais flew after them with swords drawn and chased them out of sight. Some say the sons of the North Wind slew the Harpies, but others say a messenger from Mount Olympus ordered them to spare the monsters in exchange for a promise never to trouble Phineus again. In either case, Zetes and Calais returned to the palace flushed with triumph.

The sailors then washed the filth from Phineus and fed him his first decent meal in years. In gratitude, the seer king told them of the dreaded Symplegades, or Clashing Rocks, that lay at the exit of the Bosporus and how to overcome them. Then he described the lands and peoples along the southern shore of the Black Sea until they came to the kingdom of Colchis, where the Golden Fleece lay. Safe arrival here will be but the start of your troubles, warned the king, for a great monster guards that treasure and no man has ever escaped from it alive.

Jason stood listening with growing despair and finally asked if he should turn around and go home rather than face such a difficult voyage with certain death at the end. The king rebuked him and asked what sort of hero he was if he ran away like a woman from mortal dangers.

"Put your trust in the gods," Phineus admonished, "especially Aphrodite."

The Argonauts pulled away from the land of the Thynians and made their way in great trepidation up the Bosporus. A cold fog enveloped them with silence all around, but soon they began to hear in the distance a strange and growing sound. It was like the slow pounding of a giant drum, though louder and more harsh than anything that had met their ears before. When they finally rowed around a bend in the straits, they saw the source of the clamor. It was the Clashing Rocks they had been warned of, two enormous stone sentinels that stood on opposite sides of the narrow entrance into the Black Sea. Of their own will they rushed across the waterway and crushed anything that came between them. Phineus had told them their only hope of sailing between the rocks was first to send forth a dove from their ship. If this bird could fly between the rocks and survive, there was a chance—just barely—that the *Argo* might also make it through.

The sailors all gazed in terror at the impossible obstacle before them, but to give up now would bring shame on them forever. They released the dove and watched intently as it made its way swiftly toward the Clashing Rocks. At first it seemed as if the mighty pillars would not notice such a small creature, but suddenly they began to rush together at terrific speed across the straits. The dove flew on, frantic to escape, as the rocks swiftly bore down on her. When they came together there was a sound as if the earth itself had split apart, but the dove had made it through, losing only the tip of its tail feathers at the final moment.

The Argonauts cheered for the bird as the rocks moved back to their starting points, but they knew their boat could not fly as swiftly through the passage as a dove. Still, they decided to risk everything for the glory that lay ahead, so they took oars in hand and prepared to row for their lives. Not even if Hercules had been aboard would the *Argo* have cut through the waves so fast. The sailors moved forward at astonishing speed, but the rocks were even faster. With the spray in their faces they could scarcely see, but they could hear a terrible sound rushing at them from both sides. With prayers to the gods they pulled at the oars and shouted to one another to press on even as the rocks were almost on top of them. But at the last moment, just as their strength was almost gone, they shot into the Black Sea as the Clashing Rocks met with a thunderous crash, shearing off the banner that flew from the stern of the *Argo*.

The men collapsed on the deck utterly spent, scarcely able to believe they were alive. The two giant rocks withdrew to opposite sides of the straits, never to move again, for the gods had decreed that if a ship ever sailed between them they would remain immobile. When at last the Argonauts recovered, they gazed at the unknown sea stretching before them and wondered how they would escape the new dangers that lay ahead.

As soon as they had passed the Clashing Rocks, Jason once again fell into deep despair. He told the helmsman, Tiphys, that he didn't know how they were going to make it all the way to Colchis. He confessed that he spent his nights worrying endlessly about everything that could go wrong on their voyage and wished that he had never accepted the challenge from his uncle to search for the Golden Fleece. But Tiphys assured his despondent captain that everything would turn out well in the end, especially with the help of the gods. As if to encourage this faith, at that moment they saw Apollo flying high in the sky on his way to the land of the Hyperboreans in the distant north. Everyone but Jason took this as a sign of divine favor and offered sacrifices of thanksgiving to the god.

Several days later they came to the land of the Mariandynians, where King Lycus ruled. This country was best known for a dark cave near the sea from which an ice-cold wind blew even on the hottest summer days. It was an entrance to the realm of Hades, but the Argonauts had no desire to approach it and went instead to the palace of Lycus. The king welcomed the weary travelers and feasted them in grand style, though he was disappointed that Hercules was not among them. He had wanted to see the hero who had earlier passed through his kingdom on his return from the land of the Amazons. But he was so impressed by Jason and his companions that he sent his own son to join them on their quest.

But great sadness befell the Argonauts in that land when their seer, Idmon, was mauled by a huge white-tusked boar as he hunted in the woods. His friends killed the beast, but not before it had mortally wounded the soothsayer. They mourned Idmon for a full three days and gave him splendid funeral rites, but no sooner had they said their final farewells than Tiphys suddenly died of a fever. Jason lost all hope after this double tragedy and urged that they turn back now that they had no one to steer the ship, but the rest of the sailors rallied and chose the experienced seaman Ancaeus to guide the *Argo*.

A few days later the crew passed a headland that was capped by the tomb of a Greek named Sthenelus, who had died during Hercules' expedition against the Amazons. The spirit of the dead warrior sensed that some his countrymen were passing by, so he rose from his grave as a ghost and stood dressed in full battle gear looking down on the ship. The sailors were so terrified by this sight that they pulled to shore and offered sacrifices to the lonely spirit, hoping he would let them pass in peace.

Many more miles down the coast they came to the Assyrian colony of Sinope and took on supplies. There they met three living refugees from Hercules' war on the Amazons. They were from Thessaly as was Jason and had been trying to make their way back to Greece. The three were delighted to meet their countrymen in such a distant land and gladly accepted their offer to join the crew. They advised Jason to sail away from the kingdom of the Amazons and not test their skills against these formidable foes. Luckily for the men of the *Argo*, Zeus sent a following wind that bore them safely past the coast held by the women warriors.

The Argonauts sailed for weeks past many different lands and tribes with customs strange to the Greeks. One group called the Chalybes did not sow grain or pasture sheep, but dug iron from the earth and traded it for whatever food they needed. The Tibarenians farther down the coast practiced traditional agriculture, but had a most peculiar custom regarding childbirth. When a woman was in labor, her husband would lie in their bed and groan in pain as if he were delivering the child himself. Then, when the baby was born, the exhausted mother would have to rise and take care of him. The Mossynoecians were even stranger, as they engaged in the most private practices in public places. It was considered perfectly normal for a man of their tribe to make love with a woman in the middle of the street. The Mossynoecian king lived in a high tower where he rendered judgments on various cases brought to him. If the people felt he had delivered an unjust ruling, they would lock him in and not allow him food until he had changed his mind.

The blind seer Phineus had told them they would next find an island sacred to Ares where they should stop if they wanted to receive a great blessing. But when the Argonauts attempted to land there, they were attacked by birds shooting their feathers down like darts on the helpless sailors. Most had never heard of such a thing before, but one of their number remembered that Hercules had told of similar birds he had overcome on Lake Stymphalus in the Peloponnesus. Hearing the story, Jason organized half the men to row and the other half to hold their shields above their heads while they drew near to the shore. Then when they landed on the beach, they beat their shields with their swords and shouted with all their might to scare the birds away, just as Hercules had done.

Moving inland they saw four gaunt men approaching them. These forlorn castaways turned out to be the shipwrecked sons of Phrixus, the young man who had flown to the land of Colchis years earlier on the very sheep whose fleece they were seeking. They were on their way back to Orchomenus to claim the throne left behind by their father. Jason was delighted to meet his distant cousins and invited them to join their quest, but the brothers were not enthusiastic. They warned the Argonauts that Aeetes was a cruel and clever king who would never let them have the fleece. They urged them to turn around and sail back to Greece, thankful that they had not crossed paths with such a wicked ruler. The sailors were deeply troubled by these words, but they were determined to press on. The four brothers reluctantly agreed to join them, if only to escape the island of birds where they were stranded.

Thus with a full crew, Jason and his men sailed on until they saw the Caucasus Mountains rising in the distance. At last they pulled the *Argo* into the mouth of the Phasis River, a swift stream that flowed through the heart of Colchis and the kingdom of King Aeetes. The long journey was finally over, but even the bravest warriors among them wondered if they would live to sail the *Argo* home.

The goddess Hera had been following the journey of Jason and his companions with great interest. Both she and Athena wanted the Argonauts to succeed, but like most gods they preferred to let mortals make their own way through the trials and difficulties of life. Still, even heroes need a little help now and then. The wife and the daughter of Zeus met secretly to find a way to help Jason take the Golden Fleece from Aeetes. They knew that the king of Colchis was so powerful that it would take extraordinary measures to defeat him, so they chose the one force that could melt the hearts of both men and gods—love.

They made their way to the Olympian chambers of Aphrodite and found the goddess combing her golden hair all alone. She rose and welcomed her visitors, flattered to have two such eminent goddesses as her guests. They asked if she might do them a small favor and send her son Cupid down to Colchis. They wanted him to shoot one of his irresistible arrows into Medea, the daughter of King Aeetes, so that she would fall hopelessly in love with Jason. Medea was a powerful young witch and could use her magic to help the Argonauts gain the fleece and escape back to Greece. Aphrodite gladly agreed and bribed her son to do the job by offering him a golden ball that threw a flaming trail through the air like a comet. Cupid could not resist such a bribe and flew down to Colchis to find Medea.

Jason and his companions had meanwhile left the *Argo* and were making their way to the palace of Aeetes. The four sons of Phrixus guided them, but everyone was frightened of the reception they might receive from the king. Hera helped the men by covering them in a mist so that they could approach the king's city unseen. Up from the Phasis they climbed past fruit-filled orchards. When at last they arrived at the gates of the palace, Hera blew the mist away and revealed a marvelous city built for the king by the god Hephaestus himself. At this same moment, Medea looked out her window and saw Jason below. It was then that Cupid drew his bow and let his arrow fly into her heart. Instantly she fell in love with the handsome visitor from Greece.

Jason and the Argonauts were escorted into the throne room of the king and given a cool but proper welcome by Aeetes. He had once been told by an oracle that a foreigner would be his undoing, so he scoffed at the claim that they meant no harm. Jason politely asked if he might have the Golden Fleece that had been brought to the land of Colchis by his cousin Phrixus years before. The king was not about to let his most prized possession go, but he told Jason that he could indeed have the fleece if he could pass a small test of bravery. He would have to yoke a pair of fire-breathing oxen, then use them to plow a field while he sowed dragon's teeth left over from the beast Cadmus had killed at Thebes. Hundreds of armed warriors would spring from these teeth, as they did at Thebes. Jason would have to kill them all or be slain himself. When he had accomplished all this, he could go to the grove of Ares and try to take the fleece from the murderous dragon that was guarding it.

Jason left the court and, as usual, lost all hope. He sat in a empty corner of the palace weeping and cursing the day he had ever left his home on Mount Pelion. There Medea found him and told him of her love for him. She swore that she would help him defeat the evil designs of her father and gain the fleece. Jason was overcome with gratitude and swore that he would love the beautiful princess forever. Medea then gave him a magic ointment to spread on his body that would protect him from the fiery breath of the oxen.

The next day Jason and his men, along with Aeetes and his court, arrived at the cave where the dreaded oxen lived. Jason first anointed himself with the magic elixir of Medea, then took up his sword and spear, his helmet full of dragon teeth in his hands. He found the field where Aeetes had placed the bronze yoke—wood would burn away in an instant—and fixed his spear there in the ground with his helmet hung from its point. Then with only his shield before him, he came to the dark cave reeking of sulfur and smoke. The oxen stormed out of their home bellowing fire, but Jason trusted in Medea's ointment and was not harmed. He met the sharp horns with his shield and waited until the oxen stopped to take a breath. Then, quick as lightning, Jason grabbed one ox by its horns and wrestled it to the ground. Holding this animal down he kicked the other hard on its leg and brought it to its knees as well. With the help of Castor and Pollux, he then lifted the heavy bronze yoke onto the necks of the oxen and slammed a peg into the shaft to lock them in. Then using his spear as a goad, he led the snorting animals to the nearby field to begin plowing.

As the oxen broke the sod, Jason sowed the dragon's teeth in the furrows behind him, glancing back to make sure the warriors were not springing from the ground before he was ready. When he finished, he loosed the oxen to make their way back to their cave while he put on his armor and hid behind his shield on the edge of the field. As he watched, a most amazing sight appeared before his eyes. Men were slowly rising from the earth, but only a few had fully emerged. Medea had told him what to do next, so he took a large boulder and threw it into the middle of the field. All the warriors turned toward the stone thinking they were being attacked. Some of those out of the ground began fighting with one another, but most were still unable to move. Jason then rushed into the field while the soldiers were distracted and began hacking at them like a farmer with a scythe. The newborn soldiers barely knew what was happening as he raged among them. Some tried to raise their weapons from the ground and defend themselves, but many were struck down. Most died without their feet ever emerging from the earth and fell into the bloody furrows scarcely having seen the light of day. Soon they were all dead, wilting on the earth like flowers under the summer sun, with only Jason left alive to glory in his victory.

Aeetes spent the whole night huddled together with his advisors in the palace, plotting the death of Jason and his men. He didn't doubt for a moment that Medea was behind Jason's success, for it would have been impossible to have yoked the oxen and defeated the earth-born warriors without her magic. Medea knew that her father realized she was responsible, so she made plans to flee the land of Colchis with the Argonauts. She snuck out of the palace in the darkness, bringing only what she could carry on her back and dragging her little brother Apsyrtus behind her. The sleepy child had no idea why his sister was in such a rush, but she had always been so kind to him that he trusted her completely.

Medea made her way barefoot through the empty streets hurrying Apsyrtus along until she was out of the city and at the banks of the river where the *Argo* waited. She climbed onto the deck and fell to her knees before Jason, begging him to take her with them to Greece. She would help him get the Golden Fleece that very night, but they had to act quickly before her father knew or they would all pay a terrible price. Jason gladly agreed and swore before Zeus and his companions that he would marry her as soon as they returned home. She then put her weary brother to bed on board the ship and led Jason along the river until they came to the sacred grove of Ares.

They saw the Golden Fleece hanging on a huge oak tree in the middle of the grove, but they also saw the largest snake anyone could imagine curled up around it. The serpent sensed it was no longer alone and began a hiss that sent shivers down Jason's spine. He turned to flee, but Medea held him fast and ran to the giant snake, fixing it with her eyes. The creature was mesmerized by the stare of Medea, but she knew she could not hold its attention for long. She therefore took a juniper branch and dipped it into a powerful potion, then sprinkled it on the serpent's head while she chanted incantations to make it sleepy. But even this magic had its limits on such an awesome beast, so she gave Jason a kick and told him to get the fleece right away. He quickly grabbed the prize and backed away carefully while Medea continued to work her magic on the snake. The stupefied beast slowly raised its head and bared its fangs to strike down the thieves, but the spell was too strong and it collapsed onto the ground.

Jason and Medea ran swiftly away from the grove with the Golden Fleece in hand until they came at last to the ship. He cut the ropes with his sword and ordered the crew to cast off without delay. The Argonauts did not hesitate, but manned the oars and pulled with all their might down the Phasis into the sea. They all knew that Aeetes would be close behind and would show no mercy to the foreigners who had stolen his most valued possession.

By dawn the Argonauts were well along the coast, but Aeetes had already gathered his ships and was in pursuit. The Colchians knew the waters well and soon had closed the gap between the ships to overtake the *Argo*. It was now that Medea brought her little brother onto the deck in view of their father closing from behind. Aeetes may have been ready to kill his daughter without a second thought, but he would never harm his dear son Apsyrtus. Medea then pulled out her dagger and plunged it into her brother's heart while both the Argonauts and the king watched in horror. She grabbed Jason's sword and cut Apsyrtus into little pieces, casting one of his arms into the sea behind her. Aeetes screamed in anguish and swore revenge, but ordered his ship to slow so that he could retrieve the severed limb of his son floating on the waves. Medea repeated this until little chunks of Apsyrtus were bobbing all over the sea. Aeetes had to give his son a decent burial, so he fell farther and farther behind the *Argo* as he collected the pieces of his corpse. The Greek sailors were all deeply grateful to Medea for saving them, but now wondered what sort of woman they had taken on board their ship.

Jason knew that Colchians would follow them across the southern shore of the Black Sea to the Bosporus straits, so he made instead for the mouth of the Danube River on the western coast. The king somehow suspected Jason might take this route, so he sent a warship to the Danube in pursuit, commanded by one of his sons. After a long voyage across the sea, the Argonauts entered the mouth of the Danube only to find the Colchians had arrived first and were blocking their way. Medea told Jason she could get them through if he had the courage to act without mercy. At this point, Jason was more afraid of the young witch than he was of her father's men, so he agreed. Medea therefore sent a messenger to her brother to come alone to an island in the river to discuss terms for her surrender and the return of the fleece. When the gullible brother arrived, Jason cut him down with his sword. Medea then told him to cut off the fingers and toes from the corpse and suck the blood from each three times, spitting it onto the ground. This magical rite would keep the ghost of the victim from pursuing them. With the bloody deed done, the pair returned to the *Argo* and Jason ordered his men to row up the Danube deep into the unknown wilderness that lay before them.

Stories say the voyage of the Argonauts took them through the dark forests and snow-covered mountains of Europe, far up the Danube to the foot of the Alps and beyond. Details of this journey are rather vague. Some say they arrived at the head of the Adriatic Sea, then traveled up the Po River in Italy until they came to the headwaters of the Rhine in the land of the Celts. The stories say they then crossed to the Rhone and sailed down through Gaul until they came to the Mediterranean coast of Liguria. From there they held to the Italian shore past the land of the Etruscans and the future site of Rome until they arrived at the island of Aeaea, home of the dreaded witch Circe.

Circe was sitting on the beach washing her head with seawater. She had never had such horrible dreams as that previous night, with blood dripping from the walls of her palace. She came down to the shore that morning followed by all the wild creatures she had created by magically transforming strangers who came to her island.

When she saw Jason and Medea approaching, she silently gestured for them to follow her. When they came to Circe's hall, they fell down before her with hands over their faces in the posture of those seeking to wash away the sin of murder. Out of reverence for Zeus, who watches over all supplicants, Circe began the rites of purification. First she took a suckling piglet and held it over them, then slit its throat to bathe their hands in blood. Next she prayed to Zeus to cleanse the visitors, then finally she burned cakes made without wine to propitiate the relentless Furies, who followed after those who killed their own relatives.

When Circe finished, she motioned for her guests to sit down and asked them to tell of their journey and the terrible crime for which they had sought forgiveness. She was especially eager to learn who Medea was, for she saw in her shining eyes the unmistakable fire of someone descended from the sun god Helios, her own father. In the native language of Colchis, Medea told of her lineage, that she was indeed the granddaughter of Helios and daughter of Aeetes, and therefore Circe's niece.

She told of the voyage of the Argonauts from Greece in search of the Golden Fleece and how she had helped them in their quest. Medea did not mention the murders, but Circe could now see into her heart.

"You foolish girl," she cried, "truly you have embarked on a voyage of shame. How could you slay your own brothers and expect to escape the wrath of your father? I have unknowingly purged you of this crime and cannot punish you, but your life will be full of misery. Get off my island and take this wretched fellow with you!"

Sorrow overwhelmed Medea when she heard these harsh words. As Jason took her by the hand and led her back to the ship, she pulled her robe over her eyes and wept. Only now did she begin to realize the cost of her actions. Driven to love a stranger, she had murdered her own kin and lost her home and family forever.

The *Argo* departed the isle of Circe and sailed south along the Italian coast aided by a fair wind sent by Hera. The Argonauts passed the island of the Sirens, where unfortunate men were lured to their death by sweet songs. The bard Orpheus had the foresight to begin singing loudly as they approached the island and so drowned out the voices of the deadly Sirens. The ship then passed between the monster Scylla and the giant whirlpool Charybdis with the help of the goddess Thetis, who guided the steering oar herself. They also avoided the Wandering Rocks that crushed vessels off Sicily, but ships of Colchis finally caught up with them after they entered the harbor of the kindly Phaeacians. These warships had been sent by King Aeetes through the Bosporus and all the way around Greece to catch the Argonauts as they tried to sail home. The Phaeacian queen Arete was sympathetic to the young lovers and promised her husband would not turn them over to the Colchians if Jason and Medea were properly married. That night the couple hastily went through a wedding ceremony and formally proclaimed themselves husband and wife, with Jason swearing he had not previously slept with Medea. True or not, the marriage was binding and so the Phaeacian king Alcinous extended his protection to the couple. The Colchians did not dare challenge such a powerful ruler, but they were also terrified to return home empty-handed. Alcinous therefore granted them land for a colony nearby so they would not have to face the wrath of Aeetes. With this matter settled, the Phaeacians sent the *Argo* on its way with gifts and fresh provisions.

Jason and his companions were now almost home, but no sooner had they rounded the tip of the Peloponnesus then a fierce storm arose and blew them all the way across the Mediterranean to Africa. One enormous wave picked up the ship and carried it many miles into the desert, leaving it marooned far from the sea. Not only Jason but every man on board was so depressed at this turn of events that they wrapped themselves in their cloaks and lay down in the sand to die.

Jason had gone away from the others to face his end alone in the burning heat when suddenly he thought he saw three beautiful nymphs appear before his eyes. They smiled at him and said they were the divine guardians of that land. They advised him not to worry: "Get up and rouse your comrades, Jason! As soon as Amphitrite unyokes the horses of Poseidon, then you and your companions must pay back your mother who has carried you so long in her womb. You may yet return to Greece!"

With that, they vanished. Jason thought he was losing his mind. Not only was he seeing nymphs dancing in the desert, but they were speaking nonsense. He told the rest of the Argonauts what they had said. The men were doubtful until a magnificent horse came running toward them from the direction of the sea and galloped off into the distance. Peleus then shouted with joy and said this was the horse of Poseidon loosed by his wife, Amphitrite. The mother the nymphs spoke of must be the *Argo* herself, which had carried them through so much. They should put the ship on their shoulders and bear her in turn until they came to water.

The others were dubious, but anything seemed better than dying in the desert. They picked up the ship and set out on their portage through the wilderness until after nine days they at last came to an oasis. It turned out to be none other than the Garden of the Hesperides, the very place Hercules had visited to gather the famous golden apples. The nymphs of the garden told them they had just missed the hero. The Argonauts sent out scouts, but they were not able to catch up with their former comrade even though they did glimpse him in the distance.

The sailors picked up the ship again and carried it until they came to inland Lake Tritonis and paddled around aimlessly for days. Eventually the god Triton, Poseidon's son, took pity on them and carried the ship back to the Mediterranean, where they set sail once more for Greece. Along the way they drew near to Crete to take on fresh water, but were attacked by the bronze giant Talus, who guarded the shore and threw boulders at anyone who came near. Zeus had once given Talus to Europa as a gift to protect her, but even with the unfortunate girl long dead, the monster still performed his job. The Argonauts were desperately thirsty but at a loss about what to do. Medea once again came to their rescue and cast a spell on Talus so that he struck his heel on a rock and loosed the plug that held in the magical fluid that gave him life. Once the fluid was drained from his body, the men pulled to shore and refilled their water jars for the rest of the voyage. They sailed north through the Aegean for several days until they came at last to Thessaly, to Jason's own city of Iolcus beneath Mount Pelion, from where they had set out so long ago.

There are many different stories about what happened next, but most say that Jason came to the palace of his uncle Pelias and gave him the Golden Fleece in fulfillment of his vow. The Argonauts then delivered their faithful ship to Corinth to dedicate it to Poseidon and afterward went their separate ways with fond farewells, while Jason and Medea returned to Iolcus to settle down. Jason's father, Aeson, was still alive and, at Jason's request, Medea rejuvenated him with her magical powers. This so impressed the daughters of King Pelias that they asked her to restore the youth of their own aged father. Medea was only too glad to help.

She took an old ram and cut it into pieces, then threw the parts into a large, boiling pot full of magical herbs. Moments later, the Colchian witch reached in and pulled out a spring lamb, alive and healthy. The daughters were thrilled and agreed she should do the same to their father. They entered his bedroom that very night with swords and gathered around him while he slept. Before he could wake, they cut him into little pieces, then hurried away with the still-warm flesh to Medea. She placed the pieces in the cauldron, sprinkled herbs, and chanted spells above the boiling brew. The daughters then looked into the pot with great anticipation, but all they saw was a bubbling stew with chunks of their father floating on top. Medea shrugged and apologized, explaining that sometimes the magic didn't work. She then ran back to Jason to tell him the throne was now his.

The sons of Pelias, however, had other ideas and chased Jason and Medea out of Iolcus, threatening them with death should they ever return. Jason had now lost his home in Hera's elaborate plan to punish Pelias, but Medea urged him to seek out another city so that they could start their lives anew. Corinth seemed like a good choice, since the king of that town—named Creon like the king of Thebes—admired Jason. So the two refugees made their way south along the road to the Peloponnesus with nothing but the clothes on their backs. Medea had also lost everything, but she took comfort in the fact that Jason's love for her would never fail.

Jason and Medea lived together in Corinth for ten happy years. Their lives were humble, but they found joy in the two sons that Medea bore. On days when their work allowed, they would take the boys down to the shore and show them the *Argo*, telling them stories of their great adventure.

Yet Jason was not a happy man in his heart. He longed for the life of royalty and missed the days when men looked up to him. In Corinth, the people laughed at him behind his back because he had taken a foreign wife—and a witch at that. By Greek law his sons by this barbarian woman could not even be citizens. There had to be some way he could set things right.

One day Jason came home and announced to Medea that he was going to marry shining Glauce, the daughter of King Creon of Corinth. He explained that their own marriage really didn't count since she was a foreigner, so there was no impediment to his joining the royal family. The king and his daughter were both eager to make a match with the renowned hero who had brought back the Golden Fleece almost singlehanded. Jason explained to Medea that the marriage would actually be good for her and their two sons since it would give him the means to support her. Of course, his new bride understandably didn't want his barbarian girlfriend and her illegitimate children around the city, so she would have to leave Corinth—but he was sure he could find some nice, out-of-the-way village where they could live out their lives.

Medea listened to Jason with growing incredulity until at last she exploded in outrage. He brought back the fleece? He was a pathetic pretty boy who had no more courage than a mouse. She was the one who had seized the fleece for him, as well as brought him and his companions safely back to Greece through countless dangers. Their marriage didn't count? It seemed to count just fine when it had suited his purposes. She had given up her life for him and this was how he repaid her? How dare he think he was going to get away with this!

Jason hid in a corner and claimed that she should be grateful for all that had happened. He had gotten her away from that backwater kingdom of her father and brought her to the glorious land of Greece, where civilization shone like a beacon to the world. He then ran out of their house and back to the palace.

Medea was furious beyond words. She was being shamefully cast aside for a younger woman after all she had done for Jason. She knew that both she and her boys would be little better than starving vagabonds wandering the roads of Greece, with Jason's promises of support soon forgotten. No, there was only one thing to do, no matter how horrible it might seem—only one way to have her revenge.

She sent a message to Jason at the palace saying she had acted hastily and spoken harshly out of anger. She knew he had her best interests at heart, so she wanted to try to make things right. She even had a wedding gift for the bride, a gorgeous robe of the finest cloth.

Jason was glad to see that Medea had come to her senses and accepted the gift for the princess, carrying it wrapped to her himself. But when Glauce put it on in front of the court, she went pale and staggered sideways, then started foaming at the mouth. The robe began to burn the skin from her flesh while the girl screamed and screamed. The king rushed to her and tried to rip it off, but pieces of her skin came with it. Even touching the deadly robe spread the contagion to her father, so that immediately his own flesh began to melt away. Both died in agony while Jason and the rest of her family looked on in horror.

He rushed back to the home he had shared with Medea, only to find her sitting silently with a bloody sword in her hand. He was ready to kill her for giving Glauce a poisoned cloak and destroying his dreams of a better life, but he felt a chill run down his spine and asked where their sons were. She calmly told him they were dead, killed by her own hand as they begged for mercy. It was the hardest thing she had ever done, she confessed, but she could not leave them to suffer without a proper father. Besides, she knew it would hurt Jason all the more if she left him without heirs, even half-barbarian bastards.

Jason fell to the dirt floor of their home and cried in anguish. He hardly noticed that Medea had disappeared—some say on a chariot drawn by dragons sent by her grandfather the sun god to take her to safety in Athens. Now, without a wife, sons, or hope, he had truly lost everything.

As the weeks and months passed, he was scorned by all as a man cursed by the gods. A shell of his former self, he took to sitting beneath the rotting remains of the *Argo* on the beach at Corinth. He tried to remember the old days full of adventure and romance, when he dared great deeds and was admired by all, but that time seemed so far away. At last one day as he sat beneath the decaying hulk of his old ship, the heavy oak prow from the grove of Zeus, now long silent, fell to the ground and crushed him.

TROY

It all began with an apple.

Zeus decided to honor his mortal grandson Peleus, who had sailed on the *Argo* with Jason, by giving him the hand of the beautiful sea goddess Thetis in marriage. The ruler of the gods would have gladly taken her for himself, but Prometheus had once told him that whoever lay with Thetis would sire a son greater than his father. Since Zeus was terrified of being overthrown, he gave the goddess to Peleus so her offspring would be no threat to him. It was a perfect arrangement, except that Zeus had failed to consult Thetis about the upcoming nuptials.

To help Peleus win over his divine bride, the gods told him of a secret place where she danced naked with the sea nymphs in the moonlight. Peleus snuck down to this shore and hid himself among the rocks to watch them frolic. When at last Thetis and the nymphs grew tired and lay down to sleep, Peleus quietly crept up on the goddess and grabbed her, claiming her as his wife. She was startled to be captured by anyone, let alone a mortal man, and so used her powers to change into terrifying shapes to frighten him away, but the young man hung on until the goddess finally relented and agreed to marry him.

It was a splendid wedding, staged on the wooded slopes of Mount Pelion. The Olympian gods themselves attended, seated at a glorious banquet table in a grand pavilion. The fifty sisters of Thetis sang, the Muses danced, and Ganymede, the cupbearer and boyfriend of Zeus, poured wine for all into golden goblets. Everyone who was anyone was there—except for one goddess who had not received an invitation. This was Eris, or Strife, born at the dawn of the world. Zeus had deliberately excluded her from the guest list, fearing she would bring discord to the celebration. In revenge she snuck up to the wedding feast and rolled a golden apple across the floor, which came to rest in the center of the dance floor. On it were written the words "For the fairest."

At once, Hera, Athena, and Aphrodite began to fight over the apple. They yelled and punched and tore at each one another's clothes, claiming they were most worthy of the prize, until Zeus stopped them with his voice of thunder. He declared that the matter must be decided fairly and impartially by someone who had an eye for beautiful women. He was wise enough not to judge the matter himself, but chose instead a young Trojan prince named Paris.

Troy had been struggling for many years to rebuild itself after it had been devastated by Hercules. Priam, the one surviving member of the royal family, married many wives and oversaw the restoration of his city to its former glory on the shores of the Hellespont. One of his wives was Hecuba, who first bore him a fine son named Hector. But when she became pregnant a second time, she had a dream that the child in her womb was a flaming torch. A soothsayer told her that this son would cause the downfall of Troy, so Priam and Hecuba gave the newborn infant, named Paris, to one of their shepherds to abandon in the wilds of Mount Ida above the city.

As often happens in these stories, the shepherd could not bring himself to kill the innocent baby. He raised the child as his own, teaching him to watch over flocks and drive off wild animals. The boy's skill in fighting bandits and thieves earned him the nickname Alexander, "destroyer of men." He was an extraordinarily beautiful child and very popular with the local girls when he came of age. He was also skilled with animals and took special care with a pet bull he had raised, so that it became known throughout the region. But one day men from the court of the Trojan king came to take away the bull. They said that Priam needed it as a prize for funeral games in honor of a long-dead son he had been forced to abandon in the wilderness.

Paris was indignant that his bull was being confiscated, but since he could not fight the king's men, he decided to compete in the games to win back his bull. He went down to Troy and shocked the assembled nobility by winning every contest of strength and skill. The many sons of Priam were furious that an unknown peasant could best them at anything, so much so that one named Deiphobus finally drew his sword to kill the outsider on the spot. Paris jumped up on an altar of Zeus to seek sanctuary, but at that moment Cassandra, the soothsaying daughter of Priam, declared that the young stranger was in fact the long-lost son of Priam and their own brother. Everyone believed Cassandra for once and they were so glad to see Paris alive that they forgot about the old prophecy of destruction and welcomed him into the palace.

As much as he enjoyed the pleasures of life in the Trojan court, Paris still visited the countryside around Mount Ida to keep watch over his flocks. One night while he was alone playing his flute for his sheep, the god Hermes appeared before him along with three of the most radiant beings Paris had ever seen. Hermes explained that Zeus wanted him to act as judge to decide which of the three goddesses was the most beautiful. The prince agreed and watched with great interest as Hera, Athena, and Aphrodite each removed her clothes to stand naked before him. They were all absolutely perfect in form, so there was little to help him choose among them. The goddesses saw his problem, so each came close to him to whisper in his ear.

"Choose me," said Hera, "and I will make you king of all the lands."

"Choose me," said Athena, "and I will make you the greatest warrior men have ever seen."

"Choose me," said Aphrodite, "and I will give you the most beautiful woman in the world."

Paris hesitated only a moment before he declared that Aphrodite was the fairest of the three. Hera and Athena stormed off, swearing vengeance on Paris and Troy, but Aphrodite told the young shepherd that his bride awaited him across the sea in Greece. She was Helen, the daughter of Leda and Zeus, sister of Castor and Pollux, raised by King Tyndareus as his own. She was his for the taking—except that she was already married. Her husband was King Menelaus of Sparta, brother of the great Greek king Agamemnon, though the goddess of love assured Paris this would not be a problem.

The prince was so excited he raced back to Troy and told everyone he was sailing off to Greece. He arrived at the palace of Menelaus and was welcomed as a royal guest. The king entertained him warmly and welcomed him into his home, trusting in the honor of the unbreakable vows of hospitality. But when Menelaus sailed off to Crete for an unexpected funeral, Paris came to the chambers of Helen and seduced her. The handsome young prince then told the beautiful queen that he wanted her for his own forever. If she would return to Troy with him, he would make her the happiest woman in the world. Helen did not hesitate, but threw herself into the arms of Paris and kissed him. That night, with her young daughter Hermione in hand, she left the palace at Sparta with Paris and sailed for Troy.

When Helen had reached marriageable age a few years earlier, the greatest kings and warriors from all of Greece sought to win her hand. They brought magnificent gifts to her mortal father Tyndareus hoping that he would choose them for his daughter. Some of the many suitors were Ajax and Teucer, the nephews of Thetis' husband, Peleus; Diomedes, son of Tydeus, who had died attacking Thebes; Patroclus, the best friend of Achilles; and Odysseus, the wily king of Ithaca. But it was wealthy Menelaus, brother of Agamemnon, who brought the finest gifts.

Tyndareus had found himself in a terrible predicament, for any suitors he rejected were powerful men and would be angry at him for not being chosen. He was tempted to let Helen pick her own husband, but that would go against all tradition and would not temper harsh feelings. But then clever Odysseus came to him in secret. The king of the tiny island of Ithaca realized he was too poor to compete against the other suitors in bridal gifts, so he proposed to Tyndareus a way out of his predicament in exchange for a favor. If Tyndareus would arrange for Odysseus to take Tyndareus' niece Penelope back to Ithaca as his own wife, he would draw up an oath to be taken by all those seeking the hand of Helen. They would swear by the gods to accept peacefully the choice of Tyndareus. Moreover, if any man ever took Helen by force, they would fight to regain her for her lawful husband.

This seemed like the perfect solution to Tyndareus, so he arranged for his niece to marry Odysseus, then made every suitor swear to abide by his oath if they wanted Helen. Then, to no one's surprise, he chose Menelaus, who had given him the most valuable gifts. The rest of the suitors grumbled, but they had given their word they would cause no trouble. They were now also under obligation to risk their lives and honor to defend Helen if any man tried to take her by force. They all sailed home and married other women, but as they lay beside their wives at night, they all wondered in their hearts what it would be like to share the bed of Helen.

When they heard the news that young Paris had taken Helen back to Troy while Menelaus was away, the suitors felt a mixture of emotions. Most rejoiced to see Menelaus made the fool for being so stupid as to leave his young bride home alone with a handsome foreign prince. Many were also angry at Menelaus, for they realized they were now obligated to go to war with the Trojans to get her back. But when they began to think about it, many realized the prospect of a fight with Troy was not such a bad thing. They were warriors above all with a thirst for battle and a longing to be remembered for ages to come in the songs of bards. It also didn't hurt that the city on the shores of the Hellespont was rich beyond anyone's dreams. If they could take it, the plunder in treasure and slaves would be beyond measure. Agamemnon, the brother of Menelaus and greatest of the Greek kings, was especially thrilled by the turn of events since he had long dreamed of gathering an army large enough to take Troy. It would be a glorious and highly profitable adventure—and now he had the perfect excuse to make it happen.

Agamemnon sent word to all those who taken the oath of Tyndareus to begin gathering their armies at the Greek port of Aulis on the coast of Boeotia. Most came gladly in anticipation of plunder and glory, but there were exceptions. One of these was Odysseus, who had just settled into married life with his lovely bride Penelope and was enjoying spending time with her and his newborn son, Telemachus. He also knew what the other Greeks did not. Most thought they would sail to Troy, sack the city, and be home in time for harvest, their ships full of gold and female captives to serve them in the fields or in their beds. Odysseus, however, realized the war against Troy would be long and difficult, with the outcome anyone's guess. The walls of windswept Troy were famously strong and the men of the city great fighters, especially Hector, the son of King Priam. The Trojans also had numerous allies they could call upon from all over Asia Minor. Any war against Troy would have to be won by a siege that would take years. Odysseus knew that many of the Greeks so eager to sail across the Aegean would not return home to their families. He did not want to be one of them.

When Menelaus and his comrade Palamedes arrived at Ithaca to collect Odysseus for the campaign, they found the young king wearing a floppy felt hat, plowing a field with a horse and an ox yoked together and sowing the ground with salt. Penelope broke into tears and said her dear husband had gone mad, but Palamedes suspected it was a ruse. He grabbed baby Telemachus from Penelope's arms and ran into the field, placing the infant in the path of the plow while his mother screamed at Palamedes to stop. Odysseus headed straight for his son and seemed certain to trample him beneath the hooves of the animals, but at the last moment he turned the plow aside and picked up Telemachus from the furrow. Menelaus and Palamedes then knew that Odysseus was perfectly sane and fit for duty. To his credit, once he was discovered, Odysseus accepted his fate and threw himself wholeheartedly into preparations for the war. He gathered twelve shiploads of men from his island and outfitted them for a long fight. He embraced Penelope, making her promise that she would wed again if he did not return by the time Telemachus began to grow a beard. He then kissed his wife and son, took one last look at Ithaca, and sailed away. He knew in his heart it would be a long time before he gazed on its shores again, but he swore he would somehow make it home.

The marriage of the sea goddess Thetis and her mortal husband Peleus had been a happy one until their son Achilles was born. Some say the cause of their marital problems was the day Peleus discovered his wife was secretly dipping their son in ambrosia and roasting him in a fire at night to make him immortal, as Demeter had done for a human child at Eleusis. When Peleus saw this, he cried out in terror and grabbed the boy from the flames. Thetis was so indignant that she left her husband and returned to the sea, though she always had a mother's love for Achilles. Others say that the goddess tried to make her son immortal by dipping him into the waters of the river Styx, but she held Achilles by his heel during the process so that this one part of his body did not get wet and was therefore vulnerable to weapons.

Peleus took his young son to Mount Pelion to be raised by the wise centaur Chiron, just as Jason had been. His half-human, half-horse teacher instructed Achilles in music and poetry, athletics and war, feeding him the entrails of wild animals to make him brave. While he was still a youth, he returned to his father in Phthia and completed his education under an aged tutor named Phoenix. While there, he met a young man named Patroclus, who became his best friend and, some say, his lover.

When preparations for the Trojan War began, the Greek leaders received an oracle that they needed the son of Peleus on their side to take the city. But Achilles' divine mother Thetis knew that if her son sailed to Troy, he would not return. The Fates had decreed that Achilles would either live a long, quiet life, dying in bed and soon forgotten, or he would become the greatest hero of the age and be remembered forever, though his life would be short. Thetis knew which path her son would pick if he could choose, so she sent him to the small island of Scyros in the Aegean and dressed him like a girl to keep his identity a secret.

Achilles hated this deception, for he longed to prove himself in battle, but he was an obedient son and followed his mother's wishes. Odysseus, nonetheless, received word that Achilles was hiding on Scyros and set out to find him. He came as a merchant to the palace there and spread out his wares in the courtyard for the king's many daughters to examine. Among the jewelry and perfumes he placed a fine sword and spear, hoping it would attract the eye of the missing boy. At a prearranged signal, his herald sounded a trumpet as if the palace were being attacked. The girls all screamed and ran for cover, but one especially tall and well-built young woman grabbed the weapons and ran to the walls to fight the enemy. That was when Odysseus knew he had found Achilles. The youth was relieved to have been discovered and gladly boarded the ship to sail to Aulis with Odysseus. Childhood was over and he was at last going to war.

The men who had sworn the oath to Tyndareus formed the heart of the Greek expedition against Troy, but many flocked to Aulis who had never sought the hand of Helen, all hoping for fortune and glory. Agamemnon brought a hundred ships full of men from Mycenae when he took command of the expedition, while his brother Menelaus came with sixty from Sparta. Young Achilles may have arrived late, but he brought many brave warriors from the kingdom of his father Peleus, including his friend Patroclus. Besides Ajax the son of Telamon, there was the son of Oileus bearing the same name, known to the men as Little Ajax. Old King Nestor came from Pylos leading ninety ships, while the great warrior Diomedes of Argos came with thirty ships. Menestheus brought fifty long black ships from Athens, with Agapenor leading enough men to fill sixty ships from the mountains of Arcadia. Idomeneus, king of Crete, arrived with eighty ships. Philoctetes, who had once kindled the funeral pyre of Hercules, could muster only a few shiploads of men, but he brought the weapons he had received as a gift from the great hero. Agamemnon also recruited Calchas the great prophet from Megara. Besides these, there were countless other kings, princes, and warriors gathered on the beach at Aulis to launch a thousands ships for the sake of a beautiful woman.

The vast armada set sail with great fanfare across the Aegean and in a few days arrived on the coast of Asia Minor near the Hellespont. If they had been better sailors, they might have taken the Trojans by surprise, but instead they landed and began to lay waste to the countryside. It did not take them long to figure out they were not at Troy at all but somewhere on the shore of Mysia to the south. By the time they started back to the ships, the king of Mysia, a son of Hercules and son-in-law of King Priam named Telephus, had already launched an attack on their rear and killed many of the invaders. Achilles did manage to wound Telephus with his spear when the king tripped on a vine, but it was an inglorious beginning for the Greeks.

The ships were tossed by storms on their retreat and were soon separated from one another. At last they made their way back to Aulis, where the disheartened men grumbled that this was no way to wage a war. To make matters worse, the winds had begun to blow against them so that they could not set out to sea again.

One day not long afterward, they were surprised to see King Telephus of Mysia arrive on the beach limping from his recent wound. He made his way to the tent of Agamemnon under a flag of truce and explained that he was there because of an oracle. He was in excruciating pain from the wound Achilles had given him, so he had sought the advice of Apollo, who had told him he could be healed only by that which had harmed him. Achilles protested that he was no physician, but Odysseus suggested they interpret the words of the god in a different way. It wasn't really Achilles who had injured Telephus, he argued, but his spear.

Therefore they took the weapon and scraped the rust from it into the wound. Soon the pain had ceased and the injury began to heal.

Agamemnon was actually glad to see Telephus since the Greeks had just received their own oracle saying that they could not win the war unless the Mysian king came with them to Troy. This put Telephus in a terrible predicament, since he owed a debt of honor to the Greeks for healing him, but also had familial obligations to the Trojans. He compromised by agreeing to guide the armada to Troy, but not to fight on their side. Agamemnon agreed and Telephus readied himself to lead the fleet across the Aegean—if only the wind would stop blowing.

Weeks went by in the Greek camp at Aulis while the enthusiasm of the men for the war rapidly began to wane. Food ran short, disease set in, and the idle soldiers grew more and more restless. It was a nightmare for Agamemnon, who tried to keep up the spirits of the men but knew they would have to sail soon or disband the army. He prayed to the gods and sacrificed extravagantly that they might stop the wind, but still it blew.

At last Agamemnon sent for the seer Calchas. He came, most reluctantly, and said had already consulted every sign he could think of from the flight of birds to the entrails of bulls, but the answer was always the same. Artemis was angry because King Agamemnon had once boasted during a hunt that he could hurl a spear even better than the goddess. When Agamemnon demanded to know what he must do to propitiate the goddess, Calchas hesitated and begged him to send the army home. When the king grabbed him by the throat and threatened to strangle him unless he spoke, the soothsayer declared that the only way to win the favor of Artemis and calm the contrary wind was for Agamemnon to sacrifice his own daughter, the beautiful maiden Iphigenia, to the goddess.

Agamemnon loved his daughter, but he loved power more. The other captains said they could not hold their men at Aulis much longer and demanded he sacrifice the girl for the sake of the war effort. The king reluctantly agreed. He sent a message to his wife, Clytemnestra, at Mycenae that he had decided to give Iphigenia to handsome young Achilles as his bride. The queen was thrilled with the match and quickly brought their daughter to Aulis. But when they arrived, Agamemnon seized Iphigenia and bound her for the altar. The priests first placed a gag tightly around her mouth, for the curse of a doomed virgin was powerful.

Agamemnon recited the ritual prayers and raised his hands to the goddess of the hunt that she might let them sail to Troy. The priests then lifted the maiden in her wedding dress, a bride of death, onto the altar. The girl could not believe what was happening. Would her own father, who had held her as a child in his arms, who had loved to hear her sing in his halls, really kill her? But there she was, trussed like an animal, throat bared to his sharp blade. She pleaded with him with her eyes, but he refused to meet her gaze. Tears rolling down his cheeks, Agamemnon raised the knife to the sky, then slit her throat in one quick movement.

Some say that at the last moment Artemis rescued the girl, substituting a doe for the sacrifice. These stories say the goddess took Iphigenia to live among the wild Taurian natives of the Crimea, where she became a priestess presiding over the sacrifice of strangers unlucky enough to land on those shores. But most agree that the maiden met her end there on a bloody altar at Aulis, a sacrifice to the ambition of men.

The wind died away, then the Greeks set off from Aulis to sail once again to Troy. Scrupulous in their desire to stay on the good side of the gods, they stopped at the island of Lemnos halfway across the Aegean to offer sacrifices. Philoctetes, a master archer, helped with the preparation of the sheep, goats, and oxen for the altar, but while he was busying himself around the rough-hewn stone, a snake crawled out and bit him on the foot. Soon his foot swelled to twice its normal size and began to ooze a horrid pus that smelled even worse than it looked. The men all liked Philoctetes, but they could not stand the stench and so abandoned him on the island to fend for himself. Only the kindness of a local shepherd saved him from starving to death as he passed his days in agonizing pain from a wound that would not heal.

The fleet made its way toward the Hellespont, past the small island of Tenedos just off the Asian coast, then to the mainland near the mouth of the Scamander River that flowed near Troy. The men could all see the great city in the distance, prominent on its hilltop citadel overlooking the plain above the sea. Few had ever gazed at walls so tall and strong, and none had ever seen an army like the one that had gathered to meet them. The Trojans had known the Greeks were coming ever since word of their misadventure in Mysia had reached the city. They had gathered their allies from all over Asia Minor to stand with them on the plain before their city. More than one brave man in the Greek army stared at the vast Trojan forces and wondered why he had ever left home.

The Greeks had earlier received an oracle that the first man to land on Trojan soil would die. Knowing this, everyone hung back, afraid to be the first to leap onto the beach, until at last Protesilaus, king of Phylace in southern Thessaly, set aside his fear and jumped onto the sand. Hector met him with a spear through his heart, shedding the first blood of the war. Achilles was there in an instant to drive Hector away, then he attacked Cycnus, a Trojan ally and ruler of a nearby town. His father, Poseidon, had made him invulnerable to weapons, so Achilles strangled him with the man's own helmet strap. The rest of the Greeks soon reached the shore and began to drive back the defenders to establish a beachhead. It was slow, bloody work, but by nightfall the Trojans had withdrawn to their city, leaving the Greeks to make a fortified camp on the shore. Priam and his subjects, watching from the walls, were not worried to see the foreigners holding their coast, for they knew the walls of Troy could not be breeched by any man. If the Greeks chose to stay, it was going to be a long war.

The conflict quickly evolved into a stalemate, with the Greeks unable to take the city and the Trojans unable to drive the Greeks from their shores. Battles were fought on the plain in front of the town, but neither side could gain a decisive advantage. When the Greeks realized they could not take Troy by force, they began to attack the lands of the city's allies in an attempt to disrupt Troy's supply chain. These raids also served to keep up the morale of the invaders by offering the men booty and captives as the war dragged on. The Greeks, led by Achilles, sacked over twenty cities that supported Troy, killing their men, taking their treasure, and marching their women and children back to camp as slaves.

For nine years the conflict continued with no end in sight. The Trojans still flourished behind their walls, transporting food and luxuries into the city with ease in spite of Greek efforts to stop them. Agamemnon and his army maintained a marginally profitable war due to their raids, but after so long everyone was growing weary of the increasingly pointless conflict.

It was the captive women who kept up the spirits of the Greeks on those dark nights, though in their hearts they had no wish to do so. The women of Asia were exotic compared with the wives of the Greeks back home and more willing to please since their very lives depended on keeping the Greek warriors happy. Agamemnon was particularly enchanted by a beautiful young slave named Chryseis, taken from a small town south of Troy. She was the daughter of Chryses, a priest of Apollo. Achilles also had his favorite, a young woman named Briseis from Lyrnessus near Mount Ida. He had killed her husband, parents, and brothers when he sacked their town, then bound her and put her on board his ship. When he returned to the Greek camp near Troy, she served him fearfully but faithfully in his tent.

It was the custom of the time to ransom captives for gold, if there were any relatives left alive to make such a payment. This practice was looked on favorably both by the gods and by those holding the slaves since the women were a replaceable source of profit. Accordingly, one day soon after his daughter was taken, the priest Chryses made his way to the camp of the Greeks bearing gifts and holding before him the sacred staff of Apollo. He asked Agamemnon to accept his ransom and release his daughter, as it would be pleasing to the god. The Greeks all agreed this was a reasonable request and urged their leader to accept, but Agamemnon rose from his throne and knocked the gifts from the hands of the suppliant priest, crying, "Get out of my sight, old man, and never let me see you in this camp again! I will never give up the girl! I'm taking her back to Mycenae with me when this war is over to work at the loom and share my bed."

With that, the king drove the terrified priest out of his tent. Chryses lifted his hands to the god he served and prayed, "Apollo, god of the silver bow, if ever I have offered pleasing sacrifices to you, if ever I have burned the bones of bulls and goats wrapped in rich fat at your altars, hear my prayer! Strike down these Greeks who mock your priest. Rain your arrows down upon them!"

The god heard the prayer of his faithful priest and flew down from Olympus bow in hand. He knelt on a hill above the Greek camp and shot his arrows of plague among the tents. The men began to fall, then die, and soon the funeral fires burned day and night.

At last Achilles called an assembly of the Greek leaders and said they should sail for home unless they could find out why the gods were punishing them. The seer Calchas arose and said he would reveal the truth, but first Achilles had to promise he would protect him from the wrath of the one at fault. The young warrior agreed, then Calchas said Agamemnon was to blame for spurning the ransom offered by Apollo's priest Chryses. If the king of Mycenae would return the girl, the archer god would stop the plague.

Agamemnon raged against Calchas and complained that it wasn't fair that he, the leader of the Greek expedition, should have to give up his prize while others kept theirs: "I like this young woman of mine, even better than my own wife Clytemnestra. But I'm a reasonable man. I'll give up the girl if I receive a slave of equal beauty and quality from one of you."

Achilles shot back, "And just who do you expect to give up his woman to keep you happy, you greedy pig? It's not like we have a tent full of women for you to choose from. For once think of the troops more than yourself. Surrender the girl and you can have all the women you want when we sack Troy."

But Agamemnon would not change his mind: "You're telling me how to lead an army, you young pup? I was killing men on the battlefield while you were still wetting your pants. Just to show you who's in charge, I'm going to take your prize, Achilles. Have the girl Briseis made ready and I'll send my men for her."

Achilles was going to draw his sword and kill Agamemnon then and there, but the goddess Athena, visible only to him, appeared and ordered him to stop. Achilles reluctantly agreed, but he told Agamemnon and the rest of the men present that he was withdrawing from the war along with all his men. The other leaders begged him to reconsider, but he would hear none of it. His honor had been insulted and his anger would not be mollified. They would all see the face of Hades before he or his soldiers fought the Trojans again.

Obedient to the goddess, Achilles sent Briseis to Agamemnon, then sulked in his tent until his divine mother, Thetis, came and asked what she could do. He urged her to go to Zeus and ask the ruler of the gods to help the Trojans, just to teach the Greeks how much they needed him. He wanted to see thousands of Greeks lying dead on the plains of Troy so that Agamemnon would be humbled and beg him to fight for them again. Thetis agreed and flew to Olympus, where she grasped the knees of Zeus in supplication and asked him to abandon his neutrality, at least for a little while, and aid the Trojans. Zeus agreed, though he knew it would get him into trouble with Hera, who staunchly supported the Greeks.

To urge the king into ill-timed action, Zeus sent a misleading dream down to Agamemnon telling him that if he attacked the Trojans at once, a great victory would be his. The Greek leader jumped from his bed and called an assembly, telling the soldiers he had received a vision from the gods that they would crush the Trojans and take their city that very day. Restless after years of waiting, the Greek warriors all cheered the king and put on their armor. The great battle was upon them at last.

Hector was watching the Greek camp from the walls of the city and saw the rush of activity among the tents. He knew this could mean only one thing and so marshaled the whole Trojan army to meet the enemy on the plain. Soon both sides were facing each other across a narrow no-man's-land between the armies. Agamemnon stood in his chariot at the center of the Greek lines with his brother Menelaus beside him. Ajax, Odysseus, Diomedes, and all the other Greek captains—except Achilles—were at the front of their own troops waiting for the sound of the trumpet. Hector and his brother Paris stood facing them, Trojan troops and allies gathered all around.

For nine years Menelaus had suffered the humiliation of fighting against the young Trojan who had lured Helen away. The Spartan king was a brave man and a great fighter, but he knew that the men whispered about him behind his back wondering why they were risking their lives for a man who couldn't keep his own wife. He bitterly resented playing the cuckold to Paris, so when he saw the prince standing opposite him he jumped down from his chariot and made as if he would attack the Trojan lines all by himself. Paris cringed and ran behind his brother Hector, hiding from the towering Greek warrior. Hector forced him back, calling him a coward and a fool, to which he replied, "Ah, Hector, you're right, of course. You were always so brave, while I was better with the ladies than on the battlefield. I know this whole war is because of me, so I suppose I should be the one to end it. Send a herald to the Greeks telling Menelaus that I will fight him to the death in single combat. The winner takes Helen, honor will be satisfied, and everyone can go home at last."

Menelaus was glad to take up the challenge and both armies rejoiced at the prospect of the war ending that day. Sacrifices were made and binding oaths taken before the gods that Greek and Trojans alike would respect the outcome of the fight. All swore that no man would interfere in the contest between champions and that none would launch a weapon against the other side during the sacred truce. Then the armies stood and watched as the veteran warrior of Sparta marched to the space between the lines to face the young prince of Troy. Helen herself, the prize of the contest, stood on the walls beside King Priam to see what her fate would be.

Menelaus moved first, hurling his oak spear straight at Paris. The shaft flew so fast it broke through the Trojan's shield and struck his breastplate full force, but Paris swerved aside at the last moment and avoided the deadly point. Then Menelaus drew his silver-studded sword and ran at Paris, bringing the blade down on the crest of his helmet, though his sword broke into pieces on impact. Paris was stunned but still on his feet as Menelaus stood without a weapon before the Trojan fighter. But instead of withdrawing, the Greek warrior rushed at Paris and grabbed him by his helmet strap, knocking him off his feet. He began to drag him back to the Greek lines to kill him there—but the goddess Aphrodite was watching and was not going to let Paris die that day. She snapped the rawhide strap and whisked him away to his perfumed bedroom safe inside the walls of Troy.

Paris woke to find himself lying on his bed and knew the goddess had intervened. He was thrilled to be alive and sent for Helen so that they might make love to celebrate. Menelaus meanwhile stalked up and down the lines looking for Paris. It was then that a Trojan archer named Pandarus saw his chance for glory and shot his deadly arrow at the Spartan king. The shaft found its way home and struck the king on the groin, but only a glancing blow. The Greeks shouted that the Trojans had broken the truce and rushed forward with spears in hand. The Trojans yielded not an inch and met their enemy there on the plain. All hope of a peaceful end to the war that day vanished as both sides met like two giant waves crashing together. Soon the field was littered with the broken bodies of Greeks and Trojans sprawled side by side, facedown in the dust.

No Greek warrior was more inflamed with battle lust than Diomedes of Argos. He cut through the Trojan lines taking on man after man in combat as the gods stood watching, invisible on the battlefield. He would have slain Aeneas, son of Anchises and Aphrodite, but Aeneas' divine mother picked him up before Diomedes could drive home the fatal blow. Then Athena, who favored Diomedes, lifted the mist from his eyes so that he could see the gods on the plain. She also whispered to him to stab Aphrodite with his bronze spear should the chance arise.

No sooner had the virgin goddess withdrawn than Diomedes spotted Aphrodite among the Trojan ranks and began to stalk her through the killing fields. When he was finally close enough, he lunged at her with his spear and stabbed her through the wrist, forcing her to drop Aeneas on the ground. Gods cannot die, but they can be wounded. Aphrodite shrieked and fled from the battle. Diomedes could not resist mocking her as she withdrew: "What's the matter, goddess, giving up war so soon? Maybe you should stick to ruining people's lives with your petty schemes. I don't think you'll be fighting any more today."

Soon after, Diomedes rammed his spear into the gut of the war god Ares, who was also aiding the Trojans. Aphrodite and Ares flew to Olympus to complain to Zeus that Athena was letting a mortal man attack them, then Athena joined them on the mountain to defend herself until the ruler of the gods wearied of their whining and sent them all away.

Back on the battlefield, Diomedes was about to kill Aeneas and strip him of his armor when he saw Apollo himself astride the Trojan warrior. Even before this mighty god, Diomedes did not flinch, but tried three times to drive him away. But on the fourth attempt, Apollo spoke to him: "Think, Diomedes, think about what you're doing. You are a man and I am an immortal god. We're not alike and never will be. I don't want to destroy you, but I swear I will. Stop before it's too late."

The great warrior of Argos came to his senses and ceased his attack on the god, turning his attention instead to mortal foes.

The Trojan prince Hector was in the forefront of the fighting and saw his men falling all around him. When the Greeks at last were pressing close to the gates of the city, Hector told his captains to hold the line while he went back to Troy to tell the women of the city to pray and sacrifice to the gods for salvation. He made his way through the rear of his lines and ran through the gates and up to the citadel. As he passed the rooms of Paris, he saw his brother lounging on a couch, worn out from making love to Helen, and cried, "By the gods, Paris, what are you doing here while the enemy is at our very walls? Get up and join the battle, you miserable wretch, before the city is burned to ashes around you!"

Having roused his brother, he ran to his own halls to find his wife, Andromache, and tell her to organize the women to beseech the gods. She was not in their rooms, but he found her on top of the city walls watching the battle anxiously, hoping and praying that her husband was still alive.

After they embraced and he had given her instructions, she held out their son, little Astyanax, to him. But when the child saw the crested bronze covering the face of his father, he cried in terror. Hector laughed and removed the helmet, then took the boy in his arms. Andromache held her husband and begged him not to return to battle: "Dear Hector, I am alone in this world. You are my father now, and my mother, my brother too. You are my husband, young and warm and strong. Think of your son and stay with us. I don't want to be a widow. You know what will happen if the Greeks kill you and take the city. I will be dragged back to Greece as a slave, as is the fate of vanquished women in war. Stay here, please, where it is safe."

Hector held her close to him and said, "My beloved, I must return to the battle. I would die in shame before my men if I stayed here safe on the walls while they fought below. In my heart I know there will come a day when sacred Troy will fall. My blessed father, Priam, will perish along with my brothers, while my aged mother, Hecuba, will be taken back to Greece to spin flax as a lowly slave. But none of that compares to the pain I feel when I think of some Greek tearing you away from your home to work his loom—and serve him in other ways as well. Still, I cannot give up the fight. It may well be my fate to die here, but I will never be called a coward."

With that he left his weeping wife to return to the battle.

No sooner had Hector made his way back to the field than Ajax, son of Telamon, found him and challenged him to combat. The Trojan prince did not turn away from the giant who towered over him, but put on his helmet and faced the man, not giving an inch. Men on both sides watched intently as the two great warriors faced each other. Hector threw his spear first and struck the shield of Ajax but could not pierce it. The Greek then set his spear flying through the air until it struck Hector's shield and penetrated it, tearing into the breastplate and even the shirt of his foe. Hector would have died then, but he turned away at the last instant as the mighty shaft cut through his armor. The two then set on each other with swords and fought until night began to fall on the plain. At last, heralds from both sides called on the pair to cease because of darkness. Each hated to yield, but both withdrew to mend their wounds and fight another day. After the Greeks dragged themselves back to their camp, they feasted and raised a toast to their many friends who had fallen that day. Come sunrise, they boasted, they would surely storm the walls and take the city of Troy.

It was now that Zeus remembered his promise to Thetis to make the Greeks beg Achilles for help. When Agamemnon and his men came to Troy the next morning ready to storm the city, Zeus sent down his lightning bolts like rain upon the Greeks. The shafts of fire split the earth and threw both men and horses into a panic. The wisest among them, such as old Nestor, realized at once that the ruler of the gods had turned against them. Some, like Diomedes, hesitated before the walls as the fire bolts fell, still yearning to climb the mighty towers of Troy and sack the city. But no man can fight a god like Zeus, so the Greeks fell back while Hector and the Trojans took heart and pursued them across the plain, killing countless warriors as they fled.

What seemed like certain victory for the Greeks had now turned to bitter defeat. The invaders huddled behind their ramparts on the beach praying that the Trojans would not attack them that night and drive them into the sea. All hope seemed lost as they gazed out at hundreds

of Trojan fires spreading across the plain like stars in the sky, for Hector
and his men had not even bothered returning to the city that night, but
pitched their tents before the Greek camp, ready to strike at dawn.

Meanwhile the Greek captains met with Agamemnon to decide
what to do. Many wanted to sail away that very night, but Nestor rose
and urged them to send an embassy to Achilles, begging him to return
to the fight. If only Agamemnon would set aside his pride, he counseled,
the Greeks might be able to drive the Trojans back. Agamemnon then
rose and admitted he had been wrong. Blind, he claimed, blind he had
been because of anger. He would send heralds to Achilles immediately
to apologize and offer splendid gifts to win the young warrior over. He
would send back Briseis, swearing he had never touched her, along with
magnificent treasures of gold and bronze. He would also promise Achilles
his own daughter in marriage when they returned to Greece if only he
would set aside his stubborn pride.

Odysseus led the embassy to the tents of Achilles, where they found
the great warrior playing the lyre, singing songs of glorious heroes of old.
Their host rose and greeted them warmly. He sat in the light of his fire
and listened to every word carefully, then addressed Odysseus: "Son of
Laertes, let me say this plainly and quickly. Will Agamemnon's generous
offer win me over? Not for all the world. Let him keep Briseis if he wants,
but he won't have me, for I have my honor. I'm going to sail away tomor-
row at daybreak. All of you should as well, for the Trojans are going to
crush you."

After this, aged Phoenix, who had once been the tutor of Achilles,
rose and addressed his pupil. Like all good teachers he did not lecture,
but instead told a story of another man who had also once been implacable in his anger. This was Meleager, king of Calydon, who had sailed
with Jason on the *Argo*. When he returned from that voyage, he fell in
love with and married a beautiful woman named Cleopatra. He ruled
his land with temperance and wisdom, but one day he slew his uncle
after the man tried to take the hide of the Calydonian Boar from him,
prompting his own mother to curse him for killing her favorite brother.
Meleager was so angry at her that he refused to fight when the Curetes,
his uncle's tribe, attacked his city. The enemy were at the gates, but still
he refused to leave his chambers. His family and friends came to him

begging him to reconsider, but he would not hear their words. At last
when the Curetes had breeched the walls and were on the verge of taking the palace itself, his wife, Cleopatra, came to him and urged him one
final time to rejoin the fight. She asked if he truly understood the consequences of his actions, if he really wanted to see her raped and killed
or taken away into slavery. Meleager then yielded and led his warriors to
victory, for he realized before it was too late that anger and pride would
cost him that which he held most dear.

Achilles listened to the story of Phoenix, but he did not understand
the meaning of his words. He still refused to fight and sent the embassy
of Agamemnon away empty-handed. If the Greeks were going to face the
Trojans, they would have to do it without him.

The Greek warriors hardly slept that night as fear walked among them
in the darkness. But when dawn came, Zeus sent the goddess Strife down
to the Greek camp to stir up their courage. Strife was delighted with
how events had unfolded since she had rolled the apple into the wedding
celebration of Peleus and Thetis. Now she stood on the hull of Odysseus'
black-bellied ship moored in the middle of the Greek fleet and let out a
cry, great and terrible, that put the lust for battle into the hearts of the
beleaguered invaders. Though just moments earlier the fight had seemed
hopeless, now they yearned to meet the overwhelming Trojan force—
just as Zeus intended.

The Greek captains led their men over the ramparts against the
army of Hector, urging them on with promises of glorious victory. But
soon, though the Trojans took their share of casualties, the best of the
Greeks began to fall. A Trojan spearman came up on the blind side of
Agamemnon and slashed him on the arm down to the bone, forcing
him to withdraw from battle. Next mighty Diomedes was struck in the
foot with an arrow, raw pain stabbing through his flesh and making him
retreat behind the lines. Then Odysseus was surrounded by Trojans eager
to claim the glory of slaying the son of Laertes. He fought off many, but
one soldier stabbed him with a sharp spear and cut through his armor,
tearing the skin clean off his ribs. The king of Ithaca then also withdrew,
leaving precious few Greek officers to encourage the men.

Achilles had been watching from the rampart above his tent at the far end of the line and sent his dearest friend, Patroclus, to Nestor to ask the old man for news of the battle. He had intended to sail back to Greece that morning, but could not bring himself to leave. Nestor welcomed Patroclus and told him that the Greeks were losing badly and could not keep the Trojans from the ships much longer. If they set the Greek ships ablaze, he warned, they were doomed. He begged Patroclus to join the fight himself if the pride of Achilles kept him from battle. Even the sight of Achilles' friend might be enough to drive the Trojans back.

As Patroclus ran to the camp of Achilles to ask his friend if he might fight, Hector at last smashed through the rampart guarding the Greek ships. His eyes flashed with fire as he ordered the Trojans to make for the ships, torches in hand. The Greeks fought desperately to hold the enemy back, but yard by yard the Trojans came closer to the first ship of the fleet. Idomeneus, king of Crete, led the Greeks in the drive to hold the Trojans back. He was a magnificent warrior who never slackened in his battle rage. When one Trojan prince named Alcathous charged him, Idomeneus stabbed him square in the chest and split his breastbone in two, driving the tip of his spear into his heart. Alcathous fell on his back and lay sprawling in the dust, the spear jerking in time with the final beats of his heart.

But nothing could keep the Trojans away as they broke like waves over the walls of the Greek camp. Finally they reached the closest of the Greek ships and threw their torches inside the hull. The flames rose up and engulfed it, lighting up the sky like a beacon of victory for the Trojans. The Greeks still held the enemy back from the rest of the fleet, but they all knew they would not live to see the dawn of another day.

Zeus sat on Mount Olympus and happily watched all these events unfold. He had forbidden the other gods from getting involved in the war while he turned the tide against the Greeks, but those who favored Agamemnon's men, such as his wife, Hera, could not stand to see their side losing so badly. Hera knew she could not challenge Zeus directly, so she tried a more subtle approach.

She went to her chamber and bathed in the most enticing perfumes known to the gods, then rubbed olive oil on her naked body until it glimmered. She next put on a clinging robe that flattered her perfect form and applied a magical elixir she had gotten from Aphrodite. Then she went to the god Sleep, brother of Death, and promised him one of the beautiful Graces as his wife if he would put her husband to sleep at just the right moment. At last she strolled past the mountain meadow where Zeus was sitting as if she were just passing by on the way to visit a friend.

Zeus saw her and immediately was filed with burning desire. Whatever the mortals were doing down on the plain of Troy, it could wait. He called to her, "Hera, why hurry away? Come, let's lose ourselves in love. Never have I seen a goddess or mortal woman who has made my heart pound so. Europa, Semele, Leto—they were all nothing compared to you."

But crafty Hera replied, "My lord, son of Cronus, what are you saying? We can't make love here in the open in the middle of the day. What if someone were to see us?"

Then Zeus answered her, "Not to worry. Look, I'm spreading a thick cloud about us that will cover us from sight. Take off your clothes, my dear, I've got to have you now!"

And so the pair made love on the grass, hidden from the sight of gods and men by a thick mist. Then, when Zeus was finished, Sleep poured his potion on him so that he fell into a deep slumber.

Hera was up in an instant and flying down the slopes of Olympus to the Greek camp outside Troy. She stirred the Greeks to rally and hold back the Trojans. Ajax even managed to knock Hector out of the fighting for a short time with a rock that hit the Trojan leader on the chest and spun him like a top. Back and forth the tide of battle shifted as one moment the Greeks pushed the Trojans from the ships, then the next they were driven back to the sea.

Patroclus had returned to the camp of Achilles and implored his friend to let him join the fight with their men. Achilles agreed and even gave him his own armor to wear, but warned his dear companion only to drive the Trojans back from the ships, not to take the battle to the city, for he would not be there to stand beside him. Patroclus agreed and put on the shining armor, then led many hundreds of fresh troops into the fight.

The appearance of Patroclus and his men brought hope to the Greeks and terror to their enemies. The Trojans thought that Achilles had finally put aside his anger and was rejoining the fight. With a tremendous roar, the Greeks rallied and pushed the Trojans over the ramparts and back onto the plain. The excitement was so great that the men began to believe they might take Troy itself that day. Patroclus had forgotten the warning of his friend and ordered the men to follow him to the walls of the city.

The Greeks indeed would have taken Troy then if Zeus had not awoken in anger and sent his son Apollo to stand before the ramparts of the city. The young god came up behind Patroclus and slammed him between the shoulders, stunning him like an oxen for sacrifice. A Trojan warrior named Euphorbus then struck him with a spear, but did not bring him down. Immediately Hector was there with his own bronze-tipped spear and stabbed Patroclus clean through the gut so that the blade came out his back. The fair young soldier fell into the dust, his soul flying down to the house of Hades, leaving life behind.

Hector stripped the armor of Achilles off his dead companion and would have taken his corpse back to Troy as well, but Menelaus ran and stood over him like a mother cow protecting her newborn calf. The Greek captain finally drove Hector away and put the body of his comrade into a chariot to return it to the Greek camp for proper funeral rites. Hector let him go, but gloried in his new armor and in the fact that he had killed Patroclus, one of the greatest of the Greek warriors and the closest friend of Achilles.

The son of Peleus and Thetis knew his companion was dead even before the Greeks brought the body to his tent. The wail that went up from the Greek lines told him all he needed to know. When at last the corpse of Patroclus lay before him, Achilles sat in the dust tearing his hair, weeping uncontrollably. He let loose a terrible, wrenching cry so loud that even Thetis in the depths of the sea heard it and came to comfort her son. She told him that as horrible as things seemed, he had gotten what he wanted. Agamemnon had suffered deeply for his pride and the Greeks realized they could not win the war without him.

But Achilles knew all that meant little now that Patroclus was gone. Phoenix had been right. His own pride had cost him that which he loved the most. At last he agreed to set aside his anger and rejoin the fight, with the intention to destroy Hector, even if it meant he himself would soon die. Nothing mattered now but revenge.

Achilles' mother, Thetis, flew to the home of the divine smith, Hephaestus, to ask the god to make new armor for her son. As Thetis had once rescued him when Zeus threw the god down from Olympus, Hephaestus was happy to help her. He stoked his fire and called on his handmaids—living, breathing girls made of gold who worked the forge with him. Then he set to work on a set of armor like no man had ever seen. The enormous shield was embossed with figures telling stories of two noble cities, one at war, one at peace. On it men and women fought and plowed, died and danced. There were vineyards and palaces, cattle and meadows, weddings and battles—all the world was there, encircled on the rim of the shield by the mighty river of Ocean. He also forged a breastplate gleaming like fire, a sturdy helmet, and greaves to cover the warrior's legs. Thetis thanked Hephaestus from her heart and winged backed to Troy to present the magnificent gifts to her son, who now armed himself for battle.

Zeus looked down on the plain of Troy and knew his promise to Thetis had been kept. The Greeks honored the young warrior like no other as he marched onto the battlefield to fight the Trojans. The first enemy captain he met was Aeneas, son of the goddess Aphrodite. Achilles would have killed him there, but the gods saved him. They knew it was his fate to preserve the line of Troy and found another, greater city far to the west. Achilles then turned to other Trojans and slaughtered them like sheep. The Scamander that flowed through the plain became so clogged with his victims that the god of the river rose up against the Greek warrior and ordered him to stop. When Achilles refused, the river leapt out of its banks and pursued him across the plain like a tidal wave until Hephaestus came to his aid and used fire to force the river back.

At last Achilles reached the walls of Troy and called Hector forth. His father, mother, and dear wife, Andromache, begged him not to go, but he donned his armor and went through the gates to face the greatest warrior of the age. The two fought like lions with neither gaining the advantage at first, but Hector knew he could not long match the rage of Achilles. At last he turned to flee and ran three times around the walls of Troy while Achilles chased him. Then the goddess Athena appeared to Hector in the form of his brother Deiphobus and told him they would fight together against their foe. Hector rallied and turned to make his stand against Achilles, but as the Greek warrior drew near, Deiphobus vanished and Hector knew he was doomed. He fought bravely, but finally Achilles triumphed and drove his spear deep into Hector's neck. As Hector breathed his last, Achilles gloried over him and promised the fallen soldier that the dogs and birds would soon feast on his corpse. When the soul of the Trojan had departed, Achilles pierced the tendons of his feet with rawhide and dragged his body back to the Greek camp in the dust while his family on the walls looked on in horror. No one had ever treated an enemy so, but the anger of Achilles and his grief over the death of Patroclus knew no bounds.

The funeral rites for Patroclus were splendid and included the sacrifice of horses, dogs, and Trojan captives. All the while the corpse of Hector lay unburied in the camp of Achilles, though the gods preserved it from decay. Zeus favored Achilles, but he could not allow him to dishonor the dead so. He sent Thetis to him to demand he take a ransom for the body of his enemy. Achilles reluctantly agreed, but only if some warrior of the Trojans was brave enough to cross the lines and claim him.

Later that night, King Priam had a vision telling him to go to Achilles and redeem the body of his son. His wife and family said he was mad to put himself into the hands of the monster who had so brutalized Hector, but the old man had no fear. Guided by Hermes, Priam drove a cart across the plain alone in the darkness. When he came to the tent of Achilles, he entered it and fell down on his knees before the warrior. He took the hands of Achilles—the very hands that had killed his son— and kissed them, asking him to give him the corpse for a proper burial.

Achilles was stunned to see the old king before him and was moved with pity. He thought of his own aged father, Peleus, across the sea whom he would never see again. He thought of all the young men who had fallen and died on the battlefield in hope of eternal glory, though now they were but dust and ashes. And at last he thought of his beloved Patroclus, who loved life so, but perished in the bloom of youth, never to rise again. Memory and remorse overcame both men in the tent that night, tears pouring down their faces as they realized the true cost of war.

Achilles carried the body of Hector to Priam's cart and laid him gently inside. He then bade Priam farewell and sent him back to Troy under safe conduct, granting him ten days of peace to mourn and bury his son. The women of the city keened songs of sorrow when they saw the corpse of noble Hector entering the gates. He was the best among them, both as warrior and as a man. His mother, Hecuba, embraced him, then Andromache held him close one last time. The Trojans built a great funeral pyre for their hero and burned his body as was proper. When the flames at last had died away, they gathered his white bones, wrapped them in purple cloth, and laid them at last within a golden chest in a grave.

Hector was dead, but the walls of Troy still stood and new allies were arriving to bolster the still massive army of King Priam. Penthesileia, ruler of the Amazons and a daughter of the war god Ares, rode onto the plain with her warrior women and killed many of the best Greek fighters. But Achilles mortally wounded the queen and then fell in love with her as she lay dying. Once she had breathed her last, Thersites, known among the Greeks for his biting tongue, mocked Achilles for his foolish infatuation until the warrior killed him as well. Achilles also slew Memnon, king of the Ethiopians, who had brought his army all the way from the headwaters of the Nile.

It seemed as if nothing could strike down Achilles, protected as he was by his mother once dipping him in the river Styx. But Apollo knew where he was vulnerable and guided an arrow of Paris to his heel when the Greek captain attacked the Scaean gate of the city. The greatest of the Greek warriors died there, bleeding to death beneath the walls of Troy. The Trojans would have seized his divine armor but Ajax and Odysseus drove them back and carried the corpse of their friend to their camp by the shore. There all the Greeks mourned him and burned his body on a funeral pyre, afterward mixing his ashes with those of his friend Patroclus.

The Greeks then held a contest to see who among them would receive his glorious armor. Ajax argued that he had killed more Trojans than anyone save Achilles and therefore deserved the prize, but Odysseus won the armor with his smooth tongue, claiming that his brains had helped the Greeks more than anyone's brawn. Ajax became crazed with jealousy and swore he would make the Greek captains pay. That night he rose from his bed and attacked his old friends, slaughtering Agamemnon, Menelaus, and Odysseus among others. But when dawn came, he returned to his senses and discovered he had killed only a herd of sheep. More humiliated than ever, he went to a secluded cave near the beach and killed himself with his own sword.

The Greeks were no closer to taking the city of Troy than they had been ten years earlier. When they asked the seer Calchas what they must do to win the war, he said they needed the weapons of Hercules left with Philoctetes, whom they had abandoned on the island of Lemnos a decade earlier. A delegation arrived to bring Philoctetes to the Greek camp in spite of his still-stinking wound. Once on the beach at Troy, the injured man was healed by a skilled physician and consented to use the weapons of Hercules to help his companions. This he did most prominently when he took aim at Paris and shot him dead, making Helen a widow.

Two brothers of Paris, the seer Helenus and the warrior Deiphobus, quarreled over who would be the third husband of the most beautiful woman in the world. Deiphobus won and Helenus left the town in bitter disappointment to live alone on the slopes of Mount Ida. The Greeks knew Helenus was a powerful prophet, so they sent Odysseus to kidnap him from the mountain and bring him to the Greek camp. Helenus knew secrets hidden even from Calchas, such as the oracles still protecting Troy. The disgruntled Helenus revealed that for the Greeks to take the city, they would first need to transport the bones of Agamemnon's grandfather Pelops to their camp from Greece. Second, they would need to bring Achilles' son Neoptolemus, fathered on the island of Scyros, to join them. Finally they would need to steal the Palladium, the wooden statue of Athena that had fallen from the sky, from her temple in the city. These three things are necessary, said Helenus, but they are by no means sufficient for you to capture the city. You will still have to discover for yourselves what no man or god knows—how to breech the walls of Troy.

The Greeks collected the bones of Pelops easily enough and found young Neoptolemus eager to join them, but stealing Athena's statue from her temple in the center of Troy posed more of a problem. Odysseus therefore resorted to stealth. He and Diomedes disguised themselves as beggars and snuck into the city. Some say that Helen recognized them and helped them, but others claim they stole the Palladium on their own and brought it back to the Greek camp. Now they had everything they needed to take the city of Troy—if only they could find a way to get their army through its walls.

How the idea occurred to Odysseus, no one ever knew, but when the Greeks heard it, they knew it would work. It was daring, insane perhaps, but it was so simple and cunning that Troy must surely fall at last. Odysseus instructed a master craftsman named Epeius to build a gigantic wooden horse big enough to hold fifty men in its hollow interior. It would look solid from the outside, but had a secret door that could be opened by those hiding inside.

On the evening when the horse was complete, Odysseus, Menelaus, and four dozen other Greeks climbed into the creature's belly and sealed themselves in. The rest of the Greeks burned their tents and sailed away to anchor on the far side of the island of Tenedos and await the prearranged signal.

When dawn rose the next morning, the Trojans could see the smoldering ruins of the Greek camp and a giant wooden horse in the distance. They rode out to the shore and marveled at the work, wondering why their enemies should have built such a thing. Suddenly a man came running to them from the bushes and threw himself at the feet of Priam. He said his name was Sinon and that he was a Greek. He had quarreled with Odysseus and in revenge the master conniver had arranged for him to become a human sacrifice. He had escaped, but the horse was left behind as a peace offering to Athena. The Greeks had realized at last that they could never take the city and only wanted to sail home in peace with the blessing of the goddess. Sinon begged the king to grant him sanctuary safe from his cruel countrymen.

The Trojans were moved to tears by this sad story, but not everyone was so impressed by the Greek refugee. The prophetess Cassandra declared that he was lying, but no one believed her. Laocoon, the Trojan priest of Poseidon, also mocked Sinon, throwing a spear at the horse and noting the hollow thud, perfect for hiding men inside. He warned they should never trust Greeks, especially when they were bearing gifts. But Poseidon sent a sea serpent to devour Laocoon and his sons on the beach, a sign to all to reject the words of the priest. The exultant Trojans then rigged ropes to the colossal horse and dragged it inside the city.

At the victory feast that night there was music, dancing, and more wine than anyone had ever seen. Everyone sang and drank long into the night, until at last they stumbled back to their homes to sleep the sleep of the dead.

But in the wee hours of the morning, when the city was finally quiet, a door silently opened under the belly of the wooden horse. Ropes were lowered and orders given to unbar the gates of the city. Sinon had already kindled a fire on the tomb of Achilles to signal the fleet. The Greek army had quickly sailed back from Tenedos and was waiting outside the walls.

The Greeks spread through the city slaughtering the Trojans in their beds and setting fire to their fine homes. Only Aeneas, son of Aphrodite, had his wits about him as he gathered what men, women, and children he could and escaped. But most Trojans were not so fortunate. King Priam was cut down at the altar of Zeus, where he had sought sanctuary. The lesser Ajax found Cassandra in the temple of Athena and raped her there, then gave her to Agamemnon as a slave. Hector's mother, Hecuba, was led away in chains as was his wife, Andromache, but not before his young son Astyanax was thrown from the walls to his death. The Greeks took Priam's youngest daughter, Polyxena, and cut her throat over the tomb of Achilles, a blood sacrifice to the spirit of their friend. At last, when the city was a smoking ruin, Menelaus killed Helen's new husband, Deiphobus. He was ready to plunge his sword into his former bride as well, but Helen bared her breasts to him and pleaded that she be allowed to return home to Sparta, where she would make him a very happy man. Menelaus hesitated, thinking of all the good men who had died for her sake, but then he sheathed his sword, took her by the hand, and led her back to his ship.

MYCENAE

Many years before Agamemnon led the Greeks to Troy, his ancestor Tantalus ruled as king in Lydia, not far from the city of Priam and Paris. Tantalus was a mortal son of Zeus himself and a special favorite of the god. The ruler of the gods would often invite his child to banquets on Olympus, but Tantalus took advantage of his father's hospitality, stealing the gods' own ambrosia and telling their secrets to mortals. When Zeus overlooked this misbehavior, his son became more and more bold.

One day Tantalus invited all the gods to dinner at his palace and laid before them a fine meal. But before the feast had been set, he had slaughtered his own son Pelops, boiled him in a cauldron, and served him in tasty portions to his divine guests. The king was curious to see if the gods would recognize that he had laid human flesh before them. Only Demeter was fooled, but this was because she was preoccupied mourning the loss of her daughter Persephone. She ate a shoulder of young Pelops before anyone could stop her.

Zeus rose up in anger and ordered Hermes to place the pieces of his grandson back into the pot. He reached in and pulled out a whole, living Pelops, minus a shoulder that Hephaestus later replaced with an ivory prosthesis. Zeus then cast his son Tantalus down into the darkest corner of Hades. There, tormented by thirst, he stood in a pool of fresh water, but as often as he stooped down to drink, the water vanished. In his hunger he also tried to grasp the luscious fruits that hung over his head, but whenever he reached for them, the wind blew them out of his grasp. Thus for eternity Tantalus was tantalized by food and drink he could not have.

• • •

Pelops was even more handsome after he was restored to life than he had
been before the unfortunate dinner incident. His good looks caught the
eye of the god Poseidon, who took him to Mount Olympus for a time
to serve as his cupbearer and lover. When he grew tired of the youth,
Poseidon sent him away with a parting gift of a chariot so fast some say it
could fly across the top of the sea.

Pelops had occasion to use the chariot when he heard that King
Oenomaus of Pisa near Olympia was holding races to see who could win
his daughter Hippodamia as a bride. The king had no desire to part with
her, as he had an unnatural attraction to the girl and had tried to seduce
her himself, though she refused. While he kept trying, he devised an
impossible contest for her hand as an excuse to keep her unwed. Any potential groom had to set out with Hippodamia from Pisa and race across
the Peloponnesus to the Isthmus of Corinth before the king caught up
with him. If Oenomaus did catch him—which he always did, since he
owned horses received from the god Ares—he killed the suitor, decapitated him, and hung up his head as a trophy on the walls of Pisa. Hippodamia was so beautiful that twelve warriors had already tried and died.

Pelops liked his chances in the race and decided to challenge Oenomaus for his daughter. He made his way across the Aegean Sea from Lydia
and knocked on the palace door, even as he tried to ignore the dozen
lifeless heads staring down at him. When Hippodamia saw Pelops, she fell
in love with him and decided to help the young man win the race. She
asked the charioteer of Oenomaus, named Myrtilus, to loosen the pins
from the axle of her father's chariot. As Myrtilus, too, was desperately
in love with the princess, he obliged. Thus soon after the race began,
the chariot collapsed and Oenomaus died when he was thrown onto the
rocks beside the road.

Myrtilus accompanied the happy couple as they made their way back
to Lydia, but at their first stop, the charioteer tried to rape Hippodamia
when Pelops went away to fetch her some water. The prince caught him
in the act and tossed him off a cliff, but not before Myrtilus uttered the
curse of a dying man upon Pelops and his descendants. Pelops returned
to Pisa soon after and took the crown, ruling with Hippodamia as his
queen. He was quite fond of his new land and named the entire peninsula for himself, calling it the Peloponnesus, or "Pelops Island." After

this, Pelops settled down and had many children with Hippodamia, including his two sons, Atreus and Thyestes.

After the sons of Hercules killed Eurystheus, king of Mycenae, the people of the town received an oracle that they should choose one of the sons of Pelops as their new ruler. The Mycenaeans did not know which of the sons to pick, so they sent for both Atreus and Thyestes. Atreus, as the eldest, said that he was the natural choice, but Thyestes begged to differ. He argued that whoever was able to present the citizens with the fleece of a golden lamb should be the new king.

Atreus thought this was a wonderful idea. Several years earlier he had made a vow to sacrifice to the goddess Artemis whichever lamb born to his flock was the finest. That spring an ewe gave birth to a lamb with fleece of gold, the finest anyone had ever seen. Atreus knew he should keep his vow and offer the lamb to Artemis, but he couldn't bring himself to part with such a miraculous gift. He therefore strangled the golden lamb, skinned it, and put its fleece safely away in a hidden chest.

But unknown to Atreus, Thyestes was having a passionate love affair with his brother's wife, Aerope, a granddaughter of King Minos of Crete. Aerope had secretly removed the golden fleece from her husband's chest and given it to her lover, so that when Atreus went to retrieve the fleece and prove to the Mycenaeans that he should be king, he found only an empty box. Thyestes, however, pulled the fleece from beneath his robes and presented it to the city elders, who promptly offered him the crown. Atreus was furious at this betrayal by both his wife and brother. Fortunately, so was his great-grandfather Zeus. The god sent Hermes down to tell Atreus to ask Thyestes if he would give up the throne if he could make the sun move backward. His brother laughed at such a preposterous notion and agreed. But the next day, when the sun had traveled halfway across the sky, it suddenly began to move backward and then set in the east. The people of Mycenae quickly changed their minds and decided they wanted someone who could change the course of the heavens as their king. Atreus became ruler and banished Thyestes from the land.

The new king could not forget the treachery of his brother and soon lured him and his family back to Mycenae with an offer of reconciliation.

Atreus held a great banquet and invited his brother to join him at the head of the table. But unknown to Thyestes, Atreus had taken Thyestes' three young sons and killed them, cut off their heads and limbs, then boiled the rest of their bodies in a great stew pot. After much wine, song, and tender meat, Atreus asked his brother how he liked his dinner. Thyestes replied it was the best he had ever eaten and asked what it was. Atreus clapped his hands and had a platter brought out containing the heads and limbs of Thyestes' sons, telling him he had just dined on their flesh. The younger brother recoiled in horror, cursing Atreus and his sons, then was cast out of the kingdom once again.

Alone and wretched, Thyestes traveled to the oracle at Delphi to find out how he could gain revenge against his brother. The priestess told him to do so he must father a child by his own maiden daughter Pelopia, whom he had not seen in years. Thyestes was horrified at the thought and dismissed the idea, traveling on to the land of Sicyon in the northern Peloponnesus. As he passed by a forest one evening, he happened upon a group of young women celebrating the rites of Artemis in the woods. He did not wish to profane the worship by his presence, so he hid behind a tree and watched. The leader of the dancers was a particularly pretty girl who slipped on sheep's blood in the middle of the sacrifice and left the group to wash her robes in a nearby stream. Thyestes followed her and watched as she removed her clothes to scrub them in the water. Then he snuck up behind her and grabbed her, forcing her to the ground and raping her there in the forest. The girl could not fight back against such a powerful stranger, but she did manage to steal and hide his sword before he left. Later she placed the weapon under the altar at the temple of Artemis.

Meanwhile, back in Mycenae, the crops were failing because of the blood guilt Atreus had brought on the land when he killed his nephews. He traveled to an oracle near Sicyon to seek relief for his kingdom and was told that he must bring Thyestes back to Mycenae if he wanted the land to be healed. The oracle did not specify dead or alive, and Atreus did not ask. But before he left, he saw a beautiful young woman standing near a temple and was so taken by her that he asked if she would become his wife. He did not realize that she was in fact his niece Pelopia and that she was already pregnant by her own father Thyestes. The woman agreed and journeyed back to Mycenae with Atreus, not realizing he was her uncle. A little less than nine months later, she bore a son named Aegisthus.

Years went by as Atreus continued the search for Thyestes. At last he sent his two sons, Agamemnon and Menelaus, to Delphi to ask the oracle where Atreus could find his brother. Miraculously, Thyestes was also at the oracle of Apollo still seeking a way to get vengeance on Atreus. When Agamemnon and Menelaus recognized their uncle, they couldn't believe their good fortune and took him back to Mycenae by force. Atreus was thrilled to have his brother in his hands and ordered him thrown into prison. He then ordered his other son, Aegisthus, to take a sword and kill the man in his cell.

Aegisthus was happy to be of service and so unwrapped the fine sword he had recently received from his mother, Pelopia. He went down the stairs to the damp dungeon of the palace and ordered the prisoner to kneel. Thyestes then recognized the sword the young man held and asked where he had gotten it. When Aegisthus told him, Thyestes revealed that his would-be executioner was in fact his son, conceived with his own daughter years before. Aegisthus called his mother to the prison and she confirmed the story, then took the sword and plunged it into her heart. All this was overwhelming to Aegisthus, who had just learned he was born of incestuous rape and was not in fact a son of Atreus, a man who had persecuted his true father. He took the sword stained by the blood and gore of his own mother to the throne room and presented it to Atreus. The king took it as proof that Thyestes at last was dead, but in his excitement did not notice Aegisthus come up behind him. Aegisthus stabbed him in the back.

Aegisthus then released Thyestes from prison and helped him seize the throne of Mycenae. Agamemnon and Menelaus fled for their lives and took refuge with King Tyndareus in Sparta. In time they returned to Mycenae and drove their uncle Thyestes from the kingdom once again. Agamemnon became king and in an act of remarkable kindness forgave his half brother for murdering his father. Aegisthus seemed grateful and lived a quiet life serving Agamemnon loyally, though his anger at the family of Atreus boiled just below the surface. His apparent devotion was rewarded, however, when he was left as regent of Mycenae when

Agamemnon sailed to Troy. The king left him in charge of the kingdom and ordered him to take care of his wife, Clytemnestra, until he returned. Aegisthus gladly agreed.

At the port of Aulis, Agamemnon sacrificed the maiden Iphigenia, leaving only his daughter Electra and his young son Orestes to comfort their mother during his time at Troy. Years of anger and bitterness built inside Clytemnestra until she knew what she must do. Whatever love she had once had for Agamemnon had died that day on the altar at Aulis. Now she turned to Aegisthus for comfort and found in him a willing ally in her revenge.

At last the day came when word reached Mycenae that Troy had fallen and they should await the return of the king. The news came by way of fire, when a watchman on the highest tower of the citadel saw a flame leap from a mountain peak north of the city. Clytemnestra had long ago set up a series of signal fires to be lighted when the city of Priam was taken so that she might know before any other that Agamemnon was on his way back. Her man on Mount Ida near Troy set the first fire ablaze, to be answered by his companion on the island of Lemnos to the west. That light was seen by her watchman on Mount Athos on the Greek mainland, who passed the fire on to others across Thessaly and Boeotia, down past Athens, then across the gulf at last to Mycenae. Before the burning embers of Troy had died away, Clytemnestra was preparing to welcome her husband home.

After a few weeks Agamemnon landed at the port near Argos and made his way by chariot up the road to his palace at Mycenae. Cheering crowds lined the way to admire the wagonloads of treasure he brought from Troy. Slave women who had once had servants of their own marched behind to their grim, new life. But Cassandra, the daughter of King Priam, rode beside Agamemnon as they passed the tombs of his ancestors and entered the great lion gate at Mycenae.

Clytemnestra was there to welcome him home with proper ceremony, spreading before him a path of precious crimson tapestries the color of blood so that his feet would not have to touch the ground on the way to his throne room. Agamemnon objected that such honors were more fitting to a god than a man, but his wife persuaded him that his glorious exploits at Troy had earned him this reward. He then ordered his wife to take Cassandra and prepare her for his service.

The royal entourage entered the palace except for Cassandra, left on the porch by the queen. Suddenly she began to scream, crying that she saw blood everywhere, babies butchered and served to their father, murder and murder again in this cursed household, even her own death. The people of the town assured her that such things were in the past and that the family of Atreus was now at peace. Cassandra heard none of these words, but entered the chambers of the king to meet a fate she knew she could not escape.

Then from inside the palace there was a horrible cry. The voice of a man struck down, followed by the dying moans of a woman. The citizens of the city gathered outside the palace doors until at last Clytemnestra came out with a bloody sword in her hand, proclaiming, "The deed is done, the king is dead. Long have I waited for this day, ever since he killed my precious girl to fight his war. I freely admit it, I killed him. I struck him three times, a sacrifice to the restless spirit of my daughter. His blood fell like rain on the earth. And I killed his little tart as well, good riddance. Justice is done at last."

The crowd was horrified, but then Clytemnestra's lover Aegisthus stood proudly beside her with armed men and declared that they would now rule together. The people could do nothing except bow to the new king and queen, but in their hearts they called on the gods for vengeance.

Before Clytemnestra murdered Agamemnon, she had sent away her son Orestes to a kingdom near Delphi to remove any threat to her plans. However, she kept her daughter Electra at home since a mere girl could not stand in her way. When the deed was done, Clytemnestra took the corpse of her husband and buried him near the palace, but first cut off his genitals and placed them under his armpits to render his ghost helpless to seek revenge. As the years passed, no one dared to honor his grave except for Electra, who would come secretly to pour wine for his troubled spirit.

One day two strangers appeared before the tomb of Agamemnon and brushed aside the weeds to lay a lock of hair on the grave as was the custom. One was named Pylades, while the other was his friend Orestes. While the two stood praying beside the mound, Orestes saw a young woman approach and hid himself behind a tree. It was his sister Electra, come to honor their father. She was startled to see the footprints of a man at the lonely site and an offering of hair on the grave. Both were so like her own that she knew her brother had returned. When he appeared, they embraced and Orestes sought news of what had happened in the long years of his absence. Electra told him of the darkness that had descended on her life since their father had been slain, and how their vile mother had been troubled by dreams of late. In her dreams she gave birth to a snake that slashed her with its fangs and suckled on her milk clotted with blood. Orestes said that he was that snake, sent by Apollo, who had spoken through his oracle at Delphi and told him to avenge his father. The god revealed how the spirit of their father cried out from Hades for revenge. There was something rotten in the city of Mycenae and the prince had come to kill his wicked mother and the man who had stolen his father's throne by murder. Electra rejoiced at the news and asked how she could help. Orestes told her to go back to the palace and tell no one what she had seen. He would come to the palace himself in disguise to carry out his plan.

Soon Orestes and Pylades appeared before the lion gate disguised as travelers and speaking the peculiar dialect of Delphi. They asked to see the queen, for they had a sad message to give her. When they were led to Clytemnestra, they told her that they were the bearers of bitter news. Her son Orestes was dead, nothing now but ashes in a bronze urn. Clytemnestra ran into the palace weeping, but beneath her tears there was a smile was on her face, since the one potential avenger of Agamemnon had perished. Now she and Aegisthus could live out the rest of their days without worry of Orestes returning to strike them down for their crime.

But then Clytemnestra heard a cry from across the palace courtyard. She ran out to see the young stranger with a bloody sword in his hand. He revealed that he was her son Orestes and that he had just killed Aegisthus. Now, he said, I've come for you. But Clytemnestra clasped his knees and begged for her life: "You would kill me, your own mother? I nursed you when you were a baby, cradled you in my arms. Yes, I killed your father, but only because he murdered your sister. I sought revenge for the blood of my own child!"

Orestes was torn. He had been ordered by the god Apollo to slay her, yet how could he kill the woman who had given birth to him?

With steely resolve, he raised his sword and brought it down on Cly-temnestra, judging the will of the god greater than his own ties of blood. Yet as he stood over her body, he could not believe what he had done. Would this cycle of vengeance go on forever? His great-great-grandfather had killed his own son and served him up for dinner to the gods. Then Pelops sired two sons who spent their lives plotting revenge and counter-revenge on each other amid rape, suicide, and murder. His father killed his sister on an altar, prompting his mother to slay his father. Now he had joined in by killing her, another link in an endless chain of violence and death. Who would now seek his life?

When the priestess of Apollo at Delphi arose that morning and purified herself, it seemed like it would be just another day at the temple. After praying to the earth mother Gaia, to Themis the guardian of justice, and to Apollo himself, she would sit on her tripod above a fissure in the earth while she breathed in the sacred fumes that allowed her to commune with the god. There would be farmers asking whether or not to buy an olive grove or fathers seeking advice on which suitor was the best choice for their daughters. Perhaps some foreign king would send a messenger to inquire whether or not he should invade a neighboring kingdom. The questions were always the same and the routine never varied.

But when she entered the doors of the temple, she saw a sight that made her turn and run away screaming. A man lay sleeping on the central stone, the very navel of the earth, with a bloody sword in one hand and an olive branch of supplication in the other. Around this altar of sanctuary were female creatures wrapped in black rags with hair like snakes and a stench of death that filled the air. They were the Furies, come to haunt Orestes for slaying his mother.

The god Apollo quietly entered his temple and woke Orestes, telling him to make his way to Athens to seek the intervention of the goddess Athena. When the young man had gone, the ghost of Clytemnestra ap-peared and roused the sleeping Furies. She reminded them that it was their sacred responsibility to seek vengeance against those who had shed kindred blood. Apollo then ordered them all out of his sanctuary in disgust, prompting the Furies to rail against him for not respecting their divine task. He told them to get to Athens as well, where Athena would hear their case.

Athena called a trial on the hill of the Areopagus next to the Acropolis at Athens. Orestes would be the defendant and the Furies his prosecutors. Select men of Athens would be the jury, with Athena herself presiding as judge. The Furies argued that theirs was an ancient and honorable office. Without anger at the shedding of blood, there would be no motivation for justice. The world would descend back into the chaos that reigned before the gods were born. And what could be worse than a son killing his own mother, the very woman who had given birth to him? Allow him to go free, they told the goddess, and all the bonds that hold together the society of men and gods would collapse.

Apollo spoke for Orestes and argued that the young man had only sought revenge against the woman who had killed Agamemnon. Wasn't the bond between father and son also sacred? Wasn't it justified to kill a woman who had murdered the man who sired him? The Furies declared that as wicked as Clytemnestra's crime might have been, she did not kill someone related to her. Husbands and wives were joined by pledge, not by blood. Orestes killed his mother and was therefore guilty of the greater offense.

It was then that Apollo made his most audacious argument in his defense of Orestes—a child is not really related to his mother. He argued that a woman is merely the bearer of her husband's seed, nurturing it in her body until it is ready to be born. As it is the baker who makes bread, not the oven, so a father is the true source of life for a child, not the mother. He declared that his point could be proven by the very judge who sat before them. Athena was born from the forehead of her father Zeus, not from a woman's womb.

After Apollo rested his case, Athena considered the arguments carefully. She granted that Apollo was right and that Orestes should be freed, but she acknowledged that there was a place for anger in a civilized system of justice. She therefore invited the Furies to live with her in Athens, dwelling in honor under the Areopagus. They would be the foundation of justice for her city.

The Furies found this acceptable and went to live beneath the hill of judgment. Athena then declared that the long cycle of murder and revenge that had haunted the family of Tantalus for five generations had ended at last.

ODYSSEUS

Ten long years of war at Troy, then the Greek heroes sailed for home. Some, like Agamemnon, returned to their families quickly enough, though their reunions were brief. Some were blown by storms and the wrath of the gods to distant lands, but made their way back to Greece in due course. Others met their deaths in the middle of the wine dark sea and went down to the depths of Poseidon's realm. But one man among those who fought bravely at Troy seemed neither dead nor alive. Year after year passed, but no one knew the fate of Odysseus, king of Ithaca. Some said he had offended Poseidon and perished at sea, while others said he had found a new kingdom in a distant land. No one knew for certain, least of all his wife, Penelope, and his now-grown son Telemachus. Almost a decade had passed since the victorious Greek ships sailed away from the ruins of Troy, but still Odysseus had not come home.

Telemachus sat in the courtyard of his father's crumbling estate beneath the rocky hills of Ithaca. The palace of the king, such as it was, had never been more than a large farmhouse on a poor island at the edge of the Greek world. Menelaus might drink his wine from silver cups in Sparta and the daughters of old Nestor in Pylos might wear golden jewelry, but here on Ithaca, even the nobility toiled in the fields and ate simple fare. What little the household of Odysseus had to spare had been consumed for the past few years by visiting suitors who had come to woo the beautiful Penelope—not as young as she once was, but still a radiant woman in the prime of life. Most on Ithaca agreed that Odysseus must be dead by now and that Penelope should remarry. Even her parents urged her to wed again, but Telemachus and Penelope herself still waited for the return of the king. The queen tried to put off the suitors by saying she would make a choice once she had finished weaving a shroud for

Odysseus' father, Laertes, who was old and living in the countryside of Ithaca. She would work her loom during the day, but in the darkness she would undo all she had woven. Finally the suitors discovered her deception, and though she still managed to delay her decision, the ancient laws of hospitality insisted that all guests to her home be welcomed, even if the would-be grooms ate the family's diminishing stores and seduced their slave women during the night.

The gods alone knew the fate of Odysseus. Athena, patron of war and artifice, cared most among the Olympians for the clever king, a man of many twists and turns who could think his way out of any difficult situation. Spying Telemachus sitting by himself in the courtyard while the greedy suitors feasted around him, she flew down from Olympus in the guise of Mentes, lord of the seagoing Taphians. Telemachus saw the visitor at once and sprang up to greet him, offering him an honored seat at the table and filling a cup of wine for his guest. After the man had drunk and feasted, Telemachus asked the visitor who he was and what had brought him to Ithaca. The man said he was an old friend of Odysseus come to see if he had yet returned. When Telemachus shook his head sadly, the visitor placed his hand on his shoulder as would a father giving counsel and urged him not to despair: "Odysseus is alive, my young friend, don't you ever doubt it! Nothing would stop him from returning home. He may be long delayed, but he will come. But why are you just sitting here? Get a ship and sail to Pylos to ask Nestor if there has been word. Go to Sparta and find out if Menelaus has heard anything. Good news comes to those who seek it, not those who wait. Be a man, Telemachus, and find your father. For I tell you, when he does return, he will need a man at his side to drive away these wretched suitors."

Telemachus was fired with courage by the goddess and rose to begin preparations for the voyage. He told his mother he was going and, for the first time in his life, did not give in when she told him he was too young. He gathered the elders of Ithaca and asked them for a ship and sailors to make the journey down the coast all the way to Pylos. He spoke with authority and conviction as he declared it was time the islanders knew one way or another if their king was alive. If so, he would bring back news and perhaps his father himself. If not, he would give away his own mother to a new husband. Penelope had never heard her son speak like this and was proud of the young man, though she feared losing him on the stormy seas. The suitors, led by Antinous, voiced their support, but for different reasons. They planned to lay in wait for Telemachus with their own ship so that they might kill him on his return from Pylos. With the young man out of the way, lovely Penelope would belong to one of them for certain, as would the lands and crown of Odysseus.

Telemachus set sail for sandy Pylos, journeying past the entrance to the Gulf of Corinth, then along the coast near Olympia and on to Messenia in the western Peloponnesus. At last he came to a headland at the southwestern edge of the great peninsula and there saw the citadel of Nestor rising above the waves. The king was on the shore that day offering nine black bulls to Poseidon. Athena had accompanied young Telemachus, this time disguised as Mentor, a respected elder and friend of Odysseus' from Ithaca. The goddess urged him to put away his boyish timidity and approach Nestor directly. Thus Telemachus landed and drew near to the gathering. He was welcomed by the king and by Prince Pisistratus, a youth about the same age as himself. The whole crew was invited to the banquet following the sacrifice and made welcome with roasted strips of beef and generous cups of wine.

When dinner was over, Nestor asked the strangers who they were. Telemachus rose and addressed the king, thanking him for his hospitality and giving his name. He said he was in search of news about his father, Odysseus, and would be grateful for any word they might have. Nestor was thrilled to have the son of his old friend at his feast and told him many stories of their times together beneath the walls of Troy. But alas, he could tell him nothing of his father's fate. He urged him to leave his ship on the coast and travel inland through his land to the city of Sparta. There he would find King Menelaus and lovely Queen Helen herself. Perhaps they could help him on his quest.

Telemachus thanked the old soldier and accepted his son Pisistratus as guide. The two climbed into a chariot the next morning and set off across the mountains for the journey to Sparta. Telemachus had never seen such high peaks as those that guarded the city of Menelaus, but at last they made their way through the rugged passes until they came to the beautiful valley of the Eurotas River and the city of Sparta. The splendid palace of Menelaus on a hillside overlooking the town was easy to find, so the two young men pulled up the chariot before the gate and asked for the king.

Menelaus himself was also easy to recognize with his head of bright red hair. He welcomed his visitors and took them into his halls to wash off the dust of the journey and dine at his table. When supper was finished, he asked them who they were, though at that moment his wife, Helen, entered the room and declared he could be none other than the son of Odysseus since he looked so much like his father. Telemachus confirmed that he was indeed the child of that long-lost king and asked if they might have any news of him. Like Nestor, Menelaus was overjoyed to meet the son of his dear friend and told him of all the two warriors had been through together at Troy, all the comrades they had lost on that distant shore. The king began to weep for his lost friends, as did Helen. Tears also ran down the cheeks of Telemachus as he heard stories of the father he could not remember.

Helen took her young visitor by the arm and told him of one particular incident she recalled. Odysseus had come into the city of Troy disguised as a beggar and fooled everyone—except for her. She was secretly on the side of the Greeks, she claimed, and did everything she could to help him on his spy mission. She had even hidden him in her own chambers and led him out of the walls of the city to safety.

Menelaus declared that his wife had told a fine tale, but he recounted another. He and Odysseus had hidden in the belly of the wooden horse along with their comrades after it was dragged into Troy. As they lay quietly waiting, one word would have meant discovery and death, along with the end of their plans to take the city. Then through a small hole in the horse he saw Helen approaching with Trojan warriors. She had a sneaking suspicion about the Greek gift, so three times she walked around the horse, stroking its flanks and calling out to the soldiers she suspected were inside, mimicking the voices of their own wives. Several of the Greeks almost fell for the trick and called out in response, but Odysseus was there to clasp his hand over their mouths until they came to their senses, foiling the devious plan of Helen.

The tension in the air between the king and queen of Sparta was so thick Telemachus could have touched it, but instead he spoke up and again asked if perhaps they had heard any news, rumors, even, of his father and why he had not yet returned home. Menelaus turned away from the queen and told him what he had heard on his own voyage home. He had been delayed in returning himself for several years for failing to honor the gods properly with sacrifice. The winds had blown him all the way to Egypt, where he came to a small island off the coast called Pharos. There he grounded his vessel and went looking for water and food for his starving crew. He soon met a sympathetic sea nymph who told him where to find supplies. She also told him of her father, Proteus, who lived nearby, a god with knowledge of all things. If Menelaus wanted news of what had happened at home or to his friends, he should pin him down and force him to speak.

Menelaus wanted to hear everything, so he snuck into the seaside cave of Proteus and hid among his pet seals. When the god entered the cavern and lay down to rest, Menelaus jumped on him and would not let go, even as the shape-shifting master became a serpent, a panther, a wild boar, a torrent of water, and a tree soaring to the sky. At last he resumed his original form and asked Menelaus with a sigh what he wanted. The king declared that he was in search of news of events in Greece so that he could be ready for his return. Proteus told him his own kingdom was safe, but that his brother Agamemnon had been cruelly murdered in Mycenae. Menelaus grieved at this report, but listened as the god told him of the fate of other great warriors, including crafty Odysseus. Proteus had once seen the king of Ithaca sitting on the shore of the island of the goddess Calypso, the hidden one, weeping as he pined away for the home he could not reach. That, said Menelaus to Telemachus, is all that I know of Odysseus. Whether he is still on that island, has sailed away to another land, or has gone down to the house of Hades, no man can say.

As dawn touched the top of Mount Olympus, Athena approached her father, Zeus, and bowed before him. She asked him if it wasn't at last time to let Odysseus return home after almost twenty years away from Ithaca. Hadn't he suffered enough? Wasn't the anger of Poseidon satisfied? Zeus nodded his head in assent and summoned Hermes to his side. He sent the messenger god down to the island of Calypso in the distant west to tell her she must release Odysseus. No delays, no more excuses, the exile must go home.

Hermes flew from the mountaintop to Calypso's palace and found the goddess braiding her hair surrounded by her nymphs. She welcomed him, but knew at once why he had come. She had no desire to let Odysseus go, but what choice did she have? She made her way to a beach on the eastern side of her island where the wandering hero sat on a rock, staring out toward Ithaca far across the sea, tears blinding his eyes. He spent his nights with her in her lovely bed, an unwilling lover in the hands of a goddess, but he passed his days on this rocky headland thinking of his wife and son, now grown, and of his aged father, Laertes.

Calypso told him that she had received a message from Zeus to let him go. She would even help him sail away from her island—but consider well what you do, she cautioned. I am a goddess and will never grow old. Stay with me and you too shall have immortality. What can your wife offer you better than that?

Odysseus answered, "Goddess, all you say is true. My Penelope falls far short of you in beauty. I know her hair must be turning gray by now and the first lines are touching her face—after all, she is mortal, unlike you. Nevertheless I long every day to see her again, to stroke that hair, to touch that face. Immortality? A generous offer, but what good is eternal life without the one you love? I would rather live a single lifetime with my Penelope than an eternity with anyone else."

With that he began to build a small boat with the wood that Calypso brought him. When it was ready, he stored one skin of wine and another of water aboard, along with a sack of food. Then he said farewell to the goddess and raised his single sail. Tiller in hand, he set off to the east toward Ithaca.

For eighteen days he sailed with a fair wind to his back. Then, just as his food and water were gone, he spotted an island on the horizon. But at the same moment, the god Poseidon saw him on the waves and cursed his brother on Olympus: "So, Zeus, is this how you treat me? I go away for a few days to visit my friends among the Ethiopians and you decide to let Odysseus sail home? Well, I may not be able to stop him, but I can still make his life miserable!"

With that he slammed the clouds together and stirred up a storm that sent waves crashing over the little boat. The sail was torn away and the planks began to fall apart, then lightning struck the mast and split it in two. Odysseus was thrown into the sea and his clothes were torn from him in the pounding waves. Only with the help of the sea goddess Ino, once a mortal woman, did he reach the shores of the island, though he had lost everything. Naked, exhausted, and covered in brine, he collapsed on the beach and fell into a deep and dreamless sleep.

The princess Nausicaa was tired of life in the palace. As she lay in her colorful bedroom with her handmaids near her, she decided what she really wanted was a day at the beach. But her father, the great king Alcinous, could be so old-fashioned about such things. He wanted her to spend her time weaving and learning all the things a proper young lady should know to attract the interest of a worthy husband. What she needed was a good excuse.

She jumped out of bed and told her handmaids to go to her brothers' quarters and gather all the dirty laundry they could find. Then she went to her father, who was walking in the courtyard with some of his nobles, and whispered in his ear: "Daddy dear, I hate to bother you when you're so busy, but I'm worried about your sons. Two are married, but the other three are still looking for wives. They are simply hopeless when it comes to their clothes, always leaving dirty things lying about and wearing whatever they can find. The girls will never give them a second glance if they keep looking like that. Let me take their laundry down to the beach and give it a good cleaning. It may take all day, but I'm willing to do it to help my dear brothers."

Alcinous was no fool and knew exactly what his daughter was doing, but he loved the girl and could never resist her pleas. He ordered the servants to ready a cart to take Nausicaa and her friends to the shore.

Once the princess and her companions reached the water, they gave the dirty clothes a quick rinse and threw them on the rocks to dry, then set about racing and laughing across the sand. They went swimming in the sea, then spread a picnic on the beach. They traded gossip about the young men of the court and teased each other about who their fathers would choose for them to marry. Then they lay in the sun and gloried in the fact that they had a few hours to themselves without parents to order them about.

Odysseus woke with a start when he heard what he thought were the voices of young women laughing in his dreams. He looked around and saw that he was lying in some bushes near a beach and that the sun was high in the sky. He saw that his clothes had been washed away by the storm and that he looked a fright, covered in brine and sand. Then he heard the voices again. He realized he was not dreaming, but that the boat he had made on Calypso's island had brought him to some new land. He wondered if he would ever get home to Ithaca, for he knew his island well and this was not it, pleasant though it seemed. He decided it was best to approach the girls and ask if they could direct him to the ruler of the land.

Nausicaa and her friends gasped in shock when they saw a naked man coming toward them. He looked terrible, but the princess noticed something about him, some noble bearing that stopped her from running away in fright. She stood her ground and asked what he wanted. Odysseus complimented the young woman on her beauty, then asked if he might be given a few rags to cover himself along with directions to the local palace. Nausicaa ordered her maids to give the man some of her brothers' old clothes and show him a stream where he could wash the salt and dirt from his filthy body. When he was done, she told him he was on the island of the Phaeacians, dear to the gods, ruled by her father, the wise king Alcinous. He was married to her mother, the excellent queen Arete, and had many warriors and ships at his command. She told him it wouldn't at all look proper if she led a strange man back to her home, but he could follow the road and easily find the royal dwellings.

The princess and her companions then gathered their things and headed for home, while Odysseus considered what he should do. The girl seemed friendly enough, but he had been through so much at the hands of those who had welcomed him at first. Better to be cautious and not reveal too much until necessary. But he prayed to Athena that this would be the last stop before he found his way back to Ithaca. He asked the goddess to intercede and move the king to grant him a ship to sail home to his Penelope.

As Odysseus walked toward the splendid halls of Alcinous, he saw a little girl beside the path who offered to be his guide. She told him all about the wondrous island and the virtues of the king, though she warned him that the people, descended from the god Poseidon himself, were suspicious of strangers. Fortunately a thick mist had descended on them so that they walked toward the city hidden from view. The girl told him that he should first go to the queen and clasp her knees in supplication, for Arete was known to be more welcoming than her husband. As they entered the palace surrounded by rich orchards, the girl wished him well and seemed to disappear—a fitting exit for the goddess Athena in disguise.

Odysseus gathered his courage and walked into the throne room of the king. Before anyone had seen him, he fell down before the queen and grasped her knees. "Queen Arete, after many trials I come to you to beg for mercy. May the gods grant you prosperity and may your children be the pride of your life. As for myself, I ask only a ship to take me back to my native land. If you knew how far I've come and how much I've suffered, you would be kindly disposed to the man you see before you."

The queen and king were surprised to find a suppliant appear suddenly in their court, but they knew the laws of hospitality and asked him to rise. They called for a chair for their guest and sat before him food and wine.

After he had eaten his fill, they asked the mysterious stranger who he was and where he had come from. Odysseus replied that he would prefer to withhold his name for the time being, but he could tell them that he was a man of some nobility who had been held for seven years on the island of Calypso, daughter of the Titan Atlas. He had at last escaped and come to their shores, seeking only a small ship to take him home to his native Ithaca. The king declared he would see that his visitor reached his home, but in the meantime let him rest in the palace. The next day they would have a wonderful feast to send him on his way. Odysseus thanked Alcinous and went to his chambers to sleep. Years of toil and troubles seemed almost at an end, if only he could make it back to Ithaca. He knew that he would face trials there as well, but at least he would be home.

The following evening the king held a great banquet in honor of his guest with all the nobles of the land invited. After platters of food had been served and goblets of sweet wine poured into the cups, the king called his bard Demodocus to come and entertain them. The company all rose to honor the blind singer, who bore the history and stories of their people. He knew many songs of lands beyond as well and plucked his lyre as he began. Everyone cheered as he sang of how Hephaestus had once trapped his wife, Aphrodite, in a net with Ares on Mount Olympus. Then someone asked for a tale of Troy and how the Greeks had taken that mighty city. Demodocus raised his voice with a song of the wooden horse built by the plan of the wily Odysseus and how the Trojans had dragged the ill-fated gift into their town. He told of how the Greeks had snuck from the belly of the beast that night and slaughtered the Trojans as the city went up in flames.

Odysseus sat listening to the words of the bard who sang as if he had been there himself. In his mind he saw again the horror of that night—brave men dying all around him as they tried to defend their families, mothers violated before their sons and daughters while the Greeks laughed, children screaming as they were thrown from the walls—all for the glory of war. He began to weep uncontrollably, sobbing as he fell to the ground, just like the women whose husbands he had killed that night before he dragged them off into slavery and shame. The Phaeacians watched him with great sympathy and gave him time to collect himself. Then Alcinous lifted him up and sat him gently in his own chair. He asked him again who he was.

"Great king, noble lady, kind people of Phaeacia. You ask who I am and what brought me to this land. It is a long tale full of pain, but if you want to hear it, I will tell you. I am Odysseus, son of Laertes, and I have suffered more than any man alive." And with that, he began his story.

We gladly set sail from Troy that day so long ago and the wind drove our ships west to the Thracian lands of the Cicones, allies of the Trojans. There my warriors and I sacked one of their cities and killed the men, but kept the women and children as slaves. I shared everything with my comrades and urged them to sail before more Cicones came, but they wouldn't listen, sitting on the beach drinking all the wine they had stolen until they fell asleep. The next morning the neighboring Cicones rode out of the mist and cut them down. We struggled to raise our bronze weapons against them, but they were too fast on their chariots and forced us to flee. Many men who had fought at Troy for ten years died that day because of their foolishness.

A storm blew us away from there with winds that tossed our ships for two days and nights. We were exhausted when the sun finally showed us the Peloponnesus on our starboard side. The gale had carried us just where we wanted to go—almost home! I might have seen my family soon afterward if another storm hadn't hit us then, far worse than the first, driving us for nine days into unknown seas. On the tenth morning we reached the land of the Lotus Eaters. I drew the ships up onshore to collect fresh water and sent three scouts inland to see who might live there. When they didn't return, I set off myself with a group of armed men ready for a fight. But the natives of that land meant us no harm. They welcomed us all and offered us the honey-sweet fruit of the lotus to eat. Some of my men tasted it, then lost their desire to journey home. All they wanted to do was stay and eat the lotus fruit forever. I grabbed these men by the throats and forced them back to the ships against their will, then ordered all the ships to cast off immediately and row away from that coast.

The spirits of my men were low as the ships sailed to another unfamiliar shore. It was a desolate land with rough inland hills and wild goats roaming everywhere. We found anchorage in a small harbor there and set about catching goats for our supper, then made a fine meal and slept through the night in peace. When dawn came once again, I left most of my soldiers on the beach and headed away from the shore with only a few warriors to see what kind of men inhabited the land. We hadn't gone far when we saw the entrance to a cave in the hillside with a large stone rolled away from its mouth. There were sheep pasturing nearby, larger than any in Greece. I took a skin of wine and entered the cavern, hoping to trade for food, but found no one home. The rest of my men soon discovered cheese drying on racks and spring lambs penned in the corner.

We made ourselves at home and built a fire to roast a sheep, then feasted on cheese and awaited the return of the shepherd. Late in the day, just as the sun was setting, we heard something large approaching the cave and quickly put out the fire. The creature that entered was like nothing I had ever seen before. He was a giant, taller than three men standing on top of each other, and had a single, enormous eye in the center of his forehead. He entered the cave, then rolled the huge stone across the entrance so that nothing larger than a mouse could escape. My men and I hid quietly in a corner while he milked his sheep and set aside the curds in the wicker racks for cheese. But then after he had lit his fire, the monster saw us huddled in the shadows.

"Who are you?" he demanded.

"We are Greek sailors," I answered, "making our way home from Troy. May it please Zeus, who watches over all guests, we would like to trade with you for food and be on our way."

"You are a fool," said the giant. "I am Polyphemus, a Cyclops, the son of Poseidon, and I care nothing for Zeus." With that he reached out and grabbed two of my men by their legs and smashed their heads against a stone as if they were puppies. He tore their limbs from their bodies and ate everything raw before our eyes, even the bones and entrails. We cried out to Zeus for justice, but the Cyclops ignored us and fell asleep among his flocks. I thought about stabbing him dead with my sword—but then who would move the stone away? We were trapped in a cavern with a monster who was going to kill and eat us all.

After a sleepless night for my men and me, the Cyclops left the next morning, putting the stone carefully in place to seal us in. We tried everything to move that rock, but it was no use. While my men wept and prayed to the gods, I sat down and considered what we might do. Just before sunset, I hit upon a plan and told my men to pour some of the wine we had brought into one of the Cyclops' bowls. When the giant entered that evening and closed us in once again, I spoke to him.

"Mighty Polyphemus, son of the great god Poseidon, receive this gift from our hands. It is wine, made by human hands, but a gift from the gods."

The monster took the bowl and drained it in a single gulp, then demanded more. After a second bowl, he asked my name.

"I will tell you my name," I said, "if you promise to give me a gift. My name is Nobody—that's it—Nobody."

"A strange name," said the Cyclops. "All right, Nobody, my gift to you is that I will eat you last!" Then he laughed as he grabbed two more of my men and devoured them like the first. With that he fell over in a drunken stupor and snored so loudly the cave shook.

"*Courage*," I whispered to my men. "*Now we will have our revenge.*"

I ordered them to take a long wooden pole and sharpen it, then harden the point in the fire. When all was ready, I climbed on a rock above the sleeping Cyclops and plunged the stake through his heavy lid deep into his single eye. The monster awoke screaming in agony, then groped his way to the stone and rolled it away from the door just enough to shout to his neighboring Cyclopes.

"*Help me!*" he cried. "*Nobody has attacked me! Nobody has blinded me!*"

From the distant hills came cries in response: "*Shut up, you fool! Stop making so much noise. If nobody has hurt you, why are you bothering us?*"

With that Polyphemus sank down on the cave floor and rolled the stone back in place. He tried to find us with his hands, but we moved too quickly for him. At last he settled into sleep in front of the door, whimpering from the pain even in his dreams.

The next morning the bleating sheep woke the Cyclops as they cried to be let out to pasture. I told my men each to grab quickly the underside of one of the animals and hold on if they valued their lives. Then Polyphemus rolled the stone away again and stood by the entrance, allowing only one sheep at a time to exit. He carefully felt each one to make sure it was not a man, but he didn't bother to search underneath. Holding our breath, we all made it out of the cavern clinging to those wonderful sheep.

My men were overjoyed as we ran back to our ships, still anchored in the little harbor. As they rowed away, I could see Polyphemus stumbling down the path to the shore crying out that the man who had blinded him had escaped. My warriors all urged me to keep quiet, but I couldn't help glorying over the stupid monster: "Hey, Polyphemus, you filthy cannibal, be careful you don't trip and hurt yourself! Maybe now you'll learn to treat your guests with respect. And by the way, my name isn't Nobody, you silly creature, it's Odysseus, son of Laertes, raider of cities and hero of Troy."

The Cyclops threw giant stones at us, but they splashed harmlessly off our stern. Then he fell to his knees and sent up a prayer to

Poseidon, calling down a curse upon me: "Father, if I am really your son, grant to me that Odysseus, son of Laertes, may never reach his home. But if it is his fate to do so, at least make sure that day is far off and that he returns home alone, a broken man."

So Polyphemus spoke—and Poseidon heard his prayer. Oh, that I had kept my mouth shut as we sailed away from his island! But I foolishly gave him my name to use in his curse and have suffered for it since.

From the land of the Cyclops, we came to a beautiful island with sheer rock cliffs reaching to the sky. This was the home of Aeolus, lord of the winds, whose hall was scented with the sweet smell of roasting meats all day long. He hosted us for a full month as I told him of the long war at Troy and all that had happened since. Then as we departed, he gave me a sack made from the skin of a full-grown ox, holding winds from all the corners of the earth, but the west wind he let loose to blow us home.

Nine days we sailed our ships from his island and on the tenth Ithaca was in sight! But since I had manned the rudder the whole time, I could stay awake no longer and fell into a deep sleep. My men had grown envious of the gift Aeolus had given me, thinking it was a bag of silver and gold. They took it while I slept and loosed the cord holding the top. The winds that erupted from the skin tossed the ships about in a hurricane and blew us far away from our home. Soon we found ourselves back on the island of Aeolus. Humbled, I went to the halls of the king and pleaded for another fair wind to send us to Ithaca, but he scorned me and sent us away empty-handed for seeking a gift twice. Thanks to the folly of my crew, we were as far from home as ever.

Six days we rowed through calm seas and on the seventh came to the land of the Laestrygonians. Darkness never falls there, but sunset and sunrise meet each other every day. We sailed into a deep harbor and found the palace of Antiphates the king. The people were giants, but they all seemed friendly and welcomed us to their halls. Then when the king entered, he snatched up one of my men and tore him to pieces for his dinner. The other Laestrygonians came running from every side *and speared my men like fish for their meal. Some of us fought our way back to the harbor, but only my ship sailed away from that cursed land, one of the twelve that had sailed from Ithaca many years before.*

We were sick in our hearts for our murdered comrades, but still we journeyed on. Lost and alone on an unknown sea, we spied another island and pulled up on the beach, tired to our bones. The next morning I climbed the cliffs above the ship and saw smoke rising from the heart of the island. I sent my comrade Eurylochus inland with almost two dozen armed men to see what kind of people lived on these shores and if they might help us. It was no more than a few hours later when he came running back alone to the ship and told us to launch our craft quickly into the sea. I tried to make him calm down and tell us what had happened, but he was overcome by fear. At last he said they had come across a palace in the woods with gleaming bronze doors. A beautiful woman surrounded by tame beasts opened those doors and bade them enter, but he stayed behind, sensing a trap. Alas, the others drank the wine she offered and turned into pigs.

I told my crew we were not leaving. We had lost too many men already and would make our stand here on this island. I forced Eurylochus to lead me back to the palace and then sent him away to the ship. It was then that the god Hermes, sent by Zeus, appeared to me and told me I was about to enter the halls of the great witch Circe. He gave me a magical herb to eat and said it would protect me from the witch's brew, then he vanished.

Circe met me at the door surrounded by her pets and welcomed me inside, then gave me a goblet and told me to refresh myself with her sweet wine. I drained the cup in one gulp, then threw it on the ground as I raised my sword to Circe's throat. She was incredulous that I had not been transformed into a pig, but swore by the gods she would change my men back and help me on my journey. I spared her life and watched as my men regained their human form. Circe then offered me the hospitality of her home and called her lovely nymphs to fetch the rest of the men from the ship. We had been through so many trials that they welcomed the touch of the lovely maids and the ample food and drink of Circe's house—a feast that flows on forever.

My men and I spent a year on Circe's island while we rested and they enjoyed the delights of her handmaids. I myself mounted the bed of the witch each night—so as not to offend her—and lost all track of time. But at last I roused myself and told our hostess we must leave. Circe did not try to stop us, but she warned me of what lay ahead: "Odysseus, royal son of Laertes, to sail home to Ithaca you must first make another voyage, one no ship has made before. You must journey to the house of death, the abode of Hades, and there seek counsel from the ghost of wise Tiresias."

These words crushed my heart. Sail to the land of the dead? I asked her how this was possible. She replied that an entrance to Hades' realm lay across the great river of Ocean far to the north. The spirit of Tiresias would tell me what I needed to know to complete my journey and make peace with Poseidon.

The men were overjoyed that night as they drank heavily from Circe's wine for the last time and made love to her nymphs. One of the sailors, a foolish young man named Elpenor, fell drunk from the palace roof and broke his neck in the early morning hours, but there was no time to bury him before we sailed. Once we were under way, I spoke to my crew: "Men, we are on our way to Ithaca, but there is one final journey we must first make. I ask you to trust me this last time. Circe has told me that we cannot find our way home until I have consulted the prophet Tiresias in the land of the dead."

The men thought at first I must be joking, then they saw from my face that I was serious. How could anyone travel to the land of the dead and return? they asked. Hercules had journeyed there, as had Orpheus, but they were great heroes of another age. We are just men, they cried, who want to see our families again. Even if by some miracle we could sail this ship to Hades' realm, we would be trapped there forever.

But finally, with much persuasion and not a few threats, I convinced my crew we must travel to the dwelling place of shades or never see home again. With a last look at the world of the living, we turned our ship to the setting sun and sailed into darkness.

I don't know how long our voyage lasted—weeks, perhaps months—but at last we sailed to a land where the sun never shines and endless night hangs over everything. We beached our ship on a desolate shore and disembarked, taking with us animals for sacrifice. I found a sandy spot on that lifeless coast and dug a trench with my sword, then poured milk, honey, and wine into the hole for the dead, followed by water and barley. With that I took sheep and cut their throats over the trench so that the dark blood flowed in. Then I saw a sight to freeze your soul. Thousands of ghosts appeared out of the darkness and drifted toward me. There were young brides and old men, children and warriors cut down in battle. I drew my sword and held them all back from the blood they craved until I saw the shade of young Elpenor, who had fallen to his death on Circe's island and made his way to this place faster than our ship. I let him sip the black blood so that he could speak, then he begged me to give him a proper burial if I made it back to the witch's home. I swore that I would do so and watched as he faded into the gloom.

The figure I saw next brought pity and fear to my heart so that I wept on that dismal shore. It was my own mother, Anticlea, whom I had left alive when I sailed for Troy. She was only a shade now, just a fleeting image of the woman who had raised me and loved me so. But in spite of my desire to question her, I would not let her approach the blood until I had spoken to Tiresias.

The ghost of the Theban prophet then appeared before me and motioned me to lower my sword while he drank from the trench. At last he spoke.

"Odysseus, son of Laertes, you have a difficult journey ahead of you. Many trials and much pain await you on many shores. You will come to an island where the cattle of Helios, god of the sun, graze. But no matter how hungry you are, do not touch them. If you leave them alone, you may reach home. If you do come to rocky Ithaca, you will find things are not as you left them. Even if you do become master of your house again, your journey will not be over. You must take an oar and carry it high into the mountains far from the sea. When someone at last asks you why you have a winnowing fan on your shoulder, plant the blade there and sacrifice to Poseidon. Then you will finally know peace."

The seer left me and withdrew into the darkness. Then I allowed my mother to come forward and drink the blood so that she could speak. When she had finished, I implored her to tell me of events in Ithaca and how she had come down to the house of Hades.

"My son, your home is overrun by wicked men who seek your fair Penelope as their bride. She resists them, at least for now, but she and your son, Telemachus, cannot hold them off forever. Your father, Laertes, has withdrawn in sorrow to a hut in the countryside to live like a pauper. As for me, I could not wait for you any longer. My sweet Odysseus, I died of longing for you."

Tears rolled down my face like rain as I tried three times to embrace her, but her shade passed through my hands like smoke.

Others came to drink from the trench full of blood. Mothers of great heroes, such as Leda, who bore Castor and Pollux, and Jocasta, the mother of Oedipus. Then warriors marched forward, friends I had known at Troy. The spirit of Agamemnon was there, telling me of his murder at the hands of his wife, Clytemnestra, and warning me never to trust a woman, even Penelope. Then great-hearted Achilles drank the blood as I congratulated him on being the most famous of the ghosts in Hades. But he scoffed at me: "Shining Odysseus, you are a fool if you think there is any glory here. I would rather be a living slave to the poorest farmer in Greece than rule over the kingdom of the dead."

I also saw mighty Ajax, but he turned away from me and would not drink, still angry over the armor of Achilles I had won instead of him.

I saw Tantalus there in his endless torture, reaching in vain for fruit and trying to drink water that vanished away. I saw Sisyphus pushing his rock endlessly up a hill, only to have it roll down again. I even talked to Hercules—the mortal part of his spirit that was burned away, not the god who lives forever on Olympus. I saw Theseus, Minos, the great hunter Orion, and countless others there as they pressed forward to drink the blood. But soon so many dead came surging around me that I could not hold them back. Terror gripped me and I called on my men to ready the ship before we were overwhelmed by all the shades of Hades. We cut the cables and rowed for our lives as the spirits crowded the shore, crying for blood. At last we left that dark

land behind and began our long journey back to the world of light
and life.

We returned to Circe's island and buried our companion Elpenor,
just as he had asked. The beautiful witch herself welcomed us back
from the dead, then took me aside to warn me of what lay ahead—
temptations, monsters, and death for some, though I did not tell this to
my men. The next morning we set out again for Ithaca.

A fair wind blew for many days, but suddenly we were becalmed
in a strange sea and took out our oars to row. Circe had told me what
would happen next, so I sliced beeswax into pieces and told my crew
to fix this tightly in their ears until the danger was past. I then ordered
them to bind me to the mast with double ropes so that I alone could
hear the song of the Sirens. These hideous creatures lured men to
their doom with their lovely words that no one could resist. The men
rowed with powerful strokes away from the island of these creatures,
but still I heard them singing: "Welcome, Odysseus, come closer, great
captain! We know what wonders you accomplished at Troy, we know
it all, and will sing to you of your glorious deeds. Come and lose yourself in the past."

I was driven mad by their voices and told my men to untie me so
that I could go to them. But two of my companions bound me all the
tighter for my struggling until at last we were far from their shore, covered with the bones of their victims.

Scarcely were we safe from the Sirens than we came to a narrow
strait. On one side lay the monster Scylla, once a beautiful maiden
but now a creature with six heads that snatched men and ate them
raw. We would have steered clear of her, but on the other side lay the
great whirlpool Charybdis, which dragged ships down to their doom.
Our only hope was to row as swiftly as we could between Scylla and
Charybdis, praying to the gods that not all of us would perish. Then
Scylla struck suddenly and took six of my brave men, all screaming
my name with their last breath. She dragged them back to her dark
cavern and devoured them alive, while we could do nothing. Of all
the deaths I had seen at Troy and on our voyage home, these were the
hardest to bear and most horrible to watch.

At last we found a green island and pulled up on shore. I had told

my men we should row on, for this was the island of Helios, lord of the
sun. Circe had warned me not to visit here lest my men in their hunger
eat the god's cattle. But they begged for rest and swore they would not
touch his herds. At first they kept their word, but a fierce south wind
held us on the island for a month until the food on our ship ran out.
Hunger racked our bellies while we listened to the sweet lowing of
cattle on the hills at night. At last while I slept, my men decided they
would rather face the wrath of the god than starve. They killed and
roasted one of the cattle, then ate to their hearts' content. I awoke and
told them they were fools, but the deed was done.

The next day when the wind finally died away, we set out from
the cursed island. But Helios had gone before Zeus to complain about
the violation of his herd, so the ruler of the gods struck our ship with a
lightning bolt in a storm. My men were thrown from our broken craft
and cried to me as they sank down into the waves for the last time.
I could do nothing except cling to a few broken planks as I watched
them all drown and wait to die myself. But the gods had other plans
for me. I lived to wash up on the shores of Calypso's island ten days
later, alone of all the men who had set out from Ithaca so many years
before.

That is my story, great king Alcinous and gracious queen Arete,
until I washed ashore on your island yesterday. You have heard the
whole sad tale and now I ask only that you grant me a small ship so
that I may find my way home.

The Phaeacian king and his court sat spellbound as Odysseus finished his story. Then Alcinous rose and assured him he would have his
sailors take him to Ithaca that very evening in his fastest ship. The king
called on his nobles each to give the penniless wanderer a fine gift of
gold or silver so that he would not return to his home empty-handed.
The lords of Phaeacia all agreed and had their servants place a hoard of
treasure on board the swift ship. The king and queen led Odysseus to
the docks and saw him onto the craft, bidding him a warm farewell. The
son of Laertes was so exhausted that he fell into a deep sleep as soon as
he heard the rhythmic movement of the oars. At miraculous speed, the
Phaeacian ship cut through the waters that night so that as the morning star rose in the east they spied the shores of Ithaca off their bow.

Odysseus was still dead to the world, so they carried the sleeping man to the beach and laid him gently down on the earth of his homeland. The treasure they stored safely away in a nearby cave, then boarded their ship and sailed away.

It was midmorning before Odysseus awoke and found himself again in an unknown land. He thought at first the Phaeacian sailors had left him on some desolate coast and taken his treasure for themselves, but he soon found the cave and counted his riches, blessing King Alcinous and his men for their honesty and kindness. But where was he? At that moment a shepherd boy appeared on the hill above the beach herding his goats. Odysseus hailed him and asked him what country this was. The lad laughed and said he was on the island of Ithaca. Odysseus was overjoyed to be home, but he did not show it to the shepherd. He was determined not to reveal his identity to anyone until he knew who his friends were on the island. He replied, "Ithaca? Yes, I think I've heard of it. I'm from Crete myself. I killed a man there after I returned from Troy when he tried to steal the booty I won at that great city. I fled then on a ship of Phoenician traders who brought me here."

At that moment the shepherd boy laughed again and turned into the goddess Athena.

"Odysseus, this is why I love you so. Any other man would have rushed to his house straightaway after twenty years, but you are always thinking and scheming. That's why I can never forsake you in your troubles. You're right to be careful and trust no one—not even your wife, Penelope. Test her first, test them all, before you reveal yourself. I will help you now by transforming you into an old beggar so you can move about unknown in your own household. Then I'm off to Sparta to fetch Telemachus, who has been looking for you. Be careful, Odysseus—you're not home yet. You have faced monsters and angry gods, but the dangers ahead are more treacherous."

With that the goddess touched Odysseus and shriveled his skin, turned his hair white, and clothed him in dirty rags. She gave him a staff and a beggar's sack slung from a frayed rope over his shoulder. Then she disappeared, leaving him alone.

Odysseus made his way from the beach to a nearby hut in the hills where his swineherd Eumaeus lived. The old servant welcomed the stranger—for Zeus watches over strangers—and gave him food to eat. The king did not reveal himself, but told the swineherd he was a refugee from Crete who had once served beside Odysseus at Troy. He told Eumaeus how he had fought bravely in the war, but was blown off course to Egypt on the way home, and his crew all died because of their foolish greed. He had lost everything—family, home, riches—before he washed up on these shores and only wanted directions to the local palace so that he could beg for scraps. Eumaeus told him how to find the home of the king, but warned him his lord was long absent and that wicked suitors, filthy pigs seeking the hand of fair Penelope, had taken over his home. They were beggars of a sort themselves, but they would not treat him kindly, so he had best be on his guard. Odysseus thanked the shepherd, then asked instead if he might stay with him awhile. Eumaeus consented, as he welcomed the company, and made a bed for the stranger in a corner of his hut.

Athena meanwhile had flown to Sparta to rouse Telemachus and send him on his way home. The prince thanked Menelaus and Helen, then returned to his ship at Pylos and set sail for Ithaca. By the help of the goddess he avoided the trap the suitors had laid for him and landed on the far side of the island, sending his crew on to the port, where he would join them later. The young man wanted to find his old friend Eumaeus first and question him about what had happened at the palace during his absence.

The swineherd embraced the prince like a long-lost son and brought him into his simple hut for bread and wine. The old beggar in the corner gazed at him in wonder and rose to offer Telemachus his seat, but the prince bade him sit while Eumaeus told him all the latest news. The beggar watched the young man closely as he spoke, noting his fine bearing and clear mind. When they had finished and Telemachus asked him who he was and where he had come from, the wanderer said he was nobody, just a poor castaway from Crete blown to these shores. Then when Eumaeus left to take care of the pigs, Athena removed the disguise she had placed on the king so that he stood like Zeus himself before the startled prince.

"Friend," exclaimed Telemachus, "your clothes and look have changed before my eyes! Are you a god come down from Olympus? Be kind to us here on this humble island and we will offer you rich sacrifices."

But the shining figure shook his head and said, "I am no god, but a man like yourself. Listen to me, Telemachus. You have borne a world of pain these last twenty years, but no longer. I have returned. I am Odysseus, your father."

At first Telemachus did not believe these words, but Odysseus told of what he had been through and how Athena had transformed him. Then at last the prince saw that it was true and threw his arms around his father as both stood weeping.

The two talked far into the night as Telemachus shared with his father everything that had happened and told him about each of the suitors who had come to steal Penelope. Odysseus listened carefully and finally told his son what they would do. The prince would return to his mother and let her know he had returned safely from Sparta. Then the next day when Athena had changed Odysseus back into an old beggar, the king would make his way to the palace himself. When he had learned everything he needed to know, he would drive the trespassers from his home, no matter how many there were. Telemachus was to say nothing about him to Penelope. Odysseus would reveal himself to her in his own good time.

After Telemachus left the next morning, the swineherd Eumaeus led his guest to the palace of Odysseus with another warning to be on his guard against the cruel suitors. Along the way they met Melanthius, the royal goatherd, who mocked the shabby beggar and kicked him into the dirt. For a moment Odysseus was going to take his staff and beat the man to death, but he quickly mastered his temper and let Melanthius go on his way.

The wandering king at last entered the courtyard of his palace after twenty years away. He could hardly believe the tattered look of his beloved home or the crowd of boisterous suitors he saw gathered around eating his stores. It was then that an old dog in the corner of the courtyard pricked up his ears. He was Argos, trained as a puppy by Odysseus many years before as his companion on hunts through the woods and hills. Now, with his master long gone, he lay blind and crippled on a pile of manure for warmth. Sometimes the servants threw him a scrap of food, but most of the time he slept in the manure scarcely able to move his old bones. But then he heard the voice of his old master as he entered the gate and used what little strength he still had to raise his head, though he could not even crawl forward to greet him. Odysseus saw him there, but did not dare show any recognition lest he give himself away. The faithful hound then lowered his head for the last time and quietly died, while his master, unseen by all, wiped away a tear.

The suitors saw Eumaeus bring the old beggar into the palace and railed at him for his poor manners, expecting Penelope to feed a stranger from her stores. Why, there was hardly enough for them lately, let alone some vagabond washed up on their shores. Odysseus humbly reminded them that strangers were protected by Zeus, but they only struck him with a stool and laughed as he tumbled into the dust. For their amusement they made him fight another beggar whom they used as a messenger. This toady was a former boxer with a large chest and powerful arms who looked liked he could snap an ox in half. Odysseus sized him up in an instant, then after circling him and feigning caution, he struck him below the ear with one punch and sent him crashing to the ground.

At that moment Penelope appeared on the balcony above the courtyard, radiant as a goddess. The suitors all stopped and bowed to her, each dreaming of sharing her bed. But she chastised them for their ill treatment of the old beggar and went back to her quarters in disgust. Even after she had gone, Odysseus continued to gaze up at the spot where she had stood. She was as beautiful as ever, with the same fire in her eyes. There had been so many nights he had dreamed of seeing her again, touching her soft skin and telling her how much he loved her. Now there she was, but he did not dare to reveal himself to her. The suitors were numerous and well armed. They would certainly kill him and Telemachus alike if he openly challenged them. No, it was better to wait and choose the right moment to strike.

That night after the suitors and their servants had retired to their quarters, Odysseus sat alone in the empty courtyard of his palace eating a crust of bread. A maid then came down the stairs and told him the lady of the house would like to speak with him. He followed her up to the women's quarters and found himself alone with Penelope. She gave him a stool to sit on and apologized for the treatment he had received in her home. She assured him it would not have been so in the days when her husband was lord of the house. He knew how to welcome guests, but he was gone now these twenty years and most said he was dead. Odysseus thanked her for her kindness and suggested perhaps it was time she looked for a new husband. Penelope smiled and said she had the same advice from many others, but she yearned still for her dear Odysseus. She had tried to put off the suitors using every trick she could think of, though she had now run out of time. She could not wait any longer or they might kill Telemachus and force her to marry one of them. The beggar said he understood and told her of how he had met her husband once, long ago in Crete, where he had stopped on the way to Troy. Penelope listen to his story and his description of her husband until tears ran down her cheeks like melting snow after a long winter. The heart of Odysseus went out to her as she sat just inches away. He longed to hold her and tell her everything, but for the sake of both of them as well as their son, he sat silent and cold as a stone until she withdrew to her room to find comfort in sweet sleep.

The old maid Euryclea then came to him at the bidding of her mistress and began to wash away the dirt from his feet. She had nursed Odysseus as a child and rocked him to sleep in her arms. Of the servants of the household, she was among the few who remained loyal to Penelope and her absent master. But as she bent over to place his feet in the bath, she saw a childhood scar on his leg and knew in an instant that he was Odysseus, returned at last. She started to rise and shout for Penelope to come quickly, but the cunning warrior took her by the throat and said that as much as he cared for his old nurse, he would strangle her then and there if she said a word. She swore she would keep his secret and help him however she could. Odysseus then told her to stand ready, for the day of his revenge was about to dawn.

The next morning Penelope once again stood at the top of the stairs to speak to the suitors. She declared that the long wait was over. Odysseus must surely be dead by now and she must remarry. But first her new husband would have to prove himself. She ordered her servants to take twelve long battle axes and stand them up in the courtyard in a straight line with their handles facing upward. Whoever would marry her would have to string the bow of Odysseus, then shoot an arrow through the metal loops at the end of each ax all in a row. The suitors looked at the axes and declared such a thing was impossible. Even if they could string the king's fabled bow, no man could possibly shoot an arrow clean through all twelve handles. Penelope merely scoffed and said that Odysseus had done it, then she turned her back on them and retired to her quarters while Telemachus supervised the contest.

Odysseus called his son to him and whispered that he should take all the weapons in the room and quietly lock them away. Then he was to order the gates to the courtyard barred from the outside to prevent anyone from leaving. After this he sat in the corner while the suitors tried to string his bow. One after another the warriors took the bow in hand and did their best, but could not hook the string around the end. When at last all had tried and failed, Odysseus spoke up: "Gentlemen, would you mind if I tried? Just for your amusement, of course. I'd like to see if there is any strength left in these old bones of mine."

The men told him to shut up and mind his place, but did not object as he took the mighty bow in hand. The old beggar somehow looked different as he stroked the wood and in one swift movement strung the bow. He plucked the string to make a single note like the sound of a lyre, then took an arrow, notched it, and pulled back. It sailed clean through all twelve handles and lodged in the far wall as the suitors looked on in amazement.

Before they could react, he took another arrow and shot their leader, Antinous, through the neck. The suitors raised howls of protest and moved in to kill the beggar, but he leveled his gaze at them and said, "You fools! You thought I'd never return from Troy, did you? You bled my household dry, seduced my serving women, and courted my wife while I was still alive, never fearing the gods above. Well, your time is up and you're all about to die wallowing in your own blood!"

The suitors stood shocked and unbelieving until Odysseus drew the bow again and began swiftly to cut them down. One after another they fell while Telemachus joined in the slaughter with his sword. Defenseless, some tried to escape over the walls while others made a stand, but to no avail. The last to die pleaded with the king to let them pay amends for what they had done, but Odysseus would not listen. Soon bodies sprawled about the courtyard like a battlefield. Odysseus called Telemachus and told him to have the maids clean up the mess, then send his mother down.

When all the blood and gore had been removed and the benches scrubbed clean, fair Penelope made her way down the stairs and took a seat facing Odysseus. She did not move toward him or even smile, but waited with folded hands. Telemachus asked his mother how she could be so cold, but the wily king said Telemachus should leave them alone. If his mother wanted to test his identity, then let her.

Penelope looked at Odysseus carefully and admitted he did seem like the man who had left her twenty years ago, though with a touch of gray about the temples. Still, she really couldn't be sure. She thought it would be best if her maids moved their great bed out into the courtyard for him to rest in that night since she certainly wasn't going to sleep with some stranger.

Odysseus blazed in fury at her words. Move his bed? He said that he had built that bed himself years before from the branches of an olive tree. He didn't cut it at the trunk, but shaped the bed from the living branches of the tree still in the ground. Around it he built his bedroom and around that he built his home. The bed could not be moved unless it had been severed from its roots. No one ever entered their bedroom but themselves, so no one knew about the secret of its construction. Had the bed been cut away? Was it still rooted firmly in the earth?

That was the test Penelope had laid for Odysseus. She dissolved into tears as she ran to embrace her husband. Love and longing overcame both as they held each other and cried for joy. As sailors tossed helplessly on the stormy seas weep in happiness when at last they plant their feet on solid ground again, so husband and wife clung to each other as if they would never let go. Odysseus was home at last.

AENEAS

Like the Greeks, the Romans told their own story of a refugee from the Trojan War. Their hero was Aeneas, son of Anchises and the goddess Aphrodite, who sailed from the burning ruins of Troy to found a new city in Italy. It was foretold by the gods that this second Troy would give birth to a race that would rule the world. These people were the Romans, and while they borrowed much from the myths of the Greeks, they gave their own names to the gods. Zeus became Jupiter, Hera was known as Juno, Aphrodite became Venus, and Poseidon lorded over the seas as Neptune. But by whatever names they were called, the gods still ruled the universe and played their endless games with the lives of mortals.

Juno was especially vengeful and slow to forgive. She had never forgotten that the Trojan prince Paris chose to give the apple for the most beautiful goddess to Venus instead of her. She became the implacable enemy of Troy and was still not satisfied when the city lay in ashes. It may have been prophesied that Aeneas would found a new and glorious city in the west, but she was determined to make life difficult for the Trojan fugitive—and perhaps even thwart the will of the Fates.

Seeing the Trojan fleet sailing the placid sea as it made its way toward the setting sun, Juno flew down to the island of Aeolus, king of the winds, to ask a favor of her old friend.

"Aeolus, Jupiter gave you power over the winds to calm them or raise them to a gale. Come now and do me a favor. The remnant Trojans I despise are crossing the sea on their way to Italy. Blow them far off course and I'll give you a gorgeous nymph to be your wife."

The king of the winds quickly agreed and stirred up a storm to crash against the Trojan fleet. The ships were tossed and scattered as the sky grew black, driving them away from Italian shores toward Africa.

Aeneas stood on the bow of the lead ship and raised up his hands as he shouted to the heavens: "O my comrades who died at Troy, I call you three and four times blessed to have fallen beneath our native walls rather than perish here in unknown seas. I wish I had died there too, for I just can't take any more of this!"

After a long struggle, a few of the Trojan ships were cast up together on a desert coast, though none could say where they were. The rest of the fleet was lost, with Aeneas fearing these men and their families were all dead.

Aeneas took his steadfast comrade Achates and headed inland to discover what they could learn of this unknown land. Soon they met a young girl with bow and arrows hunting in the brush. They called to her and told her not to be afraid. They were merely castaways who wanted to learn what sort of country they had come to. Could she tell them what king ruled this land and where they might find him?

The girl laughed and said there was no king in this realm but a queen—Dido, ruler of Carthage, lately come from the Phoenician city of Sidon to found a new country in the west. Her brother had murdered her husband and driven her from the city with her followers to seek safety on a distant shore. Reaching this haven, the native chiefs mockingly offered to sell her only as much land as she could cover with the hide of a bull. But Dido cleverly cut the hide into strips thin enough to circle the entire site of her new city. The chiefs were furious at being outwitted by a woman, but they could not lose face by going back on their word. The girl advised Aeneas to seek out this just and noble queen straightaway, then she threw off her mortal disguise and flew away as the goddess she truly was. Aeneas cried after her, "Mother, why does it always have to be this way? Can't we ever embrace and speak together? Why does it always have to be disguise and deception with you gods?"

Nonetheless, Aeneas followed the advice of Venus and made his way toward the city of Carthage covered in a mist the goddess wrapped around him and his companion.

The Trojan prince was impressed by what he saw as he entered the rising walls of the new town. Everywhere citizens were working like bees in a hive, some raising the citadel, others laying out building sites or digging wells. Some were dredging a harbor and carrying stones for the foundation of a theater, while the older men were meeting in their senate to draft laws and elect judges. Aeneas envied them their work and wished his own city could be under way, but it seemed now as if the dreams of the Trojans had been lost along with the missing ships. They could never establish a new home and defend themselves with only the men who had survived the storm.

As Aeneas entered the palace, he was astonished to see pictures of the Trojan War carved in stone on the temple of Juno there before his eyes. Here was the combat of Achilles and Hector, the cursed wooden horse dragged into his town, the weeping of women driven away in chains. He was losing himself in memories when the living queen suddenly appeared at the steps of the temple looking like a goddess. It was here that Dido issued decrees and justly carried out the laws of her people. Aeneas was even more amazed when he saw next to the queen none other than the captains of his missing Trojan ships. They were beseeching Dido for help in finding their leader, the great Trojan warrior Aeneas, whom they feared was lost forever in the storm. The queen pledged she would do anything within her power to aid the refugees in their search for the brave Aeneas, a man whose courage and honor were known to her and all her people.

Suddenly Venus swept away the mist covering her son and there stood Aeneas himself before the queen and his own men. He thanked Dido for her kindness and praised the fine city she was building. The queen on her part stood in awe of the Trojan hero, not just for his reputation but for the impression he made on her as a man. She invited him to send for the rest of his shipmates and join her for a feast in the royal halls. They were most welcome to stay in her city as long as they wished—even settle there if they so desired. Aeneas thanked her again and sent a messenger to all his ships to tell his men to come to the city. He was especially eager for his young son Ascanius, called Iulus, to see the splendid town of Carthage.

Venus watched all this from afar with worry in her heart. She was glad the Carthaginians were so friendly, but how long would that last? Juno would surely find a way to turn them against her son and his men, trapped as they were now in the foreign city. She also knew it was not the fate of Aeneas to live in Carthage but to found his own kingdom in

Italy. She needed a way to keep Dido friendly until her son was ready to sail. This was clearly a job for her other son, Cupid. She snatched away Iulus unseen and put him into a deep sleep in her own divine palace while Cupid took the form of the child and worked his magic on Dido. She was enchanted with the boy and fell ever more in love with him and his father, Aeneas. By the time dinner was served, she was determined to make Aeneas her husband and have Trojans and Carthaginians build the new city together as one people.

While she held Iulus in her lap, Dido asked Aeneas to tell her of his adventures from start to finish, leaving out no detail. The Trojan prince replied that he had only sorrow to share with the queen, but he would do as she wished.

It would take a man, with the silver tongue of Ulysses—or Odysseus, as the Greeks call him—to do justice to my tale, dear queen. You know what the Greeks did to my city by the help of the gods, since it is carved on the very walls of your temple, but let me share with you the fall of Troy from the other side, along with all the pain and grief we have suffered since.

You know well the story of the horse built by iron-hearted Ulysses and how the Greeks hid behind on the nearby island of Tenedos while we marveled at the wooden beast on our shore. You know how no one listened to the warnings of Cassandra or the priest Laocoon to destroy the gift of the enemy. You know as well how Sinon, that master of fraud—so typical of a Greek—deceived us with his lies of being condemned and abandoned by his countrymen. I will not retell the story of how we brought the horse inside our walls and feasted while Ulysses and his band inside its belly waited for us to fall asleep.

But that night I lay beside my lovely wife, Creusa, under the moon's quiet light when suddenly my dead comrade Hector appeared to me in a dream, warning, "Aeneas, get out of Troy now! The Greeks are already in the city burning and killing as they go. Our home has fallen and you cannot save it. Take the images of the holy gods of our fathers with you along with all the Trojans as you can gather and flee for your life. You must survive to found a new city so that Troy may live again."

I awoke with a start and leapt to my feet, running to the window.
I could see Greeks everywhere in the streets setting the homes ablaze
and slaying everyone they could find. The roar of the fire was like a
gale on a mountaintop as flames licked the sky. I grabbed my armor
and weapons, heedless of Hector's words, and prepared to fight the
invaders to my last breath. I ran into the streets and found a few
other Trojan warriors ready to make a final stand. In the darkness
it was hard to tell friend from foe. One Greek captain hailed us and
said we'd better hurry or all the booty would soon be gone. Wasn't he
surprised when we began to cut his men to pieces? We ran through the
lanes fighting like madmen with nothing to lose, then made our way
back to the palace of Priam through gates that were already breached.
It was too late to save the king, who had died after strapping a breastplate and greaves on his aged body. The cursed Greeks murdered him,
then killed all the men and raped the women, young maidens and old
matrons alike, afterward marching them back to their ships as slaves.

When I saw the body of Priam I came to my senses and thought
of my own father, Anchises, unprotected from the barbarians inside
our gates. But on my way to our quarters, I saw Helen, the cause
of all this bloodshed and grief, standing alone at the windows of her
luxurious room. I took my sword in hand, determined that she would
not live to rule again as queen at Sparta. But suddenly my mother, the
goddess Venus, appeared before me, and said, "Sheath your blade, my
son, and flee this city. Helen is not to blame for this war, nor is Paris.
The gods themselves are behind it all. Look, I will sweep away the
mortal mist covering your eyes and show you the truth."

And with that she opened my eyes so that I saw Neptune prying
loose the ramparts of Troy with his mighty trident, shaking the city to
its foundations. There was Juno leading troops through the Scaean
gate with her sword drawn. On the citadel stood Minerva, the goddess
the Greeks call Athena, her savage shield freezing the hearts of the
Trojans. Even Jupiter himself was stirring the Greeks to conquer and
burn. I realized then that what my mother said was true. All that was
left was to rescue my family, if there was still time, and escape from
Troy.

I found my rooms at the palace still untouched among the burning halls and told my loved ones we must leave, but my father shook his head. He said he had already lived too long if he was forced to see his city destroyed around him. I begged him to reconsider, as did my wife, Creusa, and our little son, Iulus, but he would not budge. Then suddenly a tongue of fire flared up on the head of Iulus and danced about, though harming him not at all. My father lifted his eyes to heaven and thanked Jupiter for the holy sign, agreeing now to escape with me from Troy. As he was crippled, I placed him on my back and carried him from the palace, with little Iulus holding my hand beside me and my wife a few steps behind. We took with us the sacred hearth gods of Troy from the temple and gathered all the survivors we could find as we made our way through the chaotic streets.

We were almost to the walls when I saw to my horror that Creusa was no longer with us. I was overwhelmed with anguish as I searched for her among the Trojan crowd, but she was not to be found. There was little time to look for her with Greek soldiers everywhere and the city an inferno, but I could not simply leave her. I told the rest to go on, then rushed back along the streets calling her name. I ran all the way back to the palace searching as the flames engulfed the city around me. I was frantic as I searched and ready to die before I turned around, when suddenly a ghost appeared before me—the ghost of my own wife.

"Aeneas, dear husband, there is nothing more you can do for me now. I'm so sorry I fell behind, but fate did not intend for me to make the long journey with you. Go now, before it's too late! Look after our son, the light of my life. Farewell, my love, farewell."

She slipped through my fingers as I tried to hold her one last time, then disappeared forever, like a dream. I ran back to the rest of my family, now outside the walls, and was struck by the number of Trojans gathered there—men, women, children—all gazing back at the smoking ruins of our city. I told them our future lay ahead of us, not behind, and ordered them to follow me. With that, I again took my father on my back and my son by the hand, then headed toward the mountains.

At a hidden spot on the coast beneath Mount Ida we built a fleet to take us far from our native shores. I knew I was to found a new city, *but I did not know yet where it should be. Trusting the gods, we hoisted the sails and set off into the unknown. Thrace seemed like a good choice since it was only a few days away and had been friendly to Troy in the past. We landed there and began to build the walls of a city, but as I was sacrificing to my divine mother something frightful happened. I saw a grove of dogwood trees nearby and was trying to tear off some green shoots to cover the altar, when dark blood began to ooze from the ground. A faint plea rose from the boughs, begging me to stop. It was a human voice saying he was Polydorus, a friend of mine from Troy, who had been sent to the Thracian king with a great weight of gold to secure him as an ally. But when the ruler heard that Troy had fallen, the faithless king slew Polydorus and threw his body in a hole here. He urged me to flee this cursed land where the laws of hospitality were not honored. After giving him a proper burial, we abandoned our walls and set out again across the Aegean.*

We came to the island of Delos, where there is an oracle of holy Apollo, and sought the will of the god. His voice shook the trees and we all fell to the ground, then he told us to seek our ancient mother, for there I would establish a dynasty that would someday rule the world. We were uncertain what the god meant, but my father, Anchises, said that our ancestor Teucer had sailed from Crete to Troy. Crete therefore must be our maternal land. It was not far, so we sailed there and again began to build the walls of a new city. But it wasn't long until plague struck our company and raged among our people for a whole year. What were we to do? Why had the god sent us to this island to die?

That night I had a dream that the sacred images of our household gods rose up before me and spoke: "Aeneas, son of Anchises, Apollo never meant for you to settle in Crete. There is a land far to the west fruitful in its soil and mighty in war. The native people call it Italy. It was the birthplace of Dardanus, your grandfather six generations past. There lies your true home."

I awoke and told the dream to my father. He groaned at the news and said he had made a terrible mistake sending us to Crete. Many times at Troy the prophetess Cassandra had proclaimed that our future lay to the west on the Italian shores, but no one ever listened to her. At last we knew our true destination was Italy, so once again we boarded the ships and set off on Neptune's sea.

A storm arose and blew us away from Crete along the southern coast of the Peloponnesus. The thunderclouds were so dark that even my faithful helmsman Palinurus couldn't tell day from night as he steered through the walls of water all around us. Finally on the fourth day the winds ceased and we came to the Strophades islands off the coast of sandy Pylos, ruled over by Nestor, that wicked old man. Here on these deserted shores the Harpies had settled who tormented Phineus until the Argonauts drove them away. But we were so desperate for solid ground that we beached our ships and kissed the sweet earth. A fine herd of cattle grazed there and we quickly killed several for a sacrifice to Jupiter and a feast for ourselves. The women among us set a fine meal, but when the table was ready the dreaded Harpies swooped down on us with shrieks before we knew what was happening and ripped at our food with their foul talons, ruining the meal we so craved. We decided to try again and killed more cattle, then took the meat to roast in a deep recess of a cliff surrounded by thick trees. We drew our swords to guard our dinner, but it was no use. The loathsome creatures again spoiled the food and left behind a trail of oozing filth. They were impervious to our blades and laughed at our efforts to stop them. Their leader, a she-monster named Celaeno, then perched on a nearby tree and spoke to me.

"My dear Aeneas, upset are we that your little picnic was ruined? Too bad for the brave warriors of Troy. You would take up arms to drive us away from our rightful kingdom? This is our home, you foolish man, and those cattle you killed belonged to us. Hear me well and remember what I say—as punishment for your trespassing, you will not find your new home until hunger drives you to eat your own plates."

With that she shrieked and flew away, leaving me to puzzle at her words.

We sailed north from there past the coast of Ithaca, rocky island of coldhearted Ulysses, and we cursed the man who destroyed our home. Up the western shores of Greece we journeyed until we saw a small harbor. We anchored there and could not believe our eyes, for beside

the banks of a stream was Andromache, widow of Hector, the best
of Trojan warriors. She thought we were ghosts as well and could not
decide whether to run or fall to her knees before us.

"Aeneas, goddess-born, is it really you? Are you a man still alive
or a spirit risen from Hades? If you come from the underworld, please
tell me of my Hector. Is he well? Is our son Astyanax with him?"

I assured her I was quite real, not a vision from the land of the
dead, and we embraced as long-lost friends. She said she had been
taken as a slave by Achilles' son—offspring of the very man who
murdered her husband—and was forced to bear him a child. Then
when he took a noble wife, he married her to a fellow Trojan, Helenus, the noted prophet and son of Priam. They had settled here with
a few other refugees from our homeland and had tried to re-create the
world they left behind.

Helenus welcomed us warmly and showed us all they had built.
As I walked through their town, I marveled at the work—and yet I
pitied them. It was a miniature Troy built of wood instead of stone.
The walls were no more than a palisade scarcely higher than a man,
with the fabled Scaean gate a simple doorway cut from local pine.
They called a dried-up creek after the great river Xanthus and honored an empty mound as the tomb of Hector. Still, we were so starved
for home that even this shadow of Troy was a glorious sight. We
feasted on their simple fare and shared stories of all that had happened
to us since that awful night when the real Troy fell.

Helenus offered sacrifice and told us by his prophetic gift what
lay ahead. We had a long voyage yet before we could establish our
city, but when we saw a sow the color of snow beneath an oak on a
riverbank nursing thirty piglets, then we would know our journey was
at an end. We must not sail the shortest route to the western shores
of Italy, for that would take us through the straits between the monster Scylla and the dreaded whirlpool Charybdis. Instead we were to
voyage all the way around Sicily and approach the blessed land from
the west. We must seek the river Tiber, but first we should go to the
prophetic Sibyl at Cumae. She would teach us of the native tribes we
must face and show us the glorious future of the kingdom I would
father.

We were anxious to be on our way, so Trojans from our ships and those from the town exchanged gifts and wished each other well. Andromache was the last to say farewell. She presented a fine Phrygian robe to my son, Iulus, and choked back sobs as she said how much he reminded her of her own little boy, thrown to his death from the walls of Troy. With great sadness we left our friends behind and let the wind carry us toward our new home.

We sailed swiftly across the Adriatic and rejoiced to at last see in the distance the shores of Italy, though our destination lay on the far side of that land. Our course took us south along the heel of that great peninsula and across its southern coast until we came to the island of Sicily, carefully avoiding the straits guarded by Scylla and Charybdis. Before us loomed the fiery mass of Mount Etna, said by some to hold the monster Typhon in its depths and by others to be the forge of the god Vulcan, known to the Greeks as Hephaestus. We pulled through the pounding waves and came at night to a small harbor to refill our jars with fresh water. We were anxious to leave that desolate place, so as dawn arose I gave the order to push off. But just then, a man came running toward us from the inland hills. He was a wretched figure, mere skin and bones, with rags covering his filthy body. He stumbled across the beach to me, then stopped when he saw I was a Trojan. I could see the hesitation in his eyes as he debated with himself about whether or not he should run away, but finally he came forward and threw himself at my feet.

"O Trojan warrior, whoever you are, strike me down with your sword if you wish. Anything would be better than another day in this horrid land. I am Achaemenides, a poor Greek from Ithaca who fought against you at Troy, abandoned here by my captain Ulysses. Do what you will with me, but cut your lines and sail away now, before Polyphemus returns!"

I raised this pitiable man to his feet and was going to ask him who Polyphemus was when we saw on the ridge above the beach a great Cyclops with his single eye gone. He had heard us and was making his way down the path to the ships with surprising speed, so I ordered my men to cast off and row for their lives. Taking Achaemenides with me—I could not leave even an enemy to such a fate—we pulled away in silence while the Cyclops blindly threw stones at us.

We sailed on along the coast of Sicily until we came to a port on the westernmost part of the island. There a great sorrow befell me when the heart of Anchises at last gave out. He who was the best of fathers had been our guide on the long journey and a source of endless comfort to me as I tried to lead my people to a new home. Tears rolled down my cheeks as we sailed away from his tomb, knowing I would never see him again unless it was in the land of the dead.

Gracious queen Dido, you know what happened after that. A storm blew us to your friendly shores so that I stand here a suppliant before you. I have lost so much already—city, wife, friends, and father—I can only pray to the gods that better days lie before us.

Dido sat in wonder at the conclusion of his story. It was late and the stars shone brightly above her palace at Carthage. She handed young Iulus, fast asleep, to his father and ordered her servants to show the Trojan leader to guest quarters near her own. In the days that followed, Dido thought more and more of Aeneas and her love for him. She was consumed by the passion Cupid had planted in her heart so that soon it became her obsession to marry him. Her sister Anna encouraged her, pointing out that with the help of the Trojans, Carthage could become the greatest city in the world.

Aeneas was also smitten with Dido and found himself thinking less and less of sailing for Italy. The hulls of his ships began to rot in the harbor as he took delight in laying out aqueducts and supervising construction projects in the city. He dined almost every night with Dido and while each maintained a proper decorum, there was little doubt among those around them that the two were in love. One evening when Aeneas and the queen were out hunting in the woods, they became separated from their followers in a fierce thunderstorm sent by Juno and sought shelter together in a cozy cave. It was clear the storm would not let up that night, so Aeneas lit a fire so that he and Dido could dry their clothes. Alone and undisturbed, the passion between them followed its natural course so that by morning the queen lay in the arms of her beloved. After they returned to the palace, she no longer hid her feelings for the Trojan hero but considered him pledged to her in marriage as she was to him.

None of this escaped Jupiter, who appreciated the warm touch of a beautiful woman himself, but fate was fate. He sent Mercury—Hermes to the Greeks—down to Carthage to tell Aeneas it was time to set sail for Italy, no excuses. Mercury found Aeneas building a home in Carthage wearing a purple robe Dido had given him. The messenger god appeared suddenly before him and did not mince his words: "Aeneas, enough of this. I come from the throne of Jupiter himself to tell you that no woman is more important than your duty. Gird up your loins and get your ship ready to sail to Italy. Your fate does not lie here at Carthage but across the sea on the banks of the Tiber. Go now!"

Aeneas was ashamed of himself and quickly ordered his most trusted lieutenants to prepare the ships—though quietly so that Dido would not know he was leaving. But no man can easily deceive a woman, especially one in love. As swift as the flight of a bird, word reached the palace that the Trojans were preparing to leave. Dido rose up in righteous fury and called Aeneas to her throne room. The brave warrior came before her presence and was about to speak, but the queen cut him off: "You sniveling coward! Did you really think you could slip away unnoticed? Is this how you repay me? I shared everything in my kingdom with you, including my bed, and now you're going to steal away in the night?"

Aeneas was afraid to look her in the eye as he tried to explain himself: "Dido, fair queen, my love, it isn't like that at all. I was preparing to depart, yes, but it's not my fault. You know I would never leave you of my own accord, but it is the will of the gods that I establish a new home for my people in Italy. It's been wonderful here with you, really, and I'd love to stay, but I can't. I thought it would be easier on you if I just slipped away quietly. And besides, it's not like we were really married."

Aeneas would have continued, but Dido threw him out of the palace. After he had gone, she went to her sleeping chamber and cried for hours on her bed. At last her sister found her there and tried to comfort the poor woman, but Dido would have none of it. She wiped away her tears and prayed to the gods that they curse Aeneas and the city he would found: *Let there be everlasting enmity between the seed of Aeneas and Carthage, until one destroys the other.*

Then Dido ordered the servants to gather a great pile of wood and place it on the highest citadel of the city where the departing Trojans and their noble prince could see it like a beacon. She then took all the gifts that Aeneas had given her and carried them to the pyre herself. Finally she ordered her men to light the fire while she knelt on the top and stabbed herself in her breast with her blade. The towering flames engulfed the queen, betrayed by love, so that even in the distance at sea Aeneas saw the great fire and knew in his heart that Dido was gone.

The Trojans sailed north away from Africa and landed again at the western tip of Sicily. Aeneas wanted to hold funeral games there at the tomb of his father, Anchises, so the ships pulled ashore and the men honored the spirit of their late patriarch with sacrifices and athletic contests according to ancient tradition. From Sicily they struck a course for Italy, finding favorable winds and calm seas all the way. But Neptune exacts a price for safe travel and so it was that the faithful helmsman Palinurus fell into the sea and was lost off the cape that later bore his name.

After mourning for their comrade, the Trojans saw in the distance the towering cone of Mount Vesuvius and soon arrived on the beach at Cumae, home of the prophetic Sibyl. Aeneas knew he must consult this oracle, but he was fearful of the path he must take. It was foretold to him that to learn the future, he must journey down to the land of the dead. Still, the captain of men entered the temple of Apollo and greeted the Sibyl, who told him first that he would face a bloody war on the banks of the Tiber before he could establish his city. All the tribes of Latium, as the land was known, would be rallied against him by a new Achilles. But help would come to him from where he least expected it.

That was the immediate future, but if he wanted to learn the destiny of the kingdom he would found, he must come with her on a fearful journey to the underworld. An entrance lay not far away, but to gain admittance he must first visit her sacred grove and seek a tree like no other. On this tree grows a branch of gold you must pluck if you can, said the Sibyl. Fate has decreed this golden bough can be torn from the tree only by the one chosen by destiny. For him, it will come away easily, but for others it will remain fixed no matter how hard they try to remove it.

Aeneas heeded the Sibyl and the bough slipped effortlessly into his hand. With this key to the underworld, he followed the prophetess to a cave in the jagged rock where they sacrificed to Hecate, goddess of darkness, along with the other powers there. Then they entered the cavern.

It was pitch black like a moonless night as the pair made their way into the gaping hole. The ancient gods born at the dawn of the world dwelled there—Death, Strife, Disease, Hunger, War, and Fear. Aeneas heard bloodcurdling shrieks and saw shadows of hideous monsters on the walls as they journeyed deeper and deeper into the earth, traveling for what seemed like days, but perhaps only minutes or no time at all.

At last they came to a river and found the boatman Charon with a vast crowd of souls seeking to cross to the other side. The gnarled old man told them to go away, as they were still alive, but the Sibyl told Aeneas to show him the golden bough. The surly ferryman grunted and motioned them aboard, though the skiff rode low in the water with the weight of their living bodies. Once on the far shore, Aeneas heard the cries of infants snatched from the breasts of their mothers by death and the moans of those unjustly condemned to die. Nearby were the fields of mourning for those who perished because of love. Aeneas wept when he saw the soul of Dido there and tried to speak to her, but she turned her back on him and faded into the darkness.

Among the countless souls Aeneas saw as he went deeper into the land of the dead were the ghosts of men he had fought with and against at Troy. Some of Agamemnon's men saw him and tried to raise a war cry against the Trojan prince, but no sound could escape from their mouths. The Sibyl led him on to a place where the path divided in two. She told him the road to the right led to the fields of Elysium, their destination, but the sinister trail to the left wound its way down to Tartarus, where the doomed souls of the wicked were punished forever.

Aeneas was pleased when they arrived at the pleasant fields of Elysium and marveled to see the happy souls gathered there on the grassy plain. But then the Sibyl pointed to one particular shade who stood watching a parade of countless spirits. This figure turned and he saw it was Anchises, his own father, looking splendid in shining robes. Aeneas tried to embrace him, but the old man laughed and explained that he no longer had a body. He was a phantom, but a happy one, especially now that he had seen his son again. Anchises led him to the crest of a hill and revealed to him all the souls that were waiting to be born, souls that would spring from the foundation he would establish in Italy.

He showed him Silvius, a boy he would father in his old age by his beautiful Italian wife Lavinia. Among the crowd were the twins Romulus and Remus, who would someday build the city of Rome. There was also Brutus, who would overthrow a hated foreign king and establish the city as a republic. The great hero Camillus marched by, savior of the city from the dreaded Gauls. The spirit of Fabius Maximus appeared next, who would wear down Hannibal and the mighty elephants he would drive over the Alps. There was Julius Caesar, greatest of Roman generals, who would cross the Rubicon to crush his enemies. Last of all Anchises showed him Augustus, who would return mankind to the age of gold lost so long ago.

The shining spirit looked at his son and said with pride, "Others in this wide world will forge bronze more skillfully and shape marble into human form. Others will speak with more elegant tongues and chart the course of the stars across the skies. But Romans will rule the people of the earth with power and justice. The gift of our people will be to establish peace, to spare the defeated, and to crush all who resist us."

With that Anchises left his son to journey back to the land of the living. Back through a radiant gate of ivory and up the long path to sunlight Aeneas swiftly climbed, eager to reach his final home and establish such a glorious future.

The Trojan fleet sailed north along the verdant coast of Italy until it came to the mouth of a river with broad trees along its banks and birds singing overhead. The captain ordered his ships to turn into this river and draw up to land. The place was so beautiful that Aeneas, his son, Iulus, and all his people took food onshore and ate their meal beneath the boughs of shady trees. The women baked wheat cakes there on the banks and heaped them with fruit they had gathered nearby. The men were so famished that they devoured not only the fruit but even the cakes on which it was served. Little Iulus laughed and said, "Look, Father, we're so hungry we're even eating our plates." It was then that Aeneas remembered the words of Celaeno the Harpy, that they would know they had reached their final destination when they ate their plates. He was even more delighted when he later saw a white sow nursing thirty piglets by the river, just as the prophet Helenus had foretold. "Make camp," he shouted to all, "this is the Tiber River! This is where we are to build our new city. We are home!"

The people all rejoiced to hear the long journey was at an end, especially as it was such a bountiful land. While he supervised the building of a fortified camp, Aeneas sent his most trusted companions to find out what king ruled this land and how they might live in friendship with him. The messengers soon found the town of King Latinus, a descendant of Saturn, called Cronus by the Greeks. He was a man of peace who had ruled many years, but had only one child, a daughter named Lavinia by his wife, Amata. The queen was a strong-willed woman who was determined to wed her child to Turnus, a powerful local ruler born of a divine nymph. But in spite of her scheming, she could not convince her husband that Turnus was the right choice, for the king had once received an oracle that he should marry his daughter to a stranger who would come from afar.

The envoys of Aeneas came to Latinus and presented him with many fine gifts. They said they were Trojans who had sailed west when their city fell to seek out a new home. They did not come as conquerors, but sought only a safe haven in which to build their city. If welcomed, they would be staunch friends of the king and allies against his enemies in war. Latinus was pleased to greet them and agreed to all they asked. Moreover, he requested Aeneas come to him personally as he suspected the man was the one foretold to take his daughter's hand in marriage. The Trojan party departed and went back to their camp to report the good news to Aeneas.

But Amata was beside herself with rage and turned on her husband as soon as they were alone.

"You old fool! You're going to make peace with these strangers and give your daughter, our only child, to some vagabond who washes up on our shore? You don't know what kind of threat these Trojans might be to your kingdom. You think they will help us defeat our enemies? By the gods, they're the ones who lost the Trojan War! I swear, Latinus, I won't stand for it!"

The anger of Amata suited Juno perfectly. The wife of Jupiter had not been able to prevent the Trojans from reaching Italy, but she might be able to kill them all yet. She went deep into the earth and found Alecto, most horrible of the Furies, and stirred her to sow discord among the Latin tribes. She enflamed Amata even more, then visited Turnus and roused him to hate the Trojans, especially Aeneas, who would steal his bride. Alecto flew throughout the land raising the cry against the invaders. Etruscans, Sabines, Volscians, and many others came together under the banner of Turnus. Before many days had passed, it seemed all of Italy had risen against the Trojans. King Latinus groaned in despair, but he was too old and weak to stand up to the tribes around him. He shut himself in his palace and dropped the reins of power.

Aeneas heard of all the tribes roused against him, and so reluctantly made preparations for war. He had come to this land in peace, following the will of the gods that he should establish a great nation here. Nonetheless he knew he could not stand against the hosts of Italy without allies of his own—but where to find them? That night as he slept fitfully beside the river, the spirit of the Tiber itself spoke to him in a dream: "Fear not, Aeneas, for help is at hand. On my banks lies a city called Pallanteum ruled over by a good man, a king named Evander, who will help you in your hour of need. He is a son of Mercury, who hails from the bountiful land of Arcadia. Do not be afraid to seek him out, even though he is a Greek."

Aeneas rose with a start and could hardly believe what the river god was telling him. Seek help from a Greek, the mortal enemies of the Trojans?

But divine commands are not to be dismissed. Aeneas fitted his best ship with troops in battle gear and began to row up the river. With a steady stroke, by midday they had come to the city of Evander beneath seven hills on the banks of the Tiber. The king and his son Pallas were gathered around an altar making sacrifice to Hercules when they saw the armed strangers pull up on the banks of the river. Pallas grabbed a spear and ran to them demanding to know whether they were friend or foe. Aeneas assured the brave lad they came in peace by the will of a god. Evander then welcomed them to his town and assured them he had no enmity against the Trojans. Dardanus himself had sailed from this land long ago to found the line that gave birth to King Priam and to Aeneas himself. He was most welcome here in the home of his illustrious ancestor.

Evander took Aeneas on a tour of the city, showing him the hill of the Capitol and the Tarpeian Rock, along with the Forum and the buildings all around it. The king explained how he had come here himself as an exile and struggled to build a home in a hostile land. He welcomed the Trojans as allies against their hostile neighbors, especially the Etruscans, ruled by cruel Mezentius. That man was a monstrous tyrant, said Evander, who delighted in wickedness, such as binding living men face-to-face with the dead until the putrid slime of decaying flesh drove the victim mad. Gladly he would stand beside Aeneas against such barbaric foes. He even asked the Trojan leader if, along with troops from his city, he would take his son Pallas with him so that the boy could learn to fight from the best. Aeneas gladly agreed and sealed a bond of friendship with Evander.

While Aeneas was away at the city of Evander, things were not going well at the Trojan camp. The warriors of Aeneas had built a stockade around their ships on the banks of the Tiber, much as the Greeks had done for their own craft at Troy. It was a strong position, but it could not hold out forever against a concerted attack. Turnus knew this and so launched an assault on the camp while Aeneas was away, hoping to provoke his lieutenants into coming out from behind their walls to face him on the open plain where he had the advantage. He taunted them, "Afraid to face us on the level field of battle, are you? Only cowards stay in camp! These are the brave warriors who fought against the Greeks at Troy? Scared to fight without Aeneas by your side?"

The Trojans gritted their teeth and endured the taunts as they were under strict orders from Aeneas not to engage the enemy until he returned. But two young Trojan warriors named Nisus and Euryalus had had enough of Turnus and snuck out that night for a little guerrilla warfare in the Italian camp, killing a number of the enemy in the dark, but both were captured and slain before dawn. Turnus put their heads on poles in front of the Trojan camp further to provoke the men of Aeneas into battle, but to no avail. Running out of patience, Turnus then launched an unsuccessful attack on the camp and even got inside the walls, fighting bravely against great odds, but was forced to jump into the Tiber to escape death.

Soon Aeneas returned to camp with Pallas and the reinforcements from Evander. It was then that the great battle began. Trojans and Italians met on the plain to fight and die in such numbers as Italy had never

seen. Each side was full of courageous men who sold their lives dearly as
they fought to make a home for themselves or to protect the homeland
they loved. Evander's son Pallas, though scarcely more than a boy, was
at the forefront of his troops, cutting down the enemy. Turnus marked
him there and came against him like a raging bull, ramming his oak
spear clean through his breastplate and chest. Turnus then stripped him
of his armor and hung the boy's sword belt from his shoulder as a trophy.

Aeneas had no time to strike back against Turnus for this outrage, as
he faced cruel Mezentius and his son in combat. He slew both, though
they fought with reckless daring. Then Aeneas turned to other foes. The
battle continued for days as one side gained the advantage, then the
other. Among the bravest of the Italians was Camilla, a warrior woman
and commander of the Volscians. She had grown up a child of the hunt
devoted to Diana, Artemis to the Greeks, and trained by her father as
a peerless fighter from her earliest days. As chaste as she was beautiful,
Camilla cut through the Trojan lines dealing death at every turn. At last
an ally of Aeneas named Arruns sent a spear ripping through her breast
and laid her low, but was soon cut down himself.

The battle raged on with Trojans and Italians dying among the
ever-rising pile of bodies on the battlefield. Soon even the gods had had
enough of the slaughter, so that Jupiter called his wife, Juno, before him
and told her the killing must end. Juno reluctantly agreed on the condition that the hated name of Troy be left behind forever and the new
kingdom be Italian in title, language, and ways. The ruler of the gods
nodded his head in consent and Juno swiftly withdrew her support of
Turnus and his men.

All the mortals on the battlefield could sense that something had
changed, Turnus most of all. He realized he now stood alone without the
favor of any god, but his pride would not allow him to surrender. He sent
a herald to the Trojan camp and asked that Aeneas come forth to face
him in single combat to end the war. Thus both men met on the bloody
field between the lines. They were evenly matched and fought each other
with great courage, though neither could gain the upper hand. Finally
Turnus picked up a rock that twelve men could barely lift to throw at
his foe, but buckled under the weight. This gave Aeneas his chance
and the Trojan captain sent his spear flying like a whirlwind through

the breastplate of the great Italian warrior, dropping him helpless to the ground. Turnus lay in the mud looking up at Aeneas and spoke to him: "Go ahead and strike the final blow, for you have fairly conquered me. I do not plead for mercy. And yet, I would be grateful if you would send me back to die in my home with my own father by my side, a man much like your own great sire, Anchises. You have won, Aeneas. Lavinia is your bride. You don't need to kill me here."

Aeneas was moved by the courage of his fallen enemy. He started to sheath his sword when suddenly he saw the sword belt of Pallas gleaming across the shoulder of Turnus. Then he knew what he must do.

"You ask a favor, Turnus, but did you give any to Pallas? Did you send him back to his father, Evander? You dare to ask for kindness when you wear the sword belt of that dear boy as a trophy?"

With that Aeneas took his sword and planted it in the heart of Turnus so that it went down deep into the Italian soil beneath him, a foundation for his new kingdom and a message to all that Rome would never yield.

ROME

ROMULUS AND REMUS

Aeneas married Lavinia and built a town named Lavinium in her honor. The Trojans and the native Italians became one people and under the name of Latins fought to maintain their freedom against all enemies. Lavinium became a large and prosperous city, but Aeneas died not long after founding it and passed the leadership to his son, Iulus. In time, however, Iulus left to establish his own settlement called Alba Longa in the hills south of the Tiber. The descendants of Aeneas and Iulus ruled at Alba Longa for many generations until Proca ascended the throne. Proca had two sons, Numitor and Amulius, but left the kingdom to gentle Numitor as the eldest when he died.

The more ambitious and ruthless Amulius plotted to take the kingship from his brother and soon deposed him, but kept Numitor alive under close supervision. The sons of the former king were not so lucky and were killed; his only daughter, Rhea Silvia, was spared on the condition she become a vestal virgin. These priestesses of the hearth goddess Vesta kept the holy flame of the city burning at all times and were not allowed to marry. Woe to any vestal who strayed from the path of chastity, for she was quickly condemned to death. Thus with Rhea Silvia sworn to virginity, Amulius conveniently removed any threat from the bloodline of his brother.

Yet one day word came to the king that his niece had given birth to twins. Furious, Amulius called the girl to him and demanded to know who the father was. Rhea Silvia claimed that she had not been with any man, but had been ravished by the god Mars as she tended the holy fire. Her uncle scoffed at this explanation and threw her into prison bound by chains. He had his men take the infants to the banks of the Tiber to be drowned. By chance the river was flooding at that time and the servants of Amulius could not approach the moving stream, so they abandoned the boys in a basket on a mud flat far from any settlement at a place beneath seven hills where the town of Evander once stood. The cries of the babies meant nothing to the cruel men who left them there, but a female wolf heard the sound and came to investigate. She found the pair wailing in hunger and so nursed them on her own teats until they fell asleep. Soon after, a shepherd found them there with the she-wolf gently licking their faces. He brought them back to his lowly hut and gave them to his wife, Larentia, to raise.

The twins were named Romulus and Remus, fine young men who grew into great hunters and warriors. They were fearless and attacked local robbers, dividing their spoils among the poor shepherds of the region, though they were just as well known for the pranks they played on anyone who offended them. The brothers gathered about them a merry band of youths to join in their adventures and became famous throughout Latium for both their courage and escapades. One group of robbers they had despoiled decided to strike back at the two and laid a trap for them one day during a festival. Romulus drove his attackers away, but Remus was captured and taken to King Amulius, for the robbers audaciously charged him with plundering the lands of Numitor they themselves had pillaged. Thus Remus was given to Numitor, his own grandfather, for punishment.

Numitor liked the boy immediately and when he heard that he was a twin who had been abandoned by the river at the same time as the children of his daughter Rhea Silvia, he quickly realized his true identity. Remus sent for Romulus and together with their followers they slew Amulius and restored their grandfather as the rightful ruler of Alba Longa. The young men were happy for Numitor, but they had a restless spirit and wanted to found their own city at the place they had been raised by the shepherd and his wife. The brothers normally got along well, but since they were twins born on the same day, neither could agree which should be king of the new city. They decided to wait for a sign from the gods and so retired to two separate hills, the Palatine and the Aventine, to watch for divine portents. Remus first saw six vultures in the sky, an impressive token from the gods, but then Romulus saw twelve. They argued about who had received the favor of the gods—Remus claimed he saw the birds first but Romulus countered that he had seen more—until the quarrel grew into a fight with drawn swords and Romulus killed his brother. Some stories say that Romulus killed Remus later when he jumped over the half-built walls of the town, but in any case, Romulus became the sole ruler of the new city and named it Rome after himself.

King Romulus gathered to his new settlement any bandits, fugitives, and runaway slaves who cared to join him. The town was soon full of wild young men who fortified their city with walls and built homes for themselves along with temples to the gods. Romulus appointed one hundred of the best men to be senators to help him govern the town and these with their descendants were known ever after as patricians. But the king had little luck recruiting wives for his new subjects, for what father would freely give his daughter to some ruffian? To solve the problem, Romulus invited several nearby villages of Sabines to a grand festival at Rome. The neighboring men were curious about the new city and hated to pass up a free meal, so they came and brought their families with them. After the food and wine were flowing, Romulus gave a signal and suddenly the Roman men grabbed all the maidens visiting their town and drove the rest of their families outside the walls.

The Sabine fathers were furious at the kidnapping of their daughters and the young women inside the walls were terrified of what lay in store for them. But the Roman men did not threaten the virginity of their captives. They confessed their undying love and explained with heartfelt pleas that they had resorted to such a crude charade only because they had no other choice. They wanted to give the women all the rights of proper wives. Together, if the women would consent, they would build a fine city and future for their children. Slowly the hearts of the women warmed to their new husbands and so they gave themselves willingly to the men who had taken them by force.

The fathers of the Sabine women who had been seized were not so forgiving. As the months passed, under their king Titus Tatius, they united to attack the city and recover their daughters. One young woman named Tarpeia agreed to sneak the Sabine advance guard into the citadel on the Capitoline Hill by night if they would give her what they wore on their left arms, meaning their gold bracelets. Once they safely held the fortress, however, the Sabines piled their heavy shields—which they also wore on their left arms—on top of Tarpeia and crushed the life from her. The cliff where Tarpeia was killed became known as the Tarpeian Rock and was a place of execution ever after for those who betrayed their country.

The army of Romulus drew up the next day in the Forum beneath the citadel held by the Sabines and invited them out to battle to settle the affair once and for all. But just as the fight was about to begin, the Sabine wives ran between the lines holding their babies in their arms and cried out that they would not be the cause of bloodshed between their fathers and husbands. Brought to their senses by the pleas of the women, both sides laid down their weapons and joined together as one people under Romulus.

The years passed and the king of Rome brought prosperity to his new city along with peace—though the Romans also became known throughout the land as the fiercest of warriors. But success in ruling breeds resentment as well as honor. One day when Romulus was holding an assembly on the Field of Mars, a great storm arose and turned the sky black. When the sun shone again, Romulus had disappeared. Some say he had been taken up into the heavens to live with the gods. Others, however, claim that jealous senators had murdered him in the darkness, then cut up his body and smuggled the pieces away under their togas. In either case, Romulus was honored afterward as a god and worshiped among the Romans as the founder of their city.

THE HORATII BROTHERS

Romulus was succeeded on the throne by Numa Pompilius, who was said to have given Rome many of its ancient religious traditions and rituals. After Numa, a great warrior king named Tullus Hostilius reigned whose goal was to incorporate the ancestral town of Alba Longa into Rome's growing state. The Albans, however, had no desire to join with their cousins and so went to war. But both sides knew an all-out con- flict would leave the two towns dangerously weak and ripe for conquest by the hostile Etruscan cities north of the Tiber. To save lives, it was therefore decided that each city would chose three men to fight to the death on behalf of all. Whichever town had the last man standing would surrender peacefully to the other. Both sides swore solemn oaths to the gods over a consecrated pig that they would abide by the outcome of the contest of champions.

Fortunately for both Rome and Alba Longa, the two cities each pos- sessed triplet brothers who were practiced warriors. The Horatii brothers of Rome agreed to stand against the Curiatii triplets of Alba Longa to determine which would rule the other. The citizens of both cities anx- iously gathered around the field of combat to see what their fate would be. At the signal, the six young men rushed at one another, all believing they would be victorious. Shields clashed and swords flew threw the air so that two of the Roman brothers soon fell dead on the ground. The remaining Horatii was surrounded by the Albans, who moved in for the kill, but the Roman warrior began to run. The three Curiatii chased him around the field until they became separated from one another by wide intervals. This was just what the Roman soldier was counting on. He turned and struck down the first Alban to reach him, then the second, and finally the third, taking on each one at a time.

A tremendous cheer went up from the Roman side, applauding the young man who had used his cunning as well as courage in battle. The Albans were understandably disappointed, but they were an honorable people and agreed to abide by the outcome of the contest. The only one weeping was a sister of the surviving Horatii brother who had been engaged to one of the Curiatii triplets. When her brother found out why she was crying, he took his sword and plunged it into her heart, saying such should be the fate of any Roman woman who weeps for the enemy. The young man was put on trial, with his father saying his daughter had been justly slain. But as the youth had acted without the authority of the state, the judges determined that he should be forced to march under- neath a yoke as a sign of shame.

ONE-EYED HORATIUS

The next king of Rome was Ancus Marcius, who established a port for the city on the sea at Ostia and built many aqueducts, along with a bridge across the Tiber. After his rule, an Etruscan king named Tarquin the Elder seized the throne and so a foreign dynasty ruled the city for the next three generations. The Romans chafed under their domination, but the city prospered and was united against other hostile Etruscan powers across the Tiber.

The most dangerous king in the region was Lars Porsenna, an Etruscan ruler just to the north of Rome. He was determined to conquer the city and so marched his army to the single wooden bridge spanning the Tiber. The Roman forces knew they could not hold the crossing against so many soldiers, so they began to tear down the bridge on the Roman side as the Etruscans approached. A guard named Horatius Cocles ("one-eyed") volunteered to stay behind on the far side and hold off the invaders to give his comrades precious minutes to complete the demolition. Two of his friends remained to help fight, but he sent them back when the timbers were almost cut. Alone, Horatius fought the Etruscan warriors until the bridge fell apart, then he dove into the river in full armor and swam to the Roman side. Afterward he was honored as a great hero who had risked everything for the good of Rome.

SCAEVOLA

Lars Porsenna, however, was a persistent king. When the bridge across the Tiber fell, he began a siege of Rome to starve the city into submission. As the weeks passed, the people of Rome grew ever more hungry and desperate. It was then that a young man named Gaius Mucius came to the senate with a plan. He would disguise himself as an Etruscan and sneak into the tent of Lars Porsenna. When he was close enough, he would kill the king and end the war. He knew it was a suicide mission, but it was worth the price if he could free Rome.

The elders agreed and so that night the Roman slipped across the river and into the Etruscan camp. He came unnoticed into the command tent, but to his horror he could not recognize the king. All the Etruscan nobility were dressed in such finery that everyone looked like royalty. He decided to take a chance and so plunged his sword into a man sitting on a regal chair. Unfortunately, this turned out to the secretary of the king. Mucius was immediately seized and held before the true king, who demanded to know the details of any plot against him. If the Roman didn't speak, he would be burned alive. Mucius laughed defiantly and said he thought not of his body but of glory. He then thrust his right hand into a brazier burning before the king until the flames had consumed his hand. All during this time, Mucius had not uttered a sound or flinched as the fire burned away his flesh.

The Etruscan king was so impressed by the young man's courage that he decided to set him free. Mucius warned him that there were three hundred other Romans who had pledged to follow in his footsteps and assassinate the king if he failed. This so troubled Porsenna that he immediately made a truce with the Romans and ended the siege.

CLOELIA

Part of the peace treaty with Lars Porsenna stipulated that the Romans must send hostages to live under guard among the Etruscans to guarantee the goodwill of Rome in the future. If the city did not behave itself, the hostages would die. Among the nobility sent to Porsenna was a maiden named Cloelia. Knowing the abuse she and the other girls could expect at the hands of the Etruscan soldiers, she organized the young women in an escape attempt and broke out of the Etruscan camp where they were held. After a harrowing chase, they made it to the Tiber and swam safely across to Rome. This escape was immediately reported to the Etruscan king, who was impressed by the girl, but demanded she be returned immediately or he would consider the treaty broken. He had no desire to harm such a brave young woman and so assured the senate that he would send her back to Rome untouched if they recognized his authority in this matter.

The Romans agreed and Cloelia returned to the camp, where she was treated well by the king. He honored Cloelia and said that as a gesture of goodwill, he would allow her to take half the remaining hostages back to Rome with her. The girl considered which to choose, then decided on the youngest boys among the group. This was because it seemed more proper for a maiden to select boys than men to accompany her, as well as her concern that young boys were more subject to abuse from their cap-tors. Thus she led the hostages back to Rome, where a statue was set up in her honor as a tribute to her courage and exemplary behavior.

LUCRETIA

The third Etruscan king of Rome was Tarquin the Proud, who started a war against the nearby town of Ardea to expand Roman power. The king's son Sextus Tarquinius fought as an officer in the conflict, as did his Roman friend Collatinus. One quiet night when they were sitting around the campfire near Ardea, Sextus and Collatinus began to argue about which of their wives was the most virtuous. Unable to agree, they decided to ride back to Rome that very night and catch the women by surprise to see what they were doing.

They found the wife of Sextus at a grand party drinking wine and celebrating with her friends, but the wife of Collatinus, a woman named Lucretia, was busy working wool in her modest home by lamplight even though it was late. After they returned to the camp that night, Sextus was ashamed of his own wife but intrigued greatly by Lucretia. Soon he decided he must have such a woman no matter the cost.

A few days later, Sextus returned to Rome alone and called at the house of Lucretia. The matron welcomed the friend of her husband and had her servants show him to a guest room after dinner. When the house was finally quiet, Sextus took his sword and crept into the bedroom of Lucretia. Holding the woman down with his left hand he ordered her to be quiet or die. He claimed he was in love with her and that he wanted only to enjoy the pleasures of her bed, but she adamantly refused. Then he said that unless she allowed him to have his way with her that night, he would kill not only her but one of her male servants and put his body in her bed. Then he would tell Collatinus that he had caught the pair in adultery and slain them both out of outrage at the behavior of his best friend's wife.

Lucretia knew she was trapped and feared for the reputation of her husband more than the sanctity of her own body. She did not resist while Sextus raped her, then cried bitter tears after he left her brutalized to return to the war. The next day she sent a message to her father in Rome and her husband at Ardea asking that they come to her home immediately. Both arrived along with her husband's Roman friend Lucius Junius Brutus. She told them all what had happened the previous night and said she was sick in her heart with guilt for bringing shame on Collatinus and her family. All the men told her that she was not to blame, but she would hear none of it. From beneath her robes she drew a sword and plunged it into her breast, falling dead to the floor.

As her husband and father held her body in their arms and wept, Brutus picked up the bloody sword and swore an oath by it that the Tarquin family would be swept away. Soon Brutus led a rebellion against the Tarquins and drove them from the city. Rome put aside rule by kings and became a republic governed by the people.

The long age of monarchy stretching back to Aeneas and the Trojan War, to the Greek tradition and the earliest tales, had at last come to an end. The classical world now entered the age of history, though the ancient myths that so shaped their lives—and still shape ours—were never forgotten.

GENEALOGIES

THE FIRST GENERATIONS OF GODS

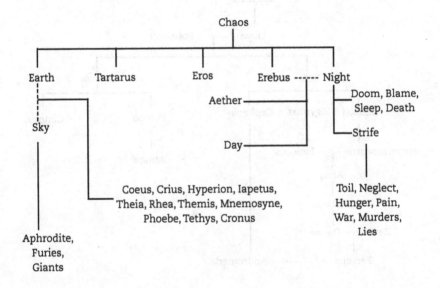

Chaos

Earth   Tartarus   Eros   Erebus ------ Night

Aether

Day

Sky

Doom, Blame, Sleep, Death

Strife

Coeus, Crius, Hyperion, Iapetus, Theia, Rhea, Themis, Mnemosyne, Phoebe, Tethys, Cronus

Toil, Neglect, Hunger, Pain, War, Murders, Lies

Aphrodite, Furies, Giants

THE CHILDREN OF CRONUS AND RHEA

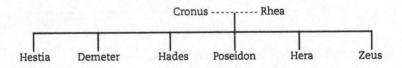

Cronus ---------- Rhea

Hestia   Demeter   Hades   Poseidon   Hera   Zeus

THE DESCENDANTS OF IO

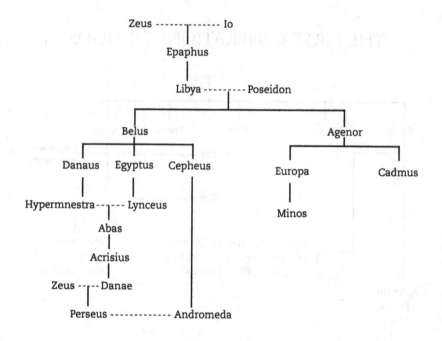

THE HOUSE OF CADMUS

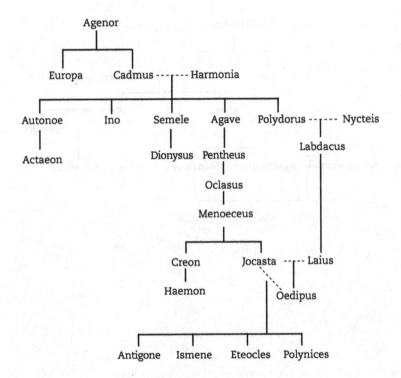

THE HOUSE OF ATREUS

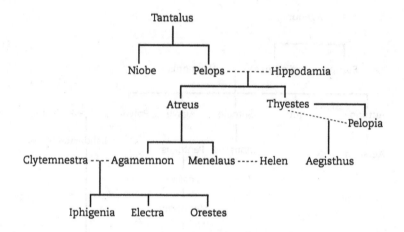

THE HOUSE OF TROY

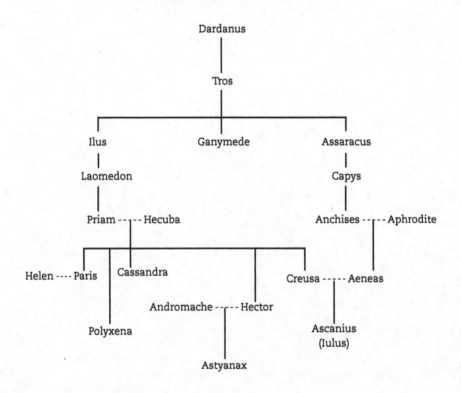

GREEK AND ROMAN GODS

GREEK NAME	ROMAN NAME
Zeus*	Jupiter, Jove
Hera*	Juno
Demeter*	Ceres
Poseidon*	Neptune
Hestia*	Vesta
Artemis*	Diana
Aphrodite*	Venus
Ares*	Mars
Hermes*	Mercury
Hephaestus*	Vulcan
Apollo*	Apollo
Athena*	Minerva
Hades	Pluto, Dis
Dionysus	Liber
Pan	Faunus
Heracles	Hercules

* The twelve Olympian gods

GLOSSARY

ACHILLES, son of Peleus and the goddess Thetis, the greatest Greek warrior at Troy.

ACRISIUS, father of Danae, grandfather of Perseus, accidentally killed by a discus thrown by Perseus.

ACROPOLIS, the high portion of any city, but most commonly referring to the famous Acropolis of Athens, home to the sacred Parthenon temple of Athena.

ACTAEON, young man turned into a deer and killed by his own hounds for seeing the goddess Artemis naked.

ADMETUS, he persuaded his wife, Alcestis, to die for him, but she was rescued by Hercules.

ADONIS, son of an incestuous union between his mother, Myrrha, and his grandfather Cinyras, he was an extraordinarily handsome lad beloved by both Aphrodite and Persephone. He was killed by a wild boar and the anemone flower sprang from his blood.

ADRASTUS, king of Argos and leader of the seven generals who fought Thebes on the side of Polynices, son of Oedipus.

AEACUS, son of Zeus and Aegina, he ruled over the island of Aegina after Zeus transformed ants into humans to be his subjects.

AEETES, son of the god Helios, king of Colchis, and father of Medea.

AEGEUS, king of Athens and father of Theseus, he aided Medea after she murdered her children and fled Corinth.

AEGINA, mother of Aeacus by Zeus and namesake of a small island near Athens.

AEGISTHUS, son of Thyestes by incest with his daughter Pelopia, he served as regent of Mycenae while Agamemnon fought at Troy and helped Clytemnestra murder him when he returned. He was slain by Agamemnon's son Orestes.

AENEAS, son of Anchises and the goddess Aphrodite/Venus, he led the surviving Trojans to found a kingdom in Italy that would give birth to the Romans.

AEOLUS, (1) king of Thessaly who is sometimes identified with (2) the ruler of the winds who tried to help Odysseus return home.

AETHER, the upper air, child of Night and Erebus.

AETHRA, mother of Theseus, who became a slave to Helen.

AGAMEMNON, son of Atreus, brother to Menelaus, he was king of Mycenae and led the Greek expedition to Troy. He was murdered by his wife, Clytemnestra, on his return home.

AGAVE, daughter of Cadmus, king of Thebes, and Harmonia, she later was punished with madness by Dionysus and murdered her own son Pentheus.

AGENOR, Phoenician king who was father of Cadmus and Europa.

AJAX, (1) son of Telemon, and a Greek warrior of immense strength in the Trojan War, he killed himself after losing the armor of Achilles to Odysseus. (2) Son of Oileus, also a gifted soldier at Troy, he was overshadowed by the previous warrior and was therefore known as Little or the Lesser Ajax.

ALCESTIS, wife who volunteered to die in place of her husband, Admetus, she was rescued from death by Hercules.

ALCINOUS, Phaeacean king, husband of Arete and father of Nausicaa, he welcomed both Jason and Odysseus to his idyllic island kingdom on their travels.

ALCMENE, mother of Hercules who became pregnant with the boy by Zeus when the god extended a night of lovemaking for three days.

ALCYONE, (1) daughter of Aeolus, she married Ceyx and was transformed into a kingfisher (halcyon) after he drowned. (2) Daughter of Atlas and the Ocean nymph Pleione, she was seduced by Poseidon and bore him several children.

ALECTO, a divine Fury who by the will of Juno stirred up the native Italians against Aeneas and his Trojans.

ALPHEUS, son of Ocean and Tethys, a river god of the Peloponnesus who pursued the nymph Arethusa to Sicily.

ALTHAEA, mother of Meleager who killed her son in anger by burning a magical log.

AMAZONS, women warriors who lived on the eastern edge of the Greek world.

AMPHION, son of Zeus and Antiope along with his brother Zethus, he avenged his mother's ill treatment at the hands of Lycus and Dirce to become coruler of Thebes.

AMPHITRITE, sea goddess pursued by Poseidon who finally yielded to him and bore him three sons.

AMULIUS, great uncle of Romulus and Remus, he drove his brother Numitor from the throne of Alba Longa and abandoned the twins on the banks of the Tiber River.

ANCHISES, father of Aeneas after he was seduced by the goddess Aphrodite.

ANDROMACHE, wife of the Trojan hero Hector.

ANDROMEDA, daughter of Cepheus and Cassiopeia, she was rescued from a sea monster by Perseus.

ANTAEUS, son of Earth, an African giant who was defeated by Hercules when the hero held him off the ground, cutting him off from the strength his mother gave him.

ANTIGONE, daughter of Oedipus who cared for her father in exile, then defied King Creon of Thebes by giving her brother Polynices a proper burial.

ANTIOPE, raped by Zeus in the form of a satyr, she gave birth to twin sons Amphion and Zethus who later avenged the ill treatment she had received from Lycus and Dirce in Thebes.

APHRODITE (Latin *Venus*), goddess of love and sex born from the severed genitals of primordial Sky.

APOLLO, son of Zeus and Leto, brother of Artemis, he was god of music, medicine, archery, and prophecy.

ARACHNE, young woman of Lydia who challenged Athena to a weaving contest and was turned into a spider by the goddess.

ARES (Latin *Mars*), son of Zeus and Hera, he was the god of war.

ARETE, Phaeacian queen and wife of Alcinous, she kindly received both Jason and Odysseus on their travels.

ARETHUSA, nymph who was chased across the sea by the river god Alpheus.

ARGONAUTS, sailors who joined Jason on the *Argo* to search for the golden fleece.

ARGOS, aged and faithful dog of Odysseus who died when he heard his master's voice on his return.

ARGUS, guardian of Io with a hundred eyes, he was killed by Hermes.

ARIADNE, daughter of Cretan king Minos who helped Theseus defeat her father and escape the maze of the Minotaur.

ARION, divine horse born from Demeter when she was raped by Poseidon.

ARTEMIS (Latin *Diana*), daughter of Zeus and Leto, sister of Apollo, virgin goddess of the hunt.

ASCANIUS (see **Iulus**)

ASCLEPIUS, son of Apollo, god of healing, he was killed by Zeus when he dared to raise mortals from the dead.

ASOPUS, river god and father of the nymph Aegina.

ATALANTA, virgin hunter who raced prospective husbands in a contest for her hand, then killed them if she defeated them.

ATHENA (Latin *Minerva*), daughter of Metis, swallowed by Zeus, she sprang from the forehead of her father. She was the virgin goddess of war and crafts, as well as patron of the city of Athens.

ATLAS, Titan who held the heavens on his shoulders until, in some stories, he was turned to stony Mount Atlas by Perseus holding Medusa's severed head before him.

ATREUS, son of Pelops and Hippodamia, brother of Thyestes, father of Agamemnon and Menelaus, he served the sons of Thyestes at a banquet and took over rule of Mycenae.

ATROPOS, one of the three Fates, she cut the thread of life.

ATTIS, beloved by the goddess Cybele; her jealousy drove him to madness so that he castrated himself.

AUGEAS, king and owner of Aegean stables cleaned by Hercules.

AUTOLYCUS, noted thief and grandfather of the hero Odysseus.

BACCHUS (see **Dionysus**)

BAUCIS, wife of Philemon, elderly peasant woman who welcomed the disguised Zeus and Hermes to her home and was rewarded along with her husband.

BELLEROPHON, son of the king of Corinth who accidentally killed his brother, he was sent to Lydia to be killed, but instead impressed the king with his heroic achievements, aided by the flying horse Pegasus.

BRIAREUS, one of the hundred-handed monsters who helped Zeus defeat the Titans.

BRUTUS, expelled Tarquin the Proud, the last king of Rome, after the suicide of Lucretia.

CACUS, monster inhabiting the future site of Rome who was killed by Hercules.

CADMUS, son of the Phoenician king Agenor, he left his home to search for his missing sister Europa and founded the Greek city of Thebes.

CAENIS, the name of the Lapith warrior Caeneus before his transformation from woman into man after being raped by Poseidon.

CALAIS, brother of Zetes and a son of the North Wind who sailed with the Argonauts.

CALCHAS, a gifted seer who accompanied the Greeks to Troy.

CALLIOPE, muse of epic poetry and mother of Orpheus.

CALLISTO, follower of Artemis and unwilling lover of Zeus turned into a bear by Hera.

CALYDONIAN BOAR, ferocious boar sent by Artemis to punish the people of Calydon for neglecting her worship. The greatest heroes of the age gathered successfully to hunt down the beast.

CALYPSO, divine daughter of Atlas who held Odysseus captive on the island of Ogygia.

CAMILLA, Italian female warrior who fought against Aeneas and his Trojans.

CASSANDRA, daughter of Trojan king Priam, she was punished by Apollo for rejecting him by granting her the gift of prophecy, but determining that no one would ever believe her. She was taken as a war prize by Agamemnon and murdered at Mycenae.

CASSIOPEIA, wife of Cepheus and mother of Andromeda.

CASTOR, brother of Pollux as well as Helen and Clytemnestra, sailed with Jason and the Argonauts.

CECROPS, first king of Athens, born with a man's body and the tail of a snake.

CENTAURS, creatures with the head and torso of a man, but the body of a horse, often portrayed as uncivilized in Greek myths, though wise centaurs such as Chiron became the tutors of heroes.

CEPHALUS, husband of Procris who tested his wife's faithfulness, but failed a similar trial when his wife came to him in disguise.

CEPHEUS, king of Ethiopia, husband of Cassiopeia, and father of Andromeda.

CERBERUS, born of the monstrous Typhon and Echidna, he was the three-headed watchdog of Hades.

CEYX, king of Trachis and husband of Alcyone, he drowned but was revived and turned into a kingfisher along with his wife.

CHAOS, the great primordial chasm from which sprang the first divine beings.

CHARON, the ferryman of Hades who transported souls across the river Styx, or Acheron.

CHARYBDIS, deadly whirlpool opposite the monster Scylla in the narrow straits between Sicily and Italy.

CHIMERA, a Lycian monster with the front of a lion, the middle of a goat, and the tail of a serpent who ravaged the land until killed by Bellerophon.

CHIONE, beautiful maiden who was raped by both Hermes and Apollo on the same night, giving birth to a son from each, though she was later killed by Artemis for boasting.

CHIRON, wise centaur who tutored Jason and Achilles.

CHRYSAOR, offspring of Poseidon after he raped Medusa, though not born until Perseus decapitated his mother and he sprang from her severed neck along with Pegasus.

CIRCE, daughter of Helios and a powerful witch who changed Scylla into a monster. She purified Jason and Medea, then entertained Odysseus after changing his men into pigs.

CLOELIA, Roman maiden who was given as a hostage to the Etruscan Lars Porsenna, but escaped back across the Tiber River.

CLOTHO, one of the three Fates, she spun the thread of destiny for each person.

CLYTEMNESTRA, wife of Agamemnon and mother of Orestes who joined with Aegisthus to murder her husband, only to be killed later by her son.

COEUS, son of Earth and Sky, he fathered Leto and Asteria with his sister Phoebe.

COTTUS, one of the hundred-handed monsters who helped Zeus overthrow the Titans.

CREON, brother-in-law of Oedipus and king of Thebes. He condemned Antigone to death.

CREUSA, (1) maiden raped by Apollo who bore Ion. (2) First wife of Aeneas and mother of Iulus, she perished at the fall of Troy.

CRIUS, son of Earth and Sky, fathered several children by his sister and wife, Eurybia.

CRONUS (Latin *Saturn*), son of Earth and Sky who castrated his own father and took his place as ruler of the universe. He was later tricked and overthrown by his own son, Zeus.

CUPID (Greek *Eros*), son of Aphrodite, he prompted irresistible desire in others with his arrows, but fell in love himself with the maiden Psyche.

CYBELE, Phrygian mother goddess adapted into Greek mythology, sometimes identified with Rhea.

CYCLOPES (singular **Cyclops**), sons of Poseidon who lived as brutes in the distant west; one of their number named Polyphemus killed some of Odysseus' men but was tricked and blinded by the hero to escape from his cave.

CYPARISSUS, handsome boy beloved by Apollo who himself loved a pet deer, which he accidentally killed. Apollo turned him into a cypress tree to mourn the animal forever.

DAEDALUS, master craftsman and father of Icarus, he built the Labyrinth for King Minos in Crete. He escaped on homemade wings with his son, but the boy plunged to his death when he flew too near the sun.

DANAE, daughter of Acrisius, king of Argos, she was the mother of Perseus.

DAPHNE, nymph beloved by Apollo, transformed into a laurel tree by Earth to save her from the god's unwanted advances.

DARDANUS, Italian-born ancestor of the Romans who migrated to Asia and became king of Troy. The Greeks claimed he was born on Crete or Samothrace.

DEIANIRA, wife of Hercules who unknowingly gave him a poisoned cloak that caused his death.

DEMETER (Latin *Ceres*), daughter of Cronus and Rhea, goddess of the bountiful earth and mother of Persephone.

DEUCALION, son of Prometheus, husband of Pyrrha, lone male survivor of the great flood sent by Zeus to destroy humanity.

DIANA (see **Artemis**)

DIDO, Phoenician founder and queen of Carthage, she was loved and abandoned by Aeneas.

DIOMEDES, (1) Greek king of Argos who fought at Troy. (2) Thracian king who was fed to his own flesh-eating mares by Hercules.

DIONYSUS (Latin *Liber*), son of Zeus and Semele, god of wine and a balanced life.

EARTH (Greek *Gaia* or *Ge*), sprung from Chaos, she bore Sky, then mated with him and produced many children, including Cronus, father of Zeus.

ECHIDNA, monster born of Earth and Tartarus who produced many terrible children of her own, including Typhon, the Chimaera, and Cerberus.

ECHO, nymph who loved and was rejected by Narcissus, she faded away into a disembodied voice that could only repeat the last words spoken by another.

EILEITHYIA, daughter of Zeus and Hera, goddess of childbirth.

ELECTRA, (1) daughter of Agamemnon and Clytemnestra who helped her brother Orestes gain revenge on their mother. (2) Daughter of Atlas who was raped by Zeus and bore two sons, Dardanus and Iasion.

ENDYMION, lover of Selene who, given whatever he wished by Zeus, chose to sleep forever, never growing old.

EOS (Latin *Aurora*), goddess of the dawn, most famous for transforming her lover Tithonus into a cicada.

EPIMETHEUS, son of the Titan Iapetus and brother of Prometheus, he accepted Zeus' gift of alluring but troublesome Pandora.

ERATO, muse of lyric poetry.

EREBUS, the dark underworld, he was born of Chaos and fathered Aether and Day with his sister Night.

ERIS (see **Strife**)

EROS (Latin *Cupid*), the primordial spirit of regeneration, born of Chaos. Later authors depict him as a son of Aphrodite.

ETEOCLES, younger son of Oedipus, killed by his brother Polynices at Thebes.

EUMAEUS, faithful swineherd of Odysseus.

EUROPA, daughter of Agenor, she was kidnapped by Zeus in the form of a bull and raped in Crete, where the god abandoned her.

EURYCLEA, loyal maid of Penelope who kept the secret of Odysseus' identity when she discovered an old scar on his leg.

EURYDICE, wife of Orpheus, rescued from Hades then lost by her husband when he turned to look at her before they left the underworld.

EURYNOME, (1) mother of Bellerophon. (2) Mother of the Graces by Zeus.

EURYSTHEUS, cowardly cousin of Hercules and king of Mycenae; Hercules was forced to complete twelve labors in his service.

EUTERPE, muse of flute playing.

EVANDER, Greek king, ally of Aeneas, and father of Pallas, who ruled at the future site of Rome before the city was founded by Romulus and Remus.

FATES, the divine rulers of human destiny, they are usually described as three in number (Clotho, Lachesis, and Atropos), though there are contradictory stories of their origins.

FURIES (Greek *Erinyes*), avenging spirits of murder, especially among blood relatives; there are multiple stories of their creation.

GAIA or **Ge** (see **Earth**)

GANYMEDE, handsome youth of Trojan royal blood, he was kidnapped by Zeus to be his cupbearer and lover.

GERYON, monstrous creature who lived in the far west, Hercules robbed him of his cattle and then slew him.

GLAUCUS, originally a mortal fisherman, he ate a magical herb and became a sea god who fell in love with the beautiful maiden Scylla.

GOLDEN BOUGH, the magical branch used by Aeneas to gain entrance to the underworld.

GOLDEN FLEECE, the priceless fleece guarded by a dragon in distant Colchis, but stolen by Jason with the help of Medea.

GORGONS, three ferocious, snake-haired creatures (Stheno, Euryale, and Medusa), the first two of which were immortal.

GRACES (Greek *Charites*), usually three in number, they were kindly divinities of various origins.

GRAEAE, ancient gray-haired hags who shared a single eye among themselves, which was stolen by Perseus.

HADES (Latin *Pluto* or *Dis*), in Greek mythology, the name for both Zeus' brother, who served as god of the underworld, and the land of the dead itself.

HARMONIA, daughter of Ares and Aphrodite, wife of Cadmus, the founder of Thebes.

HARPIES, foul female monsters with the bodies of birds, best known for ruining the food of Phineus, king of Thrace, and Aeneas on his voyage to Italy.

HEBE, daughter of Zeus and Hera who married Hercules.

HECATE, goddess of the underworld and the dark forces of the universe.

HECTOR, son of Priam and greatest hero of the Trojans.

HELEN, queen of Sparta and wife of Menelaus who went with Paris to Troy, provoking the Trojan War.

HELENUS, son of Priam and a Trojan seer.

HELIOS (Latin *Sol*), son of the Titan Hyperion, he was god of the sun and father of the unfortunate Phaethon.

HEPHAESTUS (Latin *Vulcan*), crippled god of the forge, usually described as a son of Hera.

HERA (Latin *Juno*), daughter of Cronus and Rhea, goddess of marriage and women, she joined with her brother Zeus in an often quarrelsome marriage.

HERACLES (see **Hercules**)

HERCULES, known in Greek as *Herakles* or *Heracles*, greatest hero of ancient Greece.

HERMAPHRODITUS, son of Hermes and Aphrodite who unwillingly merged with the nymph Salmacis to become both male and female.

HERMES (Latin *Mercury*), son of Zeus and Maia, messenger of the gods, and guide for the dead to the underworld.

HERO, priestess of Aphrodite and secret bride of Leander, she killed herself rather than live without him.

HESIONE, daughter of Laomedon, king of Troy, she was rescued from a sea monster by Hercules.

HESTIA (Latin *Vesta*), daughter of Cronus and Rhea, she was the goddess of the hearth.

HIPPODAMIA, wife of Pelops and mother of Atreus and Thyestes.

HIPPOLYTE, Amazon queen killed by Hercules for her belt as part of his ninth labor.

HIPPOLYTUS, son of Theseus and the Amazon queen Antiope, he died after refusing the advances of his father's wife, Phaedra.

HORATII, triplet brothers who fought as champions for Rome against three brothers from the town of Alba Longa. The last surviving Horatii brother killed the three enemy champions.

HORATIUS, called *Cocles*, or "one-eyed," he held back the entire invading army of the Etruscan king Lars Porsenna on a bridge across the Tiber.

HYACINTH, a prince of Sparta and lover of Apollo who was killed accidentally by the god, who then transformed him into a flower.

HYLAS, boy lover of Hercules who accompanied the hero on the voyage of the Argonauts until he was lured into a spring by a nymph.

HYMEN, god of marriage in later classical stories.

HYPERION, son of Earth and Sky, he was the father of Eos, Helios, and Selene.

HYPERMNESTRA, daughter of Danaus who refused her father's orders to kill her new husband, Lynceus.

IAPETUS, son of Earth and Sky, father of Atlas and Prometheus.

ICARUS, son of Daedalus who died when he flew too close to the sun while escaping Crete on wings.

INACHUS, river god in Argos, father of Io.

INO, daughter of Cadmus, sister of Semele, she became a minor sea goddess.

IO, unfortunate and unwilling lover of Zeus, turned into a cow by the god to disguise his affair from Hera, who nonetheless long tormented Io.

ION, son of Creusa after Apollo raped her, he became a priest at Delphi.

IPHICLES, mortal brother of Hercules.

IPHIGENIA, daughter of Agamemnon and Clytemnestra sacrificed at Aulis to gain a favorable wind for the Greek fleet sailing to Troy.

IRIS, goddess of the rainbow and divine messenger.

ISMENE, daughter of Oedipus and sister of Antigone.

IULUS, also known as Ascanius, he was the son of Aeneas and his first wife, Creusa.

IXION, king of Thessaly who tried to seduce Hera, but by the design of Zeus made love with a cloud and fathered the first of the centaurs.

JASON, leader of the Argonauts who retrieved the Golden Fleece with the help of Medea.

JOCASTA, mother and wife of Oedipus.

JUNO (see **Hera**)

JUPITER (see **Zeus**)

LACHESIS, one of the three Fates, she measured out the thread of life.

LAIUS, father of Oedipus who was unknowingly murdered by his son.

LAOCOON, Trojan priest of Apollo who told his countrymen to beware of Greeks bearing gifts before he was killed by a sea monster sent from Poseidon.

LAOMEDON, king of Troy who cheated Apollo and Poseidon after they labored for him for a year.

LAPITHS, a tribe in northern Thessaly who battled the centaurs at the wedding of their king, Peirithous.

LARS PORSENNA, Etruscan king and enemy of Rome.

LATINUS, elderly Italian king who at first welcomed Aeneas to his shores, then withdrew his support when hostilities began.

LAVINIA, daughter of Latinus and second wife of Aeneas.

LEANDER, secret husband of Hero who swam the straits of the Hellespont each night to be with her.

LEDA, mother of Helen, Clytemnestra, Castor, and Pollux.

LETO, daughter of the Titans Coeus and Phoebe, she was mother of Apollo and Artemis.

LUCRETIA, Roman wife who killed herself after being raped by her husband's best friend.

MAIA, daughter of Atlas and mother of Hermes by Zeus.

MARS (see **Ares**)

MARSYAS, foolish satyr who challenged Apollo to a flute contest and was flayed alive by the god when he lost.

MEDEA, daughter of Aeetes of Colchis, she sacrificed everything to help Jason retrieve the Golden Fleece, but later murdered her children in revenge when Jason abandoned her.

MEDUSA, once a beautiful maiden, she became a hideous Gorgon and was killed by Perseus, who used her head to turn his enemies to stone.

MEGARA, first wife of Hercules, murdered by the hero in a fit of madness.

MELAMPUS, Greek seer who could understand the language of animals.

MELEAGER, Greek hero who sailed with the Argonauts, the Fates told his mother he would live only as long as a certain log was not burned; later she burned it in anger.

MELPOMENE, muse of tragedy.

MENELAUS, son of Atreus, brother of Agamemnon, and husband of Helen before Paris took her to Troy.

METIS, daughter of Ocean and Tethys, she helped Zeus overthrow Cronus. Zeus then married her, but swallowed her whole when she became pregnant. Their daughter, Athena, later burst from his forehead.

MEZENTIUS, cruel Etruscan king who fought against Aeneas.

MIDAS, king in Phrygia who was granted the power to turn anything he touched into gold. In a separate incident, Apollo gave him the ears of an ass.

MINERVA (see **Athena**)

MINOS, son of Europa and king of Crete, he ordered Daedalus to build the Labyrinth to house the Minotaur.

MINOTAUR, deadly half-human, half-bull offspring of his mother, Pasiphae, and a bull.

MNEMOSYNE, wife of Zeus and mother of the Muses.

MOERAE (see **Fates**)

MUSES, goddesses who inspired poets, artists, and scholars.

MYRRHA, mother of Adonis by an incestuous relationship with her father.

NARCISSUS, beautiful son of a nymph and river god, he fell in love with his own reflection in a pool and starved to death.

NAUSICAA, daughter of King Alcinous and Queen Arete of Phaeacia, she helped Odysseus when he washed ashore on their island.

NEMESIS, goddess of retribution.

NEPTUNE (see **Poseidon**)

NEREUS, sea god and father of fifty nymph daughters, the Nereids.

NESSUS, centaur driven from Acadia by Hercules, he tricked Hercules' wife Deianara into giving her husband a cloak soaked in his poisonous blood.

NESTOR, aged king of Pylos who advised Agamemnon during the Trojan War.

NIGHT (Greek *Nyx*), born from primordial Chaos, she was the personification of darkness and the mother of many children.

NIOBE, proud and foolish mother of many sons and daughters who had all her children slain by Apollo and Artemis when she insulted their mother, Leto.

NUMITOR, grandfather of Romulus and Remus.

NYMPHS, minor female deities of various origins and types, such as Dryads (tree nymphs) and Oceanids (daughters of Ocean).

OCEAN, son of Earth and Sky, he was the great river of boundless water that encircled the world.

ODYSSEUS (Latin *Ulysses*), clever Greek warrior from Ithaca, husband to Penelope and father of Telemachus. He spent ten years fighting at Troy and an equal time trying to make his way home.

OEDIPUS, son of King Laius of Thebes and Jocasta, he unknowingly killed his father and married his own mother before discovering the truth and blinding himself.

OLYMPIA, town in western Peloponnesus where the Olympic games were founded by Hercules.

OLYMPUS, MOUNT, home of the gods, this series of peaks between Thessaly and Macedonia reaches almost ten thousand feet in height.

ORESTES, son of Agamemnon and Clytemnestra, he avenged his father's death by killing his mother.

ORION, hunter of giant size born from a bull hide soaked with urine from Zeus, Poseidon, and Hermes.

ORPHEUS, son of the Muse Calliope, he was the greatest bard in ancient Greece.

ORTHUS, ferocious hound born from Typhon and Echidna.

OTUS, with his twin brother and fellow giant Ephialtes, he launched an almost successful attack on the gods at Mount Olympus.

PALLAS, (1) a Titan born of Crius and Eurybia. (2) Son of King Evander who was killed by Turnus and avenged by Aeneas.

PAN (Latin *Faunus*), shepherd god fathered by Hermes.

PANDORA, the first mortal woman, created as a beautiful punishment for men by Zeus.

PARIS, son of King Priam of Troy, he took Helen from her husband Menelaus and precipitated the Trojan War.

PASIPHAE, wife of Minos who mated with a bull to produce the Minotaur.

PATROCLUS, best friend of Achilles killed by Hector at Troy.

PEGASUS, winged horse sprung from the body of Medusa.

PELEUS, father of Achilles by the goddess Thetis.

PELIAS, uncle of Jason who sent him on the search for the Golden Fleece.

PELOPS, son of Tantalus and father of Atreus, he was restored to life after he was cut up by his father and served to the gods.

PENELOPE, wife of Odysseus and mother of Telemachus who endured twenty years without her husband in Ithaca.

PENTHEUS, grandson of Cadmus and son of Agave, he was lured to his death by Dionysus when he refused to worship the new god.

PERIPHETES, outlaw who used his club to kill travelers, he was killed by Theseus.

PERSEPHONE, daughter of Zeus and Demeter, she was kidnapped and taken to the underworld by Hades, but later released for part of each year.

PERSEUS, son of Zeus and Danae, he beheaded Medusa, turned Atlas into a mountain, and rescued Andromeda from a sea monster.

PHAENON, handsome youth created by Prometheus and taken away by Zeus.

PHAETHON, child of Helios and Clymene, he drove his father's chariot recklessly through the heavens and was destroyed by Zeus.

PHILEMON, elderly husband of Baucis who entertained Zeus and Hermes unawares and was rewarded for his kindness.

PHILOCTETES, set fire to the pyre of Hercules at his request and was rewarded with the hero's bow and arrows. He later joined the Greek expedition to Troy, but was abandoned on the island of Lemnos because of his horrid stench.

PHILOMELA, sister of Procne who was raped by Tereus, who then cut out her tongue.

PHINEUS, Thracian seer who was besieged by Harpies until rescued by the Argonauts.

PHOEBE, daughter of Earth and Sky, she became the mother of Leto and Asteria by her brother Coeus.

PHOENIX, (1) brother of Cadmus and Europa, namesake of Phoenicia. (2) Tutor of Achilles.

PIRITHOUS, king of the Lapiths, he was trapped in Hades forever when he attempted to take Penelope from the underworld.

PITTHEUS, king of Troezen, father of Aethra, the mother of Theseus.

PLEIADES, seven daughters of Atlas and Pleione.

PLUTO (see **Hades**)

POLLUX or **Polydeuces,** brother of Castor and Helen, sailed with Jason on the *Argo*.

POLYDECTES, king of the island of Seriphus who sent Perseus to fetch Medusa's head.

POLYHYMNIA, muse of hymns and pantomime.

POLYNICES, son of Oedipus, killed by his brother Eteocles when he attacked Thebes.

POLYPHEMUS, Cyclops blinded by Odysseus.

POMONA, Roman goddess of fruit and orchards, she resisted the love of Vertumnus.

POSEIDON (Latin *Neptune*), god of the seas, son of Cronus and Rhea, brother of Zeus and Hades.

PRIAM, father of Paris and Hector, aged king of Troy during the war against the Greeks.

PRIAPUS, son of Aphrodite; a lascivious and well-endowed god of fertility.

PROCNE, sister of Philomela and wife of Tereus, she killed her son and served him to her husband when she discovered his treatment of her sister.

PROCRIS, wife of Cephalus who tricked her husband in a test of marital faithfulness, just as he had tricked her.

PROCRUSTES, outlaw who violently fit houseguests to the size of his bed before Theseus killed him.

PROMETHEUS, son of the Titan Iapetus and creator and patron of men, who stole fire from heaven for them, he was chained to a distant mountain by Zeus as punishment and had his liver eaten daily by an eagle.

PROTEUS, shape-changing god of the sea.

PSYCHE, bride of Cupid who could not resist the urge to discover who her husband really was.

PYGMALION, king of Cyprus who carved a faultless woman out of ivory, brought to life for him by Aphrodite.

PYRAMUS, young man who loved the maiden Thisbe and killed himself when he believed her dead in a lion attack.

PYRRHA, wife of Deucalion and only female survivor of the great flood sent by Zeus.

PYTHIA, name given to the priestess of Apollo at Delphi.

PYTHON, enormous guardian serpent at Delphi killed by Apollo.

REMUS, brother of Romulus and cofounder of Rome.

RHADAMANTHYS, son of Zeus and Europa, brother of Minos, he was a lawgiver made a judge in the underworld.

RHEA, daughter of Earth and Sky, wife of Cronus, mother of Zeus and other gods.

RHEA SILVIA, daughter of Numitor and a vestal virgin who became pregnant by Mars and gave birth to the twins Romulus and Remus.

ROMULUS, son of Rhea Silvia and cofounder of Rome with his brother Remus.

SABINE WOMEN daughters of nearby Sabine villages kidnapped by Romulus to be husbands for the single men of Rome.

SALMONEUS, arrogant king who pretended he was Zeus and was destroyed by the god.

SARPEDON, son of Zeus and king of Lycia who fought and died for the Trojans in the Trojan War.

SATURN (see **Cronus**)

SATYR, half-man, half-goat creatures given to drinking and unrestrained sex.

SCAEVOLA, Roman warrior who proved his bravery to the Etruscan king Lars Porsenna by thrusting his hand into a fire.

SCYLLA, once a beautiful maiden, she was turned into a horrible monster by Circe.

SEA (Greek *Tethys*), child of Earth and Sky who married her brother Ocean.

SELENE (Roman *Luna*), the moon, daughter of Hyperion and sister to Helios and Eos.

SEMELE, daughter of Cadmus who asked to see Zeus in all his glory. She died, but Zeus rescued their son, Dionysus, from her womb.

SIBYL, beloved by Apollo, she tricked the god into long life but forgot to ask for eternal youth. She was the oracle who led Aeneas to the underworld at Cumae in Italy.

SINIS, outlaw who tied travelers to two bent pine trees to pull them apart; slain by Theseus.

SINON, Greek left behind on Trojan beach to tell the Trojans the lie of the Trojan Horse.

SIRENS, women with wings of birds who lured sailors to their death with their beautiful singing

SISYPHUS, king of Corinth who was punished by the gods in Hades by forever being forced to roll a boulder up a hill, only to have it roll back down once he reached the top.

SKY (Greek *Ouranos*, Latin *Uranus*), child and husband of Earth, father of many children, including Cronus.

SPHINX, daughter of Echidna, a monster with a human head, lion's body, and eagle's wings. She killed herself after Oedipus solved her riddle at Thebes.

STRIFE (Greek *Eris*), the goddess of discord, a child of Night, created at the beginning of the world.

STYX, chief river of Hades by which the gods swore unbreakable oaths.

SYRINX, a nymph transformed into a flower to avoid the amorous advances of Pan.

TALUS, bronze giant who guarded Crete until disabled by Medea.

TANTALUS, Lydian king and father of Pelops who served his son as a dish in a banquet for the gods.

TARPEIA, vestal virgin who betrayed Rome and was crushed to death by Sabine shields.

TARTARUS, the dark region sprung from Chaos, located far beneath Hades. It was the prison of the defeated Titans.

TELEMACHUS, son of Odysseus and Penelope.

TEREUS, evil Thracian king who married Procne, then raped and cut out the tongue of her sister, Philomela.

TERPSICHORE, muse of lyric poetry and dancing.

TETHYS (see Sea)

THALIA, muse of comedy.

THEIA, daughter of Earth and Sky, mother of Eos, Helios, and Selene.

THEMIS, daughter of Earth and Sky, onetime goddess at Delphi, she was associated with order and justice.

THEOPHRANE, maiden turned into a ewe by Poseidon, then raped by him in the form of a ram. She gave birth to the ram that provided the Golden Fleece sought by the Argonauts.

THESEUS, son of Aegeus, king of Athens, and the maiden Aethra of Troezen. He had many adventures, including the defeat of the Minotaur in Crete.

THETIS, sea goddess who gave birth to Achilles by her mortal husband, Peleus.

THISBE, beloved by Pyramus, she killed herself after finding him dead.

THYESTES, son of Pelops and brother of Atreus.

TIBER, god of river that flows through Rome.

TIRESIAS, great seer of Thebes, sought out by Oedipus and Creon in life, then by Odysseus in the underworld.

TITANS, name given to the first generation of gods defeated by Zeus and his allies.

TITHONUS, handsome prince taken by Eos to her palace as a lover until she turned him into a cicada.

TITYUS, giant who attempted to rape Leto, he was punished in Hades by being staked to the ground and having his liver eternally eaten by vultures.

TRITON, sea god and namesake of Lake Triton in north Africa.

TURNUS, Italian foe of Aeneas and rival for the hand of Lavinia.

TYNDAREUS, king of Sparta and husband of Leda.

TYPHON, powerful monster sprung from Earth and Tartarus, he challenged Zeus and was beaten after the war with the Titans.

ULYSSES (see **Odysseus**)

URANIA, muse of astronomy.

VENUS (see **Aphrodite**)

VERTUMNUS, Roman fertility god who wooed and won the goddess Pomona.

VESTA (see **Hestia**)

VESTAL VIRGINS Roman maidens sworn to virginity who served the hearth goddess Vesta.

VULCAN (see **Hephaestus**)

ZEPHYRUS or **Zephyr,** god of the west wind, said to have caused the death of Hyacinth.

ZETES, Argonaut and winged son of the north wind.

ZEUS (Latin *Jupiter* or *Jove*), son of Cronus and Rhea, brother of Poseidon and Hades, and husband of Hera, he was the most powerful of the gods.

NOTES

INTRODUCTION

There are many excellent academic and popular surveys of Greek and Roman mythology. I would particularly recommend Richard Martin's *Myths of the Ancient Greeks*, Barry Powell's *Classical Myth*, and, especially for its superb photographs and illustrations, Richard Buxton's *Complete World of Greek Mythology*. For those readers who want to delve into the original sources, many of the shorter tales are collected in the *Anthology of Classical Myth: Primary Sources in Translation* edited by Stephen M. Trzaskoma, R. Scott Smith, and Stephen Brunet. There are also many good editions of classical authors from Homer to Ovid in most bookstores and libraries. I have found the essays in the *Cambridge Companion to Greek Mythology* edited by Roger D. Woodard very helpful, as well as the detailed studies by Timothy Gantz in *Early Greek Myth*. Walter Burkert offers a clear introduction to ancient ritual and worship in *Greek Religion*, while Mary Lefkowitz's *Greek Gods, Human Lives: What We Can Learn from Myths* is a wonderful exposition of why ancient mythology is still meaningful today.

Many of the Mesopotamian, Anatolian, and Egyptian stories so influential to Greek mythology are found in *Ancient Near Eastern Texts Relating to the Old Testament* edited by James B. Pritchard. *Hittite Myths*, a more recent collection by Harry Hoffner, provides a glimpse into the ancient mythology of Asia Minor. What we know of Indo-European myths is covered ably in Jaan Puhvel's *Comparative Mythology*, revealing just how little of this tradition survived among the Greeks. For stories from Italy, I recommend *Etruscan Myths* by Larissa Bonfante and Judith Swaddling, along with *Roman Myths* by Jane F. Gardner.

The names of the gods can be confusing (Hesiod lists over three hundred alone in the *Theogony*). The glossary in this book is a good start, but I also recommend a full listing of names, places, and terms such as those found in Pierre Grimal's *Dictionary of Classical Mythology*, Edward Tripp's *Meridian Handbook of Classical Mythology*, and the *Oxford Classical Dictionary*.

CREATION

The primary source for the Greek story of creation and early tales of gods and men is Hesiod's *Theogony*, though later Greek and Roman authors contribute as well. The *Theogony* (116–210) tells of the birth of the gods from Chaos and the castration of Sky by Cronus. As in the beginning of the biblical book of Genesis and in Near Eastern mythology, the world is not created from nothing (*ex nihilo*). In the opening chapter of Genesis (1.2): *The earth was a formless void and darkness covered the face of the deep, while a wind from God swept over the face of the water.*

Whereas the Babylonian *Enuma Elish* begins (1–3):

When on high heaven was not yet named
nor was the ground yet named,
there was nothing but primordial Apsu.

The conflict between generations of gods in Greek mythology is also paralleled in the Near Eastern tradition. The young Babylonian god Marduk defeats his elders along with an array of monsters to become ruler of heaven. In the *Song of Kumarbi*, a story from Hittite mythology, Alalu is king of the gods until Anu defeats him in battle, only to be overcome himself by Kumarbi, who bites off his genitals.

Modern readers are sometimes troubled by contradictory stories in Greek mythology, such as multiple origins of the Fates, who rule our destiny, the various mothers of Typhon, or conflicting accounts of the creation of humanity. The Greeks were not so bothered by discrepancies, which are often due to stories arising in different regions of Greece. In the text, I try to smooth over these differences with "Some say . . . but others say," though I cannot include all the known variants of a particular myth.

The story of the five generations of humanity is found in Hesiod's *Works and Days* (106–201), with interesting parallels to the Hebrew Bible (Daniel 2.31–35). The passage at the end of this story is one of the few examples of eschatology—an often cataclysmic story of the world's end—found in Greek mythology. Readers of the Christian New Testament (Matthew 10.34–36, Luke 12.49–53) may find the parallels instructive.

The charming story of the three types of spherical humans split apart by Zeus comes from a later source, Plato's *Symposium* (189C–194E).

The creation of man by Prometheus does not occur in Hesiod, but is described in Pausanias (10.4) and the *Odes* of the Roman poet Horace (1.16). The deception of Zeus at the banquet by Prometheus is recorded in Hesiod's *Theogony* (535–561), while his theft of fire and his subsequent punishment occur in multiple sources, including Hesiod (*Theogony*, 520–525, 565–567) and more dramatically in the *Prometheus Bound* of Aeschylus. The typically misogynistic Hesiod records the Pandora story twice (*Theogony*, 567–612; *Works and Days*, 53–104) with minor variants.

The Greek flood story has parallels with the biblical account (Genesis 6–9) and with the Near Eastern mythology, such as the stories of the righteous man Ziusudra/ Atrahasis saved by the intervention of the god Enki/Ea, and Utnapishtim saved by Ea in the *Epic of Gilgamesh*. The tale of Deucalion occurs in classical mythology in relatively late sources (Apollodorus 1.7.2; Ovid, *Metamorphoses*, 1.163–415).

GODS

Modern readers sometimes wonder if the ancient Greeks and Romans really believed in their gods. After all, how could anyone take a libido-driven divinity like Zeus seriously as a moral guide? The answer is that, yes, the people of the classical world believed in their gods—but not, perhaps, in the way some modern readers would think. The ancients saw the gods as guardians and benefactors of particular facets of life and the world, such as justice, sea travel, marriage, childbirth, and healing. The proper role of humans was to appease and bargain with the gods through sacrifices to achieve a specific goal. The Greeks and Romans would never expect the gods to love them or provide them with moral examples. Of course, there were always skeptics and atheists, but this role was generally reserved for a few intellectuals who often risked their lives in expressing their views. Some scholars did view the stories of the gods through an allegorical lens or as remnants of tales once told of actual human beings who in time came to be seen as divine (*euhemerism*), but to the average Greek or Roman, the gods were real and powerful beings neglected at great peril.

• • •

The warning from Zeus to the gods is found in Homer (*Iliad*, 8.17–27). The story of Salmoneus is from Apollodorus (1.9.7), while the tale of Ixion comes from Apollodorus (*Epitome*, 1.20) and Pindar (*Pythian Ode*, 2.21–49). The myth of Asclepius raising mortals from the dead is also from Apollodorus (3.10.3–4).

The story of hapless Io is found in many passages of Greek and Roman literature with a wide degree of variant stories. I have for the most part followed the narration of Io herself to Prometheus in Aeschylus' *Prometheus Bound* (561–886), along with scattered references in the same author's *Suppliant Women*, in Apollodorus (2.1.3), and in Ovid's *Metamorphoses* (1.568–779).

Europa is first mentioned in Homer (*Iliad*, 14.321–322) as a daughter of Phoenix, not Agenor, but I have followed the most common version of the tale from Apollodorus (3.1.1–2), Ovid (*Metamorphoses*, 2.833–3.25), and especially the Hellenistic poet Moschus (2).

The tale of Callisto occurs in many ancient authors with variations, including Apollodorus (3.8), but I have relied primarily on Ovid (*Metamorphoses*, 2.401–535). The story of Antiope likewise varies widely, with the main sources being Apollodorus (3.5), Hyginus (*Fabulae*, 7–8), and Pausanias (2.6, 9.17). The often contradictory myths involving Aegina and her son Aeacus are found in Apollodorus (1.9, 3.12), Pausanias (2.5), Hyginus (*Fabulae*, 52), and Ovid (*Metamorphoses* 7.501–660). The stories of Electra and her sister Taygete are found in Apollodorus (3.10, 12), Hyginus (*Astronomica*, 2.21), and Pindar (*Olympian Ode*, 3.29–30). The myth of Leda and her sons Castor and Pollux is from Apollodorus (3.10), Euripides (*Helen*, 16–22), Pindar (*Nemean Ode*, 10.54–91), Pausanias (3.16), and Hyginus (*Fabulae* 77–80).

The story of Phaenon is found in Hyginus (*Astronomica*, 2.42) and Ganymede in Homer (*Iliad*, 20.231–235), the *Homeric Hymn to Aphrodite* (5.202–217), and Hyginus (*Astronomica*, 2.16, 29). The name of Ganymede was corrupted via Etruscan to Latin *Catamitus*, hence the modern word *catamite*, a male who submits passively to the sexual attention of another man.

The ancient hymn is from the *Homeric Hymn to Poseidon* (22). The account of Poseidon's brief rebellion against Zeus is from Homer (*Iliad*, 1.401–406). Pausanias (10.5–6) quotes the poem about Delphi from a passage of the *Eumolpia* by the legendary Musaeus and tells how Poseidon once shared the oracle with the goddess Earth.

Pausanias tells of the fight between Poseidon and Helios for Corinth (2.1.6) and Hera for Argos (2.15.5, 2.22.4). Apollodorus (3.14.1) records the best version of the contest between the sea god and Athena for Athens, though he says Zeus appointed all twelve Olympian gods as judges rather than King Cecrops alone.

Poseidon's wife Amphitrite is rarely mentioned in ancient sources. Her disputed genealogy is from Hesiod (*Theogony*, 243, 254) and Apollodorus (1.2.2, 1.2.7), while the brief myth of her flight from her would-be husband is found in Hyginus (*Astronomica*, 2.17).

The stories of Poseidon and the unlucky objects of his affection are told in many sources. The rape of Demeter as a mare and her subsequent children by the god comes from Pausanias (8.25, 8.42) and Apollodorus (3.6.8). The assault on Medusa is from Ovid (*Metamorphoses*, 4.790–803) and Apollodorus (2.4.3). The story of Theophane is from Hyginus (*Fabulae*, 188), while the tale of Canace, her willing daughter Iphimedea, and the brothers Otus and Ephialtes is from Apollodorus (1.7.4) and Hyginus (*Fabulae*, 28). The rape and sex change of Caenis/Caenus comes from Hyginus (*Fabulae*, 14). The story of Pelops the boy lover is from Pindar (*Olympian Ode*, 1.35–45).

The tale of Poseidon's labors at Troy comes primarily from Homer (*Iliad*, 21.434–460), but also from Apollodorus (2.5.9) and Hyginus (*Fabulae*, 89).

References to both the god and place Hades are frequent in classical literature from the time of Homer, though there are few myths about him. The words of the doomed Alcestis are from Euripides (*Alcestis*, 259–264). Homer (*Odyssey*, 11) contains the fullest description of the underworld in Greek mythology. Other notable passages are Homer (*Iliad*, 8.366–368), the Homeric Hymn to Demeter, Hesiod (*Theogony*, 310–312, 758–819, 850), Aristophanes (*Frogs*, 138–140, 180–269), Apollodorus (2.5.12), Virgil (*Aeneid*, 6), and Ovid (*Metamorphoses*, 7.408–419, 10.65–67).

The alternate view in the myth of Er comes from Plato (*Republic*, 10.614b–621d). This story is not a traditional myth but a creation of the philosopher himself, yet the tale draws on ancient stories from the cult of Orpheus practiced throughout Greece and the doctrines of the famous mathematician and religious leader Pythagoras. The story of Er influenced many later writers and makers of myths, such as the Roman author Virgil.

The stories of Leto and the birth of Apollo are found in many sources, especially the Homeric Hymn to Apollo (3), but also Homer (*Odyssey*, 11.576–581), Hesiod (*Theogony*, 918–920), Apollodorus (1.4), Hyginus (*Fabulae*, 53, 140), and Ovid (*Metamorphoses*, 6.339–381). The establishment of Apollo's oracle at Delphi is from the Homeric Hymn to Apollo (3), which makes the great serpent a female, along with Apollodorus (1.4.1) and Hyginus (*Fabulae*, 140). The story of Niobe is from Homer (*Iliad*, 24.605–620), Ovid (*Metamorphoses*, 6.146–312), Pausanias (1.21.3), and Hyginus (*Fabulae*, 9, 11). That of Marsyas and Midas is from Ovid (*Metamorphoses*, 6.382–400, 11.146–193), Hyginus (*Fabulae*, 165, 191), and Apollodorus (1.4.2).

The tale of Daphne is told best in Ovid (*Metamorphoses*, 1.452–567), while the side story of unlucky Leucippus is from Pausanias (8.20). The chilling story of the Sibyl is from Ovid (*Metamorphoses*, 14.129–153) and Petronius (*Satyricon*, 48). T. S. Eliot quotes Petronius in the epigraph to his poem "The Waste Land." The myth of Marpessa and Idas is from Apollodorus (1.7.8–9), while Sinope comes from Apollonius Rhodius (2.946–954), with the addition that she successfully played the same trick on Zeus and the god of the Halys River. Cassandra's rejection of Apollo is found in Apollodorus (3.12.5), Hyginus (*Fabulae*, 93), and Aeschylus (*Agamemnon*, 1212).

The story of Hyacinth is from Ovid (*Metamorphoses*, 10.162–219), along with Euripides (*Helen*, 1465–1474) and Apollodorus (1.3.3). The transformation of Cyparissus is likewise told in Ovid (*Metamorphoses*, 10.106–142). The story of Ion comes primarily from Euripides' play *Ion*, along with Pausanias (2.14.2, 7.1.2–5). The tale of Chione is from Ovid (*Metamorphoses*, 11.291–345).

The two stories of the origin of Hephaestus are both found in Homer (*Iliad*, 1.584–600, 18.368–409), while the tale of the failed mating with Athena comes from Hyginus (*Fabulae*, 166). The humorous account of the cuckolding of Hephaestus by Ares is also from Homer (*Odyssey*, 8.266–366).

Ares appears frequently as a character in Homer's *Iliad* (the quote by Zeus is from 5.889–893) and in the genealogies of Hesiod's *Theogony*, but the genuine myths about him are as rare as those of Hades or Hephaestus. The story of Alcippe and Halirrhothius is from Euripides (*Electra*, 1258–1261) and Apollodorus (3.14.2).

Hermes appears as a secondary character in countless Greek myths, but the charming story of his theft of Apollo's cattle is from the Homeric Hymn to Hermes (4).

The birth of Pan is from the Homeric Hymn to Pan (19), while the tale of Syrinx is from Ovid (*Metamorphoses*, 1.689–712).

The sun god Helios was one of the oldest Greek deities, though he does not feature prominently in myth or cult worship. In later stories he was often identified with Apollo, but he was a distinct divinity until at least Hellenistic times. His genealogy is told by Hesiod (*Theogony*, 371–374) and his association with the island of Rhodes by Pindar (*Olympian Ode*, 7.54–76). Ovid is the source for both the story of Leucothoe/

Clytie (*Metamorphoses*, 4.167–270) and the famous tale of Phaethon (*Metamorphoses*, 1.747–2.400).

The standard story of the birth of Dionysus comes from Ovid (*Metamorphoses*, 3.253–315) and Apollodorus (3.4–5). The alternate version is recorded in Pausanias (3.24.3–4). The tale of Dionysus and the pirates comes primarily from the *Homeric Hymn to Dionysus* (7), but also from Hyginus (*Fabulae*, 134). The story of Midas and the golden touch is from Ovid (*Metamorphoses*, 11.85–145) and Hyginus (*Fabulae*, 191). The stories of initial resistance to Dionysus are from Apollodorus (2.2.1–2, 3.5.1) and Ovid (*Metamorphoses*, 4.1–54, 389–431), but the tale of Pentheus at Thebes is from the *Bacchae* of Euripides. Brief descriptions of the journey of Dionysus to Hades are found scattered throughout Pausanias and other authors, but the best sources are Hyginus (*Astronomica*, 2.5) and the early Christian writer Clement of Alexandria (*Exhortation to the Greeks*, 2.30), who takes particular delight in reporting the story of the lustful old man Hyplipnus, whom he calls Prosymnus.

The birth of primordial Eros is from Hesiod (*Theogony*, 116–122), while the complete fairy tale of Cupid and Psyche is found only in Apuleius (*Golden Ass*, 4.28–6.24). The name of Cupid and Psyche's daughter is Voluptas in the Latin of Apuleius, a word I have translated as "Happiness," but could also be "Pleasure" or "Delight."

GODDESSES

Male gods in the ancient world ruled over a multitude of realms—lightning and thunder, the underworld, horses, ironworking, and many others—but goddesses were almost all connected in some way with the primal forces of fertility and reproduction. The fruits of the harvest, sexual attraction, marriage and childbirth, hearth and home, even the hunting of wild animals—these are the concerns of female deities. Because of this, there are fewer stories about goddesses than there are about gods, such as Zeus and Poseidon, and because most myths in the ancient world were recorded by men, who told stories that their audience, again mostly male, wanted to hear. No one knows how many ancient myths told by women for other women have been lost forever.

The cultic renewal of Hera as a virgin each year is described by Pausanias (2.38.2). The shouting match between Hera and Zeus is from Homer (*Iliad*, 1.539–550), while the story of Tiresias is from Ovid (*Metamorphoses*, 3.316–338). The reference to Orion's wife Side is from Apollodorus (1.4.3), Gerana from Ovid (*Metamorphoses*, 6.90–92) and Aelian (*On Animals*, 15.29), and the daughters of Proetus from Apollodorus (2.2.2).

The story of Demeter and Iasion is briefly mentioned by Homer (*Odyssey*, 5.125–127), Ovid (*Metamorphoses*, 9.422–423), and Hyginus (*Fabulae*, 250, *Astronomica*, 2.4). The tale of Erysichthon is from Ovid (*Metamorphoses*, 8.738–878). The search of Demeter for Persephone, told in the *Homeric Hymn to Demeter* (2), is by far the most famous myth of the goddess and is a type of ritual and etiological story known as the disappearing god, found in many cultures to explain the cold, barren months of winter. The cult supposedly established by Demeter at Eleusis near Athens became a center for a well-known mystery religion in ancient times promising its initiates a path of salvation from the gloom of Hades.

The fullest account of the Actaeon tale is from Ovid (*Metamorphoses*, 3.138–252), though Apollodorus (3.4.4) briefly records the story, saying that Zeus caused the death of Actaeon for wooing Semele. Hyginus (*Fabulae*, 180–181) adds that Actaeon tried to rape Artemis at the spring. The brief story of Buphagus is from Pausanias (8.27.17), while the "Potiphar's wife" tale of Hippolytus is best told by Euripides in his play of the same name. The various versions of the Orion myth are from Homer (*Odyssey*, 5.121–124), Apollodorus (1.4.3), and Hyginus (*Fabulae*, 195, *Astronomica*, 2.34).

The story of Aphrodite and Anchises is taken from the wonderful *Homeric Hymn to Demeter.* Pygmalion is mentioned briefly by Apollodorus (3.14.3), but the tale is told fully by Ovid (*Metamorphoses,* 10.243–297).

Ovid (*Metamorphoses,* 10.519–559, 708–739) also has the longest account of the Adonis story, but Apollodorus (3.14.4) preserves several different accounts, along with Hyginus (*Astronomica,* 2.7).

The story of Hermaphroditus comes from Ovid (*Metamorphoses,* 4.285–388), while the brief tale of ill-tempered Priapus is taken from Hyginus (*Astronomica,* 2.23).

The early story praising Hecate is from Hesiod (*Theogony,* 411–452). References to her cult practices are scattered in many ancient sources, including Aristophanes (*Wealth,* 594–600) and various magical papyri.

Hestia is first mentioned in Hesiod (*Theogony,* 453–454). The passage is taken from the *Homeric Hymn to Hestia* (29).

The alternate birth stories of Athena are from Pausanias (8.26.6–7, 9.33.7) and Herodotus (4.180). The tale of defiant Arachne is from Ovid (*Metamorphoses,* 6.1–145).

The tales of Eos are mentioned in Homer (*Odyssey,* 5.121–124, 15.248–251), Hesiod (*Theogony,* 371–382, 984–991), *Homeric Hymn to Aphrodite* (5.218–238), *Homeric Hymn to Helios* (31.4–9), Hyginus (*Fabulae,* 189), and Ovid (*Metamorphoses,* 9.421–425). Some stories relate that after Cephalus and Procris were reconciled, he accidentally killed her while hunting, thinking she was a wild animal hiding in the bushes.

The nine Muses are mentioned frequently throughout classical literature, but some key passages are Homer (*Iliad,* 2.591–602, *Odyssey,* 8.62–64, 477–481, 24.60–64), Hesiod (*Theogony,* 35–115), Apollodorus (1.3.1, 3.5.8), Pausanias (9.29), and Ovid (*Metamorphoses,* 5.255–345, 662–678).

The three Fates appear in Hesiod (*Theogony,* 217–222, 901–906) with different genealogies, but I have followed the tradition that they were daughters of primal Night. The story of their deception of Typhon is from Apollodorus (1.6.3), as is the story of Meleager (1.8.2–3), with variants found in Homer (*Iliad,* 9.543–599), Hyginus (*Fabulae,* 171, 174), and Ovid (*Metamorphoses,* 8.425–525).

The song to Cybele is from the *Homeric Hymn to the Mother of the Gods* (14). The best account of the story of Cybele and Attis is from Pausanias (7.17.9–12). Among the other sources of the story and related ritual are Catullus (63), Virgil (*Ciris,* 165–167), Ovid (*Metamorphoses,* 10.99–105), and Apollonius Rhodius (*Argonautica,* 1.1092–1153). When Saint Paul in his letter to the Galatians (5.12) wishes that those advocating circumcision would "go ahead and castrate themselves," he is probably referring to the bloody rites of the priests of Cybele.

HEROES

Every true hero has a tough childhood. Moses is almost killed as a baby by pharaoh's soldiers, the Irish hero Cú Chulainn has to fight his way to a place among his young peers, while Water Jar Boy of the Tewa Indians in the American Southwest grows up as, well, a water jar. But whether King Arthur or Luke Skywalker, the struggles of overcoming childhood difficulties are part of the crucial training every hero must undergo. Greek and Roman heroes are no different. Perseus is almost drowned in a chest, Hercules has to kill snakes in his crib, and Romulus and Remus are abandoned to be raised by a she-wolf. After childhood, the challenges only increase as the hero battles monsters, defeats evil villains, and rescues the occasional princess. There is usually a happy ending—some heroes even become gods—but most have to be content with eternal glory as they are remembered forever in song and story.

• • •

The story of Perseus appears in part in many classical sources, but the most complete versions are Apollodorus (2. 4) and Ovid (*Metamorphoses*, 4.604–5.255,). The prayer of Danae in the chest is adapted from the Greek poet Simonides.

The best source for the legendary life of Theseus, is Plutarch's own *Theseus*, first in his biographical collection of leading Greeks and Romans. Other stories about Theseus are found in Apollodorus (3.15–16, *Epitome* 1), Pausanias (1.19.1, 2.22.6–7, 2.31.1), and Hyginus (*Fabulae*, 42, 47, *Astronomica*, 2.5). One alternate version of the death of Theseus' father Aegeus says the old king threw himself in the sea, hence the name Aegean.

The story of Daedalus and his son Icarus is from Apollodorus (3.15.8, *Epitome*, 1.11–15) and Ovid (*Metamorphoses*, 8.183–259).

The adventures of Bellerophon are found first in Homer (*Iliad*, 6.152–204), but also in Apollodorus (2.3) and Pindar (*Olympian Ode*, 13.55–93).

Homer (*Odyssey*, 15.225–246) first tells the story of Melampus, but the most detailed version is from Apollodorus (1.9.11–12, 2.2.2).

The female hero Atalanta is featured in Apollodorus (1.8.2, 3.9.2), Ovid (*Metamorphoses*, 10.560–738), and Hyginus (*Fabulae*, 99, 185). Other stories say that at some point Atalanta gave birth to a son named Parthenopaeus and, in hatred of this result of the sexual act, she exposed the child on a mountain just as she had earlier been left to die. This child was also rescued by shepherds and grew to be a great warrior.

The chilling story of Procne and her sister, Philomela, is told by Apollodorus (3.14.8), but the best surviving version is from Ovid (*Metamorphoses*, 6.424–674). Some sources say Philomela became a sparrow and Procne a nightingale, but it seems more fitting to give the sweeter voice to Philomela.

LOVERS

In my introductory Greek classes, I often tell the students that the language of Homer and Socrates had several different words for what we call "love." The first was *eros*, "passion" or "desire," often, though not always, with a sexual component. For a more chaste and friendly kind of love, the Greeks used *philia*, hence the city name *Philadelphia*, "city of brotherly love." The favorite word for love in the Christian New Testament is *agape*, used to mean a deeper type of affection, such as that between a loving husband and wife or between God and humanity—though it can also signify how a person feels about a really tasty dinner.

Regardless of the word used, it would be an understatement to say that Greek love stories have a distinctly tragic element about them. The phrase "and they lived happily ever after" is scarcely found in any of the ancient myths. Boy meets girl, boy loses girl, both die a horrible death is more the norm. A beautiful maiden rarely rides off to live with her beloved in a castle and the frog almost never gets kissed. The most two lovers can reasonably hope for is to be turned into some form of clinging vegetation or perhaps a pair of devoted birds.

Ovid tells the story of Narcissus and Echo in his *Metamorphoses* (3.339–510), where he also shares the tale of the two star-crossed lovers Pyramus and Thisbe (4.55–166). Shakespeare was of course familiar with Ovid in the original Latin from his schoolboy days, long before he wrote *Romeo and Juliet*.

Ovid (*Metamorphoses*, 11.266–748) is also the primary source for the myth of Ceyx and Alcyone. Pausanias (1.32.6) relates how Ceyx welcomed Hercules to his kingdom. Apollodorus (1.7.4) gives an alternate version of the Ceyx and Alcyone story, claiming that the pair offended the gods by calling each other Zeus and Hera. In this version the real Zeus turns Ceyx into a gannet and Alcyone into a kingfisher as punishment.

Scylla is best known from Homer's *Odyssey* (12.73–126, 222–259), where she eats six of the crewmen who sailed with Odysseus, but in this story, told by Ovid (*Metamorphoses*, 13.898–14.14.69), she is still a beautiful young woman, much as Medusa was before her horrific transformation at the hands of another goddess.

The primary source for the tragic myth of Hero and Leander is the tale of the same name by the late Greek writer Musaeus, though Ovid (*Heroides*, 18–19) and Virgil (*Georgics*, 3.258–263) also record parts of the story.

The bloody family tale of Danaus and his fifty daughters is told many times in classical literature, but the best sources, especially for the story of Hypermnestra and Lynceus, are Apollodorus (2.1.4–5), Ovid (*Heroides*, 14), and Horace (*Ode*, 3.11). The story of Baucis and Philemon is more pleasant and comes from Ovid (*Metamorphoses*, 8.611–724). The one-sided love affair of Alpheus and Arethusa also comes from Ovid (*Metamorphoses*, 5.572–641), as does the story of Pomona and Vertumnus (*Metamorphoses*, 14.623–771). The tale of Endymion and Selene has multiple brief sources, the most helpful being Apollodorus (1.7.5–6) and Pausanias (5.1.4).

The sad story of Orpheus and Eurydice is found in several ancient authors such as Virgil (*Georgics*, 4.453–529), Ovid (*Metamorphoses*, 10.1–85, 11.1–84), Apollodorus (1.3.2), and Hyginus (*Astronomica*, 2.7). Among the possible reasons mentioned by ancient authors for why Orpheus was torn apart by crazed nymphs are that he had dishonored Aphrodite by turning his back on love, that he preferred the company of young men in his bed, or that he had simply been in the wrong place at the wrong time.

HERCULES

The proper Greek name for Hercules is Herakles, but since the hero is known today via popular books, television, and especially movies as Hercules, I have used that name in this book. Herakles is Greek for "the glory of Hera"—an odd name for someone the goddess is always trying to kill. The Etruscans of Italy adopted him into their mythology at an early period as Hercle, due to the peculiar syncopating nature of their language. This name was borrowed in turn by their Latin-speaking neighbors as Hercules.

It is often difficult to take Hercules seriously as a hero. He carries a great wooden club and wears a lion skin as if he comes from some earlier age. He is excessive in everything he does and uses violence to solve problems when diplomacy would serve him better. He kills his wife and children in a fit of madness, cleans out filthy stables by diverting a whole river, and attacks gods when they get in his way. He is a comic figure, serving an inferior king as a slave and dressing in women's clothing. Yet in the end, he always comes out on top, either through a clever trick or by dogged determination.

It's hard to find a piece of classical literature that doesn't mention Hercules, but the two relatively complete sources for the life of the hero are Apollodorus (2.4.8–7.7) and Diodorus Siculus (4.9–39).

Some of the many other important sources for the conception and early life of Hercules are Homer (*Iliad*, 19.96–133), Hesiod (*Shield of Herakles*, 1–56), Ovid (*Metamorphoses*, 9.280–323), and Hyginus (*Fabulae*, 29). His short and tragic marriage to Megara is described by Euripides in his play *Hercules*.

Some ancient authors say there were ten labors, but most agree there were twelve. Many involve the classic folk motif of slaying or capturing a fearsome monster, though in almost every case Hercules has to use his innate cleverness to accomplish the deed.

The variants in the stories of the labors are too numerous to list completely, but are not particularly important in any case. Notable are whether Eurysthius ruled in Mycenae or Tiryns, the number of the original heads of the Hydra (anywhere from one to a hundred), who if anyone accompanied him during each task, and the overall order of the labors.

Important sources for the labors aside from the passages of Apollodorus and Diodorus above are Homer (*Iliad*, 5.395–402, 20.144–148, *Odyssey*, 11.601–625), Hesiod (*Theogony*, 313–318, 523–534), Herodotus (4.8–10), Sophocles (*Women of Trachis*, *Philoctetes*), Hyginus (*Fabulae*, 30–31, *Astronomica*, 2.3, 6, 23–24, 38), Euripides (*Alcestis*), Pausanias (1.27.9–10, 5.1.9–5.2.2, 8.22.4), and Virgil (*Aeneid*, 8.190–269).

On the European side of the world, in Spain, the northern Pillar of Hercules is the Rock of Gibraltar, while its African counterpart is Jebel Musa in Morocco. Although these were traditionally the western limit of the world, the Greeks did sail beyond them, at least as far as the land of Tartessus in southwestern Spain at the mouth of the Guadalquivir River. The Phoenicians traveled much farther, both south along the African coast and north perhaps as far as the British Isles.

Virgil tells the story of the encounter of Hercules and Cacus, whose name is simply the Greek adjective *kakos* ("evil, bad"). The setting is the site of the future city of Rome.

The closing hymn to Hercules is from the *Homeric Hymn to Herakles* (15).

OEDIPUS

"It was God's will," says the believer when tragedy strikes. The ancient Greeks would have understood this sentiment, though they wouldn't have attributed the slings and arrows of outrageous fortune to the workings of a single divinity or even to the inhabitants of Mount Olympus. Fate was bigger than the gods, who themselves were subject to it, though they might try to delay it on occasion. Zeus, for example, considered sparing his mortal son Sarpedon from imminent death on the battlefield of Troy, but Hera and Athena convinced him that tampering with the all-powerful Fates would unleash chaos in the cosmos.

As with many aspects of life, the Greeks saw fate in agricultural terms. The word *moira*, most commonly used for fate, means "share" or "portion" in the sense of a plot of land to plow. It may be fertile and well watered or it may be rocky and parched, but it is unavoidably yours, so you better learn to live with it. To try to act "beyond fate" is asking for trouble. Many Greeks, like some modern believers, took comfort in the idea that the universe had assigned them a particular destiny. The details may be flexible, but the general outline of their lives was fixed. This was a blessed assurance to Odysseus, who knew his destiny was to reach his home in Ithaca no matter what trouble Poseidon might cause along the way. But if you were Oedipus—doomed unwittingly to kill your father and marry your mother—fate could be an unbearable burden.

The story of Cadmus and the foundation of Thebes is told in Apollodorus (3.4.1–2), Pausanias (9.5.1–2, 12.1–4), and Ovid (*Metamorphoses*, 3.1–130). References to the life of Oedipus are numerous in Greek and Roman literature as early as Homer (*Odyssey*, 11.271–280), but the prime sources are two plays of Sophocles, *Oedipus Rex* and *Oedipus at Colonus*. The fate of the sons and daughters of Oedipus are also best told in Athenian tragedy, namely in the *Seven Against Thebes* by Aeschylus, Euripides' *Phoenician Women*, and *Antigone* by Sophocles. The later *Thebaid* of Statius is also an excellent but often overlooked epic concerning the seven warriors who fought against Thebes.

ARGONAUTS

The Greeks were great wanderers, sailing the Mediterranean for trade as early as the Mycenaean age. But it wasn't until the eighth century B.C. that colonization from various city states on the Greek mainland and Asia Minor really took off. Perhaps it was population pressures at home that drove the first colonists to leave Corinth, Phocaea, and other towns to establish new homes in sometimes hostile lands from the northern edge of the Black Sea to Italy, Africa, Gaul, and even Spain. Jason and his Argonauts visit many of these sites on their mythical travels, making the story a kind of ancient travelogue of Greek colonies.

But like most modern colonizers, wherever the Greeks went they ran into native people who had been there long before them. Sometimes the relations were good and commerce prospered between the coastal settlers and the hinterland, sometimes not. It didn't help that the haughty Greeks saw themselves as innately superior to the natives. The Greek colonists called the native people *barbaroi*, since their languages sounded like blabbering nonsense (*bar-bar*) to the refined ear of a Greek speaker. These barbarian peoples, whether Celts, Africans, or natives of the Caucasus like Medea, became the proverbial Other of Greek culture and literature. They were crude and warlike, but also daring, brave, and clever—and definitely not to be underestimated.

The most extensive source for the voyage of the Argonauts is the somewhat tedious third-century B.C. epic poem *Argonautica* by Apollonius of Rhodes. Two other ancient authors who wrote extensively on Jason and his adventures are Apollodorus (1.9.1, 16–28) and Pindar (*Pythian Ode*, 4). The short accounts in the *Fabulae* (12–25) of Hyginus are also helpful. The story was well established in the popular imagination even in the eighth century B.C. as shown in Homer (*Odyssey*, 12.66–72). The best source for the post-voyage love life of Jason is Ovid (*Metamorphoses*, 7.1–424) and the tragic play *Medea* by Euripides.

TROY

You can't blame Hollywood for loving a story that has adventure, true love, sex, bravery, sacrifice, and lots of bloody violence. The Greeks felt the same way, making the tale of the fall of Troy their national epic. For schoolboys from Sparta to Athens, studying Homer's poetic account of that war was a foundation of their education. Everything a boy needed to know about being a man was found in Homer's *Iliad*. And yet, read carefully, the story is much more a tragedy than a glorification of combat.

But was there a really Trojan War? For the purposes of mythology it doesn't matter, but since ancient times readers have wondered how much truth lies behind the tale. Homer's site of Troy near the coast at the entrance to the Hellespont was certainly a strategic choke point for commerce between the Mediterranean and the Black Sea, as well as a major land route between Asia and Europe. Whoever ruled this area could quickly become rich by controlling trade. Archaeologists excavating a site known as Hisarlik in northwest Turkey at this location have found a hill overlooking the Hellespont containing the remains of at least nine fortified cities sitting on top of each other like layers on a cake, the earliest dating to about 3000 B.C. and the latest to the Byzantine era. The level known as Troy VIIa was destroyed about 1190 B.C.—just the right time for Homer's story—with evidence of fallen masonry, fire, and bodies in the street. If there was something like a historical Trojan war on which the Greeks based their legend, these could well be its remains.

Homer's *Iliad* is of course the primary source for the Trojan War, but the main action covers only a short period of time toward the end of the conflict. The rest of the story from the wedding of Peleus and Thetis to the trick of the Trojan horse is found in many other ancient sources, including Homer (*Odyssey*), Hesiod (*Catalogue of Women*, 154), the fragments of the Epic Cycle (*Cypria, Little Iliad*), Aeschylus (*Agamemnon*), Sophocles (*Ajax*), Euripides (*Iphigenia at Aulis, Trojan Women, Andromache*), Apollodorus (3.10.8), Hyginus (*Fabulae*, 78, 81, 91–108), and Virgil (*Aeneid*).

MYCENAE

The descendants of Tantalus are the ultimate dysfunctional family. Their story begins with the slaughter of Pelops by his own father to serve him at a banquet, then over the years moves beyond cannibalism to incest, adultery, murder, rape, and suicide—most of these more than once. Just when Agamemnon thinks everything has calmed down after his victory at Troy, he is murdered by his own wife and the violence begins anew. But their son Orestes, five generations removed from Tantalus, at last finds a way to escape the cycle of vengeance that has plagued his family for so long. By making the anger of the Furies the foundation of civic law, he brings the endless trail of blood to a peaceful end.

The sordid story of Tantalus is told by Homer (*Odyssey*, 11.582–592) when Odysseus travels to the underworld, as well as by Hyginus (*Fabulae*, 82–83). The adventures of his son Pelops are found in Apollodorus (*Epitome*, 2.3–9), Hyginus (*Fabulae*, 83–84), Pindar (*Olympian Ode*, 1), and Pausanias (5.13.1–7, 6.22.1). The complicated and bloody drama of Atreus and his brother Thyestes is found in several ancient authors, including Apollodorus (*Epitome*, 2.10–14), Hyginus (*Fabulae*, 86–88), and Aeschylus (*Agamemnon*). The best source for the remainder of the family tragedy is the *Oresteia* trilogy of Aeschylus (*Agamemnon, The Libation Bearers*, and *The Furies*, also known as *The Eumenides*).

ODYSSEUS

"There's no place like home," says Dorothy when she closes her eyes and taps her ruby slippers together three times to leave Oz for Kansas. Homer understood that universal longing and used it to create in his *Odyssey* the greatest story ever told of a journey home. But the tale of Odysseus is about so much more than just battling monsters and vengeful gods to find one's way back home. The most powerful obstacles to Odysseus' return are the temptations on the journey—beautiful women, happy forgetfulness, and even immortality. And let us not forget his patient wife, Penelope, who undergoes her own odyssey without ever leaving her house. The forces she faces—loneliness, despair, and relentless suitors—make her journey to an ultimate reunion with her husband every bit as trying as his. The story of Odysseus is an epic adventure, but its most enduring lesson is that the greatest power of all is love.

The story of Odysseus and Penelope occurs in many classical authors with interesting variations—the Romans and even some Greeks could be quite hostile to the wandering hero—but the beginning and the end of ancient sources is Homer's *Odyssey*. I can never do justice to his marvelous tale in my retelling, though I hope I have captured something of its original spirit.

AENEAS

Arma virumque cano . . . —"arms and the man I sing": so begins the *Aeneid* of Virgil, as generations of Latin students have learned. Readers are sometimes surprised that the Romans would choose the loser of a war as their ancestor, but the greatest poem in Latin takes as its theme the voyage of the Trojan prince Aeneas to establish the line that would give birth to Julius Caesar and Augustus. One thing that drew the Romans to the Aeneas legend was that the Trojans were the implacable enemies of the Greeks, full of nobility and honor, whereas Odysseus and his countrymen were seen as conniving and surreptitious. This fit nicely with the Roman self-image and how they looked at the Greeks of their own day. Aeneas is everything a good Roman should want to be—aware of his human failings yet brave in battle, full of filial piety, and devoted to his country above himself.

Aeneas appears several times in the *Iliad*, but it is the prophecy of Poseidon in Homer's poem (20.307–8) saying he would survive the war and become king of a new race of Trojans that was the seed of later legend. The Romans claimed the Trojans as their ancestors at least by the third century B.C., though it is in the first-century B.C. *Aeneid* of Virgil that the story comes to full fruition. The Latin poet and friend of Augustus borrowed heavily from Homer's *Iliad* and *Odyssey*, but he created a uniquely Roman story.

ROME

Whatever else myth might be, it is a window into the values and culture of a people. Americans see themselves as an honest people, so we tell the story of George Washington confessing to his father that he cut down the cherry tree. The Romans likewise told stories of their early history illustrating the importance they placed on bravery, honor, action over contemplation, and devotion to the good of the state above all. When Romulus has trouble finding women for his new city, he takes them by force from his neighbors. Scaevola burns off his hand without flinching to show his fearlessness to an enemy king. Then there is the innocent Lucretia, the ideal Roman matron who weaves late into the night and kills herself to prevent bringing shame to her husband and family. In the words of Shakespeare, from his *Rape of Lucrece*, she blames the foul Tarquin for her condition:

> She utters this, "He, he, fair lords, 'tis he
> That guides this hand to give this wound to me."
> Even here she sheathed in her harmless breast
> A harmful knife, that thence her soul unsheathed.

Some early Roman writers such as Fabius Pictor recorded early myths as part of their histories, but these survive only in fragments. Our best source for stories from the age of kings is the Latin historian Livy, who wrote in the days of Caesar Augustus. The Greek biographer Plutarch, who lived over a century later, also provides important details. The saga of Romulus and Remus is found in Livy (1.3–16) and Plutarch's *Romulus*. Livy (1.22–26) tells the story of the battle between the Horatii and Curiatii triplets, as well as the later tale of Horatius Cocles heroically defending the bridge across the Tiber (2.10). The tale of fearless Scaevola is also found in Livy (2.12), as is that of modest Cloelia (2.13) and tragic Lucretia (1.57–60).

FURTHER READING

Bonfante, Larissa, and Judith Swaddling. *Etruscan Myths*. Austin: University of Texas Press, 2006.

Bulfinch, Thomas. *Myths of Greece and Rome*. New York: Penguin Books, 1981.

Burkert, Walter. *Greek Religion*. Cambridge, Massachusetts: Harvard University Press, 1985.

Buxton, Richard. *The Complete World of Greek Mythology*. London: Thames and Hudson, 2004.

D'aulaire, Ingri, and Edgar D'aulaire. *D'aulaire's Book of Greek Myths*. New York: Doubleday, 1962.

Gantz, Timothy. *Early Greek Myth: A Guide to the Literary and Artistic Sources*. Baltimore: The Johns Hopkins University Press, 1993.

Gardner, Jane F. *Roman Myths*. Austin: University of Texas Press, 1998.

Grant, Michael. *Myths of the Greeks and Romans*. New York: Meridian, 1995.

Graves, Robert. *The Greek Myths*. New York: Penguin Books, 1992.

Grimal, Pierre. *The Penguin Dictionary of Classical Mythology*. New York: Penguin Books, 1991.

Hamilton, Edith. *Mythology: Timeless Tales of Gods and Heroes*. New York: Meridian, 1989.

Hansen, William. *Classical Mythology*. Oxford: Oxford University Press, 2005.

———. *Ariadne's Thread*. Ithaca, N.Y.: Cornell University Press, 2002.

Harris, Stephen L., and Gloria Platzner. *Classical Mythology: Images and Insights*. New York: McGraw-Hill, 2008.

Hendricks, Rhoda A. *Classical Gods and Heroes*. New York: HarperCollins, 2004.

Hoffner, Harry A., Jr. *Hittite Myths*. Atlanta: Scholar's Press, 1990.

James, Vanessa. *The Genealogy of Greek Mythology*. New York: Gotham Books, 2003.

Kerényi, C. *The Gods of the Greeks*. London: Thames and Hudson, 1980.

Kirk, G. S. *The Nature of Greek Myths*. New York: Penguin Books, 1974.

Lefkowitz, Mary. *Greek Gods, Human Lives*. New Haven: Yale University Press, 2003.

Martin, Richard P. *Myths of the Ancient Greeks*. New York: New American Library, 2003.

Newman, Harold, and Jon O. Newman. *A Genealogical Chart of Greek Mythology.* Chapel Hill: University of North Carolina Press, 2003.

Powell, Barry. *Classical Myth.* New York: Pearson/Longman, 2009.

Puhvel, Jaan. *Comparative Mythology.* Baltimore: The Johns Hopkins University Press, 1987.

Segal, Robert A. *Myth: A Very Short Introduction.* Oxford: Oxford University Press, 2004.

Tripp, Edward. *The Meridian Handbook of Classical Mythology.* London: Plume Books, 2007.

Trzaskoma, Stephen M., R. Scott Smith, and Stephen Brunet, eds. *Anthology of Classical Myth.* Indianapolis: Hackett Publishing, 2004.

Woodard, Roger D., ed. *The Cambridge Companion to Greek Mythology.* Cambridge: Cambridge University Press, 2007.

INDEX